How to Do Everything with

Everything

with

Microsoft Office Access 2007

About the Author

When Grace Hopper, the originator of the concept of program compilers, told **Virginia Andersen** in 1948 that there was a future for women in high-speed digital computers, she responded, "In *what*?" Nevertheless, after graduating from Stanford University, Virginia pursued the idea and carved out a career applying computers to many challenging projects such as mapping the moon's surface in preparation for the Apollo landing; managing large industrial construction projects; conducting undersea surveillance; simulating navy weapon systems; and building reliability mathematical models. She also found time to teach computer science, mathematics, and system analysis at the graduate and undergraduate levels at several Southern California universities.

Since retiring from the defense industry, Virginia has written or contributed to more than 38 books about personal computer–based applications, including database management, word processing, and spreadsheet analysis. She tells the story of her varied uses for computers over the last 50 years in her book *Digital Recall: Computers Aren't the Only Ones with Memory.*

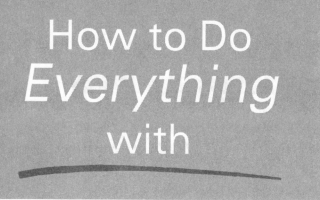

How to Do
Everything
with

Microsoft® Office
Access™ 2007

Virginia Andersen

New York   Chicago   San Francisco   Lisbon
London   Madrid   Mexico City   Milan   New Delhi
San Juan   Seoul   Singapore   Sydney   Toronto

The **McGraw·Hill** Companies

McGraw-Hill books are available at special quantity discounts to use as premiums and sales promotions, or for use in corporate training programs. For more information, please write to the Director of Special Sales, Professional Publishing, McGraw-Hill, Two Penn Plaza, New York, NY 10121-2298. Or contact your local bookstore.

How to Do Everything with Microsoft® Office Access™ 2007

34567890 CUS CUS 12 11 10

ISBN-13: 978-0-07-226346-6
ISBN-10: 0-07-226346-6

Sponsoring Editor Megg Morin	**Copy Editor** Julie M. Smith	**Illustration** International Typesetting and Composition
Editorial Supervisor Jody McKenzie	**Proofreader** Raina Trivedi	**Art Director, Cover** Jeff Weeks
Project Manager Rajni Pisharody	**Indexer** Kevin Broccoli	**Cover Designer** Pattie Lee
Acquisitions Coordinator Carly Stapleton	**Production Supervisor** Jean Bodeaux	
Technical Editor Jocelyn Fiorello	**Composition** International Typesetting and Composition	

Contents at a Glance

PART I   **Get Started**

1	Get Acquainted with Access 2007	3
2	Create a Database	27
3	Create and Modify Tables	45
4	Relate Tables	79
5	Enter and Edit Data	97

PART II   **Retrieve and Present Information**

6	Sort, Filter, and Print Records	135
7	Extract Information with Queries	157
8	Create Advanced Queries	199
9	Understand Form Report Design Basics	221
10	Create Custom Forms and Subforms	259
11	Create and Customize Reports and Subreports	301
12	Create Charts and Graphs	347

PART III   **Improve the Access 2007 Workplace**

13	Customize the Workplace	375
14	Speed Up Your Database	407
15	Automate with Macros	423
16	Customize the User Interface	449
17	Customize the Navigation Pane and Create Switchboards	473

PART IV   **Exchange Data with Others**

18	Exchange Database Objects and Text	505
19	Exchange Data with Outside Sources	537
20	Share with Multiple Users	557
21	Secure a Database	571
Appendix	Convert to Access 2007	585
	Index	591

Contents

Acknowledgments xvii

Introduction xix

PART I **Get Started**

CHAPTER 1 **Get Acquainted with Access 2007** **3**

Start Access and Open a Database 4

Take a Tour of the Access Window 6

Open a Database 7

Open the Sample Database 9

Tour the Navigation Pane and the Object Window 12

Look at the Ribbon 16

Use Shortcut Menus 18

Open a Table 18

Take a Tour of the Datasheet View 19

Check Out the Subdatasheet 22

Get Help When You Need It 24

Use Microsoft Access Help Window 24

Ask What's This? 25

Get Help with What You're Doing 26

CHAPTER 2 **Create a Database** **27**

Design an Efficient Database 28

Determine the Goals of the Database 30

Distribute the Data Among the Tables 30

Identify the Data Fields 31

Specify Key Fields 31

Define Table Relationships 33

Complete the Database 34

Create a Database with a Template 36

Run the New Application 41

Start with a Blank Database 42

CHAPTER 3	**Create and Modify Tables**	**45**
	Create a New Table from a Template	46
	Create a New Table in Datasheet View	46
	Add Fields to the New Table	47
	Use a Field Template	49
	Add Fields from an Existing Table	50
	Save the New Table	51
	Create a Table from Scratch in Design View	52
	Tour the Table Design View	52
	Add Fields	53
	Choose a Primary Key	63
	Create Other Indexes	64
	Save the Table Design	66
	Modify the Table Design	67
	Switch Table Views	67
	Add or Delete Fields	67
	Change the Field Order	68
	Change a Field Name or Type	69
	Change a Field Size	69
	Modify or Delete the Primary Key	70
	Ensure Data Validity	71
	Define Field Validation Rules	72
	Define a Record Validation Rule	73
	Require an Entry and Prevent Duplicates	74
	Handle Blank Fields	74
	Assign a Default Value	76
	Copy an Existing Table Structure	77
CHAPTER 4	**Relate Tables**	**79**
	Define a Relationship	80
	Use the Relationships Window	80
	Use the Field List Pane	91
	View and Edit Relationships	93
	Hide or Delete a Table	93
	Modify or Delete a Relationship	93
	Change a Table Design from the Relationships Window	94
	Print the Relationships	94
CHAPTER 5	**Enter and Edit Data**	**97**
	Enter New Data	98
	Copy and Move Data	98
	Insert Pictures	103
	Insert Hyperlinks	105
	Attaching Files to a Field	108

Customize Data Entry 110
    Add Custom Input Masks 110
    Create Lookup Fields 113
Change the Datasheet Appearance 119
    Move and Resize Columns and Rows 119
    Freeze and Hide Columns 121
    Change the Font 122
    Change Gridlines and Cells 123
    Set Datasheet Default Options 124
Change Table Definition 125
    Insert/Delete a Column 125
    Change Field Names 126
    Insert/Delete a Subdatasheet in Design View 126
Find and Edit Record Data 127
    Locate Records 127
    Find and Replace Data 131
    Delete Data 132

PART II   **Retrieve and Present Information**

CHAPTER 6   **Sort, Filter, and Print Records** **135**
Sort Records 136
    Sort on a Single Field 136
    Sort by Two or More Fields 137
    Save the Sort Order 137
Filter Records 137
    Filter by Context 139
    Use the Filter Command 142
    Filter By Selection 143
    Filter By Form 146
    Filter with Advanced Filter/Sort 152
    Save a Filter 153
    Remove and Clear Filters 155
Preview and Print Sorted or Filtered Table Data 155

CHAPTER 7   **Extract Information with Queries** **157**
Create a Select Query 159
    Use the Simple Query Wizard 160
    Tour the Query Design Window 162
    Without the Wizard 164
    Relate Multiple Tables in a Query 165
    Add/Remove Fields 168
    Run and Save the Query 171

Hide and Show Fields 172
Specify the Record Order 173
Show Highest or Lowest Values 174
Add Selection Criteria 175
Use Wildcards and Operators 176
Use a Single Criterion 176
Use Multiple Criteria 177
Get Help from the Expression Builder 180
Set Query Properties 182
Modify a Query 183
Insert a Field and Change the Field Order 183
Change Field Properties 183
Perform Calculations in a Query 185
Add a Calculated Field 185
Summarize with the Wizard 188
Summarize with Aggregate Functions 188
Summarizing in Datasheet View 192
Create Special Queries with the Query Wizard 193
Create a Find Duplicates Query 193
Create a Find Unmatched Query 194
Create a Crosstab Query 195

CHAPTER 8 **Create Advanced Queries** **199**
Create Special Purpose Queries 200
Parameter Queries 200
AutoLookup Queries 204
Design Action Queries 206
Update Query 206
Make-Table Query 210
Append Query 211
Delete Query 213
Look at Structured Query Language (SQL) 215
Review SQL Statements 215
Create a Subquery 217
Define a Criterion 217
Define a New Field 218

CHAPTER 9 **Understand Form Report Design Basics** **221**
Use Simple Form and Simple Report Tools 222
Common Form and Report Design Elements 224
Understand Controls 224
Work in the Design Window 225
Start a New Design 225
Tour the Design Window 228

Add Controls 232
Starting a New Form in Layout View 238
Modify Controls 238
Select Controls and Other Objects 239
Move and Resize Controls 243
Align and Space Controls 245
Use Property Sheets 246
Use the Font Group 250
Format Conditionally 251
Change a Control Type 253
Delete Controls 254
Modify Form or Report Properties 254
Change the Record Source 254
Apply Filters and Sort Orders 256
Use AutoFormat 257

CHAPTER 10 **Create Custom Forms and Subforms** **259**
Create a New Form Design 260
Use the Form Wizard 260
Create a Form Without the Wizard 263
Modify the Form Design 264
Add Form Header and Footer Sections 264
Place and Customize Data-Related Controls 266
Add Yes/No Controls 275
Add User-Interactive Controls 278
Use the Form for Data Entry 282
Navigate in the Form 282
Change the Tab Order 283
Locate Records 284
Sort and Filter Data in a Form 284
View Multiple Records 285
Create a Multiple-Page Form 285
Add a Page Break 285
Add a Tab Control 287
Customize a Tab Control 288
Add Special Controls 288
Add Calculated Controls 288
Add an AutoDialer Control 289
Create a Hierarchical Form 290
Use the Form Wizard 291
Use the Subform Wizard 293
Use the Hierarchical Form 296
Modify a Subform 296

Add Custom User Guidance 297
Add Data Validation 298
Validate with Properties 298
Validate with Events 299

CHAPTER 11   **Create and Customize Reports and Subreports** **301**
Start a New Report 302
Use the Report Tool 303
Use the Report Wizard 304
Preview and Print the Report 308
Work in the Print Preview Window 309
Print the Report 311
Modify the Report Design 313
Examine the Report Sections 314
Set Report and Section Properties 314
Change the Report Style 316
Add Page Numbers and Date/Time Controls 316
Save the Report Design 317
Filter, Sort, and Group Records in Layout View 318
Filter Records in Layout View 319
Change the Sort Order 320
Add Group Sections 322
Modify and Add Groups 326
Create a Summary Report with the Report Wizard 329
Print an Alphabetic Index 332
Add a Subreport 335
Create a Subreport with the Report Wizard 335
Create a Subreport Control 336
Insert an Existing Subreport 339
Link the Report and Subreport 339
Modify a Subreport Control 340
Design a Multiple-Column Report 340
Print Mailing Labels 342
Use the Label Wizard 343

CHAPTER 12   **Create Charts and Graphs** **347**
Choose a Chart Type 348
Create a New Chart with the Chart Wizard 348
Select the Data for the Chart 348
Use the Microsoft Chart Wizard 352
Save the Chart 354
Link the Chart to Record Data 355

Add an Existing Chart to a Form or Report 356
Modify the Chart 358
Modify with Access 358
Edit with Microsoft Graph 364

PART III **Improve the Access 2007 Workplace**

CHAPTER 13 **Customize the Workplace** **375**
Personalize the Workplace 376
Work with Objects in the Navigation Pane 376
Using the Ribbon 380
Create a Shortcut 380
Set Access Options 381
Popular Options 382
Set Options for the Current Database 384
Set Datasheet Options 388
Set Object Designers Options 388
Set Proofing Options 393
Set Advanced Options 395
Customize the Toolbar 401
View and Manage Add-Ins 402
Choose Trust Center Options 404
Search Additional Resources 405
Customize the Status Bar 406

CHAPTER 14 **Speed Up Your Database** **407**
Optimize a Database 408
Use the Analyzer Wizards 408
Optimize Tables and Queries 414
Optimize Filter By Form 416
Optimize Forms and Reports 416
Optimize Controls 418
Back Up and Restore a Database 418
Compact and Repair a Database 419

CHAPTER 15 **Automate with Macros** **423**
Create a Simple Macro 424
Choose Macro Actions 426
Set Action Arguments 427
Test and Debug a Macro 429
Start the Macro 429
Step Through a Macro 430
Modify a Macro 431

Assign a Macro to an Event Property 432
    Decide Which Event to Use 433
Add Conditions to a Macro 434
    Create a Macro to Display a Warning 435
Create Other Commonly Used Macros 437
    Set Control Values and Properties 438
    Change the Flow of Operations 441
    Filter Records 443
    Create an AutoExec Macro 444
Create a Macro Group 445

CHAPTER 16   **Customize the User Interface** **449**
Work with the Ribbon 450
    Resize the Ribbon 450
    Hide and Restore the Ribbon 451
    Use Keyboard Shortcuts for Ribbon Commands 451
Customize the Quick Access Toolbar 452
    Move the Quick Access Toolbar 452
    Add Commands to the Toolbar 452
    Remove Commands from the Toolbar 457
Use Existing Customization 458
    Show Startup Switchboard 458
    Use Custom menus and toolbars 458
Create a Custom Dialog Box 460
    Design the Form 461
    Create and Attach the Macros 464
Create a Dialog Box for User Input 469
    Set the Input Form Properties 469
    Create the Macros 470
    Modify the Query 470

CHAPTER 17   **Customize the Navigation Pane and Create Switchboards** **473**
View Objects in the Navigation Pane 474
    Change Categories and Groups 474
    Hide/Restore Groups and Objects 480
    Search for an Object 482
Customize the Navigation Pane 484
    Plan the Custom Groups 484
    Hide/Restore Custom Groups and Objects 489
Create Switchboards 490
    Use the Switchboard Manager to Create Switchboards 491
    Modify the Switchboard 498

PART IV   **Exchange Data with Others**

CHAPTER 18   **Exchange Database Objects and Text** **505**
   Copy Objects among Access Databases 506
      Copy and Paste 506
      Drag and Drop 507
   Import or Link Access Data 508
      Import Objects 509
      Set Import Options 512
      Link Access Tables 513
   Import from or Link to Other Data Sources 515
      Use Data from dBASE or Paradox 516
   Work with Linked or Imported Tables 517
      Rename a Linked Table in Access 517
      Change Linked Table Properties 517
      Update Links with the Linked Table Manager 518
      Unlink Tables 520
   Import and Link Text Files 520
      Use Delimited Text Files 520
      Use Fixed-Width Text Files 526
      Change Import Specifications 527
   Export to an Existing Access Database 529
   Export to Another Database Format 530
   Export to Text Files 531

CHAPTER 19   **Exchange Data with Outside Sources** **537**
   Copy or Move Records 538
      Copy or Move Data from a Word Processor 538
      Copy or Move Data from a Spreadsheet 540
      Copy or Move Records from Access to Another Application ... 541
   Save Access Output as an External File 542
   Work with Word 545
      Save in Rich Text Format 545
      Use Merge It with Microsoft Word 546
   Work with Excel 548
      Import from and Link to Excel Spreadsheets 549
      Export a Table or Query to Excel 554
   Mailing Access Objects 555

CHAPTER 20	**Share with Multiple Users**	**557**
	Share a Database on a Network	558
	Share an Entire Database	558
	Split the Database	559
	Prevent Exclusive Access	563
	Manage the Database in a Multiuser Environment	564
	Control Data Editing	565
	Update Records with Refresh and Requery	567
	Edit Shared Database Objects	568
CHAPTER 21	**Secure a Database**	**571**
	New Security Measures	572
	Enable/Disable Database Content	572
	Encrypt the Database	573
	Encrypt with a Password	574
	Use the Trust Center	575
	Create a Trusted Environment	575
	Trust Macros	578
	Trust Add-Ins	580
	Security with Earlier Version Databases	581
	Create a Certificate	582
	Code-sign the Database	583
APPENDIX	**Convert to Access 2007**	**585**
	Decide on a Conversion Strategy	586
	Convert a Database to Access 2007	586
	Convert a Workgroup Information File (MDW)	588
	Convert a Secured Database	588
	Convert a Replicated Database	588
	Convert to an Earlier Version	589
	Open an Earlier Database	589
	Share a Database Across Several Access Versions	590
	Index	**591**

Acknowledgments

It has been a treat to be involved in the continuation of this book series, and it is also a pleasure to revise *How to Do Everything for Microsoft Office Access 2007*. My thanks go to the great staff at McGraw-Hill for all the help they provided. I note especially Megg Morin, my sponsoring editor, who, with skill and patience, guided me in the structure and tenor of this book. She is a pleasure to work with, as is all her staff. Carly Stapleton, my acquisitions coordinator, skillfully juggled her many responsibilities, all the while being responsive and helpful.

I also owe many thanks to Jody McKenzie, editorial supervisor, for keeping the book's production on track, and to Rajni Pisharody, project manager, for all her help in moving the many chapters through the complex editing and production maze. The other editorial staff, including technical editor Jocelyn Fiorello and copy editor Julie Smith, were very conscientious in pointing out glitches in the logic and lapses in the style. My sincere thanks also go to Raina Trivedi for proofing, to Kevin Broccoli for indexing, and to International Typesetting and Composition for a great job illustrating and laying out the book.

I must mention how much I appreciate the unrelenting efforts my agents at Waterside Productions, who have put in to keep me from wasting my time by lolling around on the beach for the last 16 years.

Finally, I have my husband, Jack, to thank for providing quiet and peaceful surroundings, amenable to writing. I also thank him for helping me find all the figures that needed recapturing after the "technical refresh," a.k.a. "de-bugging."

Introduction

The Microsoft Office Access 2007 database management system can be a powerful tool for you whether you need to handle business or personal information. The concept of distributing data among related tables is not new, but the way the concept is implemented in Access 2007 makes information management a snap. Access 2007 is extremely flexible and can be applied to any environment.

With Access, you can design and build complete applications with virtually foolproof data entry and retrieval functions and adaptable user-interactive vehicles.

Access's main features are the objects that you can create and combine to produce a complete information management system:

- *Tables* are the containers for the data. They consist of fields that can contain data of many different types.

- *Queries* are the questions you ask of the database. They can extract specific data from multiple tables or even perform actions such as inserting, updating, or deleting certain records.

- *Forms* display data from one or more tables in an informative design. Forms are used for data entry and display.

- *Reports* are used for distributing printed information from one or more tables.

- *Macros* are lists of actions that work together to carry out a particular task in response to an event.

The new user interface with ribbons and tabs, instead of the previous menus and toolbars, offers a more user-friendly atmosphere. With ribbons, all the actions you may want to take for what you are doing are visible to you without investigating menu lists and toolbar buttons.

As an integral member of the Microsoft Office 2007 family, Access 2007 has become very cooperative in working smoothly with the other members. For example, it can provide the mailing list for Word's Mail Merge document or send data to Excel for analysis and charting. Access can also easily import and link to data in other program formats and interact smoothly with Microsoft SharePoint services.

Who Should Read this Book?

This book is especially designed and written for readers who want an effective guide to all the Microsoft Office Access 2007 features, as well as for those who need a complete step-by-step walk-through to learn how to get the most out of Access. It is written for anyone who has a need to organize information efficiently and accurately, whether to fulfill personal or business objectives. The book is appropriate for beginners to Access who are familiar with computers and other programs but who would like to become proficient in information management. It is also highly useful for beginner-to-intermediate readers who are migrating from other database management systems or earlier versions of Access.

This book focuses on how you can get the most out of Access, whether you are responsible for your company's complete information system or just want to keep track of personal information on your home computer.

What's in Each Part of the Book?

The book is divided into four parts, each of which addresses a specific aspect of Access database management in a logical sequence, from a simple beginning to complex multiple user environment.

Part I gives you a general overview of Access, and addresses the basics of creating a new database with related tables, and then entering data in those tables.

Part II gets to the meat of database management by describing how to build queries to extract just the information you want—in the form you want it. Part II also shows you how to create forms and reports for displaying and distributing data. One of the chapters even describes how to analyze data with visual charts and graphs.

Part III diverts from database management to discuss personalizing your workplace and improving database performance. It describes how to create custom Navigation Pane groups, as well as switchboards and dialog boxes. Macros are also introduced in this part.

Part IV looks outward from Access and investigates the exchange of data with other programs, including database applications. It also addresses the sharing of an Access database among multiple users, and describes various means of securing the database from intentional and unintentional disruption.

The Appendix shows how to convert a database from previous versions of Access. In addition, it describes how to deal with sharing a database across several different versions.

What Features and Benefits Are Included?

Many helpful editorial elements are presented in this book, including the chapter-opening checklist of How To topics that are covered in the chapter. If you are new to Access, you may want to start at the beginning of the book and read each chapter carefully. Work the step-by-step exercises as much as possible to gain important "hands-on" experience. If you have used earlier versions of Access, you may want to skim through the How To lists for material that is new to you.

You will find all the information you need to perform a specific task clustered together in a single chapter with cross-references to other chapters that may contain related information.

In addition to the explanations in the text, every chapter presents relevant and interesting figures and illustrations that clearly depict the activity under discussion. Other elements are included such as:

- *Tips* with graphics and text that point out alternative ways to use a feature.
- *Cautions* that warn the reader of pitfalls and workarounds that can avoid problems.
- *Notes* that contain ancillary information related to the current topic but not part of the action.
- *How To and Did You Know? sidebars* that contain additional, peripheral information about the process at hand.

The following conventions are used in this book:

- *Click* means to click an item once, using the left mouse button.
- *Double-click* means to click an item twice in rapid succession, using the left mouse button.
- *Right-click* means to click an item once, using the right mouse button.
- Procedural steps that are numbered must be carried out in the prescribed order.
- Optional choices are presented as bulleted lists from which to choose.

Download the Databases

The databases used in this book are available at Osborne.com. You can download the entire databases to examine and work with the finished products or download only the tables with which you can build your own databases. At the site, select Free Downloads and once you reach the page where book titles are listed, select *How To Do Everything with Access 2007*. Once you click on the book's title, the download will begin automatically.

Part I

Get Started

Chapter 1

Get Acquainted with Access 2007

How to…

- Start Access
- Open a database
- Tour the Navigation Pane and object window
- Use ribbons, command tabs, galleries, and shortcut menus
- Open a table
- Navigate in Datasheet and Subdatasheet view
- Get help

In this data-centric world, there has never been a more urgent need for immediate and accurate access to the information pool. In order to be successful in the expanding information age, you must be able to manage and maintain your data, no matter what profession or business you are in. To do so, you must store the information in such a way that you can keep it up to date, get to it when you need it and make sense out of it. Microsoft Office Access 2007 is the top-notch database management system for all your information management needs, from a simple address list to a complex, multiple-location inventory management system. It offers all the necessary tools for storing, maintaining, tracking, retrieving, and interpreting your data as well as keeping it up to date and sharing it with others. Furthermore, these tools are a breeze to comprehend and employ.

Relational databases, such as the ones Access provides, make a lot of sense by distributing the data among tables, with each table referring to a specific aspect of the database such as customers, products, or orders. The tables are closely related so you can retrieve the information you need from all of them and in any arrangement you want.

With a single copy of each data item in its source table, you need to update it in only one place, which improves the probability of correct and consistent data. In smaller, less complex, and more focused tables, information is easier to find. Conversely, in one large table containing a conglomeration of information, it can be difficult to find just the information you need.

This chapter starts Access 2007 and gives you a tour of the Access workplace. If you are already an experienced user of an earlier version of Access, you will be amazed at the new, visually upgraded user interface.

Start Access and Open a Database

You can start most software built for the Windows environment in the same way: from the Start button. Depending on how you installed Access 2007, the program's name may appear as a separate item in the Programs (or All Programs if you are using Windows XP) list or as one of the programs in the Microsoft Office menu. If you don't see Microsoft Access in the Programs list, choose Microsoft Office, then click Microsoft Access.

To start Access:

1. Click the Start button and point to Programs or All Programs in the Start menu.

2. Click on Microsoft Office Access 2007 in the list of programs.

When you open Access, the window displays the Getting Started with Microsoft Office Access window containing four options (see Figure 1-1):

■ Start a new database with one of the Access templates. The left pane lists available templates and samples.

■ Start with a new blank database.

Microsoft Office button   Quick Access toolbar

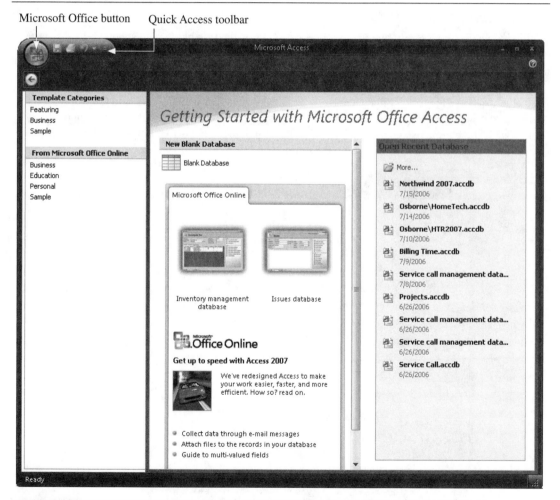

FIGURE 1-1   The Microsoft Office Access opening window for getting started.

■ In the center tab of the screen you can connect to Microsoft Office online. The database templates offered online may differ each time you start Access 2007.

■ Select a recently used database from the list in the right pane (no doubt your list will be different).

Take a Tour of the Access Window

The Access window shows a title bar with several buttons you can use to start work or manipulate the window. Before we get to the business of creating and using an Access database, let's take a quick tour of the Access 2007 window and get acquainted with its features. It is a great advantage that many of the Access features are common to other Office programs so you may already be familiar with them.

The Microsoft Access Title Bar

In addition to displaying the program name, Microsoft Access, the title bar contains the Microsoft Office button, a small Quick Access toolbar, and the buttons that you can use to manipulate the window.

The Microsoft Office button at the left end of the title bar offers you a choice of eight menu items that you can use to work with a database, such as New, Open, Save, Save As, and Close Database. The other three menu items deal with managing the database, printing documents, and sending email. The button also displays a list of recently used documents. Two buttons at the bottom of the display let you set specific Access options or exit Access altogether.

The buttons on the Quick Access toolbar offer shortcuts to three of the commonly used menu commands: Save, Undo and Can't Undo. You can rest the mouse pointer on the button and see its name displayed below the button in a ScreenTip. You can use the Customize button on the right of the Quick Access toolbar to add more commands to the toolbar, so that all of the actions you need are at your fingertips. You'll find out how to customize the toolbar in Chapter 16.

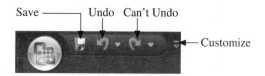

Three buttons appear at the right end of the title bar. These buttons are common to all Windows applications. You can use them to maximize, minimize, restore to the previous non-maximized size, or close the window. If the window is not maximized, the lower-right corner of the window becomes a resizing handle that you can drag to change the height or width of the window. You can also drag one of the window borders to change the height or width.

The Status Bar

Once you get going with a database, the status bar, located at the bottom of the Access window, provides a running commentary about the ongoing task and clues to the Access working environment. The center of the status bar also shows boxes that indicate the presence of a filter that limits the displayed records and the status of various toggle keys such as INSERT, CAPS LOCK, SCROLL LOCK, and NUM LOCK. The right end of the status bar contains tool buttons that can change the view of the current object. For example, change an open form from Form view, where you see data in the form, or to Design View where you can make changes in the form design.

Open a Database

Now let's get down to business. If the database you want to open is listed in the Open Recent Database pane that appears when Access starts, you can open it by simply clicking the filename. If the one you want is not on the list, click More. The Open dialog box appears, as shown in Figure 1-2. (Your list of folders and files will be different.)

TIP   *If Access is already running, you can open a recently opened file by clicking the Microsoft Office button and selecting the filename from the list.*

The Favorite Links pane at the left contains a list of places to look for the database. Select Documents to see a list of available documents in the current folder or click the Folders arrow to browse through all the folders in your computer. You can also click the Folders down arrow to begin the search of the folders in your hard drive.

The trick is to know where you have stored your database. If you have used other Windows applications, such as Word or Excel, you know how to find the file you want with the Open

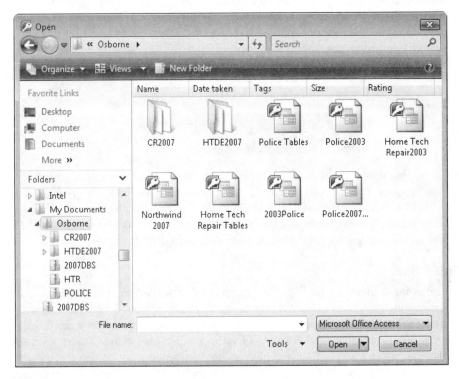

FIGURE 1-2 Choosing a database from the Open dialog box.

dialog box. Use the "look in" box (the left text pane in the title bar) to zero in on the folder that contains the database, double-click the folder name or icon to open it, then select the file you want from the list. You can also enter the file name in the Search box and click the Search button.

The Open dialog box contains several buttons that help you find the file you want to open. You can see the name of each button by resting the mouse pointer on the button in the command bar.

The Views drop-down list offers different ways to show the document list. As you drag the scroll button on the left margin, the display gradually changes to match the currently high-lighted view.

If you want to work with a different file type, click the down arrow next to Microsoft Office Access and choose from the list of 24 types or All Files. The default file type for Access 2007 is Microsoft Office Access, which includes all Access databases and any other Office documents

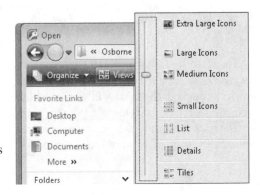

that have been linked to an Access database such as an Excel spreadsheet or a Word document. Other Access file types are available from the list.

Once you have tracked down the database you want to open, double-click the name or select it and then click Open.

The Open button offers other ways to open the database such as read-only, exclusive, or both. You can also use one of the Open check boxes to limit the use of the opened database. You will learn more about these options in later chapters.

Open the Sample Database

To get started working with a database in Access 2007, let's open the Northwind sample database that comes with Microsoft Office Access 2007. The Northwind database is an order processing application that demonstrates the power and usefulness of a relational database. Although the focus seems simple enough—taking and filling orders from customers for the company products—a lot of data actually is involved.

The easiest way to install and open the Northwind database is through the Access Getting Started window.

1. In the From Microsoft Office Online section of the left pane, double-click Sample. The Sample window displays a thumbnail for accessing the Northwind database (see Figure 1-3).

2. Click the thumbnail to see the option. It offers to download the database file into your default folder. E.g. C:\\Documents and Settings\Virginia Andersen\My Documents\..

NOTE *If you have already downloaded the Northwind database, you will see another thumbnail offering to create another copy on your hard drive.*

3. Click the folder icon to browse for a different destination.

4. Enter a different database name, if desired.

5. Click Download (or Create). Figure 1-4 shows the opening Northwind Traders window.

FIGURE 1-3   Choosing the Northwind sample from the Sample pane.

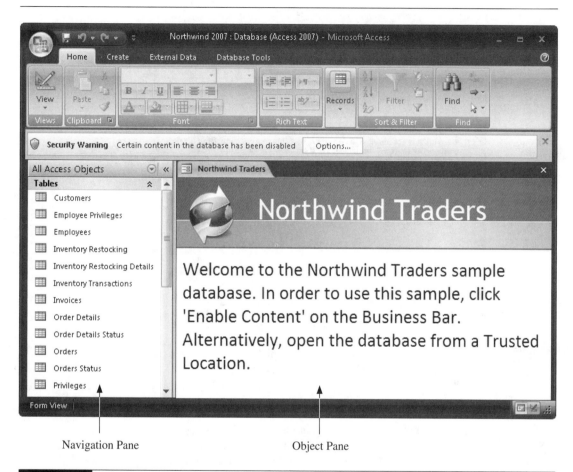

Navigation Pane   Object Pane

FIGURE 1-4   The Northwind Traders database in the startup window.

New security features have been added to Access 2007. In previous versions, when you opened a database containing macros or VBA code, you were asked whether you wanted to enable them. In Access 2007 you see a Security Warning message across the window between the opening ribbon and the database itself. To enable the contents:

1. Click the Option button.

2. In the Microsoft Office Security Options dialog box (see Figure 1-5), check Enable this content.

3. Click OK.

The Microsoft Office Security Options dialog box gives you the chance to enable the content in the database.

More about security and how you can keep your database safe in Chapter 21.

Now you are ready to sign on to the Northwind Traders database. Click Login as an employee in the Login Dialog box to get started with the database. Figure 1-6 shows the Home page of the Northwind Trader database. The tab shows the object name, Home.

Tour the Navigation Pane and the Object Window

The left pane labeled All Access Objects is the new Navigation Pane which replaces the Database window used by previous versions of Office Access and is the door to your database objects. With the Navigation Pane, you can see the complete list of objects without having to tab to other object windows as was required in a Database window. You can also open any of the database objects from the Navigation Pane.

To see all the ways you can group and view your database objects in the Navigation Pane, click the down arrow next to All Access Objects.

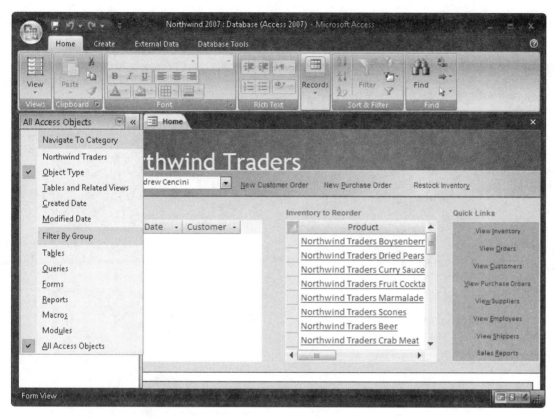

The upper section of the Navigation Pane, Navigate to Category, shows a list of five options or categories for accessing objects.

- **Custom Groups**   Shows the objects that you have placed in custom groups usually by way of the current database. These can replace switchboards used in previous versions. More about this in Chapter 17.

- **Object Type**   Allows you to select to show only specific types, such as tables, queries, forms, or all types.

- **Table and Related Views**   Shows all objects related to the tables you choose. For example, if the table is used as the basis for a form or report, is the subject of a query, those objects appear also.

- **Created Date**   Displays the selected object types sorted by date of origin with the older objects at the top of the list.

- **Modified Date**   Similar to Created Date but sorts by date of last modification, including today.

Microsoft Office button   Quick Access toolbar   Shutter Open/Close button

FIGURE 1-6   The Home page of the Northwind Trader database.

The lower section offers the option to filter the objects by a specific type, such as to see only table names, or to include all objects in the display. For now, let's leave the Navigation Pane to show all objects grouped by type.

You can resize the Navigation Pane by dragging the right border. You can also hide the Navigation Pane if you need more screen space by clicking the Shutter Bar Open/Close button in the upper right corner of the Navigation Pane. Or just press F11. To reopen the pane, click the button or press F11 again. If you want more information about the objects, right-click in the title bar or in the blank space at the bottom of the Navigation Pane and point to View By and click Details. (See Figure 1-7). You can also sort objects in the list in alphabetic order or by creation or modification dates by pointing to the Sort By command.

The Navigation Pane replaces the common switchboard user interface by allowing you to place specific actions in a custom group in the pane. More about this in Chapter 17.

NOTE *If you have an established switchboard that you want to keep, you can turn off the Navigation Pane and use the switchboard as before.*

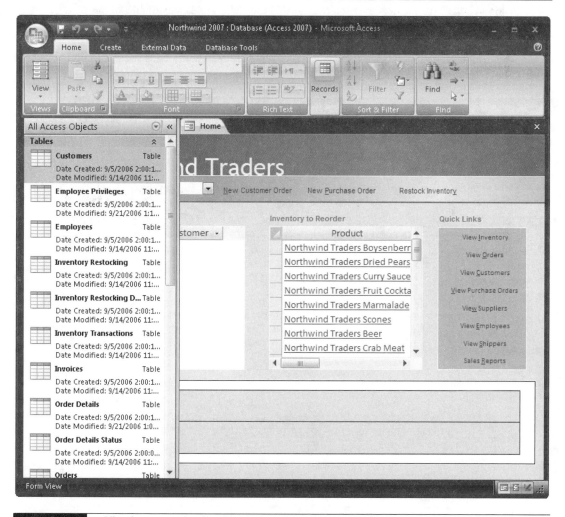

FIGURE 1-7   Viewing more details about objects listed in the Navigation Pane.

The Object Window where you view the database objects represents what Microsoft calls the "single-document interface model." All open objects are placed in the window, each marked with a tab. Refer to Figure 1-5, where the only open object is the Home form in Northwind Traders database, as you can see on the tab. With more than one object open, however, you can use the tabs to switch from one object to another.

Look at the Ribbon

While you are browsing around in the window, you might as well take a look at the new Access ribbon. The new ribbon replaces the stacks of menus and toolbars found in earlier versions of Access.

The major advantage of the new user interface is that the ribbon makes available all the tasks related to the current activity. So rather than searching through a series of menus for the action you want, all the appropriate commands are right in front of you. For example, if you are building a report, the ribbon includes a logical group of report-related commands such as Report Wizard, Labels, Report Design, and so on.

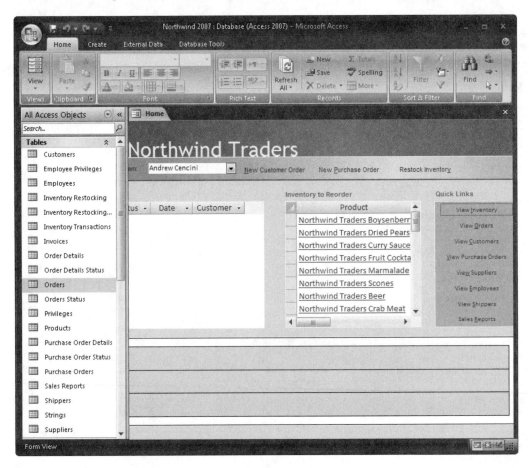

The standard Home ribbon appears in the Access window when you open a database. Not all of the options are available to all of the database objects, and some, such as the Save command, are not available until a table or other object is opened. It also makes sense that the Paste command is dimmed until you have copied something to the clipboard.

Each ribbon appears with a series of tabs relating to the current activity. For example, the ribbon shown above has four tabs: Home, Create, External Data, and Database Tools. When you click on a tab, the ribbon changes to show groups of commands related to that activity. For example, if you click the Create tab, you will see groups of commands you can use to build a new database object.

The commands on each tab are arranged in the ribbon with a group designation at the bottom of the group. For example, the Clipboard group on the Home ribbon includes Cut, Copy, Paste, and AutoFormat commands. The Font group includes all the style, alignment, foreground (text) and background color settings, and grid lines.

The command tabs also vary depending on the currently active object. For example, if you open a table, you will also see a Datasheet contextual command tab. If you switch to table Design view, Access automatically changes the ribbon from the Home tab to the Design tab where you can find all the actions you need to work on the table design.

To see what a ribbon command will do, rest the mouse pointer on the button and look at the ScreenTip that appears briefly. A lot of the ribbon commands also have shortcut keys that might show in the ScreenTip or with the command name. See Chapter 16 for more information about showing shortcut keys.

When you change the size of the Access window, the ribbon will change to match. For example, with a wide window, the ribbon shows commands in one or two rows. If you shrink the width of the window, the ribbon will compress to three rows and may even remove the textual explanation of the commands and leave only the image.

You can still use your earlier version keyboard shortcuts to execute a command. To see what keyboard shortcut works with a command on the ribbon, press and release ALT. The keytips appear over each feature that is currently available.

If you need more display space, you can hide the ribbon and leave only the command tabs in view. To hide it, double-click the active command tab or press CTRL+F1. Repeat to restore the ribbon.

Choose from Context Menus

A command in the ribbon that shows a down arrow provides additional commands in a context menu. Click the View down arrow to choose from the list of available views, depending on the current document. For example, the Northwind Traders Home page is a form so the choices in the View context menu are Form View, Layout View, and Design View.

Many other context menus are available, as you will soon see for yourself as you create tables and other database objects.

Check out the Galleries and the Mini Toolbars

The ribbon contains a new control type, called the *gallery*. A gallery presents the optional results of a specific command. For example, with a table open, if you click the down arrow next to the Gridlines command, you can select from the displayed arrangements—horizontal, vertical, both, or none.

A mini toolbar is a temporary display of text formatting options. After you select the text you want to format, the automatic mini toolbar appears above the text. Move the mouse pointer closer to the toolbar and you can use it to apply italic, bold, font size, color, and other formatting options. When you select a formatting option, the selected text adopts it and you can see how it will look without actually changing it. If you move the mouse pointer away from the mini toolbar, it disappears.

Use Shortcut Menus

Shortcut menus didn't get that name by accident—they really are shortcuts to a lot of actions. Shortcut menus are context-sensitive menus that appear when you click the right mouse button. The commands in the menu depend on where the mouse pointer is and what is going on when you click the button. Click anywhere outside the menu to close it.

Figure 1-8 shows the shortcut menu that appears when you right-click on a table name in the Navigation Pane. Only the most commonly used commands are included in the shortcut menu, but they also might include commands from several different ribbon tabs.

To choose a command from a shortcut menu, click the command or type the letter that is underlined in the name of the command, called the *access key*. If the command shows a right arrow, such as the Import command in Figure 1-8, it leads to a submenu that contains more commands. Rest the pointer on the arrow to open the list of commands, then choose one from the list. If the command shows an ellipsis (…), it opens a dialog box when you click it.

See Chapter 16 for information on how to get wild and crazy with the Navigation Pane, ribbons, toolbars, and shortcut menus, in order to create your own workplace style.

Open a Table

To get started working with the data, let's open a table. To open one of the tables in the current database, first expand the list of tables in the database by clicking the expansion arrow next to Tables in the Navigation Pane. Then, to open the Orders table, do one of the following:

- Double-click the Orders table name.
- Right-click the name and choose Open from the shortcut menu.

The table appears with the data in rows and columns much like a spreadsheet. This view of table data is called *Datasheet view*.

Figure 1-9 shows the open Northwind Orders table in Datasheet view. Each row contains a single record with the information for one order. Each column contains values for one field. Each field has a unique name—for example, Order ID—and contains a specific item of data, such as the customer name or order date.

NOTE *Notice that the Home form is still open and showing the Home tab. You can return to it by clicking the tab.*

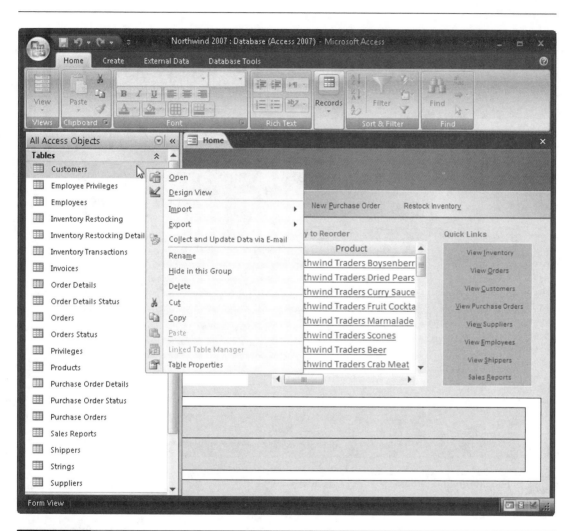

FIGURE 1-8   Shortcut menus help speed up database work.

Take a Tour of the Datasheet View

You probably noticed that some changes occurred in the window when you opened the table. For example, the window now shows the name of the open table in the tab above the table document. The Home tab of the ribbon now shows more available commands in the contextual command groups, that is, they are no longer dimmed.

Navigate Among Records and Fields

You need to be able to get to your data if you want to enter new information or edit existing records. As always, you can choose from several ways to move the cursor around the records and

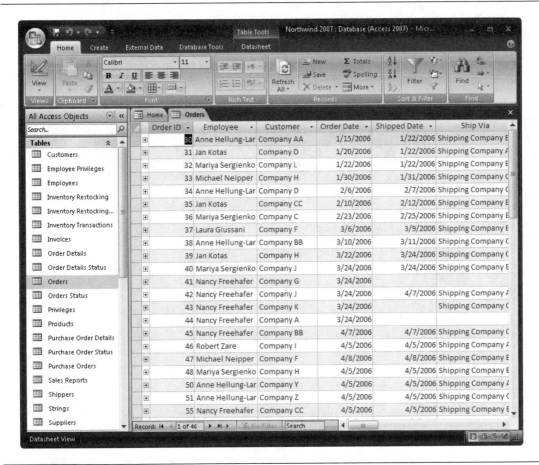

FIGURE 1-9 The Northwind Orders table in Datasheet view.

fields in your table, including simply clicking in the desired location if it is visible. You should try them all and settle on the one that works for you. The other methods are as follows:

- Using keystrokes such as TAB and the arrow keys (more about shortcut keys later)
- Clicking the record navigation buttons at the bottom of the datasheet to move to a specific record in the datasheet
- Dragging the vertical and horizontal scroll boxes
- Clicking Go To in the Find command group at the right end of the Home ribbon to move to the first, last, next, previous, or an empty, new record similar to the buttons on the navigation bar

The record navigation buttons at the bottom of the datasheet window give you the same options as the Go To ribbon command, the right arrow in the Find group. You can also enter a specific record number (if you know the number of the record you want to see) in the text box between the navigation buttons and then press ENTER. This area also tells you what record the cursor is in and the total number of records in the table.

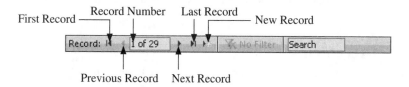

You can also find a specific record by placing the cursor in the column you want to search and then entering the desired value in the Search box in the navigation bar. The cursor immediately moves to the record containing that value.

If this is a filtered subset of the table, such as only those orders from a specific customer, the word "(Filtered)" appears after the total number of records, which is the number of records remaining after the filter has been applied.

To scroll to a particular record in the table, drag the scroll box to that record. As you drag the scroll box, a helpful ScreenTip appears next to the pointer. It tells you the number of the current record and the total number of records in the table. You can also use the horizontal scroll box at the bottom of the window to drag to other columns in the datasheet.

⊞ Nancy Freehafer	Company BB	4/7/2006	4/7/2006	Shipping Company C	1
⊞ Robert Zare	Company I	4/5/2006	4/5/2006	Shipping Company A	1
⊞ Michael Neipper	Company F	4/8/2006	4/8/2006	Shipping Company B	1
⊞ Mariya Sergienko	Company H	4/5/2006	4/5/2006	Shipping Company B	1
⊞ Anne Hellung-Lar	Company Y	4/5/2006	4/5/2006	Shipping Company A	1
⊞ Anne Hellung-Lar	Company Z	4/5/2006	4/5/2006	Shipping Company C	1
⊞ Nancy Freehafer	Company CC	4/5/2006	4/5/2006	Shipping Company B	1
⊞ Andrew Cencini	Company F	4/3/2006	4/3/2006	Shipping Company C	1
⊞ Anne Hellung-Lar	Company AA	4/22/2006	4/22/2006	Shipping Company B	1
⊞ Jan Kotas	Company D	4/22/2006	4/22/2006	Shipping Company A	1
⊞ Mariya Sergienko	Company L	4/22/2006	4/22/2006	Shipping Company B	1

Shortcut Keys

If you are mouse-phobic, you can use the shortcut key combinations to move around the datasheet once you get used to the correlation between the keys and the resulting cursor movement. Here are some examples of what happens when you press various key combinations:

- The UP or DOWN ARROW moves to the same field in the previous or next record.
- RIGHT ARROW or TAB moves right one field in the same record. If you are in the last field in the record or the Add New Field blank column, the cursor moves to the first field in the next record.

- LEFT ARROW or SHIFT-TAB moves left one field in the same record. If you are in the first field in the record, the cursor moves to the last field in the previous record.

- PGUP or PGDN moves up or down one screen of records.

- HOME or END moves to the first or last field in the same record.

- CTRL-HOME or CTRL-END moves to the first field of the first record or the last field of the last record.

Change the Current View

With a table open, the Datasheet view status bar shows four buttons at the right end that can change the current view of the table data:

- Datasheet view shows records in rows with fields in the columns.

- PivotTable view shows a summary and analysis of table data.

- PivotChart view shows a graphical analysis of table data.

- Design view shows the table design.

See Chapter 3 for more information about the viewing the table data and design.

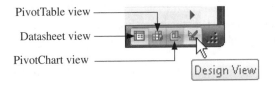

Check Out the Subdatasheet

In a relational database, it is important to be able to view information related to the current data on the screen. The related data is displayed in a *subdatasheet,* which can easily be opened. If the records shown in Datasheet view display a plus sign at the left end of the row, there is additional information in another table in the database that is related to that record. To see this data, expand the subdatasheet by clicking the plus sign. The plus sign changes to a minus sign when the subdatasheet expands. To collapse the subdatasheet, click the minus sign.

You can expand as many subdatasheets as you want in a single Datasheet view. Each subdatasheet contains records that correspond to one record in the datasheet. You can expand them individually or set a table property that automatically expands all of the subdatasheets when the table opens in Datasheet view. See Chapter 3 for information about setting table and other properties.

Figure 1-10 shows the Northwind Orders table with three subdatasheets expanded to show the products from the Order Details table, which were included in three of the orders in the Orders table. Notice the plus and minus signs that indicate the current state of the subdatasheet.

NOTE   *If fields have not been specified to link records in the subdatasheet with records in the datasheet, you will see all the records in the related table when you expand the subdatasheet. See Chapter 2 for more information about relating tables and what that can do for you.*

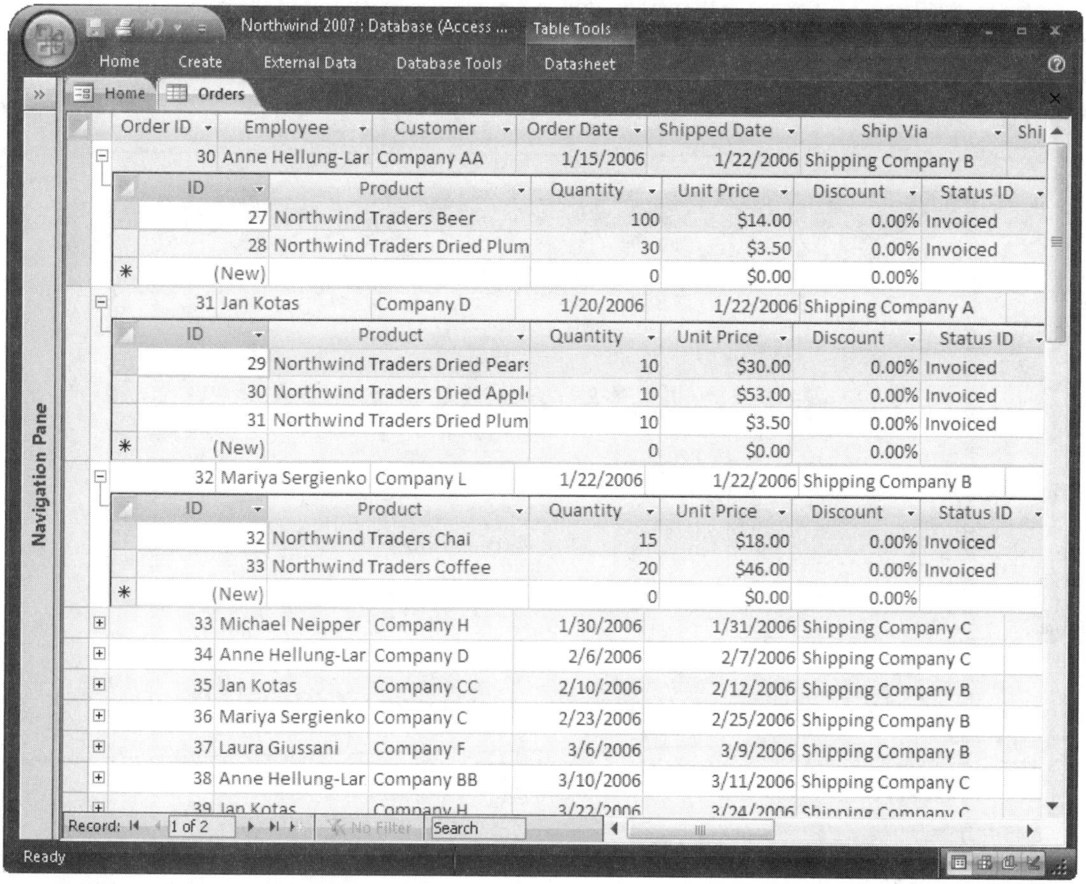

FIGURE 1-10   Viewing subdatasheets in the Orders table in Datasheet view.

Get Help When You Need It

No matter how easy Access makes database management, you can't possibly remember how to do every task. That's where the Access Help feature comes in. There are two ways to get help with what you are doing:

- Click the question mark icon at the right end of the ribbon
- Press F1

Use Microsoft Access Help Window

When you press F1 or click the question mark button in the upper right corner of the ribbon the Access Help window opens showing the list of subjects you can reach through the Access Help and How-to window. (See Figure 1-11) You can click on a topic to see the information or you can type specific words in the Search box at the top of the screen then click Search.

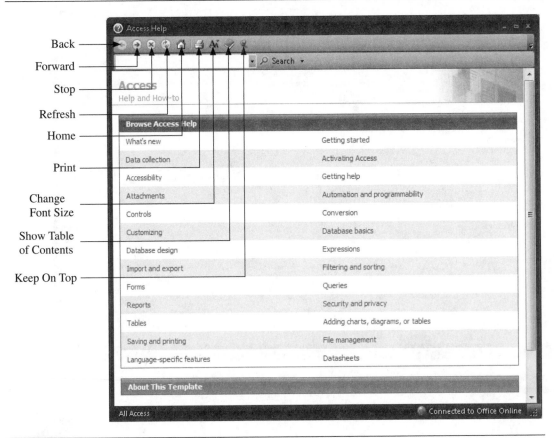

FIGURE 1-11 Browse in the Access Help window for information.

The Access Help window has its own toolbar with buttons that you can use to browse for help.

If you want to browse through the Help file table of contents, click the Table of Contents toolbar button. The Table of Contents pane displays a list of topics marked with the closed book icon. Click these to expand the topics into individual Help articles (see Figure 1-12).

If you are currently connected to the Internet, you also have access to all the up-to-date Help topics. Additional online help includes assistance, training courses, the latest product updates, clip art and media, and a research library.

Ask What's This?

Many of the Access dialog boxes include the What's This? tool, which gives you quick and short information about a specific element or choice in the box. Activating the What's This? help feature is a two-step process. First, click the ? button in the dialog box title bar. The mouse pointer changes to an arrow accompanied by a question mark. Then, click the element you want to know more about.

To return the mouse pointer to its normal state without opening What's This?, press ESC.

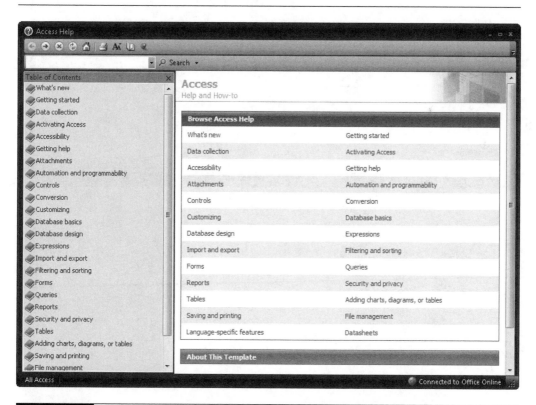

FIGURE 1-12   Open the Table of Contents pane to find more information.

Get Help with What You're Doing

Without opening the Help window, Access gives you many hints and clues while you're working. The status bar offers information about the current activity or position of the cursor. Many design windows include hint boxes that tell you about aspects of the design. Other windows and dialog boxes include samples or previews of the selections made.

For example, when you are working in the table Design window, status bar information tells you how to move around the Design view and get help. The hint box on the right describes what should appear in the Field Name column.

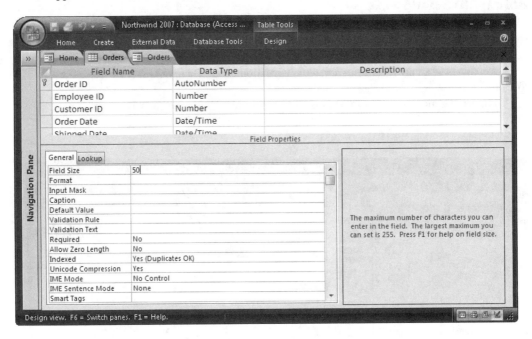

Chapter 2

Create a Database

How to...

- ■ Design an efficient database
- ■ Create a database with a previously designed template
- ■ Run the new application
- ■ Start a new database from scratch

In this chapter, you'll get started with Access by learning how to design a relational database. You will see the elements of a successful relational database system. The information in a relational database system is distributed among related tables to optimize information storage and retrieval. Related tables have fields in common so that information can be extracted from several tables together and presented in useful ways. If properly designed and constructed, a database can be an essential tool in tracking and managing personal or business information.

Design an Efficient Database

The design process begins with an analysis of the tasks that will be required of the database. First, find out what the prospective users intend to do with the system. Interview each user and get thorough descriptions of their expectations. It is essential to keep in mind that the design process also is an iterative one: as the users get used to a new system, they will think of more features they can use, such as an additional data entry form, a special query, or a calculated field.

The database design process can be broken down into seven steps, each with specific goals and products, such as assigning data to tables and relating the tables. Then you may want to design other tools, such as data entry forms, reports, analytic tools such as charts and graphs, and other end user requirements. Each of these steps is described in more detail in later sections.

1. Determine what the users want from the database and the data that is needed to provide the basis for those results.

2. Plan the data distribution among the related tables in the database. For example, customers in one table, employees in another, while workorders in another table relate to both customers and employees.

3. Identify the fields for each table.

4. Assign a unique field for each table to ensure that no two records are the same.

5. Determine how the tables are related to one another.

6. Review the design and step through procedures with users.

7. Create tables and enter data.

Although numbering the steps in a process implies that one step is completed before the next begins, in reality the design process is more fluid, with each step overflowing into the next. You can return to a previous step anywhere along the line.

We will use the Home Tech Repair database as our first relational database example. Home Tech Repair is a small company that specializes in maintenance and improvement of home structures. Its specialties are electrical, plumbing, structural, painting, and heating and air conditioning systems in the home. Figure 2-1 shows an example of the manual record keeping system in use before the development of the Access database.

Home Tech Repair

Order #_____	Date/Time_____
Customer_____	
Address_____	
_____	
Phone _____	Taken by_____

Description _____
_____
_____
_____

Bid Number_____   Total Bid_____   Date_____

Supervisor_____

Work in Progress   Date Started_____

Date Finished_____   Supervisor_____

Labor			Costing Data	
Hours	Rate	Cost	Parts	_____
_____ x _____		= _____	Sales Tax _____	
_____ x _____		= _____		
_____ x _____		= _____	Sub Total _____	
_____ x _____		= _____	Labor _____	
_____ x _____		= _____		
Total Labor:		_____	Total _____	
Cost Estimate _____ Date _____			Amount Paid_____	

FIGURE 2-1   The Home Tech Repair manual workorder record.

Determine the Goals of the Database

A poorly designed database is of less than no value. You can lose data, have duplicate data that can't be updated consistently, or even be unable to extract the complete and accurate data that you need. The more time you spend on task and data analysis, the better the results will be. To begin the database design, start at the end point. Find out what the end user expects of the database, then go about structuring the design to provide these requirements.

To do so, answer the following questions:

- What do the users want to get from the database?
- What kinds of reports are needed (how do users want the information arranged and summarized)?

Then follow these directions:

- If adequate data collection forms already exist, use them as patterns for the Access forms.
- Look at other databases that address similar information management situations and see whether they can provide any guidance with the design of your own.
- Once the tasks have been defined, develop a list of the required data items.

The main purpose of the Home Tech Repair database is to maintain up-to-date information about current workorders. To do this, it must relate the individual workorders to specific customers or employees. It also must include forms for data entry and for viewing of all table data.

In addition to the workorder tracking, the owner would like to be able to conduct financial analyses; for example, to determine how much revenue has been generated by each employee or to review the total sales on a monthly basis. These analyses can include summary reports with charts and graphs depicting trends and proportional distributions of types of jobs over a period of time. Such studies are helpful when planning for future work.

Distribute the Data Among the Tables

Distributing data is the cornerstone of relational databases. The efficiency and effectiveness of such a database relies on the proper distribution of data among the tables that make up the database. This is not as easy as it sounds, but here are some guidelines to follow:

- The information in a table should be limited to a single subject, such as workorders or customers. This allows you to maintain data about each subject independently of the others.
- Tables should not contain duplicate information among its records. With only one copy of each data item, you need to update it in only one place and the current data is available to all. A field in a related table contains a link to the data item, not the entire value. For example, the Employee table has an Employee ID field as well as all the other information about the employee. Any table related to the Employee table has only the Employee ID field as a link, not the name, address, and so on.

In the Home Tech Repair case, employee and customer information is repeated on several manually prepared workorder sheets. To reduce the redundancy, pull out both sets of information and put them in separate tables named Employees and Customers. Employees and Customers both have ID fields that can relate them to workorders. Keeping payments in a separate table will also add flexibility, especially if the work is paid for in installments, such as a deposit at the start of the contract and the remainder while the work is being completed.

If specific parts are routinely used, such as plumbing fixtures or electrical devices, the list should be kept in a separate table, each part with an identifier such as an ID or an SKU. The data in the parts table can be accessed by the form or report that brings the workorder expenses together.

Other peripheral data can be included in separate small tables, such as shipping or payment methods. The Home Tech Repair company information also can be kept in one separate table, accessible to the report that prints the invoice. This table can include the company address, phone and FAX numbers, Internet address, and any short standard message to include in correspondence.

Identify the Data Fields

All the fields should relate directly to the subject and not include any information that can be derived from other fields. Include all the information you need—nothing extra. Break up the information into small, logical parts, such as First Name and Last Name fields, rather than a single Full Name field. Name the fields so you will be able to locate specific records and sort by individual field values. You can always combine the fields later for finding and searching if you need to.

Table 2-1 lists the fields in each of the Home Tech Repair tables and shows the type, the size, and a brief description of the data that will be stored in the field. Access can handle a wide variety of data, including text, numbers, currency, date/time, and variable length text in memo fields. It can also use special types of data such hyperlinks to outside locations and OLE objects including photos and drawings.

After arranging the data in the tables, review the distribution carefully to remove any redundancies, such as the customer's name and address repeated in the Workorders table. Also, make sure all fields in each table apply directly to that subject. For example, the overhead and the total work order costs are calculated fields, and thus are not included in the Workorders table.

Specify Key Fields

Each of the three main tables of the Home Tech Repair database has a field that uniquely identifies a record: Workorder Number, Employee ID, and Customer ID. Such a field is called the primary key field and no two records may have the same value in that field. The values in these fields can be entered by the user or assigned by Access in the form of an incremental AutoNumber.

Field	Data Type	Field Size	Description
Workorders Table			
Workorder Number	Number	Integer	Uniquely identifies work order
Customer ID	Number	Integer	Customer ID
Bid Number	Text	5	Original bid number
Start Date	Date	N/A	Scheduled start date
Completion Date	Date	N/A	Expected completion date
Supervisor	Number	Integer	ID of employee in charge
Principal Worker	Number	Integer	ID of employee who is second in charge
Helper	Number	Integer	ID of helper
Material Cost	Currency	2 decimals	Cost of materials
Labor Cost	Currency	2 decimals	Cost of labor
Description	Memo	N/A	Description of work order
Drawing	Hyperlink	N/A	File of drawing, as required
Employees Table			
Employee ID	Number	Integer	Uniquely identifies employee
First Name	Text	20	Employee's first name
Last Name	Text	25	Employee's last name
SSN	Text	10	Social Security Number
Specialty	Text	25	Special labor skills
Address	Text	50	Employee's home address
City	Text	50	City
State	Text	2	State
ZIP	Text	9	ZIP code
Work Phone	Text	12	Office phone or pager
Home Phone	Text	12	Home phone
Hourly Rate	Currency	2 decimals	Salary hourly rate
Billing Rate	Currency	2 decimals	Customer's billing rate
Comments	Memo	N/A	Additional information
Badge Picture	OLE Object	N/A	Employee picture

TABLE 2-1 Distributing Data Among Home Tech Repair Tables

Field	Data Type	Field Size	Description
Customers Table			
Customer ID	Number	Integer	Uniquely identifies customer
First Name	Text	20	Customer's first name
Last Name	Text	25	Customer's last name
Billing Address	Text	50	Address to send bill to
City	Text	50	City
State	Text	2	State
ZIP	Text	9	ZIP code
Phone Number	Text	12	Customer's phone
FAX Number	Text	12	Customer's FAX number
Notes	Memo	N/A	Additional customer information

TABLE 2-1   Distributing Data Among Home Tech Repair Tables (*continued*)

If the number has no other significance, such as identifying the general location of the job, let Access enter the number and you can be sure there are no duplicates.

Define Table Relationships

To relate two tables, you must use common fields. The linking field in the main table usually is the primary key field—for example, the Customer ID field in the Customers table. The linking field in the other table is called the foreign key and usually is not a primary key—for example, the Customer ID field in the Workorders table. The linking fields need not have the same names, but should be the same data types and contain matching values.

The relationship between the Customers and Workorders table is one-to-many because one customer might contract for more than one job. The relationship between the Employees table and the Workorders table also is one-to-many because one employee can work on more than one job at a time and in one of three slots—supervisor, principal worker, helper—in a single job.

Figure 2-2 shows the Home Tech Repair tables in the Access Relationships window. The field lists have been lengthened to display all the fields. The figure also shows a fourth table, Bid Data, which you can add later.

NOTE   *There are three instances of the Employees table in the Relationships window because it is linked to three separate fields in the Workorders table. Chapter 4 contains information about working in the Relationships window and defining relationships.*

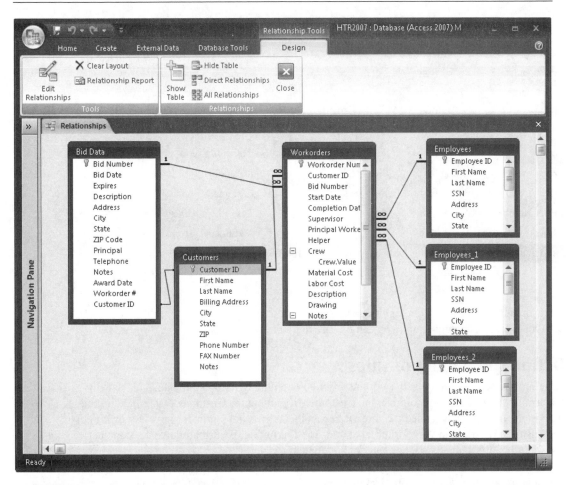

FIGURE 2-2 The Home Tech Repair tables.

Complete the Database

Now is the time to consult with the users for additional comments and suggestions. Step through the operations you plan to carry out with the information. Then, armed with the "go-ahead," do the following:

1. Gather just enough data to test the application. You can complete the tables later.

2. Design the forms, reports, and queries. If the database is for inexperienced users, you can group the forms and reports by company user to make their jobs easier.

3. Carefully test the entire system. Time spent refining and verifying the design now can save time revising the database after it has been populated with data. In addition, if serious design changes are needed later, you may have to discard the data and start over with the new design.

After the design is established, Access gives you two ways to create a new database. You can do this by

■ Downloading a pre-designed database template

■ Starting from scratch with a blank database

You Can Relate Tables Three Different Ways

One-to-Many

This is the most common relationship between tables. One record in one table can have many matching records in another table. The table on the "one" side often is called the *parent* table and the other is the *child* table. For example, the Customers table would have one record for each customer, whereas the Workorders table might have more than one work order for the same customer. Both tables would include a field with a value that represents that specific customer and links the two tables.

One-to-One

This relationship is more like a lookup tool in which each record in one of the tables has a matching record in the other table. Both tables have the same standing and neither table is designated as the parent. The key fields in both tables are the primary keys. One good use for this type of relationship is to store additional, seldom-referenced information about an item, such as an abstract of a book or the details of a work order in the first table.

Many-to-Many

The many-to-many relationship is not exactly permitted as such in a relational database. Many records in one table have the same values in the key field as many records in the second table. If you relate tables in this way using Access, you must create a third table, called a *junction table,* to place between the first two, then relate the two original tables to the junction using two one-to-many relationships. For example, the relationship between the Employees and the Customers tables is many-to-many, and the Workorders tables could serve as a junction table between them.

Create a Database with a Template

If you don't want to bother designing your own database and if you need the database for a common personal or business purpose, one of the Access templates can get you started. Once you have created the database, you can add your own data and make modifications to the forms and reports that came with the turnkey application. If none of the templates seem to fill your needs, you can start with a blank database.

The Getting Started with Microsoft Office Access window shows a couple of templates in the center pane. If you double-click on one of the thumbnails, you can see a sample form in the right pane along with instructions for downloading the template. For example, enter a name for the database and click the folder icon to change to a different destination directory.

To see more templates, double-click one of the subjects in the Template Categories group in the left pane. Figure 2-3 shows eight different templates available in the Business category. Double-click a template thumbnail again to get more information.

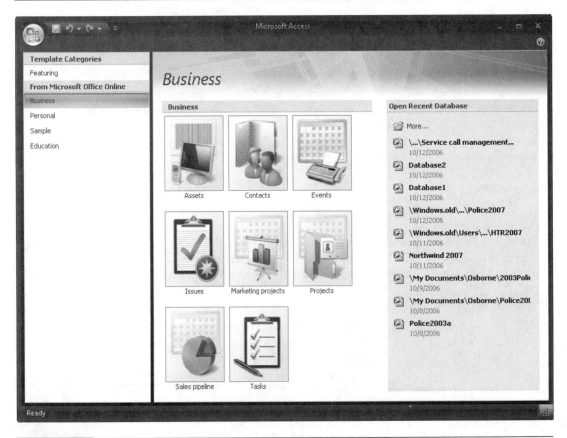

FIGURE 2-3 Database Templates in the Business category.

If none of these options match your requirements, you can browse online for more templates, some from earlier versions of Access:

1. Scroll down to the bottom of the center pane in the Getting Started with Microsoft Office Access window.

2. Click on Templates under More on Office Online.

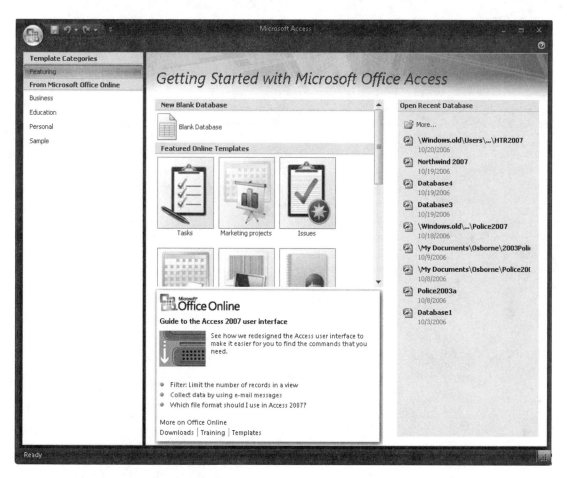

3. Scroll to the bottom of the window and enter Databases in the Search text box and select Access from the Program list.

4. Click Search. (See Figure 2-4)

For Home Tech Repair, the best template seems to be the Service Call Management database. To download the template, select the database in the search list (see Figure 2-5) and click

FIGURE 2-4   Searching for database templates online.

Download Now. You can change the file name and select a different destination folder. Microsoft Office downloads the file automatically to your default directory and opens the database.

As before, when the downloaded database opens you will see the Security Warning message and are then prompted to enable the contents of the database. Click the Option button, then in the Microsoft Office Security Option dialog box, check Enable this Content and click OK.

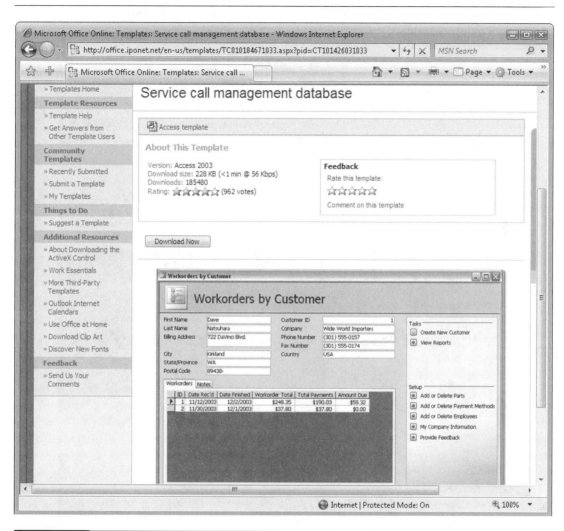

FIGURE 2-5   Preparing to download the database template.

You can move and rename the new database and then convert it to Access 2007. To convert the database to Access 2007, once you have downloaded it, do the following:

1. Click the Microsoft Office button and choose Convert in the drop-down menu.

2. Enter the file name in the Convert Database Into dialog box.

3. Accept Save as type Microsoft Office Access 2007 Database and click Save.

You can learn more about converting to other versions of Access in Appendix A. For now, let's view the database in Access 2007 as shown in Figure 2-6 with the main form in the document pane and the objects listed in the Navigation Pane.

NOTE *If you don't see tabs in the document pane after converting the database to Access 2007, you can restore the option. Click the Microsoft Office button and click Access Options. On the left pane, choose Current Database. In the Application Options group, check Tabbed Documents then click OK. Close and restart the database to have the change take effect. More about setting workplace options in Chapter 13.*

You can now add more objects and delete the ones you don't need or change the names to fit your business. You can also add and remove fields from the tables and change report and form styles and content. You may need to change relationships if you remove a related table or field that

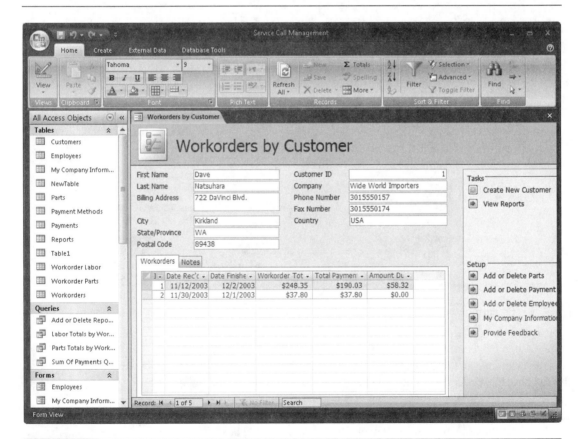

FIGURE 2-6   The new Service Call Management database in Access 2007.

is used as links. All of these actions are covered in the next chapters. Right now, it is important to know that you have a great deal of flexibility with respect to a downloaded template.

Once you have tailored the database to fit your needs, you can create custom group categories in the Navigation Pane that include related activities. For example, place all the Workorder-related forms and reports in a group named Workorders. The group would include:

- Workorder by Customer form
- Workorders form
- Invoice report
- Print Invoice form
- Payments form

A second custom group, named Preview Reports would include the following reports:

- Revenue by Employer
- Sales by Month
- Finished Workorders in House
- Unfinished Workorders
- Workorder Summary

A third custom group, named Other Information would include the following forms for data viewing and entry:

- Parts
- Payment Methods
- My Company Information
- Employees

See Chapter 17 for ways to customize the Navigation Pane.

Run the New Application

At startup, the Home Tech Repair application automatically opens the main form for the application Workorders by Customer, as shown in Figure 2-6. It is here that you can enter new work orders, edit existing records, or view details of specific work orders.

To see individual workorder information, select the workorder in the subform and click the View Workorder command button (see Figure 2-7). The information contains specifics about a single workorder, including the parts needed for the job, and (on the Labor tab) the employees who worked on the job, their billing rate, and the hours spent. The costs are calculated and

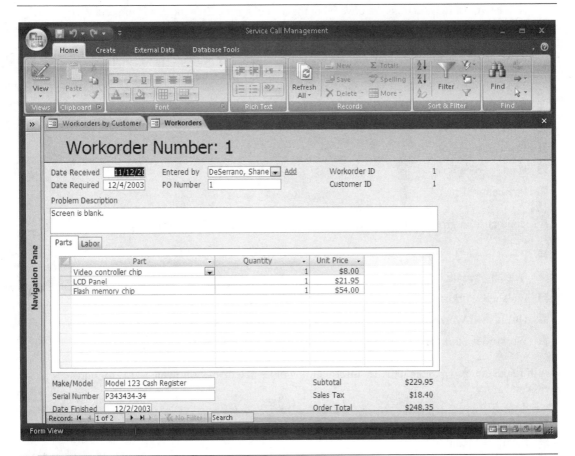

FIGURE 2-7   Reviewing the details of a workorder.

displayed with payments credited to the workorder and the remaining balance computed. Close this form to return to the previous form.

Many changes are required to have the template database conform to the needs of the Home Tech Repair Company. Some fields are unnecessary and should be removed; others are renamed. Any disturbed relationships must be restored. Additional forms and reports that depend on different queries, filters, or sort orders might be necessary. All of these changes can be made to the Home Tech Repair database built from the Service Call Maintenance template.

Start with a Blank Database

If you don't find a template that comes close to the database you have in mind, you can create your own by starting with a blank one and adding the tables you need one at a time. Once you have the skeleton database, you can import objects from other databases or create the tables and other objects yourself.

First, let's start by creating a new blank database as follows:

1. Click the Microsoft Office button and choose New, then select Blank Database in the center pane of the Getting Started window.

2

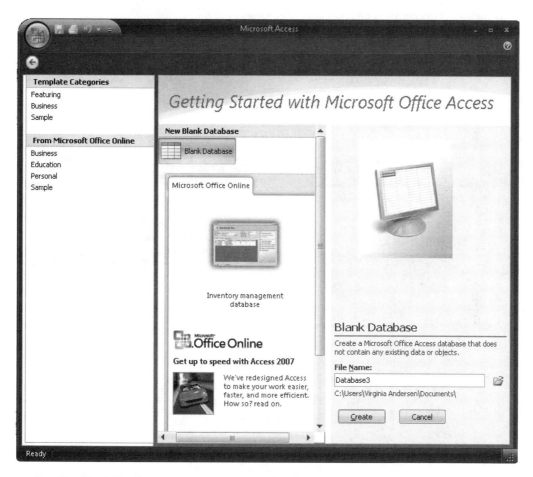

2. The Blank Database pane opens at the right of your screen where you can enter a name for the new database and click the folder icon to browse for the folder in which you want to store it.

3. After entering a custom name for the new database and opening the folder where you want to store the database, click Create.

A new empty table is started for you in the tabbed document window and the new table name, Table1, is listed in the Navigation Pane. The Datasheet ribbon tab is active and contains all the tools you need to build the new table in Datasheet View.

All you need to do now is:

- Enter data in the new table and save it with a name or
- Switch to Design View and build the table structure.

In the next chapter, you will learn how to create and modify new table structures. The many field properties that determine the appearance and behavior of the data are also discussed. Additionally, you will learn how to improve the value of the information in a database by adding validation rules, default field values, and other features.

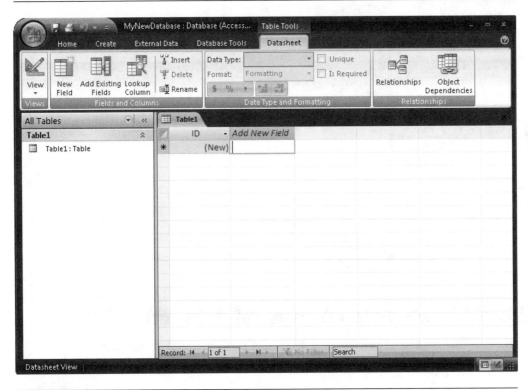

FIGURE 2-8   Starting with a new blank database.

Chapter 3

Create and Modify Tables

How to...

- Create a table from a template
- Create a table from scratch in Design or Datasheet view
- Modify a table design
- Ensure data validity
- Copy an existing table structure

Tables are the essential building blocks of a relational database: the development of a database begins with building the tables to store the data distributed among them. If you carefully design your table structures, you can have a smooth-running, error-free information system instead of a total disaster.

In this chapter, you will return to the Home Tech Repair database introduced in Chapter 2. See Appendix A for instructions for downloading the database from the Osborne web site.

Create a New Table from a Template

Access 2007 provides several built-in table templates that you can use to start a new table structure. Not only are the table templates appropriate for common office usage, they are compatible with the Microsoft SharePoint Services lists of the same name.

To start a new table from a template, open the database and on the Create ribbon tab in the Tables group, click the Table Templates command.

Look over the list of templates and click the one that best suits your needs. (Figure 3-1 shows a new table built from the Contacts template.) The new table that you have chosen will now be added to your database. You can make changes in the fields and their properties as described later in this chapter.

Create a New Table in Datasheet View

When you start a new database, Access automatically creates a new table for you and displays it in Datasheet view. If you have already started the database and want to add a new table, use the Create tab again. Then click the Table command in the Tables group.

A new table now opens in Datasheet view in the object pane with two fields showing:

- ID, which is the automatic primary key field
- Add New Field, where you begin entering data.

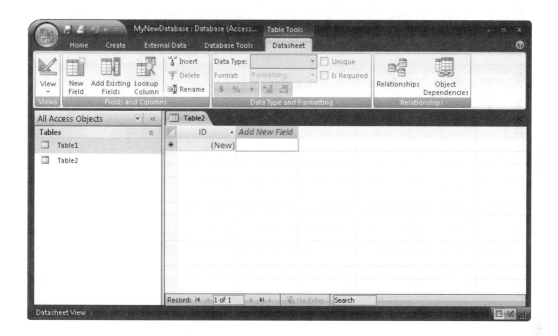

Add Fields to the New Table

You build a new table in Datasheet view by entering the data in the cell just below Add New Field in the column header. As you enter data in each new field, Access chooses the appropriate data type for the field, such as Text, Number, or Date/Time. For example:

- John Brown results in a Text field
- 1/15/07 results in a Date/Time field
- 12.99 results in a Number, Double because of the digits to the right of the decimal point
- $15,000.00 results in a Currency field

NOTE *See the section called "Create a New Table from Scratch in Design View" for a list and description of all the Access data types.*

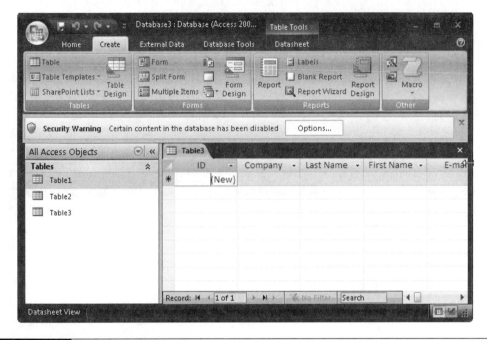

FIGURE 3-1 Creating a new table from a template.

Change Data Types and Formats

To check up on what data type Access has assigned to a field, do the following:

1. Click the Datasheet tab and select the field you want to change.
2. In the Data Type and Formatting group click the Data Type command.
3. If you want the field to have a different data type, choose the type from the list. The selected data type must be compatible with the data you have already entered in the field.

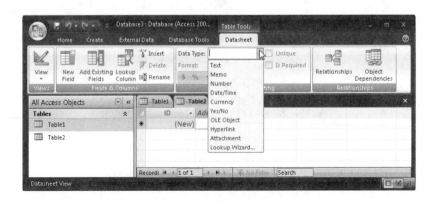

You can also change the default data format by clicking the Format command in the Data Type and Formatting group. Then choose from the list of formats that apply to the selected field's data type.

Change Field Names

As you enter the new fields, Access automatically names the fields Field1, Field2, and so on. To change a field's name to something more meaningful, right-click the field header and select Rename Column in the shortcut menu. You can also use the Rename command in the Fields and Columns group of the Datasheet tab. Then enter the new name in the column header.

Field names can have up to 64 characters, including letters, numbers, and spaces. Don't begin a field name with a space, however. You also cannot use any of the characters Access attaches special meanings to, such as periods, exclamation marks, or brackets. Using a mixture of uppercase and lowercase letters can help explain the field to the user, but Access doesn't differentiate between cases in field names.

Use a Field Template

Access 2007 has included the field templates from previous versions and grouped them in the table templates. You can save time by placing these templates in your new table. To see the list of the templates you can add to your table in Datasheet view, do the following:

1. On the Datasheet tab in the Fields and Columns group, and click the New Field command.

2. In the Field Templates pane, click a plus sign next to one of the table template names to see the fields in that table.

3. When you find the field you want, click and drag it to the table. Drop the field when the insertion line appears.

4. When finished, click the Close button in the Field Templates pane.

You can select more than one field from the Field Templates pane and drag the group to the Datasheet view. To select contiguous fields, select the first field in the list and hold down SHIFT *as you select the last field. If the fields are not contiguous, hold down* CRTL *as you select them individually. They will appear in the table in consecutive columns.*

Add Fields from an Existing Table

When you build a relational database, the related tables will have fields with matching data types. If you have already built one of the tables and are working on a new one, you can add fields from the existing table, whether or not the new table is related.

To do this, you need to see the list of all existing fields in all the tables in the database. In the Fields and Columns group on the Datasheet tab, click Add Existing Fields. The Field List pane opens (as shown in Figure 3-2) showing the names of all the tables currently in your database. The list contains two categories of tables:

■ Fields available in related tables that list all of the tables to which the current table is related.

■ Fields available in other tables that list tables not yet related to the current table.

To see the list of fields in a table, click the plus sign by the table name. If you want to add one of the fields in the list, drag the field name to the Datasheet view and drop it when you see the insertion line. This starts the Lookup Wizard that you can use to add Lookup columns to the table that contain the values from the field you chose. You'll learn more about the Lookup field later in this chapter, and you can also see Chapter 5 for details about using the Lookup Wizard in Design view in order to create Lookup fields.

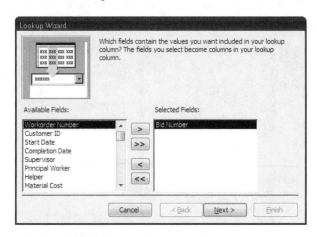

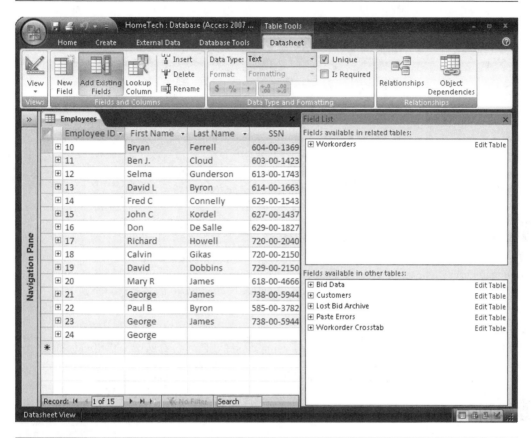

FIGURE 3-2 Selecting fields from existing tables.

Save the New Table

When you are satisfied with the new table structure, you can give it a name and save it in the database. The table name can contain up to 64 characters, including spaces. You have three ways to save the table:

- Click the Microsoft Office button and click Save
- Right-click the table document tab and click Save in the shortcut menu
- Click Save on the Quick Access toolbar

If you have not already assigned a name to the table, enter the name in the Save As dialog box and click OK.

 *It is actually a good idea to save a new object several times during development, especially if the process takes a while, just in case the worst happens.*

Create a Table from Scratch in Design View

The easiest way to start a new table from a blank table design is to click the Table Design command in the Tables group on the Create tab. An empty table appears in the Table Design window, as shown in Figure 3-3. The ribbon automatically changes to the Design tab.

Tour the Table Design View

You have two panes to work with in the table Design window. The upper pane is the field entry area where you enter the field name, the data type, and an optional description. In this upper pane, you can also specify the field that will serve as the primary key for the table. The lower pane is devoted to specifying the individual field properties for the field selected in the upper pane. Properties such as size, display appearance, validity rules, and many more appear in the list of properties in the lower pane.

The list of properties you see depends on the type of field you are entering. To the right of the Field Properties pane is a description of the currently active area of the screen.

There are some new commands on the Design tab of the Table Tools ribbon that relate to the task of creating and modifying a table definition. You will use many of these commands in later sections in this chapter.

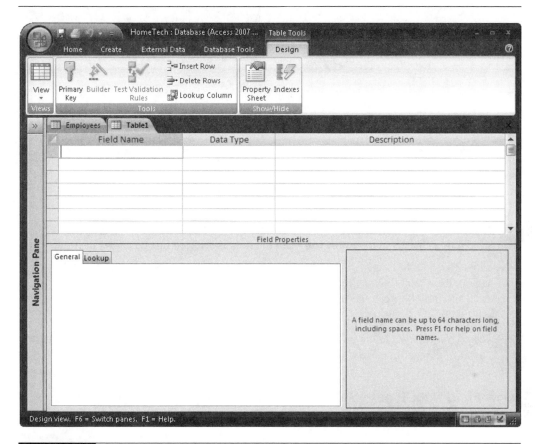

FIGURE 3-3   Starting a new table in Design view.

Add Fields

To begin adding fields to your new table, do the following:

1. Click in the first row of the field entry area and type the first field name.

2. Choose an appropriate data type from the Data Type drop-down list. Because the most commonly used field type is Text, Access automatically specifies a new field as a Text field by default. To change it to another type, select from the drop-down list in the Data Type property box.

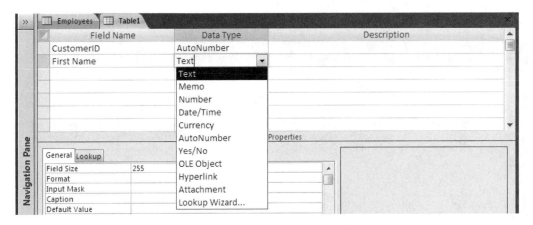

3. Enter an optional description to provide additional information about the field. The description appears in the status bar when the field is selected in a datasheet or form.

4. Move to the Field Properties pane and change the default properties, if necessary. Otherwise, repeat steps 1 through 3 to add other fields. You can also press F6 to jump back and forth between the field list and the property pane.

Once you get used to the names of the available data types, you can simply type the first letter of the type name and Access will fill it in.

Specify Field Data Types

Several factors come into play as you decide on the data types you want to use; for example:

- What kind of values do you plan to allow in the field?
- What are you going to do with the data? You can count the number of records containing a specific value in a field specified as most of the data types, but you can add up values only from Number and Currency fields.
- Will you want to sort or index records? You can sort or index on any field type except Object Linking, Embedding (OLE) Objects, and attachments.
- Will you want to group records for a report or query? You can group on any field type except Memo, Hyperlink, OLE Object fields, and attachments.

You can use the field templates to help add new fields to your table. Simply click in an empty row in the table design and then click the Builder command in the Tools group (the one that looks like a magic wand). The list of field templates contains the same sample table and field lists shown in an earlier section. The predefined fields come with complete names, data types, and other common properties.

The following sections introduce you to each of the eleven data types and how they are used.

Text   The Text data type is the most common data type, and it can contain any combination of up to 255 characters and numbers (the default size). You use the Text type for storing values that contain combinations of numbers and letters such as addresses and job descriptions. If you expect the field to contain more than 255 characters, consider using the Memo field type instead, which can hold much more data.

Memo   Use a Memo field to store long but variable-length text, possibly relating to other field data. Of course, not every record will include memo data, but when it does, the text can vary in size from a few words to up to 65,535 characters. Memo fields also support rich text format (rtf) editing.

Number   Select the Number data type when you plan to sort based on numeric values or use them in calculations, such as adding up the labor hours for a plumbing job or the hours that a certain employee has worked during the fall season. Fields that contain numbers but that will never be used in calculations are better specified as Text data types. For example, a Social Security Number stored without the dashes, or the first five digits of a Zip code.

If you are working with dollar sales figures, it is better to use a Currency type because you can choose from several monetary display formats.

Date/Time   The Date/Time type is very useful when you want to be able to sort your records chronologically by the value in the field. You can also use a Date/Time field in your calculations in order to determine elapsed time. With the Date/Time data type, you also have a variety of ways to display the data—for example, 25-Dec-2007, 12/25/2007, or December 25, 2007.

Currency   Use the Currency type when you want to store monetary values, such as the cost and bid price of contracted jobs. You can use Currency fields, just like Number fields, in arithmetic calculations.

AutoNumber   When you specify an AutoNumber field, Access guarantees that each record in the table has a unique value in the field, thereby creating a field that you can use confidently as a primary key. Access automatically generates a unique value for the field as you enter and save each new record.

Yes/No   The Yes/No field is useful when you want the equivalent of a checkmark in your records. For example, suppose you want to know if a transaction has been posted or a job has been completed. By default, a Yes/No field appears as a check box control in a datasheet and in forms and reports. You can choose to display Yes or No, On or Off, or True or False. You can also create your own custom display for Yes/No fields.

OLE Object   When you want to embed or link an object from another source in your table, use an OLE Object type field. With this type of field, you can acquire data from such objects as an Excel spreadsheet, a Word document, a graphics or sound file, or other binary data.

Hyperlink When you want the field to jump to another location or connect to the Internet or an intranet, store the hyperlink address in a Hyperlink field. The hyperlink can link to a web address (URL), a file on your own computer, or a file on an intranet or LAN. A hyperlink field contains four parts: the text you want to display, the target address, a subaddress if necessary, and an optional ScreenTip.

Attachment An Attachment field is used to store pictures, images, files from other Office programs, and binary files, This data type is similar to attaching files to an e-mail message. An Attachment field offers more flexibility that the OLE data type because you can store all types of documents or even binary files. You can also put multiple attachments in a single record.

Lookup Wizard The Lookup Wizard is not exactly a data type. It is a wizard that creates a field that is limited to a list of values that are valid for the field. Some examples might include a list of employees or current projects. When you select this option, a wizard helps you create the list and actually attaches it to your table. You can type in the values you want to use or have the Lookup Wizard consult another table for the set of valid values. When you enter table data, you can choose the value you want from a drop-down list.

Set Field Properties

You can set field properties to control how the values in the field are stored and displayed. Each type of field has a particular set of properties. For example, you might want certain currency values displayed with two decimal places, a dollar sign, and a comma as the thousands separator. Or, you could specify that the currency values be rounded off to the nearest whole dollar. While you can set some of the field properties in Datasheet view, it is more efficient to use the Design view.

 *When you click in a field property, you can see a description of the property in the lower-right pane of the table Design view. You can also press F1 to see the related Help topic.*

Access attaches some default properties to every field. You can accept or change the settings to customize your fields. Because Text fields are the most common and most of the field properties apply to the Text data type, let's take a look at their properties first. Table 3-1 describes the properties of a Text field, most of which are also available to other types of fields, although they will have different default settings for different data types.

To specify a property setting:

1. Select the field in the field entry pane (the upper portion of the window) in Design view.

2. Click the desired property in the Field Properties pane.

 *You can also press F6 to move to the Field Properties pane then use the Up and Down keys to move among the properties.*

3. If you see a down arrow next to the property, click it to display a list of property options from which you can choose. In most cases, you can also type in the setting you want.

Property	Effect
Field Size	Specifies the maximum number of characters allowed in the field. For more details, see the "Choose a Field Size" section.
Format	Determines the display appearance, such as forcing uppercase or lowercase characters. No default format is specified for text fields. See "Format Field Data" for more information.
Input Mask	Provides a template for data that follows a pattern, such as telephone numbers or Social Security numbers, and can add literal characters to the field if needed. Used to control data entry. Default is none.
Caption	Displays a name other than the field name in datasheets, forms, and reports. Default is none.
Default Value	Automatically enters the specified value in the field. Default is none.
Validation Rule	Specifies an expression that will check for invalid data. Default is none.
Validation Text	Displays this message if the entered data fails the validation rule. Default is none.
Required	Indicates that this field may not be left blank. Default is No.
Allow Zero Length	Differentiates between a blank field and a field containing an empty string of text (""). Helpful when a value is known not to exist (such as a FAX number). Default is Yes.
Indexed	Indicates that the table is indexed on this field. Default is No. See section, "Create Other Indexes" for more information.
Unicode Compression	Allows string data that now is stored in Unicode format to be compressed to save storage space. Default is Yes.
IME Mode	Sets the IME (Input Method Editor) mode for a field when focus is moved to it. IME is a program that enters East Asian text into programs by converting keystrokes into complex East Asian characters. Default is No Control.
IME Sentence Mode	Sets the type of IME sentence. Default is None.
Smart Tags	Specifies which Smart Tags to apply to the field. Smart Tags are new to Access and provide links to other information about the field.
Text Align	Specifies the default alignment of the field in a control. Default is General.

TABLE 3-1   Text Field Properties

Other properties, such as Input Mask and Validation Rule, include a Build button that appears as a button displaying three dots (...) to the right of the property text box. You can click on this Build button to get help with the property. If you don't need help building an expression, you can just type it in the property box. If the expression is invalid, Access will let you know.

Choose a Field Size

The Text, Number, and AutoNumber field types are the only ones that you can specify a field size, as Access automatically sets field sizes for the other types. A text field that will contain only a few characters, such as a postal code or job number, doesn't need to take up the default 255 characters of disk space. You can change the size of the field by entering a different number in the Field Size property. Another reason to specify the field size is to prevent data entry errors by limiting the number of characters that can be entered.

Number fields are sized a little differently because they specify the name of the specific numeric type rather than the number of characters. The options are:

- **Byte**   Stores small positive integers (whole numbers) between 1 and 255
- **Integer**   Stores larger positive and negative integers, between –32,768 and +32,768
- **Long Integer**   Stores the default Number field size, which is used to store even larger signed integers between roughly –2 billion and +2 billion
- **Single**   Stores single-precision floating-point numbers in IEEE format
- **Double**   Stores double-precision floating-point numbers in IEEE format
- **Replication ID**   Stores a global unique identifier (GUID). Replication is not supported in the new Access 2007 accdb file format, but it is still supported in mdb files used in Access 2007.
- **Decimal**   Makes the Precision and Scale properties available to control number entries

NOTE   *AutoNumber fields are limited to Long Integer and Replication ID field sizes.*

If you change the size of a Number field, you are only changing the way that the numbers are stored, not the appearance of the numbers. To change their appearance, you need to change the Format property.

Format Field Data

The Format property is used to specify the appearance of the value when it is displayed, and it has no effect on the way the value is stored nor does it check for invalid entries. The Format property makes sure that all the field values look alike no matter how you entered the data.

When you set a field's Format property in Design view, Access applies that format to the values in Datasheet view and in any new forms and reports based on the table. Fields that were added to the form or report design prior to setting the custom formats are unaffected. Table 3-2 describes the custom formatting symbols that can be used with all data types.

Other custom formatting symbols are valid for only specific data types as described in the following paragraphs.

Symbol	Effect
!	Enters characters from left to right instead of right to left, forcing left alignment.
(Space)	Enters a space as a literal character when the SPACEBAR is pressed.
"xyz"	Displays the characters or symbols within the quotation marks.
*	Fills available space with the character that follows.
\	Indicates that the character that follows should be treated as a literal character. The back slash is often used with reserved symbols and characters.
[color]	Displays the field data in the color contained within the brackets. You can use black, blue, green, cyan, red, magenta, yellow, or white.

TABLE 3-2   Custom Formatting Symbols

Text and Memo Fields   Text and Memo fields use the same format symbols, some of which are character placeholders that apply to individual characters, while others affect the entire entry. Table 3-3 describes the symbols you can use with Text and Memo field data.

Custom Text and Memo format settings can have two sections, separated by a semicolon. The first section applies to fields containing text and the second to fields that are blank.

The following are some examples of using the Text and Memo format settings:

Format Setting	Entered As	Displays
@@@@@-@@-@@@@	123456789	123-45-6789
@@@@@@@-&&&&	92118	92118-
>	Jimmy	JIMMY
<	JIMMY	jimmy
@@@\!	Hello	Hello!
@@@;"No Data"	horse	horse
@@@;"No Data"	(blank)	No Data

Symbol	Effect
@	Indicates that a character or a space is required
&	Indicates that a character or a space is optional
<	Converts all characters to lowercase
>	Converts all characters to uppercase

TABLE 3-3   Text and Memo Format Symbols

Number and Currency Fields You can format your Number and Currency data with one of Access's predefined formats or create your own using the special formatting symbols. The Format property of a Currency field is automatically set to Currency, but you can change it to any of the other settings if you like. The Format property of a Number or Currency field displays a list of the predefined formats as described in Table 3-4.

TIP *When you specify the Percent format for a number field, you have to change the Field Size property from the default Long Integer to Single. Otherwise, the field displays only the integer portion of the number you enter and leaves off the fraction. For example, if you enter 1, the field will display "100.00%," but if you enter 1.25, the field will still display "100.00%."*

Date/Time Fields Date/Time fields include seven predefined format settings and some symbols you can use to create your own custom formats. Table 3-5 describes the formats that Access provides. Date and Time format settings are specified according to the setting in the Regional Setting Properties dialog box in the Windows Control Panel.

Yes/No Fields Access automatically displays a default check box control when you specify a Yes/No data type and ignores any format settings you make.

Setting	Effect
General Number	Displays the number as entered. This is the default setting for Number fields.
Currency	Displays the number with a currency symbol and thousands separator. Negative values appear in parentheses. Default is two decimal places. This setting is the default for Currency fields.
Euro	Displays the number with the Euro currency symbol and a thousands separator. Negative values appear in parentheses. Default is two decimal places.
Fixed	Displays at least one digit. Default is two decimal places.
Standard	Displays the thousands separator. Default is two decimal places.
Percent	Displays the value multiplied by 100 with an added percent sign (%). Default is two decimal places.
Scientific	Uses standard scientific notation with exponents. For example, 243 displays as 2.43E+02.

TABLE 3-4 Number, AutoNumber, and Currency Predefined Formats

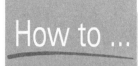

Include Literal Characters with Date/Time Values

You can use characters other than the date and time separators with the Date/Time values, in order to present dates and times with text. To do this, close the text and spaces in quotation marks. Some examples of using these special formatting symbols are:

Setting	Displays
ddd," "mmm d," "yy	Mon, Jan 15, 07
dddd," "mmmm d," "yyyy	Monday, January 15, 2007
h:n:s AM/PM	9:15:35 AM

In addition, you can add other characters to the display format by enclosing them in quotation marks. For example, entering the value **5/25/07** in a field with the format setting
"Today is " "dddd" " in week number " "ww"""."
displays
Today is Friday in week number 21.

Notice the spaces within the quotation marks that separate the characters in the string from the date values and the period added to the end of the expression.

You can create almost any display format using special characters to represent the hour, minute, and second in a time format and the day, week, month, and year in a date format. For example, the letter *d* can display the day of the month as one or two digits or as the full name, depending on how many *d*s you use in the string. The letter *m* can also be used to represent the month from one or two digits to the full name. Refer to the Access Help topic "Format Property–Date/Time Data Type" for details of the many formatting symbols you can use with Date/Time fields.

To change a Yes/No field format, you need to use the field's Display Control property in the table design:

1. Open the table in Design view.
2. Select the Yes/No field.
3. Click the Lookup tab in the Field Properties pane.
4. Select Text Box from the Display Control list.
5. Return to the General tab to choose the desired display format.

Setting	Description
General Date	Combines Short Date and Long Time settings. This is the default setting. If no time is specified, then only the date is displayed; if no date is displayed, only the time is displayed. Examples: 5/21/07 3:30:00 PM (US) 21/5/07 15:30:00 (UK)
Long Date	Uses the Long Date Regional setting. Examples: Friday, May 25, 2007 (US) Friday, 25 May 2007 (UK)
Medium Date	Example: 25-May-07
Short Date	Uses the Short Date Regional setting. Examples: 5/21/07 (US) 21/5/07 (UK)
Long Time	Example: 3:30:00 PM
Medium Time	Example: 3:30 PM
Short Time	Example: 15:30

TABLE 3-5   Date/Time Predefined Format Settings

The Yes/No custom format contains up to three sections separated by semicolons. The first section is not used, but you still need to enter the semicolon before entering the second section. The second and third sections specify what to display when the value is Yes and No, respectively. For example, the format

```
;"Yes, indeed!"[Green];"No, never!"[Red]
```

displays

```
Yes, indeed!
```

in green when the value is Yes, and

```
No, never!
```

in red if the value is No.

NOTE

If you choose Combo Box as the Display Control property instead of Text Box, more properties appear on the Lookup page. It's here that you can set the appearance and values of the list that the combo box will display. For more about using combo boxes and lookup lists, see Chapter 5.

Set the Number of Decimal Places

The Field Size, Format, and Decimal Places properties of Number and Currency fields are all related. The Field Size property determines whether the number is stored as an integer or with fractional values and specifies the degree of mathematical precision.

The Format property adds display features such as dollar or percent signs and commas as thousands separators.

The Decimal Places property determines how many digits to display to the right of the decimal point in a Number or Currency field. The default Decimal Places setting for Number and Currency fields is Auto, which displays two decimal places for fields with Format property settings of Currency, Fixed, Standard, Percent, and Scientific. If you want to change the number of Decimal Places in the display, click the arrow in the Decimal Places property box and choose a number from the list or just enter the number you want. The Decimal Places setting has no effect on the precision of the stored number, only on the display.

If the value is stored as an integer (Byte, Integer, or Long Integer data type), you will see only zeros to the right of the decimal point—no matter what you set in the Decimal Places property—because only the integer portion of the number is stored. If you keep the default Long Integer property, the values will be rounded to the nearest integer no matter how many decimal places you specify for the display.

To change the number of decimal places stored in the field, change the Field Size property to one of the settings for real numbers, such as Single, Double, or Decimal.

Include a Caption

If someone else will be using the database and you think the field names are not descriptive enough, you can use the Caption property to change the column heading in the Datasheet view. A caption can contain up to 2,048 characters in any combination of letters, numbers, special characters, and spaces.

The new caption will also appear in queries and replace the text in the field labels attached to controls in report and form designs. The field names remain the same; only the labels show the new caption text.

 If you rename the field later in Datasheet view, the Caption property is deleted. To prevent this, rename fields only in table Design view.

Choose a Primary Key

In a relational database system, it is important to be able to gather and retrieve related information from separate tables in the database. To do so, each record in one table must be unique in some way. The field or fields that contain the unique value is the *primary key*. Access does not permit duplicate values in the primary key nor does it permit blanks. There must be a valid, unique value in the primary key in every record. In Design view, you can tell which field contains the primary key by the key icon in the left margin.

When you create a new table in Datasheet view, Access automatically adds the first field and assigns it as the primary key with the AutoNumber data type.

Let Access Set the Key

The AutoNumber field type is an Access tool that can guarantee unique records in a table. Designating an AutoNumber field as the primary key for a table is probably the simplest way to set the key. You needn't worry about inadvertently entering duplicate values, though, because Access uses unique numbers to identify each record. Once the number is generated, it can't be changed or deleted. Access will also ensure that no other record contains the same value in that field.

You can choose to have incremental numbers or random numbers. With incremental values, Access adds 1 to the value for each record you add. When you choose random numbers for the AutoNumber field format, Access uses a random number generator to create the value. Replication ID numbers, also called GUIDs, are not supported in the 2007 accbd file format but can still be found in mdb file format.

When you finish a table design without having designated a primary key, Access asks if you want it to create one for you. If you answer Yes, Access either applies the primary key to an AutoNumber field—if one exists—or creates an AutoNumber field, which it then designates as the primary key. You can also respond No and leave the table without a key for the time being.

Set a Single-Field Primary Key

You've seen the Table Wizard pick a primary key and now it's your turn. If your table has a field that you are sure will not contain any duplicate values, you can use that field as the primary key. The AutoNumber field type is an Access tool that can guarantee unique records in a table.

Designating an AutoNumber field as the primary key for a table probably is the simplest way to set the key. You don't have to worry about inadvertently entering duplicate values because Access uses unique numbers to identify each record. Once the number is generated, it can't be changed or deleted.

In the table Design view, click in the field row that you want to use as the primary key, then on the Design tab in the Tools group the click Primary Key command. To remove the primary key designation, repeat the step.

Create Other Indexes

Indexes help Access find and sort records faster, just as an index helps you find topics in a reference book: an index in Access contains a pointer to the location of the data rather than the data itself. The primary key in a table is automatically indexed, so the indexes that you can create are secondary indexes created with other fields. An index can include a single field or multiple fields. You can index any field except an OLE or Attachment field.

To help you decide which fields to use as indexes, look at the fields you expect to search frequently or that you think you will want to sort. Also, if you expect to use a field to create a relationship with another table, you might want to create an index on the field to improve performance.

> **TIP**   *A field that has many records containing the same value is not a good candidate for an index because an index on such a field won't speed things up much.*

Add a Single-Field Index

To set a single-field index, simply change its Indexed property to Yes and decide whether to permit duplicate values. If you decide to allow duplicate values, choose "Yes (Duplicates OK)." If not, choose "Yes (No Duplicates)."

   To take a look at the indexes that have been specified for a table, on the Design tab in the Show/Hide group, click the Indexes command . The Customers table in the Home Tech Repair database includes two currently defined indexes. The primary key, Customer ID, is listed with the key icon as the first index in the list and a single-field index based on the customer's last name as the second. Notice that the primary key properties, shown in the Index Properties pane, specify the index as Primary with Unique values and that the Ignore Nulls property is marked No.

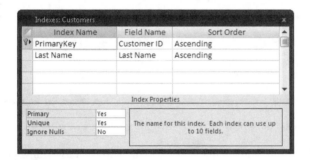

Create a Multiple-Field Index

Often, you may want to search or sort records based on more than one field at once. Creating a multiple-field index allows you to do just that. When you sort records using a multiple-field index, the records are sorted initially by the first field in the index. If Access finds duplicate values in the first field, it sorts by the next field, and so on. For example, you want to see records for customers in particular areas of the city. To do this, you can create an index using both the City and ZIP code fields.

   To create a multiple-field index, follow these steps:

1. With the Customers table open in Design view, on the Design tab in the Show/Hide group, click the Indexes command.

2. Click in the first empty row in the Indexes window.

3. Enter a name for the new index, such as **City Region**, and then press TAB to move to the Field Name column.

4. Click the down arrow and select City from the list of available fields.

5. Accept Ascending as the sort order for the City field and click in the Field Name in the next row (leaving the Index Name blank because both fields will be used in the same index).

6. Choose ZIP from the field list and change the sort order, if necessary.

7. If the index is intended to be the primary key, set the Primary property to Yes. (You will have to click the first row of the index containing the index name to display the Index Properties pane.) If you want the index to contain unique values for each record, change the Unique property to Yes. Leave the Ignore Nulls property set to No because a primary key cannot allow null values.

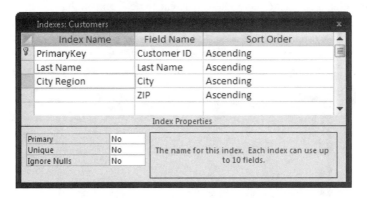

8. Close the Indexes dialog box and then save the changes to the table.

You can specify up to ten fields in one index with a mixture of ascending and descending orders for the fields.

Save the Table Design

The table design does not have to be complete before you save it. In fact, it is a good idea to occasionally save the design during the design process to guard against catastrophes. But Access does require you to save the design before you can switch to Datasheet view to enter data. To save the table design, do one of the following:

■ Click the Save button in the Quick Access toolbar

■ Right-click the table tab and choose Save in the shortcut menu

■ Click the Microsoft Office button and choose Save

The first time you save a new table, Access prompts you for a name. The table name can have up to 64 characters in any combination of letters, numbers, and spaces. It may not begin with a space, however. You can include special characters except those that have a special meaning to Access, such as a period (.), exclamation point (!), accent grave (`), or brackets ([]). You cannot use any control character with an ASCII value between 0 and 31.

TIP

If you want to undo the changes you have just made to the table design, close the table design and respond No when Access asks whether you want to save the changes.

Modify the Table Design

Even though you have tried to include all the necessary features and properties in your table design, you will undoubtedly find things that need changing. You might want to:

- Change the order of the fields in the table so that the ones you want to see most often appear on the screen without scrolling to the right.
- Add a new field or delete one that is not needed.
- Change the field size or type.

You can make any of these changes to an empty table with no problems, but after you have entered data, you risk losing data with some of the changes. Adding fields, increasing a field size, and rearranging the field order will not cause any data loss.

But if you decide to delete a field or reduce a field size in a table that already contains data, Access will display a warning if data loss might occur. Problems can also occur when changing a field type or renaming the field. It is always a good idea to make a backup of the data before making any changes to the table design.

Switch Table Views

If you are entering data in Datasheet view and you decide that you need to make some changes in the table structure, you can quickly return to the Design view by one of the following ways:

- Right-click the document tab and click Design view
- Click the Design button in the Access status bar
- On the Home tab in the Views group, click the View command and choose Design view.

Add or Delete Fields

You can add a new field to the bottom of the list of fields or insert one anywhere among the existing fields. To add one to the bottom, click in the first blank field and enter the field definition. To insert a field among existing fields, click in the row below where the new one is to appear, then do either of the following:

- On the Design tab in the Tools group, click the Insert Rows command
- Right-click the row and choose Insert Rows from the shortcut menu

The new blank field row is inserted above the row that contains the cursor, and all the fields below are moved down one row. The insertion point is in the new row.

Another way to add a new field that will inherit the same properties as one already in your table, is to copy the existing field to the clipboard and then paste it in an empty row. Of course, you must change the new field's name before you can save the table, because no two fields can have the same name. Only the field definition will be copied; previously entered data is not. (Earlier in the chapter you learned how to drag a field from another table in the database.)

If you want to add several rows at once, select the number of contiguous rows in the table design equal to the number of new fields you want to insert, and then use one of the previous methods. A number of new blank rows equal to the number of rows you selected appear above the top-selected row.

When you delete a field from the table design, you are not only deleting the field name but any data that has been entered in the field. Before deleting a field that contains data, Access warns that you will permanently lose the data and asks whether you really want to delete the field.

To delete a field click the row selector for the field in Design view and on the Design tab in the Tools group, click the Delete Rows command. You can also right-click in the row and choose Delete Rows from the shortcut menu. To delete several rows at once, select them all and then delete them as a group.

You can cause a problem by deleting a field that you have used in a query, form, or report. Be sure that you remove any references to the field you are about to delete from the other objects before you try to delete it. Access will not let you delete a field that is a link in a relationship to another table without deleting the relationship first.

Change the Field Order

If you want to change the order of fields in both the stored table and the Datasheet view, you can rearrange them in Design view. To move a field to a new position in the table design, click the row selector to select the row you want and then drag the row selector to move the field to its new position.

You can move several contiguous fields at once by selecting them all, and then dragging them as a group. To select more than one, click in the top field row selector and then drag through the row selectors until they are all selected. Alternatively, you can click the top field row selector and hold down SHIFT while you click the field row at the end of the group.

Although you can select noncontiguous field rows by holding down CTRL as you select the rows, you cannot drag the group to a new position.

If you want to keep the field order in the stored table but would like to view them in a different order in the datasheet, you can rearrange the datasheet columns without disturbing the table design. See Chapter 5 for information about changing the appearance of a datasheet.

Change a Field Name or Type

Earlier, you learned how to change the name that appears in the column heading in Datasheet view by changing the field Caption property. If you like, you can also change the actual field name in the design. Changing the field name has no effect on the data already entered into the field. However, it might cause problems with references to the field in other objects, such as queries, forms, and reports, or in an expression. To change a field name in Design view, simply type the new name. After changing the name, you must save the table again.

If there is no data in the table, you can safely change any field data type, but it is a little more complicated if the table already contains data. You might be trying to convert to a type quite different from the data already in the table. For example, you try to convert a text field to a number data type but the text fields contain alphabetic characters that are not permitted in number fields. Some types convert easily to another type, but other conversions might result in loss of data.

If the change will cause data to be lost, Access displays a message showing the number of values that will be affected before it makes the changes. If you have used the field in an expression, you might need to change the expression as well.

To change a field type in Design view:

1. Select the field.

2. Click the Data Type arrow and select the new data type.

3. Save the table design. If Access displays a warning message, respond No to cancel the changes or Yes to go ahead and make the changes. If you have no data in the table, Access doesn't display any warnings.

You will not encounter any difficulties converting other data types to text. Memo fields that are too long are truncated. Number fields convert to text with a General Number format, whereas Date/Time fields convert to text with the General Date format. Currency fields convert accurately to Text fields but without the currency symbols. Converting from text to other data types requires only that the text values conform to the new data type. You cannot change an Attachment field to another type.

 If the field you are converting is a primary key field or a unique index and the conversion would result in duplicate values, Access deletes the entire record. Access warns you first so you can prevent the deletion if necessary.

Change a Field Size

Changing the Field Size property has no effect on the data if you are increasing the size. Obviously, if you want to reduce the field size, especially for a Number field, you should make sure no values are larger than permitted by the new field size. If the values are too large to fit the new field size, they are replaced with Null values. If the new field size doesn't permit the number of decimal places currently specified, the values are rounded off.

Modify or Delete the Primary Key

You might find that the field you chose as the primary key does not always have a unique value after all and decide to use a different field or create a primary key with two or more fields.

To change the primary key, select the row you want as the primary key and on the Design tab in the Tools group, click the Primary Key command. The key icon is removed from the old key field and appears in the new one.

To add another field to the existing primary key, select both the old and new key fields, then click the Primary Key command. The key icon appears in the row selector of both rows.

There might be times when you want to temporarily disable the primary key—for example, when importing records from another table, some of which might contain values that duplicate your original table. You must remove any duplicates in the new data before restoring the primary key. This has no effect on the data stored in the field designated as the key; it just removes the key field feature temporarily.

To remove the primary key designation effectively, select the primary key field and click the Primary Key command. If the key is used in a relationship, you must delete the relationship before you can remove the key.

Name AutoCorrect
Can Fix Your Mistakes

Starting with Access 2000, you no longer need to be so careful about changing the names of fields that are used in forms and other database objects. The Name AutoCorrect feature automatically corrects most side effects that occur when you rename the fields, tables, queries, forms, reports, and controls that are included in form and report designs. When you open a form or other object, Access searches for and fixes any differences between the form and the fields and controls on which the form depends. By checking the date/time stamp for the last revision of the table and the form, Access can tell whether any names have changed since the last time the form was saved. If the stamps are different, Access automatically performs Name AutoCorrect.

By default, Name AutoCorrect is automatically set on in any database you create in Access 2003. If you convert a database from a version of Access before 2007, you must turn it on in the Options dialog box. In Chapter 13, you can find more information about Name AutoCorrect and other options to customize the workplace.

Modify or Delete an Index

To delete a single-field index, change the field's Indexed property to No. This removes only the index; it has no effect on the field itself or the underlying data.

In the Indexes dialog box, you can add or delete fields from a multiple-field index, change the sort order for any field in the index, or change the index properties. You can also change the field order in the index.

- To remove a field from a multiple-field index, display the Indexes dialog box, select the field row, and then press DEL.

- To remove the entire index, display the Indexes dialog box, select all the rows in the index, and then press DEL.

- To insert an additional field into the index, display the Indexes dialog box, select the field below where you want the new field to appear, press INSERT, and then enter the new field name.

- To change the field order in a multiple-field index, select and drag the field selector to the desired position, except the first position that shows the index name, in the index definition.

- To change the sort order for any of the fields in the index, choose from the Sort Order list.

After making changes to the table's indexes, you must save the table.

Ensure Data Validity

You have seen how Access can ensure that the values entered in your database are valid. For example, the data type you choose for the field can limit the values to date and time values. You can also limit the number of characters in a Text field and prevent duplicate values. A more direct way to ensure valid data is to set some rules that the values must obey.

You can specify two kinds of data validation rules: *field validation* and *record validation.* A field validation rule can limit the value to a few specific values or to a range of values. Access checks the rule when you try to move to another field in either the same record or another one. For example, a rule could limit a numeric value to a range between 1 and 100 or insist that a date value fall in 2007.

A record validation rule is handy for comparing the values in two fields in the same record. The rule is checked when you move out of a record and Access attempts to save the record. Access will not save a record with a conflict between fields. For example, a record validation rule could prevent saving a record in which the job cost is greater than the bid price. Another record validation rule could ensure that the elapsed time between dates in two separate fields does not exceed a specific value.

When either type of rule is broken, Access displays a message in a warning box that explains the violation and alerts you that you can't move to another field or record. The message you want to display is the Validation Text property in the table or field property. If you don't enter message text, Access creates a standard default message such as the one shown next. As you can see, a more meaningful message would be of more help to the user.

Define Field Validation Rules

To define a field validation rule:

1. Select the field name in the upper pane of the Design window, then click Validation Rule in the General tab of the Field Properties pane.

2. Type the expression you want in the property box. For example, if the value must not exceed 100, enter **<=100** (less than or equal to 100).

3. Then move to the Validation Text property box and enter the message you want to display when the rule is broken.

The Validation Rule property has a Build button that you can use to open the Expression Builder if you need help with the expression. See Chapter 7 for information about using the Expression Builder.

You can also include wildcards in the expression. These are the same placeholders that are used in search strings: ? stands for a single character, and * stands for any number of characters. When you enter an expression with a wildcard, Access converts it to an expression using the Like operator and adds quotation marks.

For example, if you type **C*** in the property text box, it turns into Like "C*" when you move out of the property box. This expression means that all values entered in the field must begin with the letter *C* or *c*. The expression is not case sensitive.

A validation rule defined for a Date/Time field also includes special symbols when translated by Access. To enter a rule specifying that the date entered must be earlier than January 1, 2007, you type **<01/01/07** and Access converts it to <#01/01/07# to make sure it is not confused with a Number value.

Figure 3-4 shows the Bid Data table structure with a validation rule added to the State field. The rule specifies that the State value must be CA, AZ, or NV; if the rule is violated, the message "Bid contracts only in California, Arizona or Nevada" displays in an information box.

The State validation rule in the previous example will also cause a violation if the field is left blank because it insists on one of three values. If you want to be able to leave the field blank, add Null to the list of valid values. You can also create a more complex record validation rule that insists on a value only if there is no value in the corresponding City field (to allow for customers who deal solely over the Internet instead of by mail).

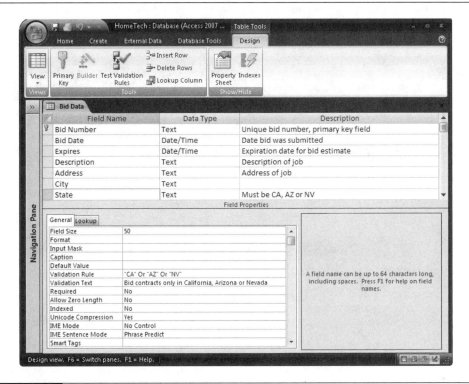

FIGURE 3-4   Setting new State field properties

Define a Record Validation Rule

A record validation rule is a table property rather than a field property. You can define only one record validation rule for a table, but if you want to apply more than one criterion, you can combine them in an expression using the AND or OR operators.

The record validation rule is applied whenever you enter or edit table data. When you move to another record, Access checks the new record against the rule you defined. As with field validation rules, if you define a record validation rule for a table that contains data, Access will ask whether you want to apply it to the existing data when you save the table.

To add a record validation rule to a table open the table in Design view:

1. On the Design tab in the Show/Hide group, click the Property Sheet command or right-click anywhere in the table Design view and choose Properties from the shortcut menu to open the Table Properties dialog box.

2. Enter the validation rule expression in the Validation Rule property; for example, **[Bid Date]<[Expires Date]**. Enclose the field names in brackets so Access knows you are referring to fields in your table.

3. Enter the text to display when the rule is violated in the Validation Text property—for example, **Bid date must be prior to Expires date**.

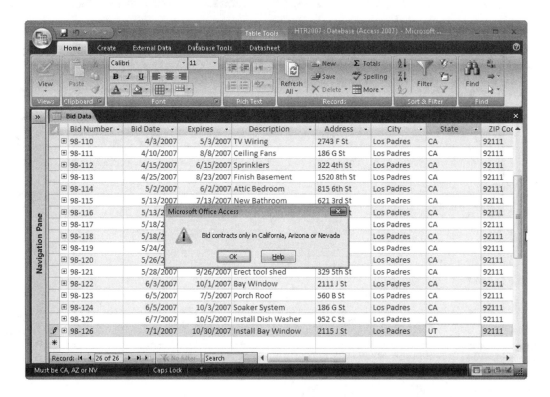

Require an Entry and Prevent Duplicates

One of the field properties is Required, which is set to Yes or No. The default value is No, but you can change it to Yes if the field should never be left blank. For example, every employee record must have a Social Security number, so you would change the field's Required property to Yes.

You can use the Indexed property to help prevent duplicate values. A single-field primary key field already requires unique values, but you can have only one such field in a table. To require other fields to contain unique values, change the field's Indexed property to Yes (No Duplicates). If you open the Indexes window, you will see the new single-field index with its Unique property set to Yes. This works with multiple-field indexes, too. Once the index is created, change the Unique property in the lower pane of the Indexes window to Yes; this means that no two combinations of the values in these fields can be the same.

Handle Blank Fields

In a database, blank fields can pose quite a problem if not handled properly. It is very important to understand why the field is blank and to correct or prevent blank fields when they cause a problem.

How to ...   **Build Validation Rules**

You can set more than one criterion in a validation rule for the same field by combining them using the And or Or operators. Combining two criteria with the And operator demands that both criteria be met, while the Or operator will accept either criteria being met. Here are some examples of validation rules, the corresponding Access expression, and an appropriate Validation Text message:

Rule	Access Version	Typical Message
<>0	<>0	Value must not be 0 but it might be negative.
100 Or 200	100 Or 200	Value must be either 100 or 200.
C*	Like "C*"	Value must begin with "C" or "c."
C* Or D*	Like "C*" Or Like "D*"	Value must begin with "C" "c" "D" or "d."
C??t	Like "C??t"	Value must be four characters long, begin with "C" or "c" and end with "t" or "T."
>=01/01/04 And <01/01/05	>=#1/1/04# And <#1/1/05#	Value must be in 2004.
Not CA	Not "CA"	Field can contain any value but "CA."

You can use two special field properties to control how blank fields are handled. The Required property determines whether or not a blank field is acceptable. The Allow Zero Length property, when set to Yes, permits zero-length strings.

These two properties work together as follows:

- If you want to be able to leave the field blank and don't care why it is blank, set both the Required and Allow Zero Length properties to No.

- If you never want to leave a field blank, set Required to Yes and Allow Zero Length to No. You cannot leave the field without entering a value, even if it is only "Don't know" or "None."

- If you want to be able to tell why the field is blank, set Required to No and Allow Zero Length to Yes. Then you would leave the field blank if the information is not known or enter quotation marks ("") to indicate that the field doesn't apply to the current record (there is no pager).

- If you want to leave the field blank only if you know the field isn't relevant to a record, set both properties to Yes. In this case, the only way for you to leave the field blank is to enter a zero-length string by typing "" or pressing the SPACEBAR.

Assign a Default Value

If one of your fields usually has the same value—for example, the City field for a list of local customers—use the Default Value property to have that value automatically entered when you add a new record. You can still change it to a different value when you enter data, but a default value can save time during data entry, especially if it is a long value such as Sacramento or Indianapolis. A newly assigned default value does not affect values already entered in the table, only new entries.

A default value can be assigned to any type of field except an AutoNumber, an OLE Object or an attachment. To assign one, enter the value in the Default Value property for the field. The type of value you enter depends on the data type. The value must also conform to the property settings and data type requirements.

If you assign or change a default field value after entering record data, you can change the existing values to the new value by pressing CTRL-ALT-SPACEBAR with the insertion point in the field.

 **Test the Rules**

As you add validation rules to a table, you can test them against existing data to see whether any of the field values will violate the new rule. To do this, on the Design tab in the Tools group, click the Test Validation Rules command or, if the Design window is not maximized, right-click in the Design window title bar and choose Test Validation Rules from the shortcut menu.

Access warns you that the process also will check the Required and Allow Zero Length properties and might take a long time and asks whether you want to do it anyway. If you respond Yes, you are told you must save the design before testing the rules. Choose Yes to save the design and continue testing. If Access finds no violations, it displays a message saying that all the data was valid for all the rules you have defined. If a violation is found, Access stops checking and displays a message indicating which rule was violated and asks whether you want to continue with the rule testing. You can then build a query to find any records that violate the rule.

See Chapter 7 for more information about building queries.

Copy an Existing Table Structure

If you already have a table with a structure similar to what you need now, you can save time by copying the structure to a new table without the data. Then change the field names and properties as necessary.

To copy the table structure without opening the table:

1. Right-click the existing table name in the Navigation pane and select Copy from the shortcut menu.

2. Right-click the Tables group title bar in the Navigation pane and select Paste from the shortcut menu. The Paste Table As dialog box opens.

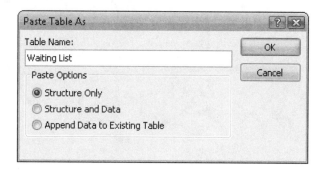

3. Enter a name for the new table and choose Structure Only, then click OK.

The new table inherits the field properties from the original table.

Now that you know how to build tables and define the fields they contain, in the next chapter you will see how to relate the tables into a relational database.

Chapter 4

Relate Tables

How to...

- Define a relationship
- View all relationships
- Modify and delete relationships
- Print the database relationships

There are many advantages to relating tables in a database. At the top of the list is the reduction of data redundancy. Having a single copy of each piece of information not only reduces required disk space, but also speeds up processing and helps prevent errors caused by inconsistent data. You need to update the data in only one place and it is available to all forms and reports.

For example, the Customers table contains the customer's full name, address, phone number, and other information. It also has a unique CustomerID field as the primary key. The Workorders table has all the job information as well as the CustomerID field, which serves as the foreign key that relates the job to the customer. By relating the two tables with the CustomerID field, information from both tables can be accessed. Each customer may be linked to more than one job with the CustomerID field.

You can define relationships between tables at any time, but the best time is when the tables are new and contain no data. When you design the database, an important step is to decide on the relationships between the tables and figure out the fields that they have in common.

Define a Relationship

To define a relationship between two tables, specify which fields the tables have in common. In a one-to-many relationship, the field in the parent table is called the *primary key* and must be either the table's primary key or a unique index. The field in the child table is called the *foreign key* and does not need to have a unique value within the child table; however, data retrieval is faster if the child table is indexed on the foreign key.

Defining table relationships at the table level keeps the relationships active and makes the database easier to use. You can link two tables temporarily in a query when you want to draw information from more than one table, but the permanent relationship is preferred—you can break it later if necessary.

Use the Relationships Window

The Relationships window has all the tools you need to define and work with database relationships. To open the Relationships window, on the Database Tools tab in the Show/Hide group, click the Relationships command.

If no relationships have been defined in the current database, the Show Table dialog box appears in a blank Relationships window. The dialog box displays a list of all the tables and queries in the current database.

If you have already examined the relationships between tables in this database, Access goes directly to the Relationships window without displaying the Show Table dialog box. To open the Show Table dialog box, on the Design tab in the Relationships group, click the Show Table command.

To add the tables you want to relate from the list in the Show Table dialog box, do one of the following:

- Double-click the table's name or select the table and click the Add button.

- To select multiple adjacent tables, select the first table to be included, then hold down SHIFT as you select the last table in the list to be included, and then click the Add button. If the table names are not adjacent in the list, hold down CTRL while you select the names.

- Click the Queries tab to add a query to the Relationships window. A query limits records from one or more tables to a specific subset depending on the criteria you have set.

- Click the Both tab to have access to a combined list of tables and queries.

When you have added all the tables and queries you want to work with in the Relationships window, click Close.

Tour the Relationships Window

The Relationships window shows the field lists of the tables you have chosen. The lists display the primary key field with a key icon. Use the scroll bars to see all the fields, or resize a field list box by dragging the bottom border to see more names or the right border to see complete field names.

You also can drag the field list boxes around in the window for better viewing. In the following diagram, four Home Tech Repair tables appear in the Relationships window. Relationships exist only among the first three.

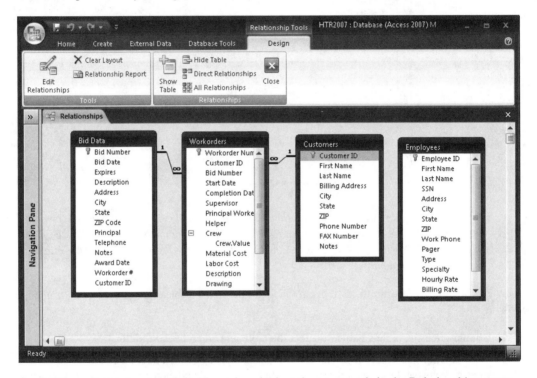

Before going on to relate the tables, take a look at the commands in the Relationships group on the Design tab.

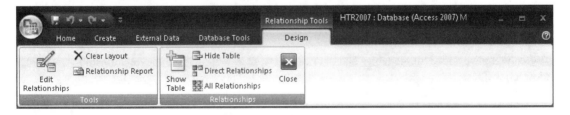

- Show Table opens the Show Table dialog box
- Hide Table removes the selected table from the layout
- Direct Relationships displays the relationships for the selected table
- All Relationships displays all relationships in the current database
- Close closes the window after asking if you want to save changes to the layout

Draw the Relationship Line

It couldn't be easier to relate two tables. You simply drag a field (usually the primary key) from one table and drop it on the corresponding field (the foreign key) in the other table, or vice versa. The field names do not need to be the same but they usually need to be the same data type and contain the same kind of information. If you intend to enforce referential integrity, the fields must be the same data type. If the fields are Number fields, they also must have the same Field Size property. See section, "Enforce Referential Integrity" for more information.

One exception applies to the requirement to match data types when you relate an AutoNumber field to a Number field. An AutoNumber field with the New Values property set to Increment can be linked to a Long Integer Number field. AutoNumber values are stored as four-byte numbers, so for the foreign key to have a matching value, it must contain a number of the same size—a Long Integer.

Here's how to relate the Employee table to the Workorders table by EmployeeID:

1. Click the EmployeeID field in the Employee field list and drag it to the Principal Worker field in the Workorders field list.

2. Drop the linking field into the child table. The Edit Relationships dialog box will now open.

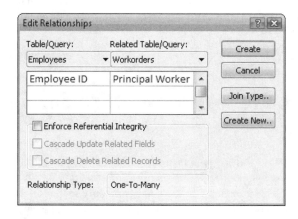

TIP
Notice that Access recognizes this relationship as one-to-many because one of the fields is a primary key and the other is not. If both fields are primary keys, Access recognizes the relationship as one-to-one. If neither field is a primary key nor has a unique value, Access calls the relationship Indeterminate.

3. Verify the field names that relate the tables, and then do one of the following:

   ■ If you want to change the field at either side of the relationship, select a different field from the drop-down field list under the table name.

   ■ If you want to add another relationship between the same tables, but which relates two different fields, move to an empty row in the grid, click the down button, and then choose from the list for each table. For example, relate the EmployeeID field to the Principal Worker field as well as the Supervisor field in the Workorders table.

   ■ If you have chosen the wrong foreign key, choose Cancel in the Edit Relationships dialog box and start again in the Relationships window.

TIP
If you type the first few letters of the field name in the Edit Relationships dialog box grid, Access will fill in the rest for you.

4. To complete the relationship, choose Create and return to the Relationships window. Figure 4-1 shows the Relationships window with the new link drawn between the tables.

5. Repeat the preceding procedure to draw the relationship line from the EmployeeID field in the Employees field list to the Supervisor field in the Workorders field list.

Enforce Referential Integrity

Referential integrity is an optional set of rules that keeps a database complete, and with no loose ends. It guarantees that the records are valid and that the database will remain accurate and

How to ... Relate to Two or More Foreign Keys

If you need to create relationships from a primary table to two or more foreign keys in the same table, Access will create additional instances of the table in the Relationships window. You do not have two copies of the table in the database—only in the Relationships layout. Figure 4-2 shows the Relationships window with three copies of the Employees table with the EmployeeID primary key field relating to the Supervisor, Principal Worker, and Helper foreign keys in the Workorders table.

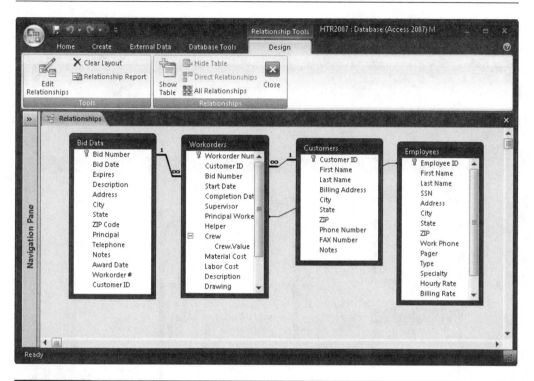

FIGURE 4-1   A new relationship line is drawn between the two tables.

complete as data is entered, edited, or deleted. No related records can exist without a parent. When you want Access to enforce the referential integrity rules on the relationship you are defining, check Enforce Referential Integrity in the Edit Relationships dialog box.

To summarize the basic integrity rules that Access can enforce:

- You cannot enter a child record for which no parent exists (in this case, start a workorder without a customer).

- You cannot delete a parent record if related child records still exist (meaning, remove a customer before the job is completed).

- You cannot change a child record so its foreign key doesn't have a match in the parent table (change the customer field in a work order record to a nonexistent customer).

- You cannot change the primary key value in a parent table as long as related records are in the child table (in other words, change a customer link before the workorder is finished).

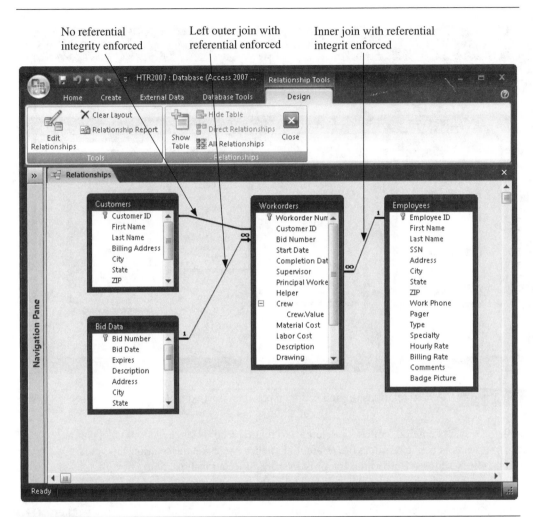

No referential integrity enforced

Left outer join with referential enforced

Inner join with referential integrit enforced

One table is related to three fields in another table.

Before you can set referential integrity, you must make sure you meet the following conditions:

- The matching field in the parent table is the primary key or at least has a unique value, such as an AutoNumber field.
- Related fields are the same data type, except for AutoNumber fields relating to Number fields, as mentioned earlier.
- Both tables are in the same Access database. You can set referential integrity between linked tables, providing they are both in Access format and you can open the database that contains the linked tables.

Two options that let you override some restrictions have become available: Cascade Update Related Fields and Cascade Delete Related Records. When you set these options, you can perform delete and update operations that normally would not be allowed.

4

TIP *If the tables already violate one of the rules, such as when related fields are not of the same data type, Access displays a message explaining the violation and does not apply the enforcement.*

With both of these options checked, if you delete a record from the parent table or change one of the primary key values, Access will automatically make equivalent changes to the child table to preserve referential integrity. If one of these options is not checked and you try to change the parent's primary key field or delete the parent record when child records still exist, Access displays a warning message.

The Cascade Update Related Fields option lets you change the value in the primary key field in the parent table, and Access automatically changes the foreign key value in the child table to match. For example, if you change the CustomerID value in the Customers table, all records for that customer in any related table will automatically be updated to the new value. This option preserves the relationship.

TIP *If the primary key in a table serves as a link to more than one table, you must set the Cascade Update Related Fields property for each of the relationships.*

The Cascade Delete Related Records option allows you to delete a parent record; Access then automatically deletes all the related child records. When you try to delete a record from the parent table of a relationship with this option selected, Access warns you that this record and the ones in related tables will be deleted.

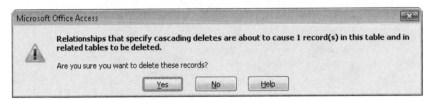

 *Setting the Cascade Delete Related Fields property can be dangerous. If you delete records using a Delete query, Access automatically deletes the valid related records without issuing the warning.*

Create a One-to-One Relationship

There might be times when you want to store information about an employee separate from the main pieces of information. For example, you might have data about an employee such as name, address, and Social Security Number readily available in one table but keep other data such as the resume and employment history in another table. These two tables are related by primary keys using a one-to-one relationship because only one record in each table matches one record in the other table.

To relate two tables in a one-to-one relationship, do the following:

1. On the Database Tools tab in the Show/Hide group, click the Relationships command.

2. If the tables you want to relate do not appear in the Relationships window, click the Show Table command.

3. Select each table in the Show Table dialog box and click Add; then choose Close.

4. Drag the primary key field from one table and drop it on the key field on the other table. It doesn't matter which direction you go; the same one-to-one relationship is created.

Specify the Join Type

One of the most powerful Access tools is the query that extracts and brings together data from more than one source. For example, you might want to see how much time each employee spends working on a job for each current customer. To do so, you need information from the Workorders, Employees, and Customers tables. Once the data is extracted, the query adds up the hours for records with matching employees and customers.

When you define the relationship, you also can specify the type of join you want for the tables. The join type specifies which records to display in a query based on related tables when they don't correspond exactly. For example, do you want the customer record to appear only if there are corresponding workorder records or do you want to see all customer records even if there are no related workorders?

 *The join type does not affect the relationship; it simply tells Access which records to include in the result of a query.*

To modify the relationship between the Employees and Workorders tables and set the join type:

1. In the Relationships window, right-click in the middle of the relationships line joining the Employees table with the Workorders table and choose Edit Relationship from the shortcut menu. The Edit Relationships dialog box opens.

2. Click the Join Type button to open the Join Properties dialog box.

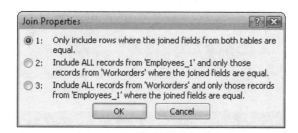

3. Select option 2 as the type of join for this relationship because you want to see all the Employee records, even if they have no related records in the Workorders table. Notice that the explanatory text is specific to the tables you have related.

4. Click OK in the Join Properties dialog box.

5. Click OK in the Edit Relationships dialog box.

Understanding Joins

You can specify three types of joins through the Join Properties dialog box:

- Option 1 includes only records where both parent and child have the same values in the linking fields (no orphans and no childless parents). This is called an *inner join* or an *equijoin,* and it's the default join type.

- Option 2 includes all the records from the table on the left, even if no corresponding values are in the other, and only the matching records from the table on the right. This is called a *left outer join* (all parents, including the childless, but no orphans).

- Option 3 is the opposite of option 2 and includes all the records from the table on the right and only matching records from the left table. This is called a *right outer join* (all children but no childless parents). If Referential Integrity is enforced, there will be no children without a parent.

Right and left refer to the position of the tables in the Edit Relationships dialog box, not their position in the layout.

If you select an outer join, an arrow at one end of the relation line points to the table whose value must match to be included in the query results. In a one-to-many relationship, the "one" side is considered the left table and the "many" side is the right table.

Figure 4-3 shows the completed layout for three tables in a database that tracks bid data, workorders, customers, and employees. The relationships that include referential integrity show a 1 on the "one" side and an infinity sign (∞) on the "many" side. Relationships with no referential integrity enforcement appear as lines with small dots at each end. Relationship lines with no arrows represent inner joins. An arrow on a relationship line means the join is an outer join and the arrow points to the table whose values must match to be included in the query results. The relationship between Bid Data and Workorders tables is a left outer join with referential integrity enforced.

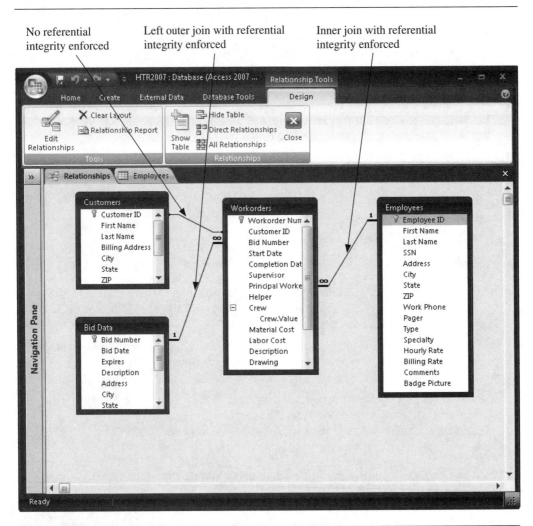

FIGURE 4-3   This layout now contains four related tables.

Save the Relationships Layout

All relationships are saved when you create them. You also can save the arrangement of the field lists in the Relationships window (the layout). Saving the layout has no effect on the tables in the database. To save the layout, right-click anywhere in the Relationships window (except on a field list), and then choose Save Layout from the Relationships shortcut menu.

If you have made changes in the layout and try to close the Relationships window without saving the layout, Access prompts you to save it. If you want to discard the changes, choose No. When you open the Relationships window again, the previously saved layout is displayed.

Use the Field List Pane

Once you have added tables to your database, it is time to build their relationship. Or if you have already created some relationships but need more, you can do this using the Field List Pane. For example, you want to add another field to the Workorders table that will name extra helpers on the job. To do this, open the Workorders table in Datasheet view and open the Field List as follows:

1. With the table open in Datasheet view, on the Datasheet tab in the Fields and Columns group, click the Add Existing Fields command.

2. Find the table in the Field List pane that contains the data you want to use in the relationship (Employees in this case). The tables are listed as available from related table or unrelated tables. Then click the plus sign to the left of the table name to see the complete list of fields in the table.

3. Click Employee ID field and drag it to the datasheet. Drop the field when the insertion line appears. The Lookup Wizard dialog box opens showing the Employee ID field in the Selected Field list.

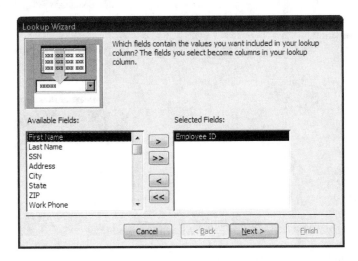

4. You will want to see the Employee's name instead of the ID, so select Last Name and click the right arrow and then click Next.

5. Skip the Sort Order options by clicking Next, accepting the Hide Key Column option and click Next.

6. Enter a new name for the Lookup field, such as Crew2, and click Finish.

7. Close the Field List Pane and on the Database Tools tab in the Show/Hide group, click Relationships. Figure 4-4 shows the new relationship between the Employees table and the Workorders table.

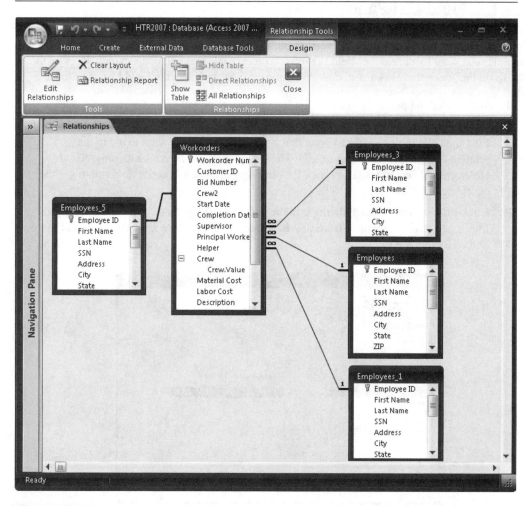

FIGURE 4-4 Building a new relationship using the Field List Pane.

View and Edit Relationships

You have a choice of viewing either all the relationships that you have set in your database or only those involving a specific table. In the database window, open the Relationships window as before and on the Design tab in the Relationships group, do one of the following:

■ To view all the relationships in the current database, click the All Relationships command.

■ To see only the relationships for the table selected in the database window, click the Direct Relationships command.

If all the relationships already appear in the Relationships window and you want to see only one table's relationships, do the following:

1. Clear the layout by clicking the Clear Layout command in the Tools group and click Yes to confirm the action.

2. Click the Show Table command, double-click the table name in the Show Table dialog box, and then click Close.

3. In the Relationships window, click the Direct Relationships command.

All tables related to the first are added to the layout and the relationship lines are drawn.

Hide or Delete a Table

If the Relationships window becomes too crowded, you can temporarily hide a table or delete it entirely from the layout. To hide the table, select the table and in the Relationships group click Hide Table, or right-click the table and choose Hide Table from the shortcut menu. The next time you view the Relationships window, all the tables will reappear unless you save the layout with the changes.

To delete the table from the layout, select the table and press DEL, or click the Delete command in the Records group on the Home tab. This affects only the display of the layout and does not remove the relationship or the table from the database.

To restore the relationship's layout to its previous arrangement, close the window without saving the changes. When you reopen the window, the old layout returns. If you want to keep the window open and restore the relationships, click the All Relationships command in the Relationships group.

Modify or Delete a Relationship

Relationships are not cast in concrete. There will be times when you need to make some changes such as altering the linking field or modifying the type of join. You can use the same Relationships window to edit a relationship that you used to create one.

To modify an existing relationship:

1. Open the Relationships window as before.

2. If you don't see the relationship you want to change, choose Show Table from the Relationships menu, double-click the missing table, and choose Close.

3. Double-click the relationship line or right-click the line and choose Edit Relationship from the shortcut menu to open the Relationships dialog box.

4. Make the changes you want, and then click OK.

To delete a relationship, click the join line to select it and press DEL. You also can right-click the line and choose Delete from the shortcut menu.

Access asks for confirmation before permanently deleting the relationship no matter which method you use.

Pressing DEL with a table selected only removes the table from the layout, whereas pressing DEL with a relationship line selected permanently removes the relationship between the tables.

Change a Table Design from the Relationships Window

You might need to make a change in a table design to be able to create the relationship you want. For example, the primary key might be a Text field and the foreign key a Number field. This design may suffice unless you want to enforce referential integrity, which requires the same data type in both fields. You can open the child table design and change the field type to Text.

If you have already set a relationship between the tables, you must delete the relationship before you can change the table design. You also might want to add a secondary index on the foreign key in the child table to speed up processing.

To switch to the Table Design view from the Relationships window, right-click in the title bar of the table's field list box and choose Table Design from the shortcut menu. When you finish changing the table design, save the changes and close the window; then return automatically to the Relationships window.

Print the Relationships

Documentation is always helpful, especially if you work with several databases or develop applications for others. Once you have defined all the relationships for the database, it is easy to document the structure graphically by printing it.

To print the table relationships diagram:

1. In the Relationships window, right-click in an empty area and choose Show All.

2. When all tables appear in the layout, on the Design tab in the Tools group, click the Relationships Report command. Figure 4-5 shows the printed layout of the Home Tech Repair database relationships.

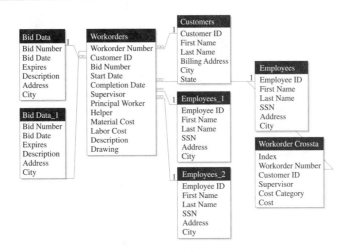

FIGURE 4-5   Printed database relationships diagram.

TIP

You might need to run Page Setup and reduce the left and right margins or change to landscape orientation to be able to print the entire diagram on one page.

If you want more precise information about the relationships you have established in the database, including the attributes such as referential integrity and the relationship type, you can use the Database Documenter, one of the Access analytical tools. See Chapter 14 for information about using the Database Documenter and other analysis tools.

Chapter 5

Enter and Edit Data

How to...

- ■ Enter new data
- ■ Customize data entry
- ■ Change the datasheet appearance
- ■ Edit data in a table
- ■ Find and replace data

Once you have figured out how to distribute your data and have built the tables to hold it, it's time to enter the data and get to work. In the last chapter, you saw some design features that keep errors out of your database. This chapter discusses more tools that can block data errors and speed up the data entry process.

Enter New Data

When you open a new table, it appears in Datasheet view, ready for data entry. To add a new record, do one of the following:

- ■ On the Home tab in the Records group, click the New command
- ■ Click the New (blank) Record button in the record navigation bar.
- ■ Right-click in a record selector box at the left end of the row and choose New Record from the shortcut menu.
- ■ Right-click the Datasheet View button in the upper left corner of the datasheet and choose New Record from the shortcut menu.

TIP   *You can also simply scroll down to the blank record at the end of the table and start typing.*

When the insertion point moves to an empty field, type in the data. If you have specified a custom display format, the entered value will adapt to that format when you move to the next column. If you have created an input mask for that field, the mask appears when you enter the field. See the section "Add Custom Input Masks" later in this chapter for details about input masks and how they compare with display format settings defined in the table design.

You can enter date/time data in any format valid within your language setting; Access will then convert it to the format you've specified in the field property. However, do not try to enter decimal fractions in number fields that are defined as integers because you will lose the decimal by the rounding off to the integer equivalent.

Copy and Move Data

Access provides some shortcuts for entering repetitive data by copying or moving existing data. You can copy or move all the data from one record to another or to individual fields or you can move or copy specific items using the Clipboard group of commands on the Home tab. You also can display the clipboard side pane and use it to copy and paste items.

When you collect items by copying or cutting them from their source, they are placed on the Office clipboard, which is shared by all Office programs. The Office 2007 clipboard is a Task pane that can hold up to 24 items with previews of the text or pictures that have been copied. You can paste them to a new location singly or as a group. If you place a 25th item on the clipboard, the first item is deleted. If you don't see the Clipboard pane, on the Home tab click the Clipboard Task Pane launcher next to the group name.

Clipboard Task Pane Launcher

The first item on the Office clipboard is also on the Windows clipboard, and you can paste it into almost any other Windows program. Similarly, cutting or copying from a non-Office program puts an item on the Windows clipboard (see Figure 5-1), and you can then paste it into any Office program, including Access.

- ■ To paste a selected item from the clipboard, place the insertion point where you want to paste it then click the down arrow next to the item and choose Paste from the shortcut menu.

- ■ To delete an item from the clipboard, move the mouse pointer to the item, click the down arrow to the right of the item and then choose Delete from the menu.

- ■ To close the Clipboard pane, click the Close button in the upper-right corner.

- ■ To display the clipboard later, click the Clipboard Task Pane launcher again.

- ■ To paste all the items to the same document, click Paste All in the Clipboard pane.

The Options button at the bottom of the pane gives you control over the behavior of the clipboard. The options include Show Office Clipboard Automatically, Show Office Clipboard When Control-C Pressed Twice, Collect Without Showing Office Clipboard, Show Office Clipboard Icon On Taskbar, and Show Status Near Taskbar When Copying. You can also move, resize, or close the pane using the Clipboard title bar down arrow.

Copy and Move within the Same Table

You can copy or move one or more records within the same table. Once you copy a record, you can add it to the table or replace an existing record with the one you copied.

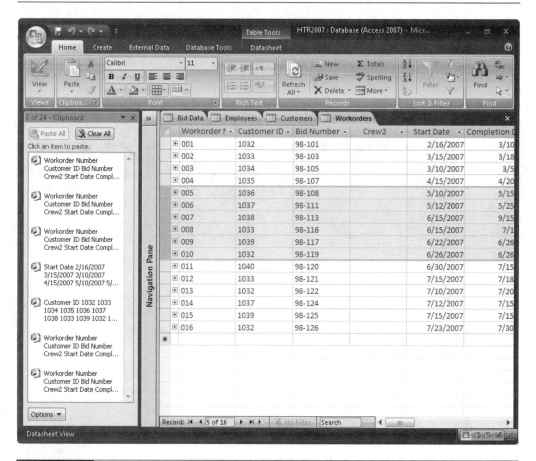

FIGURE 5-1 Copying items to the Clipboard.

To copy a record within the same table:

1. Select the record you want to copy by clicking the record selector (the small gray box to the left of the record).

2. On the Home tab in the Clipboard group, click the Copy command (or press CTRL-C).

3. Click the record selector in the record you want to replace and click the Paste command (or press CTRL-V).

4. If you want to add the copy as a new record rather than replace an existing one, select the empty record at the bottom of the datasheet, then click Paste (or press CTRL-V). You can also right-click the selected record and choose Paste in the shortcut menu.

Access tries to save the copied record when you move out of it. If the table has a primary key or a unique index, Access won't let you leave the new record until you have replaced the duplicate value with a unique one.

TIP *If the primary key field is an AutoNumber data type, Access automatically increases the number rather than copying the original number—another good reason to use an AutoNumber field as the primary key.*

To copy more than one record, do the following:

1. Select all the records you want to copy before clicking the Copy command.

2. When replacing records, select the same number of existing records as you have placed on the clipboard, then click Paste.

3. To append the new records to the table instead of replacing existing ones, select the new empty row at the bottom of the datasheet and click the down arrow under the Paste command and choose Paste Append.

Access asks for confirmation when you try to paste multiple records.

If the table has a primary key or a unique index that is not an AutoNumber, you will not be able to paste multiple records until you remove the key or index. Unlike pasting a single record, Access would create records with duplicate values in the field. If you try, Access objects by displaying the information message shown here.

If you just want to repeat the value in a single field to the next record while you are entering data in a new record, you don't need to paste it to the clipboard. You can quickly copy the value by pressing CTRL-' (apostrophe) after moving to the field.

If you want to move one or more records rather than create another copy of the data in the record, click Cut instead of Copy. This removes the record completely and places it on the clipboard. Then use the same paste or append process as described previously for copying records. If you have enforced referential integrity, you may see a message about a violation when you delete a record.

Copy and Move from Another Table

If you want to copy or move records from another table, select the records in the source table and click Copy or Cut. (If you click Cut, you will be asked to confirm that you wish to delete the record or records from the source table.) Switch to the destination datasheet and select the blank row at the bottom of the datasheet. When you click Paste, the new records are added to the destination datasheet.

Fix Paste Problems

When errors occur during a paste operation, Access creates a Paste Errors table and displays a message advising you of the errors as each is added to the table.

To view the Paste Errors table, double-click the table name in the Tables list in the Navigation pane. When you open the Paste Errors table, you might be able to correct the problems one by one and paste the data in the destination table field by field.

Here are some of the problems you might encounter when trying to paste data into a datasheet:

- Values are incompatible with the destination data types.
- The value is too long for the destination field.
- The destination is in a hidden column. See the section "Freeze and Hide Columns" later in this chapter for information about hidden columns.
- A value violates one of the destination field property settings. For example, you are trying to paste a text value in a Date/Time field.

The fields in the copied records are pasted in the same order as they appeared in the original datasheet, regardless of the field names. You might need to rearrange the columns in the destination datasheet before pasting, so that they will correspond with the incoming fields. Inconsistent data types or sizes between the incoming and the destination records can result in problems.

If you want to replace certain records in the destination datasheet with records from another table, select the records you want to replace before clicking Paste. To append records from another table to the existing datasheet, choose Paste Append as before. If the source table has more fields than the destination table, the excess fields are not pasted.

Insert Pictures

The Home Tech Repair Employees table has a field reserved for the employees' badge pictures. The Badge Picture field is an OLE (Object Linking and Embedding) Object data type and will store a file containing the digitized photograph. The Badge Picture photos are OLE Objects created by a scanner and contained in image files such as .tif, .gif, or .pcx. Because the photos are not expected to change, they are embedded in the table. Additionally, they represent the value stored in the Badge Picture field, which means they are bound to the table records.

TIP

Objects you expect to be edited often are better left in the source program and linked to your table. You can store the pathname or filename of the picture or other object in the Text field and won't have to reimport it when changes occur.

To insert an image in the Badge Picture field:

1. Place the insertion point in the Badge Picture field and right-click the field and choose Insert Object from the shortcut menu.

2. In the Insert Object dialog box, choose Create from File.

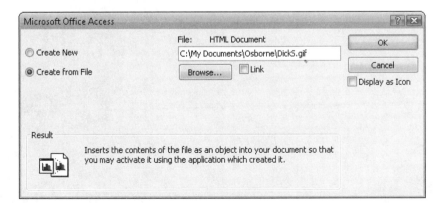

3. Type the path and filename of the image file in the File box or click Browse and look for the object.

4. After entering the file name, choose OK to embed the picture in the field.

When you return to Datasheet view, the field now contains the word, "Package." To see the image, on the Create tab in the Forms groupclick the Form command. Figure 5-2 shows an Employee record with the badge picture embedded.

NOTE   *The form has been slightly formatted in order to show the full picture.*

FIGURE 5-2   Viewing a picture inserted into a record.

5

You might need to double-click the added object to activate the OLE source program associated with that type of file before you can see the image.

Insert Hyperlinks

A *hyperlink* is a connection to an object in the same or another Access database, a document created in another program, a document on the Internet, or your local intranet. The *hyperlink field* contains the address of the target object, and when you click the hyperlink, you jump to it. If the object is the product of another application, that application is automatically started.

In the Home Tech Repair database, the Workorders table contains a hyperlink field that links to the engineering drawings for that work order. The scanned drawings are saved as .gif files in the same folder as the database itself.

Define the Hyperlink Address

A hyperlink address can contain up to four parts, separated by the pound sign (#), as in

   displaytext#address#subaddress#screentip,

of which only the address is required. If you want the hyperlink to jump to a specific location in the target object, a subaddress is also required.

- The *displaytext* is optional and can be displayed in the field in place of the actual address. If you don't include display text, the hyperlink address or subaddress appears instead.

- The *address* is either a *Uniform Resource Locator* (*URL*) such as a web address, or *Universal Naming Convention* (*UNC*) path to the document. An *absolute path* starts with \\ and describes the exact location on the system or local area network (LAN). A *relative path* is related to the current path or the base path specified in the database properties. An address is required unless you added a subaddress that points to an object in the current database.

- The *subaddress* contains a named location within the target object, such as a bookmark in a Word document, a particular slide in a PowerPoint presentation, or a cell range in an Excel spreadsheet.

- The *ScreenTip* is the text that appears when you rest the mouse pointer on the hyperlink. If you don't specify a ScreenTip, the address is displayed.

The scanned drawings for the Workorders Drawing field are stored in the Home Tech folder with the database. Use the Insert Hyperlink tool to enter the hyperlink address:

1. Right-click in the Drawing field in the Workorders datasheet and then point to Hyperlink in the shortcut menu. Then, choose Edit Hyperlink to open the Insert Hyperlink dialog box.

Browse the Web

Up one folder

Browse for file

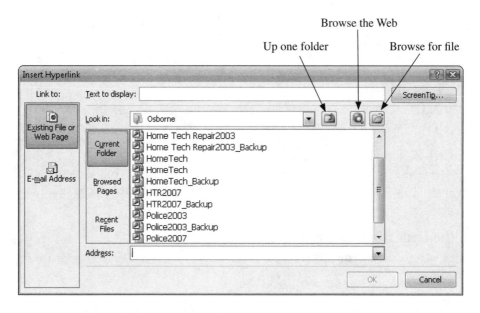

2. Click the Existing File or Web Page button under "Link to" if not already chosen. Then do one of the following:

   ■ Type the path to the drawing file in the Address box; for example, **c:\My Documents\Osborne\fireplace.gif**.

   ■ If you have accessed the target of this hyperlink before, you can select it from the list of Recent Files or Browsed Pages.

   ■ Click the Browse for File button (the open folder) and locate the file in the Link to File dialog box and click OK.

3. Back in the Insert Hyperlink dialog box, enter the text you want to show in the field in place of the address in the "Text to display" box. For example, you could enter **Fireplace**.

4. If you want to show a ScreenTip, click the ScreenTip button and enter the text in the Set Hyperlink ScreenTip dialog box, then click OK.

5. Click OK to finish inserting the hyperlink and return to the Workorders datasheet where the hyperlink appears in the Drawing field. When you rest the mouse pointer on the hyperlink, you will see the ScreenTip.

6. Click the hyperlink to test it; Microsoft Picture Library (or whatever program handles your .gif files) opens, displaying the scanned fireplace drawing, as shown in Figure 5-3.

Edit and Delete Hyperlinks

Editing a hyperlink address is a little different from editing normal text because if you click on the address, you jump to the target. There are two ways to edit the address:

- Right-click on the hyperlink, point to Hyperlink in the shortcut menu, and click Edit Hyperlink in the submenu; then, edit the address directly in the Edit Hyperlink dialog box.
- Press TAB to move to the field and press F2 to switch to Edit mode. To see the full address, press SHIFT-F2 to open the Zoom box.

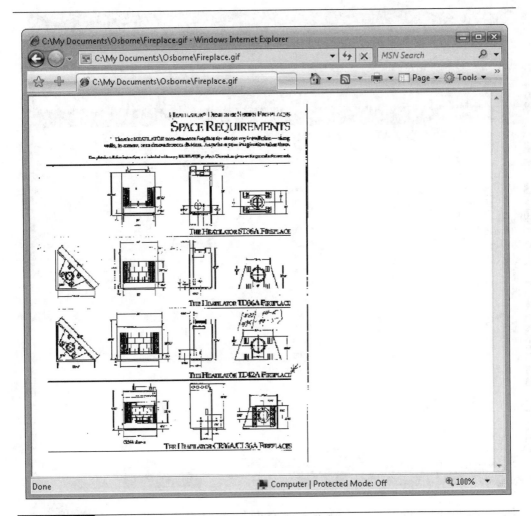

FIGURE 5-3 Viewing the target of the Fireplace hyperlink

To delete a hyperlink from a field, right-click the hyperlink and choose Cut from the shortcut menu. You can also point to Hyperlink in the shortcut menu and then click Remove Hyperlink. If you want to delete all the hyperlink addresses you have inserted in a field, delete the field from the table design.

Attaching Files to a Field

To add a file to an Attachment field, open the table in Datasheet view and double-click in the Attachment field. The Attachments dialog box appears displaying a list of files already named as attachments. You use this dialog box to add or remove attachments, open one of the attachments in its native program, or save changes you have made to them.

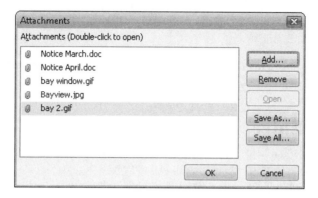

5

1. Click Add to open the Choose File dialog box.

2. Go through the folders to find the one or more files you want to attach to the field.

3. Select the file or files and click Open to return to the Attachments dialog box.

4. After attaching all the files you need, click OK to return to the datasheet.

Back in Datasheet view, you see the paper clip icon followed by the number of files currently attached to the field.

If you want to look at the attachment directly from the Access table, you need the program that originated, or at least supports, the file installed in your system.

Customize Data Entry

Access offers many tools that help improve the efficiency and accuracy of data entry. Some minimize the process, others assist in navigation in a datasheet or give you access to special symbols. For example, input masks guide the user with data input and help to prevent data errors, while lookup fields offer a list of valid values for selection.

Add Custom Input Masks

An *input mask* is a field property similar to the Format property you set in the table design but with a different purpose. An input mask displays a fill-in blank for data entry, whereas a format is used to display field data with a consistent appearance. Setting the Format property affects how data is displayed after it is entered and offers no control over or guidance for the data being entered. Input masks can be used with Text, Number, Date/Time, and Currency fields. An Input Mask Wizard can help you with Text and Date/Time fields.

Return to Chapter 3 for information about the field Format property.

To decide between a Format property and an Input Mask property, use the following guidelines:

- If you just want to make sure the field values look the same when displayed, use the Format property to specify the desired appearance.

- If you want to guide data entry and make sure it is entered properly, use an input mask.

An input mask appears before any data is entered, when the insertion point reaches the field. The mask displays fill-in blanks with literal characters separating them. When you use an input mask, you can be sure the data will fit the specifications you set by limiting the number of fill-in spaces. Depending on the characters you use in the mask, you can leave some fill-in spaces blank but you cannot enter more characters than there are spaces.

To create an input mask with the Input Mask Wizard:

1. Move the insertion point to the field in the table Design view. For example, the Phone Number field in the Employee table.

2. Click in the Input Mask property, then click the Build button (...).

3. Select a mask in the Input Mask Wizard dialog box, as shown in Figure 5-4, and click Next.

4. You can make changes to the mask, such as changing the placeholder that displays as the fill-in blanks (the default is an underline character). Then click Next.

5. Choose to store the literal characters with the data, if desired, by adding them to the Input Mask text box. This uses more disk space but the symbols are already available when you want to use the value in a form or report.

6. Click Finish to close the wizard.

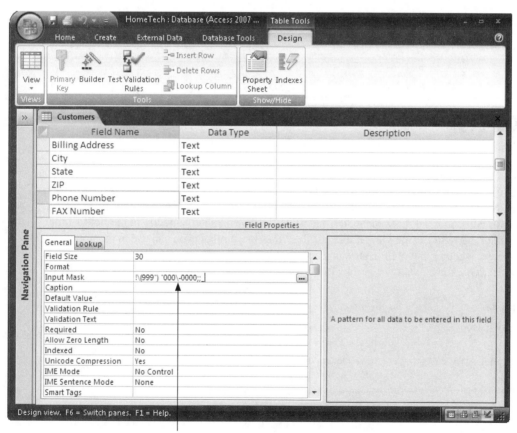

Input mask for Phone Number field

If you have a customized field whose input mask is not part of the Input Mask Wizard's repertoire, you can easily create your own mask manually using special symbols. The special symbols are placeholders that specify which entries are required and define the type of characters

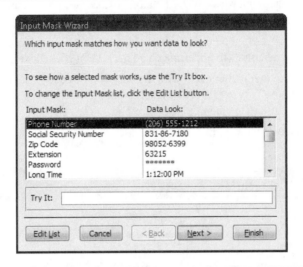

FIGURE 5-4 Choosing from pre-designed input masks.

that can be entered at each position in the mask. You can even add a custom mask to the wizard's list of predefined input masks. You cannot create an input mask for a Memo, AutoNumber, Yes/No, OLE Object, attachment, or Hyperlink field.

To build an input mask manually, enter the desired characters directly in the field's Input Mask property in Design view. Table 5-1 describes the symbols you can use in an input mask and indicates whether they will require an entry in that position.

Here are some examples of the effects of input masks:

Input Mask	Description	Sample Valid Value
00000-9999	Uses zeros to represent required entries. The 9s are optional.	92118-2450 or 92118-
(999) AAA-AAAA	Allows letters or digits. The area code is optional.	(301) 555-CALL
!>L0L 0L0	Converts all letters to uppercase, and fills the mask from left to right.	N0C 1H0
>L<??????????	Converts required initial letter to uppercase. Other characters are optional and converted to lowercase.	Henrietta
>LL0000-000	Converts the two required letters to uppercase, which are followed by the seven required digits.	BT5430-115

Symbol	Entry	Entry Required?
0	Displays a digit (0 through 9) with no + or – sign. Blanks display as zeros.	Yes
9	Displays a digit with no + or – sign. Blanks display as spaces.	No
#	Displays a digit with + and – signs. Blanks display as spaces.	No
L	Displays a letter (*A* through *Z*).	Yes
?	Displays a letter.	No
A	Displays a letter or digit.	Yes
a	Displays a letter or digit.	No
&	Displays any character or space.	Yes
C	Displays any character or space.	No
<	Converts letter to lowercase.	N/A
>	Converts letter to uppercase.	N/A
!	Fills the mask with the characters that the user types into the mask, from left to right. Can appear anywhere in the mask.	N/A
\	Treats the next character as a literal.	N/A

TABLE 5-1   Input Mask Symbols

To make a change in one of the wizard's pre-designed masks, first select the mask in the Input Mask Wizard dialog box, click Edit List and then proceed, as you did in the preceding examples, to make the desired changes.

Create Lookup Fields

A *Lookup field* is an Access tool that makes entering data quicker and more accurate. A lookup field displays a list of values from which to choose. The most common type of Lookup field, called a *lookup list*, gets its values from an existing table or query. The advantage of this type of Lookup field is that the tables actually are related and as the source list changes, the current values are available to the Lookup field.

The second type of Lookup field gets its values from a list that you type in when you create the field. This type is called a *value list* and is best used when the list is limited to a few values that do not change often, such as a short list of product categories or employee status.

You can add either type of Lookup field in Design or Datasheet view. If the field already exists in the table design and you want to change it to a Lookup field, you must change the data type in Design view. To add a new Lookup field to a table, do one of the following:

- In Design view, add a new field row and select Lookup Wizard from the Data Type list.

- In Datasheet view, click in the column to the right of where you want the new Lookup field, then on the Datasheet tab in the Fields and Columns group, click the Lookup Column command.

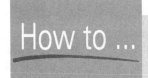
Create a Custom Input Mask

If you have a field that commonly appears in your tables or forms, such as the Canadian postal code, you can create a new input mask and save it in the Input Mask Wizard's list of predefined masks, as follows:

1. In table Design view, click the Input Mask property for the field, then click the Build button to open the Input Mask Wizard dialog box.

2. Click Edit List. The Customize Input Mask Wizard dialog box shows the Phone Number input mask.

3. Click the New (blank) Record navigation button at the bottom of the dialog box to show a blank form.

4. Enter a description of the new mask, the mask itself, the symbol you want to use as the placeholder, and a sample of the data you intend to enter into the field.

5. Select the Text/Unbound Mask Type. The definition for the Canadian postal code input mask is complete.

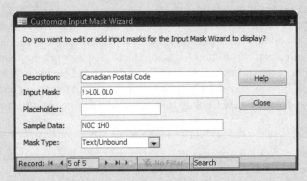

6. Click Close. The new definition appears in the list of predefined masks.

Both methods start the Lookup Wizard, which displays a series of dialog boxes where you specify the details of the Lookup field. In the first dialog box, decide which type of Lookup field to create: a lookup list that relates to a table or query, or a value list that you type in.

Specify a Lookup Column

As an example of defining a Lookup field that gets its values from another table, let's insert a new field in the Workorders table of the Home Tech Repair database. The Workorders information is easier to enter and read if a Lookup field is used for the Supervisor, Principal Worker, and Helper fields. The Last Name will be displayed, but the Employee ID will be stored.

> **NOTE**   *You may be asked to delete table relationships before you can change the field to a Lookup field.*

5

To add a Lookup field to the Workorders table:

1. Open the Workorders table in Design view and insert a field named Supervisor between Completion Date and Principal Worker, choosing the Lookup Wizard data type.

2. In the first Lookup Wizard dialog box, choose the first option, "I want the Lookup column to look up the values in a table or query." Click Next.

3. Select Employees from the list of tables and click Next. You could also select a query as the source of the values.

4. In the next dialog box, double-click the Employee ID and Last Name fields in the list of available fields in the Employees table (see Figure 5-5). Click Next.

5. In the next dialog box, you can specify the sort order for the fields in the Lookup list. Click Next.

6. The next dialog box (see Figure 5-6) shows you how the field values will look in the Lookup column. Drag the right edge of the column header to adjust the width if necessary. Also check the "Hide key column (recommended)" option so you need not view the Employee ID key value, only the last name. If you have no data in the column yet, accept the default column width. Click Next.

7. Accept the name Supervisor for the Lookup column and click Finish. Access prompts you to save the table so that the relationships can be completed.

8. Choose Yes. Access returns you to the table Design view.

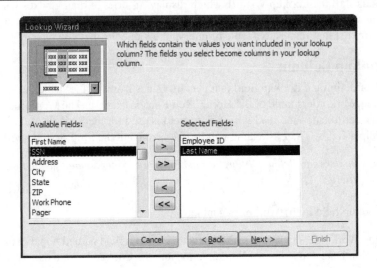

FIGURE 5-5   Selecting the fields for the Lookup field.

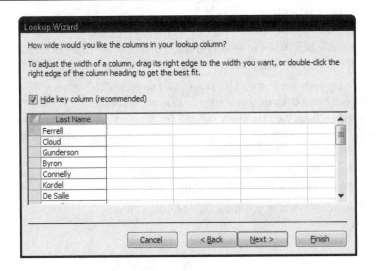

FIGURE 5-6   Changing the Lookup column appearance.

The Lookup Wizard has set the properties for the new field based on your selections in the dialog boxes, which you can view on the Lookup tab of the Field Properties pane.

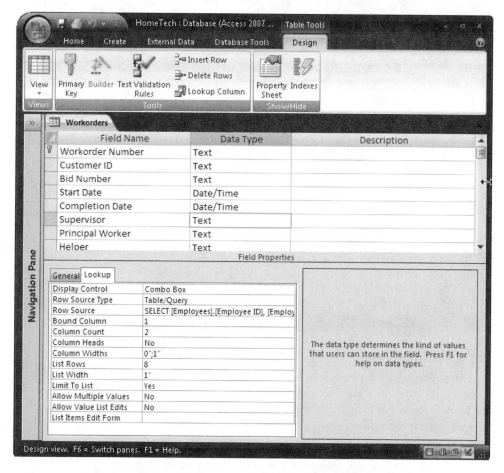

Take a look at the Lookup properties that specify the appearance and behavior of the lookup field when it appears in a datasheet or a form. As you click in each property on the Lookup tab, look at the description in the right pane.

The Workorders table shows the new lookup field used to locate employee names in the Employee table. The lookup field links the Employee table to the Workorders table by the Employee ID field. The employee's last name is displayed, whereas the foreign key (Employee ID) is not displayed but it is stored in the field.

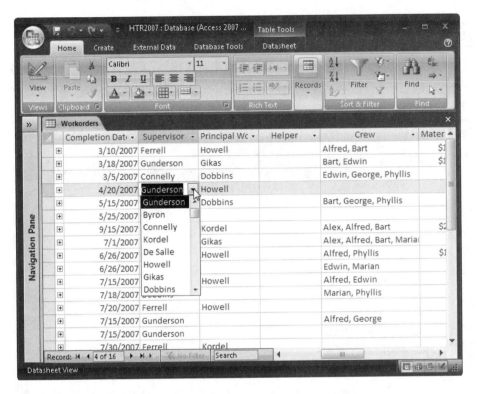

Specify a Lookup List

A list of acceptable values can be helpful when entering data in the Employees table. Because only a few values are valid in the Specialty field, it is a good candidate for streamlining. Start with the Lookup Wizard as before, and in the first Lookup Wizard dialog box, choose the second option "I will type in the values I want." Then move to the next dialog box, shown here, where you enter the values for the list.

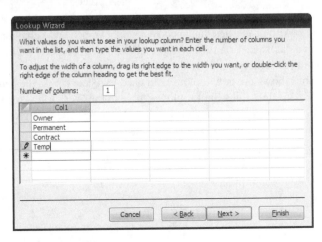

The Row Source property on the Lookup tab for the Specialty field now shows the list of values you typed in instead of a SELECT statement.

Change the Datasheet Appearance

Datasheet properties include the layout of the fields and records—the order in which the fields appear, the dimension of the rows and columns, and the column headings. Other properties are the font size and style, the colors of the text, the background, and special cell effects such as raised or sunken borders.

You also have the option of hiding some fields from view if the data shouldn't be visible to all users of the database. Finally, if you have too many fields to view on the screen at once, you can keep one or more key fields on the left of the screen, so that as you scroll right some information is always in view.

NOTE   *All of these changes in datasheet appearance can also be applied to subdatasheets.*

Move and Resize Columns and Rows

Access displays the data fields in columns in the same order as the fields appear in the table design unless you change the column order. By default, the columns are all the same width, so you might not be able to see the whole field name or value. Other columns might be wider than necessary and waste screen space. The rows also are standard height. You can change any of these datasheet properties using the elements of the datasheet itself.

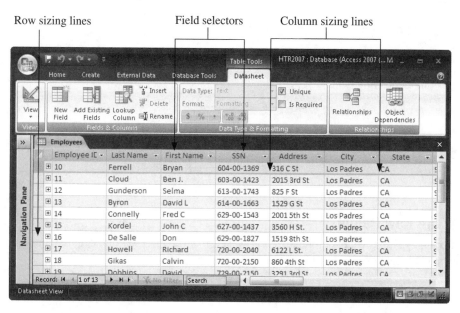

Rearrange the Columns

To move a column, click the field selector. Then click the field selector again and the mouse pointer changes shape to an arrow with a small rectangle. Drag the column to the desired position.

As you move the column, a dark vertical line moves with it, showing you where the left boundary of the moving column is at that moment. Release the mouse button to reposition the column. Changing the relative position of a column in the datasheet has no effect on the way the fields appear in the table design or the way they are stored on the disk.

Change the Column Width

There are three ways to change a column width:

- Drag the sizing line at the right border of the field selector button
- Double-click the column sizing line to fit the contents
- Set the precise width in a dialog box

TIP   *If you drag the right boundary all the way left until it reaches the left boundary, the column disappears. This is one way to hide a column. You will learn more about hiding columns in the section "Freeze and Hide Columns."*

If you need to specify a column width more precisely, you can set the exact width in the Column Width dialog box after selecting one or more columns by doing one of the following:

- On the Home tab in the Records group, click More and choose Column Width from the shortcut menu.
- Right-click the field selector and choose Column Width from the shortcut menu.

Then type a new value in the Column Width text box or click Best Fit. The Best Fit option resizes the selected column or columns to fit the longest data string currently in the field or the text in the column heading, whichever is longer.

Change the Row Height

You can change column widths individually; however, rows are all the same height, thus when you change the height of one, you change them all.

To change the row height:

1. Move the mouse pointer to any one of the row sizing lines in the record selector area.
2. When the pointer changes to a plus sign with arrows, click and drag the line until the rows reach the desired height.
3. Release the button. All rows will be the same height.

To set a more exact row height, on the Home tab in the Records group, click the More command and choose Row Height from the shortcut menu to open the Row Height dialog box. (The insertion point can be anywhere in the datasheet.) You also can right-click in a selected row or a row selector and choose Row Height from the shortcut menu. The Row Height dialog box is similar to the Column Width dialog box except there is no Best Fit option. The height is measured in points; the default height depends on the default font size.

Freeze and Hide Columns

Two other properties of a datasheet deal with the display of the data. *Freezing* a column keeps the data on the screen as you scroll right to see other fields in a long record. *Hiding* a column keeps the data from displaying in the datasheet. Again, neither of these properties changes the way the data is stored, only the way it is displayed.

Freeze and Unfreeze Columns

When you freeze a column on the screen, the column and its contents are automatically moved to the left of the datasheet and are kept on the screen as you scroll right.

To freeze a column, right-click in the column header and choose Freeze Columns from the shortcut menu.

To freeze several adjacent columns, select them all before choosing Freeze Columns. If you want to freeze non-adjacent columns, freeze them one at a time in the order that you want them to appear at the left of the screen. Access will move them one by one to the left side of the datasheet. To unfreeze the columns, on the Home tab in the Records group, click More and choose Unfreeze from the context menu.

TIP   *Unfortunately, Access doesn't return the thawed column to the position it was in before you froze it and moved it to the left. You have to move it back yourself, or close the table without saving the changes in the layout, if you want to restore the original arrangement.*

Hide and Unhide Columns

If your table contains information that is not relevant to the current activity, you might not want it to take up space on the screen. In this case, you can hide one or more columns from view. Again, this changes only the appearance of the datasheet, not the actual data that is stored in the table. To hide a column, right-click in a selected column or in the field selector and choose Hide

Columns from the shortcut menu. The column immediately disappears from the screen. If you want to hide several adjacent columns, select them all first. If you want to hide non-adjacent columns, you can reposition them so they are adjacent, then hide them as a group or simply hide one at a time. The More shortcut menu in the Records group also provides commands to hide and unhide columns.

 *If you try to copy or move records to a datasheet that currently has hidden columns, the data will not be entered and you will get paste errors. Be sure to unhide all the hidden columns before attempting to copy or move records.*

To return the hidden columns to the datasheet display, right-click any column header and choose Unhide Columns from the shortcut menu. The Unhide Columns dialog box appears with a list of all the fields in the datasheet. Check marks next to the field names indicate the fields currently in view. If a field does not show a check mark, it is currently hidden. To return a field to the datasheet display, check the box next to its name. Choose Close when you have returned all the desired fields to the display.

 *While you are unhiding columns with the Unhide Columns dialog box, you can hide columns at the same time by removing the check marks next to the columns you want to hide.*

Change the Font

Access uses 11-point Calibri as the default font for its datasheets. This font setting applies to all the characters in the datasheet—data and captions alike. You might want to reduce the font size to get more data on the screen or enlarge it to make it more visible if a group will be viewing the screen from a short distance. The row height and column widths are automatically adjusted to accommodate the font changes.

To change the datasheet font, on the Home tab in the Font group, click the down arrow next to the current font setting and choose a font from the list. You can use the other commands in the Font group to select font size, alignment, special effects, and colors.

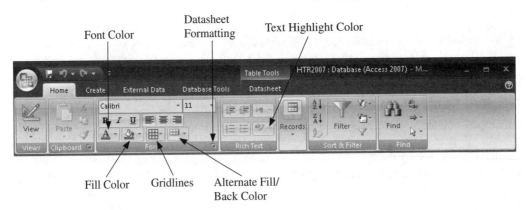

Change Gridlines and Cells

Now comes the fun part: making some dramatic changes to the appearance of the datasheet with colors and special effects. The *grid lines*—the horizontal and vertical lines that separate the datasheet into rows and columns—are displayed by default, but you can remove the horizontal or vertical lines, or both. You also apply special coloring effects for alternate rows in the datasheet.

The *cells* are the boxes at the intersection of the rows and columns. In addition to changing the appearance of the grid lines, you can apply special effects to the cells to make them appear raised or sunken.

To change these datasheet properties, on the Home tab in the Font group and use the following commands to change the properties:

■ Click the Gridlines command and choose to show either or both horizontal and vertical gridlines or none at all.

■ Click the Alternate Fill/Back Color command to select row colors from the palette. Every other row will show the color in the background.

Clicking one of the color commands displays a palette of colors from which to choose. As you make changes with the Font group, the combined effects are shown in the datasheet itself. If you don't like the results, close the datasheet without saving them.

To make more changes in the datasheet format, click the Datasheet Formatting button in the lower right corner of the Font group. The Datasheet Formatting dialog box opens where you can choose several other settings such as the cell effect and line styles.

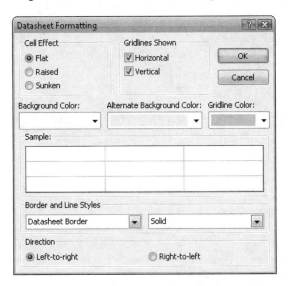

As you make the changes, a sample of the results is displayed in the Sample pane. When you are satisfied with the appearance, click OK. To save the new datasheet appearance, save the layout with the table.

Set Datasheet Default Options

To save the new datasheet appearance, save the layout with the table. To create a custom datasheet layout for use with all the tables in the database, you'll need to change some of the default datasheet options. Click the Microsoft Office button and then click Access Options to open the Access Options dialog box. Next, click Datasheet in the left pane to see the datasheet view options, as shown in Figure 5-7.

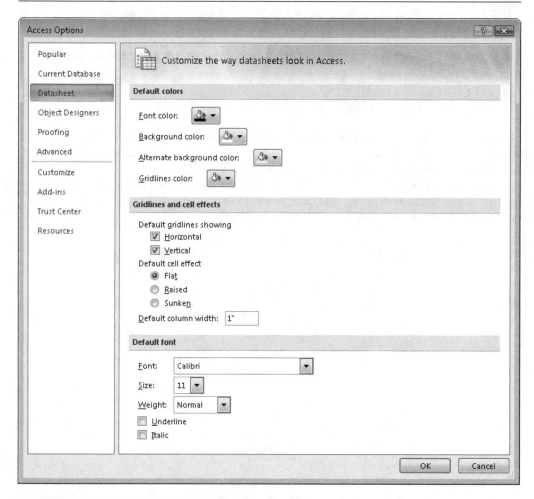

FIGURE 5-7   Setting datasheet default options.

The default options include:

- **Default colors**   Displays a palette of colors you can use for the font, background, alternate background, and gridlines.
- **Default gridlines showing**   Displays or hides horizontal and vertical gridlines. Gridlines appear displayed in the color set in the Default Colors box.
- **Default cell effect**   Specifies one of three cell effects, either Flat, Raised, or Sunken.
- **Default column width**   Sets the standard width for all the columns in the datasheet.
- **Default font**   Specifies the font, weight, size, and style. The text appears in the color set in the Default Colors box.

Change Table Definition

Although the best place to modify the table definition is in Design view, you can make some limited changes in Datasheet view. You can add or delete columns, as well as change field names in Datasheet view.

Insert/Delete a Column

To insert a column in the datasheet, place the insertion point in the column to the right of where you want the new one, then on the Datasheet tab in the Fields and Columns group, click Insert. A new blank column appears and the columns to the right move over. Double-click the field selector, usually labeled Field1, and rename the column with the appropriate field name.

> **NOTE**   *If you want to change the data type that Access assumes for the field, define a validation rule, or change other properties, you must switch to Design view.*

As discussed earlier in this chapter, the commands in the Fields and Columns group offer three special column sources: New Field, Add Existing Fields, and Lookup Column.

- Choosing New Field opens the Field Templates pane at the right of the datasheet where you can choose the field template closest to what you need.
- Choosing Add Existing Fields opens the Field List pane where you can choose fields from other tables in the current database.
- Choosing Lookup Column starts the Lookup Wizard.

To delete a column in Datasheet view, click anywhere in the field and on the Datasheet tab in the Fields and Columns group, click the Delete command. Access warns you that the deletion will be permanent. (This is one of those cases where Undo doesn't work.) Choose Yes to go ahead with the deletion or No to cancel. You can delete contiguous columns by selecting them and then clicking the Delete command.

 *You cannot delete a field that is part of a relationship without first deleting the relationship. Either open the Relationships window to delete the relationship or accept Access's offer to delete it for you.*

Change Field Names

In Datasheet view, you have three ways to rename an existing column. All three methods place the insertion point in the field name text, where you can replace or edit the existing name. Be warned that this also deletes the caption you might have specified:

- Double-click the text in the field selector and type the new name.
- Select the column and on the Datasheet tab in the Fields and Columns group, click the Rename command.
- Right-click the field selector and choose Rename Column from the shortcut menu.

Insert/Delete a Subdatasheet in Design View

The Subdatasheet Name is one of the table properties. If you like, you can open the table's Property Sheet and change the settings. To insert or delete a subdatasheet, open the table in Design view. Then, right-click anywhere in the table design and choose Properties from the shortcut menu. You can also on the Design tab in the Show/Hide group, click the Property Sheet command.

To insert a new subdatasheet, click the down arrow in the Subdatasheet Name property and choose a new table or query from the list.

The Link Child Fields and Link Master Field properties are automatically set based on the object relationships. These properties contain the names of the linking fields in the related tables.

> TIP
>
> *If the new subdatasheet shows the same data for all the rows in the datasheet, you might not have specified the linking fields correctly.*

To delete the subdatasheet, delete the name in the Subdatasheet Name property. The subdatasheet is removed only from the display. The data is not affected and the relationship remains intact.

Find and Edit Record Data

5

To move to another record you can either use the Go To command in the Find group of the Home tab or use the navigation buttons at the bottom of the datasheet: First, Previous, Next, Last, or New. The TAB key and the RIGHT ARROW and LEFT ARROW keys can also move you to another field.

To change the entire value in a field, select the field and enter the new value. To edit only part of the value, change to Edit mode by clicking in the field or pressing F2. Once in Edit mode, the RIGHT ARROW and LEFT ARROW keys move the insertion point through the characters instead of among the fields.

> TIP
>
> *You can tell you are in Edit mode when the insertion point is in the text and the whole value isn't selected. If the whole value is selected, you are not in Edit mode.*

Locate Records

If your table doesn't contain a lot of records, you can probably find the record you want by scrolling down through the records in the datasheet or form, especially if the records are sorted by the field you are searching. However, if your table contains hundreds of records, that method is rather time-consuming, so Access provides the Find feature. This way you just tell Access what you want to find, where, and how to search for the value. The search can apply to the complete value in the field or only to certain characters within the field.

> NOTE
>
> *If you are looking for values in a datasheet with a subdatasheet or a form with a subform, Access searches only the object that contains the insertion point.*

Find an Exact Match

When you want to edit a specific value in a field in the table, you need a method to locate all the records that contain that value. You can find them one at a time and make the changes you want or ask Access to make the changes for you automatically.

To find a record with a specific value in one of the fields, for example, a record with Plumbing in the Specialty field, you should do the following:

1. Place the insertion point anywhere in the Specialty column on the Employees table of the Home Tech Repair database.

2. On the Home tab in the Find group, click the Find command. The Find and Replace dialog box opens.

3. Enter Plumbing in the Find What box.

4. Click Find Next. The insertion point moves to the next record with that value (see Figure 5-8).

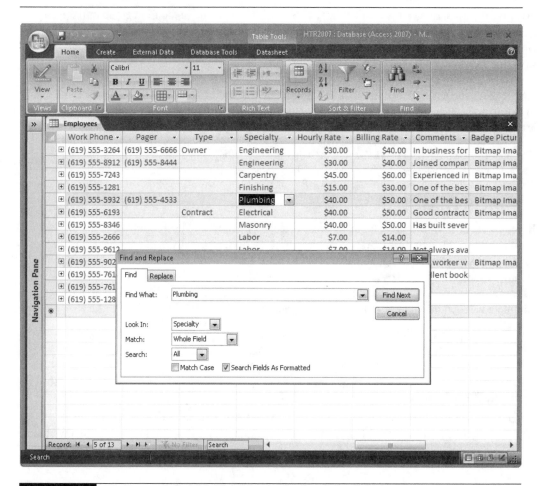

FIGURE 5-8   Finding records with Plumbing in the Specialty field.

5. Click Find Next again to find subsequent records with the same value in the field. After Access has found the last record that matches the value, choosing Find Next displays an information dialog box indicating that there are no more records with that value.

6. Click OK to close the message and click Cancel to close the dialog box.

Limit or Expand the Search

By default, Access searches only the specified field in all the records. In the Look In box, you have a choice between the field that contains the insertion point or the entire table. By choosing the whole table, you can have Access search for the value in all the fields in the table. This is slower than limiting the search to a single field, but it comes in handy for finding specific values in all fields, especially when you want to replace one value globally with another. The Search option drop-down list includes:

- **All** Is the default setting; begins at the current record, searches to the end of the table, and begins again at the first record until all records are examined
- **Up** Searches from the current record toward the first record
- **Down** Searches from the current record through the remaining records

The Match Case option, when checked, treats upper- and lowercase letters as different characters. For example, if you enter the value **plumbing** in the Find What box and check Match Case, Access will not find *Plumbing*. The Search Fields As Formatted option looks for the field based on the displayed format rather than the stored value.

Find an Inexact Match

Access offers two ways to find an inexact match in a Text or Memo field: setting the Match option to limit the search to only part of the field or using wildcards in the search string. The Match options specify whether to require a complete and exact match or to accept a match with only part of the field. There are several Match options that you can choose from:

- **Whole Field** This is the default and it only finds records containing values that exactly match the search string.
- **Any Part of Field** Finds records whose field contains the search string anywhere in the field. For example, if you want to find all workorders that have the word *heater* somewhere in the description, you would ask Access to find a match anywhere in the field.
- **Start of Field** Specifies the first one or more characters to match with the field values. For example, if you want to locate records for all customers whose last name begins with *A*, you would use the Start of Field Match option.

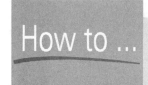

How to ... Look for Wildcard Characters

The field value you are looking for might include one of the characters Access recognizes as a wildcard, such as an asterisk (*), a question mark (?), a number sign (#), an opening bracket ([), or a hyphen (-). If you use the character directly in a search string, Access handles it as a wildcard.

When you use wildcards in a string to look for one of these characters, you must enclose the item you are looking for in brackets. For example, to find a value that begins with *?B*, you would use the string **[?]B***.

But if you are looking for a hyphen along with another wildcard character, you must treat it a little differently. Access interprets a hyphen or tilde as an indication of a sequence of acceptable characters. You must put such a character before or after all the other characters inside the brackets, not between them. If you have placed an exclamation point (!) inside the brackets to indicate a match excluding the characters within the brackets, place the hyphen right after the exclamation point.

If you are searching for an exclamation point or a closing bracket, you don't need to use the brackets at all. Just place the characters in the string with the rest.

Several wildcard characters can be used in the search string to represent one or more characters. You can mix and match wildcards to create the string combination you need. Most of them can also be used in queries and expressions, as you will see in Chapter 7. Look at Table 5-2 for more ways to use wildcards.

Wildcard	Matches	Example
*	Any number of characters.	**b*** finds *bird, belt*, and *blueberry*
?	Any single character.	**b??l** finds *ball, beal, bell, bowl*, and so on
[]	Any character within the brackets.	**b[aeo]ll** finds *ball, bell*, and *boll*, but not *bill* or *bull*
!	Any character not in the brackets.	**b[!ae]ll** finds *bill, boll*, and *bull* but not *ball* or *bell*
- (hyphen)	Any character in the specified range of characters. The range must be in ascending order.	**B[a-d]t** finds *bat, bbt, bct*, and *bdt*
#	Any single numeric character.	**10#** finds *100, 101, 102*, and so on but not *10A*

TABLE 5-2 Wildcard Characters

Wildcards can appear anywhere in the search string in the Find What box. For example, you can enter the string **12##*[BC]*** to find all addresses in the 1200 block of any street that begins with *B* or *C*.

Find Blank Fields

You can use Find to locate records with blank fields. This is useful when you enter incomplete record data because all the information wasn't available. Then, when more data arrives, you can quickly look for the records that need to be filled in.

To find blank fields, enter Null or Is Null in the Find What text box. When Access finds a record with a blank in the field, the record selector moves to the record but the field is not highlighted. When you close the Find and Replace dialog box, the insertion point appears in the blank field, ready for you to enter data.

If you have created a custom format for a Text or Memo field that specifies a certain display when the field contains a Null value and a different display when it contains a zero-length string, be careful how you apply the Search Fields As Formatted option.

Also, be sure to select Whole Field in the Match box when you are looking for either a Null value or a zero-length string.

Find and Replace Data

A variation of the Find feature is the Replace tool, which lets you specify a value that you want in the field in place of the one that is already there. The search options are the same. The only difference between the Find tab and the Replace tab is the addition of the Replace With box where you type the replacement value. For example, to replace all occurrences of the word *Lost* in the Award Date field of the Bid Data with the words *Not Awarded*:

1. Place the insertion point in the Award Date column.

2. If you already had the Find dialog box open, click the Replace tab.

3. Enter **Lost** in the Find What box and **Not Awarded** in the Replace With box.

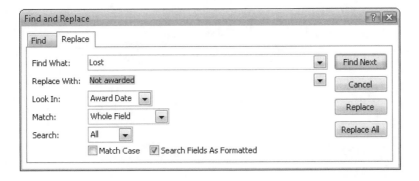

4. Click Find Next, then do one of the following:

  ■ Choose Replace to replace this instance of *Lost*. Access replaces the value and moves automatically to the next occurrence.

  ■ Choose Find Next to skip replacing this occurrence and move to the next.

  ■ Choose Replace All to replace all the values without reviewing them individually.

5. Access displays a message when it has finished searching the records. Click Cancel to close the dialog box.

Delete Data

To delete individual characters, you can place the insertion point in the field and then press DEL to remove the next character or press BACKSPACE to remove the previous character. To delete all data in the field, select the field and press DEL or BACKSPACE. You can restore characters deleted from a field by clicking Undo on the Quick Access toolbar.

To delete an entire record, select the record and press DEL or on the Home tab in the Records group, click the Delete down arrow and choose Delete Record from the shortcut menu. A deleted record cannot be restored, so Access warns you before deleting the record. To delete several records, select them all, then proceed as previously described. To delete a record without selecting it, place the insertion point anywhere in the record and click Delete Record.

TIP   *If you have a lot of records to delete, you can save time by using a delete query. See Chapter 8 for information about this special query.*

Part II

Retrieve and Present Information

Chapter 6

Sort, Filter, and Print Records

How to...

- Sort records by values in one or more fields
- Filter records
- Use the Advanced Filter/Sort feature
- Remove/clear or save a filter
- Preview and print filtered or sorted table data

Once you have stored all the information in the related tables of your database, you must be able to retrieve specific data and arrange it in meaningful ways. The Access Sort & Filter features help you do that. Sorting arranges the records in a specified order; filtering hides records. Combining these two tools gives you the power to display only the records you want, in the order you want.

Sort Records

Access automatically sorts records by the value in the primary key field. During data retrieval and presentation, there will be times when you will want to arrange the records in a different order.

In Datasheet view, you can sort up to 255 characters in one or more fields to achieve a sort within a sort. In Form view, records can be sorted by only one field with the Sort feature.

In ascending order, Yes/No fields sort by Yeses first, and then by Nos. Use descending order to reverse the order of the sort. You can sort on Memo fields using the first 255 characters. Access sorts Hyperlink fields by the Text to Display (if any) or the address. You cannot sort on OLE Object or Attachment fields.

Sort on a Single Field

To see records grouped together in Datasheet or Form view, you can sort the records based on the value in a specific field. To sort by a single field in a datasheet or form, click in the field by which you want to sort, then on the Home tab in the Sort & Filter group, do one of the following:

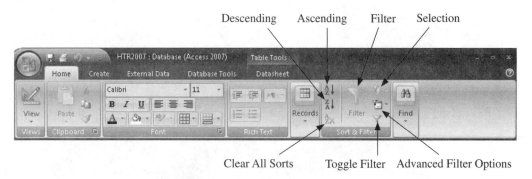

■ Click the Sort Ascending or the Sort Descending command.

■ Right-click in the field and choose Sort A to Z or Sort Z to A from the shortcut menu.

To restore the records to their original order, on the Home tab in the Sort & Filter group, click the highlighted Sort command or click the Clear All Sorts command.

NOTE *To sort records in a subdatasheet, display the subdatasheet by clicking the expand indicator (the plus sign in the left margin), then proceed as with a datasheet. When you specify a sort order for one subdatasheet in Datasheet view, all the subdatasheets of that level are also sorted accordingly.*

Sort by Two or More Fields

To sort by more than one field, the fields must be adjacent in the datasheet. Access uses a sort precedence from left to right, so that the records are sorted first by the values in the left column. If duplicate values appear in that column, a secondary sort is performed on those records by the values in the next column.

If the columns involved in the sort are not adjacent or are in the wrong relative position in the datasheet or subdatasheet, move the columns before sorting the records. Once they all are in position, select the columns you want to sort on and then click one of the Sort commands as before or choose from the shortcut menu.

NOTE *When you sort records by two or more fields, Access performs a "simple" sort in which all the values in the fields are sorted in the same order, either ascending or descending. To mix sort orders, you must use the Advanced Filter/Sort operation described in the section "Filter with Advanced Filter/Sort" later in this chapter. Or use a query instead, as described in Chapter 7.*

Save the Sort Order

If you close the table after sorting the records, Access asks if you want to save the changes to the design (which includes the sort order). Responding Yes saves the sort order with the table; the next time you open the table, the records will appear in that order. The fields will also appear in the order you selected for sorting. Responding No saves the table in the original, primary key order.

Filter Records

When you want to see only certain records in your datasheet, subdatasheet, or form, you can filter out the ones you don't want to see. The *filter* process does just that: it screens the records and lets through only those that meet your criteria. A filter doesn't actually delete any records, it just hides them. The *criteria* are a set of specified conditions that limit the display to a certain subset of records.

There is a difference between finding records and filtering records. When you order Access to find a record, the cursor moves to the specified record, but leaves all the rest on the screen. With a filter, the non-compliant records are removed from the screen, leaving only the records you want to see.

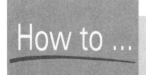

Access reminds you that you are not viewing the entire table. The status bar shows Filtered, indicating that a filter is in effect, and the navigation bar gives you the number of records qualified by the word (Filtered). The Toggle Filter command appears pressed and the ScreenTip for the button has changed to Remove Filter.

In Access, you have four ways to filter records, depending on the conditions you want to set and whether you want the records sorted in a particular order.

- **Context filters** These are available in the shortcut menus depending on the field type.
- **Filter By Selection** Leaves either only the records with the same value as the one you select in one of the records or the records that don't include the same value.
- **Filter By Form** Screens records with the criteria you enter into a table skeleton.
- **Advanced Filter/Sort** Gives you, in addition to filtering, the capability to sort the records by two or more fields using different orders, ascending or descending.

If you also want the records sorted as part of the filter process, you must use the Advanced Filter/Sort. You can, however, sort the results of the other types of filters after applying the filter by clicking one of the Sort commands in the Sort & Filter group.

How to ... Pick a Filter Type

To decide what type of filter you should use, think about what you want it to do:

- If you want to retrieve records that meet more than one criterion at once (combined with AND), you can use any of the four types of filters. Using Filter By Selection, you must specify and apply the criteria one at a time.
- If you want to combine criteria with the OR operator or enter expressions as criteria, you must use Filter By Form or Advanced Filter/Sort. An OR filter returns records that meet at least one of the criteria.

Filter by Context

Access 2007 provides many common filter options that are type-specific. These common filters are available in every view that displays data. The set of specific filters that are available depends on the type of data and the values in the selected column. All you have to do is right-click in the field and choose from the context menu. You can filter by the displayed value or by a selected partial value in the field.

Context filters are not available for Yes/No, OLE Object, or Attachment fields.

Filtering by Complete Value

As an example of filtering by a complete value, open the Workorders table in the Home Tech Repair database and place the insertion point in a Supervisor field with the value "Ferrell." Then right-click in the field and choose from the four options:

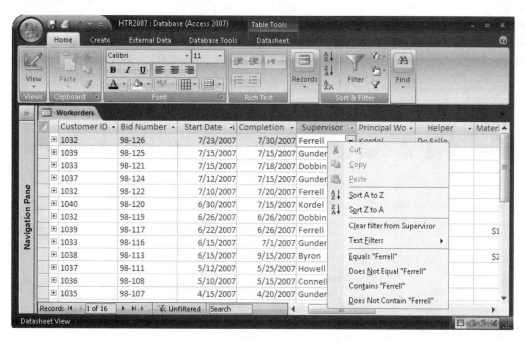

- **Equals** limits the display to exact matches
- **Does Not Equal** displays all records without "Ferrell"
- **Contains** displays all records in which "Ferrell" is included in the field
- **Does Not Contain** displays all records without "Ferrell" anywhere in the field

If you want to see additional options, point to Text Filters. You have several more choices in the context menu for matching with the selected value.

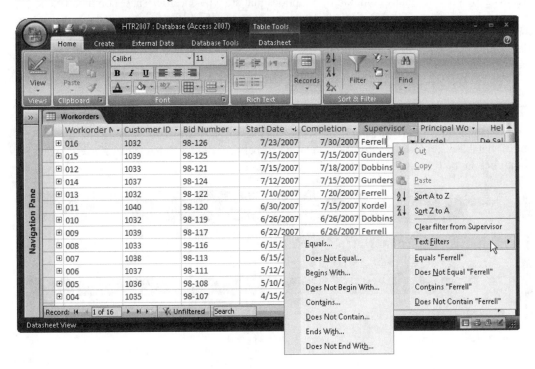

When you choose one of the Text Filter options, such as Equals, a Custom Filter dialog box opens where you can enter the value you want to use as the filter.

When you filter by a Date field, the context menus offer relevant options. For example, right-click in the Completion Date field and choose from the same four options as applied to the

Text field. If you want more options, point to Date Filters where you can choose from the type-specific filters.

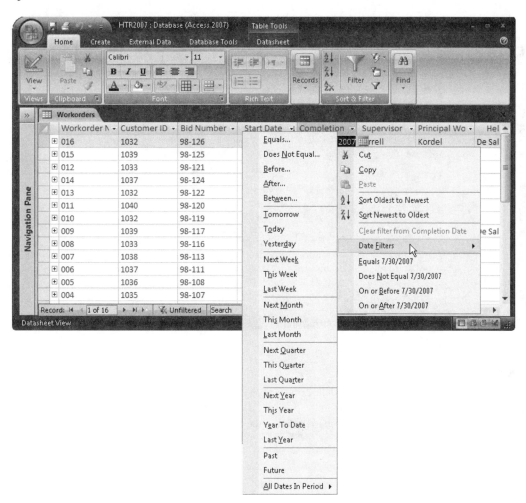

Filter by a Partial Value

If you want to filter on only part of the value in a field, select the characters you want to use and then right-click in the field. You can choose records with the selected characters somewhere in the field or at the beginning or end of the field. If you select characters embedded in the value, you only have the choice of displaying records containing or not containing the selected value.

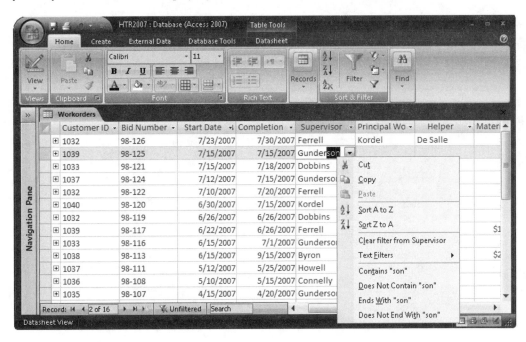

Use the Filter Command

With the insertion bar in a field in the datasheet, you can use the Filter command to limit records by individual values. On the Home tab in the Sort & Filter group, click the Filter command. All the values are checked in the list and will be included in the filter unless you uncheck them. You can do that one at a time or, if you only want a short list of values, uncheck Select All and check just the ones you want to see. Use the vertical scroll bar, if necessary, to see all the values for the field.

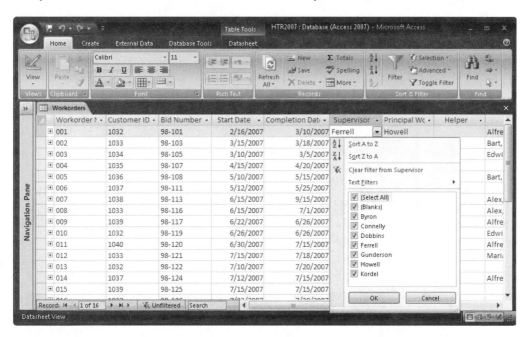

You can also click the Filter icon in the column header to see the list of values and the other options.

If the field is a Date/Time data type, you also have the option of screening by date criteria. Rest the mouse pointer on Date Filters to see the options. If it is a Text data type, you can use the Text Filters options.

The Filter command also offers to clear any filters from the selected field.

Filter By Selection

Filter By Selection provides another quick and easy way to limit the records to those with the currently selected value. If you want to filter the Workorders to those for a particular customer, click in the row that contains the customer's ID and on the Home tab in the Sort & Filter group, click the Selection command. You will see the same choices that appear when you right-click in the field.

Date/Time fields offer more choices. If you want to see which workorders will be completed during the month of July 2007 do the following:

1. Open the Workorders table in Datasheet view and click in the Completion Date field in any row.

2. On the Home tab in the Sort & Filter group, click Selection.

3. Choose Between to open the Between Dates dialog box.

4. Enter the Oldest and Newest dates or use the Calendar buttons to select the dates.

5. Click OK to return to the table now filtered to show workorders that are scheduled to be completed in July 2007 (see Figure 6-1).

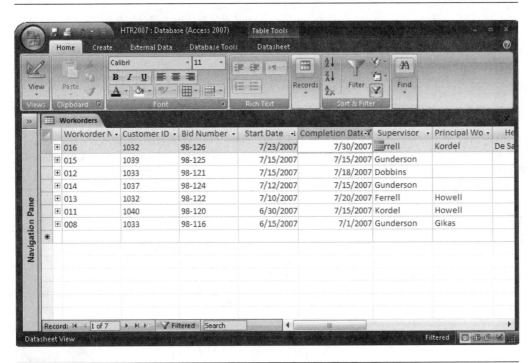

FIGURE 6-1 Filtering to workorders to be completed in July 2007

You can also use the Filter By Selection to filter to a few selected characters or numbers. This works the same as when you use the context filters. The filter choices include special options that depend on where the selected characters appear in the value.

- If the characters are at the beginning of the value, the choices are Begins With or Does Not Begin With as well as Contains and Does Not Contain.

- If the characters are within the value, the choices are Contains or Does Not Contain.

- If the characters are at the end of the value, the choices are Ends With or Does Not End With as well as Contains and Does Not Contain.

As an example of filtering to a partial value, filter the Bid Data table so you see only records that contain the word "heater" in the Description field:

1. In the Bid Data datasheet, select the "heater" part of Replace Waterheater in the Description field of the Bid Number 98-102 record.

2. On the Home tab in the Sort & Filter group, click the Selection command and choose Ends with "heater" in the context menu. Two records remain, both with the word "heater" at the end of the Description field.

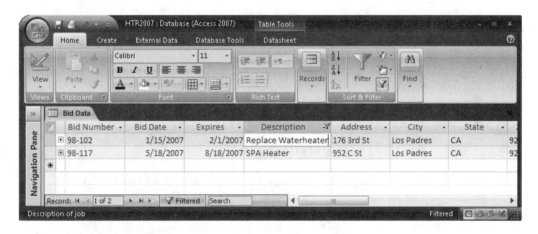

3. To remove the filter, click the Filtered button on the record navigation bar. All filters are removed and all records return to the datasheet. The filter is not deleted—it is just no longer active. You can reapply the filter with the Toggle Filter command.

If the field is a Date/Time data type, you also have the options specifying a time interval by entering beginning and ending dates as before.

You cannot filter Multivalued fields using a partial selection. The Selection command is not available for attachments.

Filter By Selection applies only one filter condition at a time. If you need to filter based on a combination of two or more values, you can apply the second Filter By Selection criterion to the records that remain after the first filter is applied. This is equivalent to combining the filter criteria with an AND operator.

Filter By Form

Filter By Form is one of the choices in the Advanced Filter Options context menu. Filter By Form is not much different from Filter By Selection. Instead of selecting a value from the datasheet or subdatasheet as a filter criterion, you enter the value in a filter grid. The grid is a table skeleton that resembles a blank record showing all the filterable fields in the table with space to enter filter values.

One advantage of using Filter By Form is that you can combine filter criteria in one operation. You can specify two or more conditions so that a record must meet any one or all of them to survive the filter. The multiple criteria can apply to a single field or to more than one field.

Enter Filter Criteria

When you click the Advanced Filter Options command and choose Filter By Form, the table grid appears on the screen. The most recent filter that has been saved with the table shows in the filter grid.

To create a new filter, right-click in the document below the grid and choose Clear Grid from the shortcut menu to remove any existing filter. Then move to the field where you want to specify a value. When you move the insertion point to a field in the grid, an arrow appears in the field.

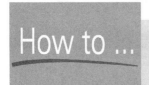

Filter Memo, OLE Object, and Hyperlink Fields

When you apply Filter By Selection to a Memo, OLE Object, or Hyperlink field, you can see all the records with the same value in the field. With the other filter operations, you can filter based only on whether the field has a value or is empty.

When you filter on a blank memo field with the Selection command, your choices are Equals Blank and Does Not Equal Blank. If the field has a value, you also have the options, Equals and Does Not Equal the selected value.

When you choose Selection for an OLE Object, your only option is Is Not Blank whether the field has a value or not. For a hyperlink field with a value, your choices are Equals, Does Not Equal, Contains, and Does Not Contain the selected value. If there is no value in the field, the choices are Equals Blank and Does Not Equal Blank.

When you click the drop-down list in one of these fields, the only available options are Equals Blank and Does Not Equal Blank.

Clicking this arrow displays a list of unique values that currently exist in the field, sorted in ascending order. Here you see a list of values in the Completion Date field in the Workorders table.

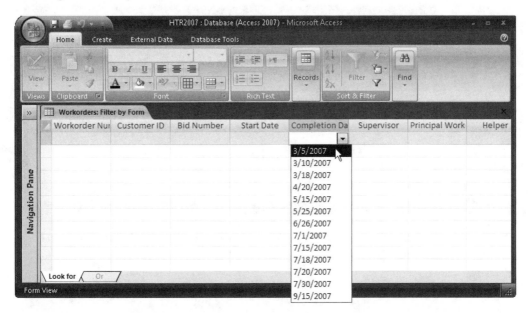

To filter on one of these values, select the value and click Toggle Filter command. This is equivalent to using Filter By Selection.

 If the table has a long list of unique values in the field, Access might not build the list. Instead, you may see only two choices: Is Null and Is Not Null.

Now try filtering the Workorders records by using an expression to show only those whose scheduled completion date is before July 1, 2007:

1. On the Home tab in the Sort & Filter group, click the Advanced Filter Options command and choose Filter By Form in the context menu.

2. If there are entries in the filter grid, select the entry and press DELETE or right-click below the grid and use the Clear Grid command to remove them.

3. Place the insertion point in the Completion Date field and select 7/1/2007 from the value list. Access automatically adds the date/time delimiter symbols (#) to the date you select from the list.

4. Place the insertion point at the beginning of the date and enter < (less than).

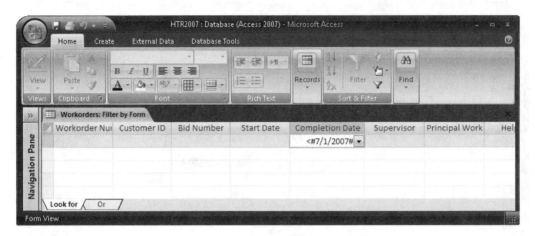

5. Click the Toggle Filter command. Only the eight records of Workorders scheduled to be completed before July 1, 2007 remain on the screen.

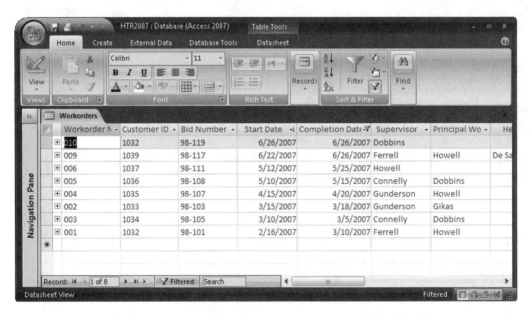

6. To remove the filter and restore all records, right-click in the filtered column and choose Clear Filter from *field name* in the shortcut menu. To clear all filters, click the Advanced Filter command and choose Clear All Filters from the context menu.

Use Wildcards and Expressions in a Filter

You can use wildcards in filter criteria for Text and Memo fields; refer to Chapter 5 for examples of using wildcards. In a search, wildcards can be applied only to character strings. You can use wildcards to replace individual characters or groups of characters.

You can also enter an expression as the filter criterion, such as the earlier example of <7/1/2007 entered in the Completion Date field in the Filter By Form grid. To use an expression as a criterion, enter it directly in the filter grid. Open the Access Help topic, "Examples of expressions used in queries and filters," to see some useful expressions. However, there are a few rules you must obey when entering expressions in a filter condition, whether you're using the Filter By Form or the Advanced Filter/Sort method:

- If a Text field value contains a space, any punctuation, or an operator character, the value must be enclosed in quotation marks. If the entry is one of the values in the list, Access adds the quotation marks for you after you leave the criteria grid.

- To filter a Memo field, use the asterisk (*) wildcards to filter on embedded text.

- For Number, Currency, and AutoNumber fields, do not include characters such as the currency symbol or the thousands separator. Decimal points and minus signs are okay.

- For Date/Time field values, abide by the options set on the Date tab of the Regional and Language Settings Properties dialog box of the Windows Control Panel. These options control the sequence of the month, day, and year values within the field. Access encloses the date or time value in pound signs (#).

- For Yes/No fields, you can enter Yes, -1, On, or True to filter for Yes values, and No, 0, Off, or False for No values.

Combine Filter Criteria with AND

The Filter By Form process can accept more than one criterion. To combine two filter conditions with the AND operator which limits the records to those that meet both conditions:

1. In the Workorders datasheet, on the Home tab in the Sort & Filter group, click the Advanced Filter Options command and choose Filter By Form in the context menu.

2. Right-click and choose Clear Grid in the shortcut menu to remove the previous filter conditions then click in the Material Cost field.

3. Type **<=1000** and press TAB to move to the Labor Cost field and type **>=500**, then press ENTER.

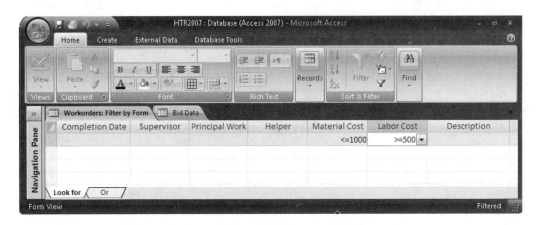

4. Click the Apply Filter command. Four records meet the combined filter conditions that show the labor-intensive contracts.

5. Click Toggle Filter to restore all the records in the datasheet.

 *If your filter doesn't return any records and the table does have data, you might have set conflicting criteria that were impossible to meet.*

Combine Filter Conditions with OR

The OR operator expands the resulting record set by including records that meet either of the conditions, not necessarily both. The Filter By Form window contains two tabs at the bottom of

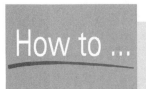 **Use AND in One Field**

The preceding example combines filter conditions in different fields with the implied AND operator. You also can combine filter conditions in the same field with AND by typing AND between the expressions. For example, if you enter the filter condition >=500 AND <=1000 in the Material Cost field, you would see only the records for work orders requiring between $500 and $1,000 worth of materials, inclusive. Another way to express the same criterion is to use the Between...And...operator: Between 500 And 1000.

the window: Look for and Or. Enter the first filter condition and any others you want to combine with it using AND on the Look For page. The records must meet all the criteria on a each tab to be capable of inclusion in the resulting recordset, but not on both tabs combined.

If you want to add an OR filter condition, click the Or tab and enter the condition on the second page. If you change your mind and want to delete the Or tab, select it then right-click in the grid and choose Delete Tab from the shortcut menu.

NOTE   *Another Or tab appears when you begin to add a filter to the first Or page.*

To combine two filter conditions with OR so that you can see all the Bid Data records for jobs on B or H Streets:

1. In the Bid Data datasheet, on the Home tab in the Sort & Filter group, click the Advanced Filter Options and choose Filter By Form in the context menu. The Filter window opens showing the last filter condition in the grid.

2. Click Clear Grid, then enter *** B*** (with a space before the *B*) in the Address field on the Look for page and press ENTER. Access translates the expression to *Like "* B*"*.

3. Click the Or tab at the bottom of the window. The Or page opens with the same empty grid as the Look For page. Notice a third Or tab now shows at the bottom of the window.

4. Place the insertion point in the Address field and enter *** H***, then press ENTER. The expression is changed to *Like "* H*"*.

5. Click Apply Filter on the toolbar. The datasheet now shows the five jobs with addresses on B or H Streets.

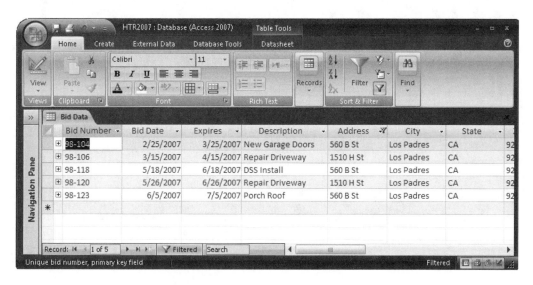

6. Click the Remove Filter command to restore all the records.

If you don't include a space before the H in the filter criterion, you will see all records with the letter H anywhere in the Address field. Examples include addresses on any street with "th," such as 5th or 6th.

Filter with Advanced Filter/Sort

The Advanced Filter/Sort feature is the most flexible and comprehensive of the Access filtering tools. It includes all the features of Filter By Form and allows you to specify mixed sort orders for different fields in the table. You enter all of the filtering and sorting specifications in a single window.

The Advanced Filter/Sort window is divided into two parts. The upper part contains the field list. The lower part is the design grid where you specify which fields you want to filter, the values to use as filters, and how you want the records sorted in the resulting recordset. If you have applied a filter recently, the criteria will appear in the Criteria row of the grid. Right-click and choose Clear Grid in the shortcut menu to remove it.

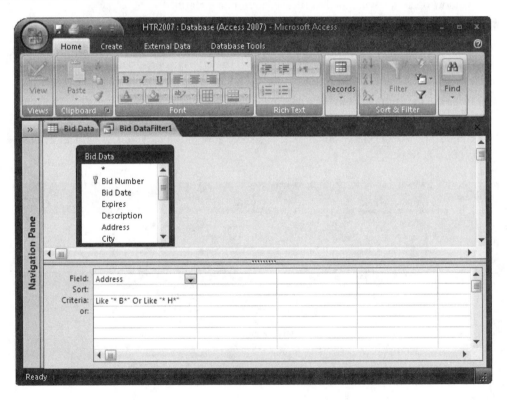

The process of creating an Advanced Filter/Sort is nearly identical to that of creating a query. Chapter 7 contains all the details for creating queries that you can use to build an Advanced Filter/Sort that can accomplish tasks such as the following:

- Selecting the fields to filter or sort
- Specifying filter criteria
- Setting the sort orders

Apply the Advanced Filter

At any time during the design of an advanced filter, you can apply it to see if you are getting the data you want. Access gives you two ways to apply the filter:

- On the Home tab in the Sort & Filter group, click the Toggle Filter command.
- Right-click anywhere in the upper section of the Design window and choose Apply Filter/Sort from the shortcut menu.

Filter by Lookup Fields with Advanced Filter/Sort

Filtering on a field that gets its value from a lookup list with Advanced Filter/Sort can present a slight problem. When you choose to filter records by values in a Lookup field in Filter By Form, you pick from the value list that contains all the values in the lookup list created by the Lookup Wizard. What you don't see in the list are the values that are actually stored in the field. It is the value in the primary key field of the lookup list that is stored instead of the more informative displayed value.

When you use Advanced Filter/Sort, you do not choose from the lookup list because there is only one table in the Filter window. This means that you must enter the stored value in the Criteria row to filter on a Lookup field. For example, using Filter By Form to filter on Ferrell in the Supervisor field of the Workorders table, you can select Ferrell from the list or type **Ferrell** in the grid. To do the same in Advanced Filter/Sort, you must enter **10**, Ferrell's Employee ID number, in the Criteria row.

Save a Filter

The most recent filter is saved with the table—not as a separate object—if you respond Yes to save the table changes. When you reopen the table, the filter is no longer in effect but you can reapply it by any of the methods discussed earlier.

If you want to have more than one filter available to a table or want to save a filter permanently, you must save it as a query, which is stored as a separate Access database object. When you want to use the filter again, you can bring it back from the query to the Filter window or simply run it as a query.

To save an advanced filter as a query and load it again in the Filter window:

1. With the Filter tabbed document displayed, right-click anywhere in the design grid and choose Save As Query in the shortcut menu.

2. Name the query and choose OK.

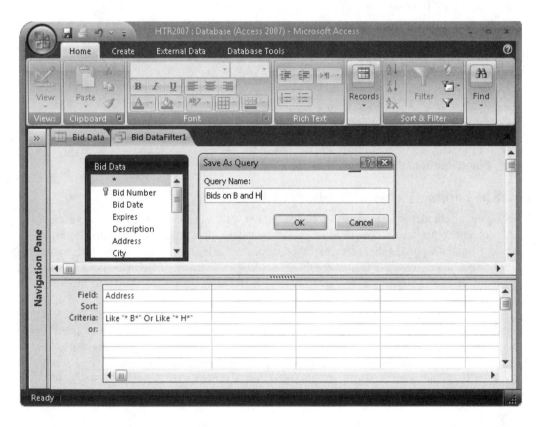

To restore the specifications to the Filter window, then do the following:

1. Right-click in an open blank Advanced Filter/Sort window and choose Load From Query in the shortcut menu.

2. The Applicable Filter dialog box shows a list of all the queries that are based on the Bid Data table.

3. Choose the query you want and click OK. All the filter parameters are returned to the grid, where you can choose to apply the filter or make changes to it.

If all you want to do is filter the records, simply run the query you saved from the filter.

Remove and Clear Filters

There is a difference between removing and clearing a filter. Removing a filter simply returns all the records to the datasheet or form, and you can reapply it later. Clearing the filter erases the filter criteria, and the filter cannot be reapplied unless you reconstruct it. (You saw how to remove a filter earlier in the chapter.)

To delete a filter entirely, you need to clear the filter grid and apply the empty filter to the datasheet. On the Home tab in the Sort & Filter group, click the Advanced Filter Options command and choose Clear All Filters from the context menu.

Preview and Print Sorted or Filtered Table Data

You don't have to create a fancy report to print your table data. You can print the datasheet as it appears in the Datasheet view or print in the default report format. To print a single copy of the entire datasheet, click the Microsoft Office button, point to Print and choose Quick Print from the context menu.

If you want to see how the filtered or sorted table data will look when it is printed, click the Microsoft Office button, point to Print as before and choose Print Preview. The Print Preview tab includes some commands that offer options for viewing the printout. The Print Preview window shortcut menu contains many of the same options. See Chapter 11 for details of how to use the Print Preview window.

Figure 6-2 shows the Bid Data datasheet previewed in two pages. If you change the page orientation to landscape, it will also be two pages.

If you want to adjust the margin settings, the paper size, or the page layout, use the Page Setup dialog box. If you want to choose other print options such as multiple copies or selected pages, open the Print dialog box. See Chapter 11 for information about running Page Setup and setting Print options.

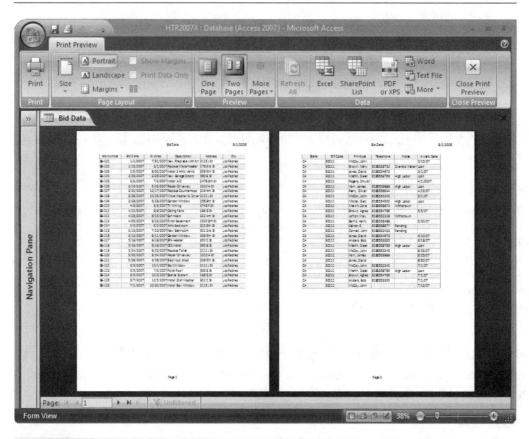

FIGURE 6-2   Previewing the Bid Data datasheet printout.

Chapter 7

Extract Information with Queries

How to...

■ Create a select query with help from the Query Wizard

■ Create a select query without the wizard

■ Add selection criteria

■ Set query properties

■ Modify a query

■ Perform calculations with a query

■ Create special queries with the Query Wizard

When you work with information in an Access datasheet, you can filter and sort the records in many ways, but you have even more flexibility with queries. You can limit the records to a specific subset and specify only the fields you want to see in the result.

 ## Decide between a Query and a Filter

Usually you will use a filter to view or edit records temporarily in a datasheet or form. If you want to return to the subset of records later, you should use a query. Queries are separate database objects that appear in the Navigation Pane whereas a single filter is saved with a table.

Use either a query or a filter when you want to do the following:

■ Use the results as a basis for a form or report

■ Edit data in the result if editing is allowed

Use a query if you want to do the following:

■ Add another table and include those records in the result

■ Select only specific fields to include in the result

■ Store the data as a separate Access object in the database

■ See results without opening the underlying table, query, or form

■ Include calculated values in the result

The results of both filters and queries can be used as the source of data for forms and reports. You also can sort the results of both and save the sort order for use in a later work session. Both methods let you edit the data displayed in the results if editing is otherwise permitted.

An Access query is a set of explicit specifications that tell Access exactly what information you want to see and how you want it arranged or manipulated in the results. Access provides several types of queries ranging from the popular *select query,* which extracts specific data to the more exotic *action queries,* which can insert, update, and delete records. You will see how the different types of queries work later, both in this and in the next chapter.

The results of both filters and queries can be used as the source of data for forms and reports. You can also sort the results of both and save the sort order for use in a later work session. Both methods let you edit the data displayed in the results if editing is otherwise permitted.

Before getting down to business, you need to understand a few new terms. When you run a query, the resulting group of records is called a *recordset,* which may or may not be editable, depending on the type of query that produced the recordset. If the records can be edited, the resulting recordset is called a *dynaset.* Simple select queries produce dynasets. If not editable, it is called a *snapshot.* Crosstab queries and any queries with groupings or calculated fields produce snapshots. See the Access Help topic, "When can I edit data in a query?" for more information.

7

Create a Select Query

As usual, Access gives you a choice of methods to begin a new query design. You can either start from scratch in an empty query design or call upon one of the Query Wizards for help. On the Create tab in the Other group, click either the Query Design or the Query Wizard command.

When you choose to use a wizard, you can choose to create four types of queries. To create a select query with the wizard, choose Simple Query Wizard, which will guide you through choices about the basic design of the select query. You can then go to the Design window to customize the query design if necessary.

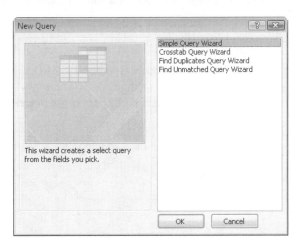

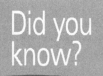

Specific Types of Select Queries

The Access select queries include the following:

- **Simple Select queries**   Display data from one or more tables sorted in a specific order. You also can perform many types of predefined or custom calculations on values in all records or within groups of records.
- **Crosstab queries**   Summarize data between two or more sets of field values.
- **Parameter queries**   Display all records that match a criterion you enter at a prompt.
- **Find Duplicate queries**   Display all records with duplicate values in one or more specified fields.
- **Find Unmatched queries**   Display records in one table that have no related records in another table.

Use the Simple Query Wizard

The Simple Query Wizard displays a series of dialog boxes in which you specify the fields and records you want to include in the query and enter a name for the same query. You can include fields from any of the tables or other queries in your database.

Let's use the Simple Query Wizard to build a list of current work orders and include information from the Workorders and Bid Data tables:

1. On the Create tab in the Other group, click the Query Wizard command.
2. Select Simple Query Wizard from the New Query dialog box and click OK.
3. Select Table: Workorders from the Tables/Queries list box (see Figure 7-1) and then use one of the following methods to move the Workorder Number, Supervisor, Material Cost, Labor Cost, and Description fields to the Selected Fields list.
   - Double-click the field name.
   - Select the field in the Available Fields list and click the right arrow (>).

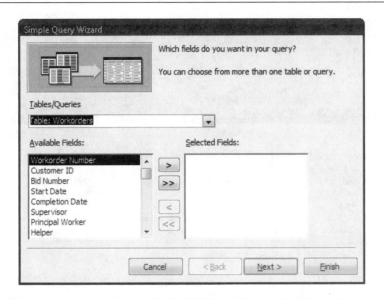

FIGURE 7-1   Choose the fields in the Simple Query Wizard dialog box.

TIP   *To add all the fields from a table, click the double right arrow (>>). If you change your mind about including a field, double-click it in the Selected Fields list or select it and click the left arrow (<).*

4. Select Table: Bid Data from the Tables/Queries list box and add the Address, Bid Number, and Principal fields to the Selected Fields list.

5. Click Next and accept the Detail option, which will then show every field of every record, then click Next.

6. Enter Current Workorders as the name for the new query and then accept the default option to open the query to view information.

7. Click Finish. The query results appear in a datasheet showing not only the eight fields you selected but all the records (see Figure 7-2). The column widths have been adjusted in the figure to show all the information.

The wizard has helped you with the basic query definition; now it is up to you to add the final touches, such as adding selection criteria to limit the records, changing the query and field properties, adding another table, specifying a sort order, or adding calculated fields.

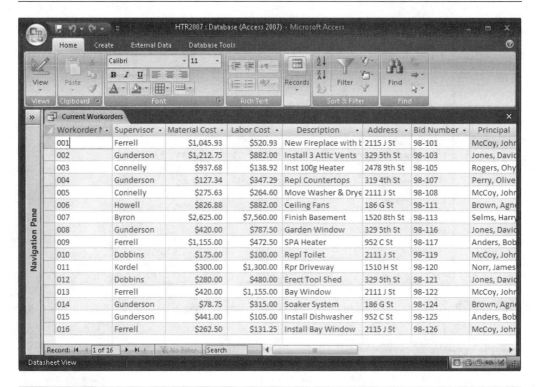

FIGURE 7-2 The results of the Current Workorders query.

Tour the Query Design Window

A query, like a table, can be viewed as a datasheet or a design. The Datasheet view shows you the data that results when you run the query. The Design view is where you can look at the query structure and make changes to the query design or even create a new one. The third query view, not available to tables, is the SQL view, which shows the SQL statements that Access creates behind the scenes to implement the query. The SQL view has no counterpart with table objects.

To switch to Design view, right click the Query document tab and choose Design View from the shortcut menu. Or on the Home tab click the View command and choose Design View in the Context menu.

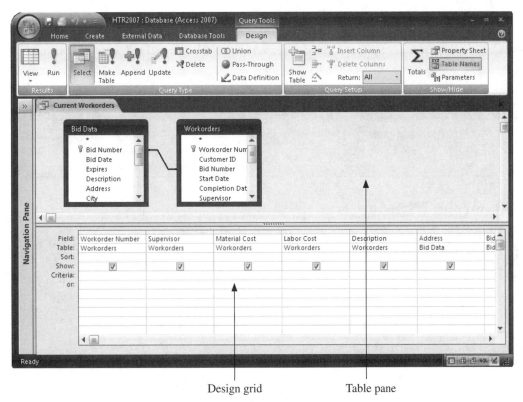

Design grid   Table pane

- ■ The upper pane is the table pane, which displays the field lists for all the tables in the query and shows the relationships among the tables.

- ■ The lower pane is the design grid, which shows the elements of the query design.

The table pane for the Current Workorders query shows the two tables from which you selected fields: Bid Data and Workorders. Access has accepted the relationship between the tables joining the Bid Numbers.

The design grid shows the field names you selected in the wizard dialog box and includes the name of the table they came from. Here is where you specify which fields to include, any filter criteria or sort orders, and whether to show the field in the query result. The check marks in the Show row indicate which fields are to appear in the query result. Clearing the check mark hides the field from the query result. This is helpful when you want to filter or sort the results based on a field that you don't want to appear in the query results.

The Query Design ribbon has some new groups and commands. The Results group has commands that change the query view or run the query to see the results before saving the query. The Query Type group offers commands to create all types of queries. The Query Setup group has tools to modify the query design and limit the query results as well as a command to start the Expression Builder. The Show/Hide group includes commands to summarize data, view and change query properties, take the table names off the design grid, and create a parameter query. As you work with queries in this and the next chapter, you will see how these commands are put to use.

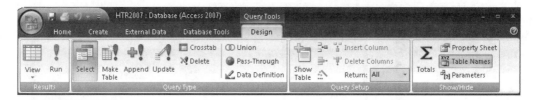

Without the Wizard

To bypass the wizard and create your query from scratch, on the Create tab in the Other group, click the Query Design command. The Show Table dialog box opens where you will select the tables or queries you want to work with.

As an example of creating a new query without the wizard, Home Tech Repair needs a list of work orders showing the following fields from the Bid Data and Workorders tables arranged in the following order:

- Bid Number (Bid Data)
- Supervisor (Workorders)
- Job Address (Bid Data)
- Description (Workorders)
- Award Date (Bid Data)
- Start Date (Workorders)
- Completion Date (Workorders)

Later we will add the customer's Last Name and Phone Number from the Customers table. We'll also add the cost data; compute the total cost; and add criteria based on start date, total cost, and other factors to limit the records in the result.

Now you'll create the new query:

1. On the Create tab in the Others group, click the Query Design command.
2. The new Query Design document opens with the Show Table dialog box. The dialog box has three tabs that display a list of Tables, Queries, or Both in the current database.

3. On the Tables tab, select the Bid Data table (if it is not already selected) and choose Add. You can see the field list added to the query table pane behind the dialog box.

4. Double-click Workorders in the Tables list and choose Close. Figure 7-3 shows the query design with the two tables. (Field lists have been resized in the figure so you can see the linking fields.)

5. Keep the Query window open to add fields to the design grid.

The next task is to choose the fields that you want to appear in the query result and arrange them in the desired order; let's first take a look at the relationships that Access shows for the two Home Tech Repair tables and add a third table to the design.

Relate Multiple Tables in a Query

To add a table to an existing query, in the Query Setup group, click the Show Table command or right-click the table pane and choose Show Table from the shortcut menu. If the tables are already related at the table level, Access automatically displays the join lines when you add the table to the query design. You can tell by the appearance of the line whether referential integrity is enforced, and which table is the "one" side and which is the "many." The one side shows a "1" while the many side shows an infinity (∞) symbol.

If the tables are not related before you add them to the query, Access often assumes a relationship between them based on fields with the same name and data type, especially if one is a primary key. When Access joins the tables, referential integrity is not enforced.

In the Home Tech Repair database the relationship between the Bid Data and the Workorders table was defined as one-to-many, linked by Bid Number, with referential integrity enforced. The Workorders table is related to the Bid Data table by Customer ID but referential integrity is not enforced. You can see these relationships in the query table pane. Let's add the Customers table to the new query and include the Last Name and Phone Number in the results so we won't have to look them up to reach the customer.

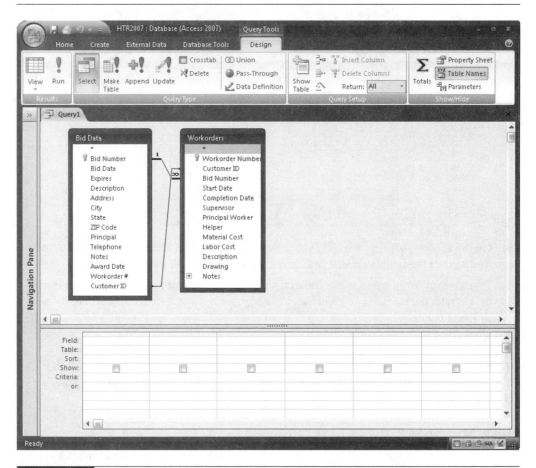

FIGURE 7-3 Tables added to the query design.

To add the Customers table:

1. Click the Show Table command to open the Show Table dialog box.

2. Double-click the Customers table and click Close. Referential integrity is enforced on the relationship with the Workorders table, but not on the relationship with the Bid Data table (see Figure 7-4). (The tables have been rearranged slightly in the figure to show the relationships more clearly.)

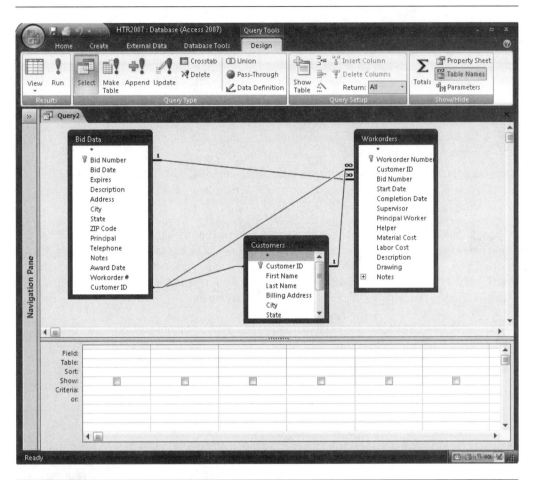

FIGURE 7-4   A third table is added.

NOTE

To remove a table from the query design, click on the field list in the table pane and press DEL or right-click the field list. Next, choose Remove Table from the shortcut menu. The table is removed from the query design but remains untouched in the database. Any fields from that table that you have already placed in the design grid are also removed.

Add/Remove Fields

You can add all the fields at once, add a selected group of fields, or add one field at a time. To add all the fields in a table to the grid at once, do one of the following:

■ Double-click the asterisk (*) at the top of the field list. This method places the table or query name in the Field row of the column followed by a period and an asterisk, as in the following example: Customers.*

■ Drag the asterisk from the field list to an empty column in the grid. This method does the same as the previous one.

■ Double-click the field list title bar to select all the fields and drag the group to the grid. Access places each field in a separate column across the grid in the order in which they appear in the field list.

There is an advantage but also a disadvantage to using the asterisk method of adding all the fields to query. The advantage is that if fields are added or deleted from the underlying table or query, this query will automatically make corresponding changes to the design. The disadvantage is that if you want to sort or filter using one of the fields, you must add it separately to the grid.

To add fields to the grid one at a time, do any of the following:

■ Double-click the field name to place it in the first empty column.

■ Drag the field to an empty column or insert it between filled columns.

■ Select the field name from the Field row drop-down list (see Figure 7-5). The list in a blank column contains all the fields in all the tables in the table pane and the table names with a period and asterisk.

To add a group of fields to the grid at once, select them and drag them as a group. The standard use of SHIFT and CTRL to select adjacent and non-adjacent field names works here the same as with filters. When you drag the block of selected field names to the grid, Access spreads them to empty columns, beginning where you drop the group. If there are already fields in the grid, the ones to the right of where you drop the group move over to make room.

To delete a field from the grid, click the column selector and press DEL or in the Query Setup group, click the Delete Columns command. If you remove the check mark from the Show cell in a column with no Sort or Criteria entries, the field will be removed from the grid the next time you open the query.

You can adjust the column widths and drag a column to a new position just as in a datasheet. Changing the column width has no effect on the query results datasheet unless you reduce the column width to zero.

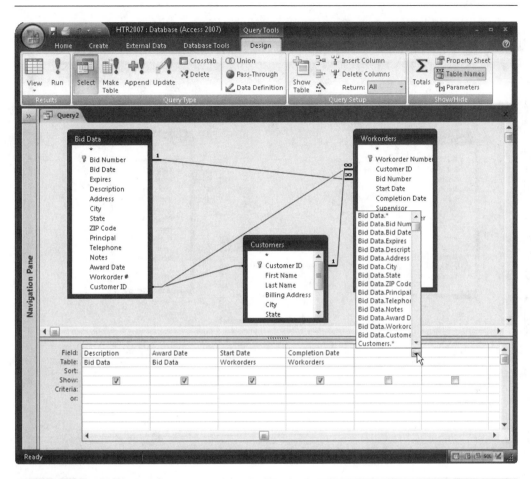

FIGURE 7-5 Choosing fields from the list.

> **NOTE** *To adjust a column width to fit its longest visible entry in the design grid, move the mouse pointer to the right edge of the column selector and double-click when the pointer changes to a two-way arrow. If you enter a longer value in the column later, you will need to readjust the width to see it all.*

Figure 7-6 shows the new query, still unnamed, with all the required fields in place. The columns have been resized to fit their contents and some are out of sight.

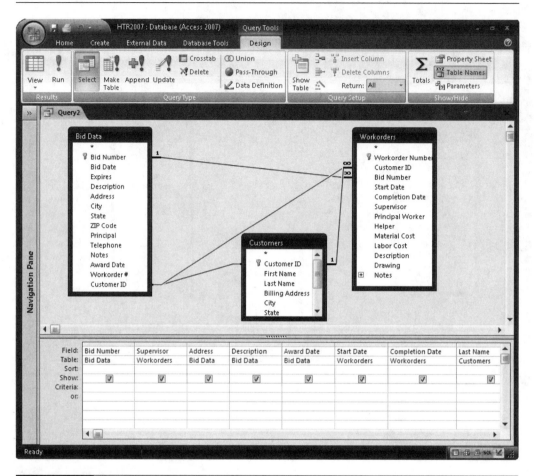

Fields added to the new query.

When you want to add a multivalued field to a query, you have two ways of displaying it in the query result:

- All entered values in a single cell in the record row in the datasheet
- Each value in a separate record row in the datasheet

For example, if you want all the Crew names for one workorder to appear in one cell separated by commas, place the Crew field name in the design grid (see Figure 7-7).

If you want each Crew name on a separate line, choose Crew. Value from the field list instead.

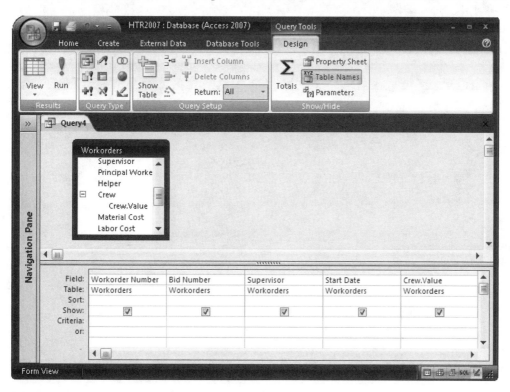

 You can't sort on a multivalued field when you have chosen the Value version. If you try, you will get an error message when you try to switch to Datasheet view.

Run and Save the Query

As you progress with the query design, it's a good idea to run the query now and then to see if you are getting the information the way you want it. You have three ways to run the query:

■ In the Results group, click the View command and choose Datasheet View in the context menu.

■ In the Results group, click the Run command.

■ Right-click the query document tab and choose Datasheet View in the shortcut menu.

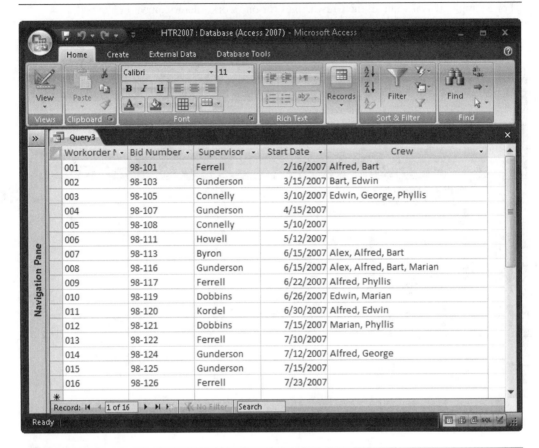

FIGURE 7-7   Placing all the multiple values in a single cell.

When you try to close the query from the Design view or one of the query result views, Access will prompt you to save the design. To save the new query design before adding the sort order and filter criteria:

1.   Right-click the Query Design document tab and choose Save in the shortcut menu.

2.   Enter **Workorder Cost Sheet** in the Save As dialog box, then choose OK.

Hide and Show Fields

There might be one or more fields that you want to use in filtering or sorting the query results, but don't want to appear in the results. The check box in the Show cell of the design grid

How to ...   Optimize Query Performance

If you have created an important query but it seems to take a long time to run, there might be ways to streamline it:

■ Make sure all the foreign keys in the related tables are indexed. If a field cannot be indexed, try not to sort on it.

■ Include in the design grid only those fields that are necessary in the results. Extra fields take more time to display.

■ Make sure you are not using exorbitantly large data sizes. Unnecessarily large fields waste disk space and slow processing.

determines whether the field values will be displayed. Clear the check mark to hide the field; check it to show the field.

TIP   *When you reopen the design of a query in which you have hidden some of the fields, you might think they have been removed. Actually, Access moves the hidden fields to the rightmost columns in the design grid when you save the query, so they might be off the screen. However, if there are no Criteria or Show entries, the field indeed is removed from the design.*

Specify the Record Order

To set a sort order in the query design, choose from the Sort cell list box in the column containing the field by which you want to sort. If you want to sort on more than one field, make sure you have the fields arranged in the proper order from left to right; they need not be adjacent.

A sort order will be saved with the query if you specify it in the design. Any new form or report based on the query then inherits the sort order. The order need not be applied but it is an inherited property of the form or report.

Sorting on a Lookup field can have confusing results. For example, Figure 7-8 shows the results of sorting the Workorder Cost Sheet records first by Supervisor, then by Completion date. The lower window shows the underlying query grid with both fields sorted in ascending order.

The Completion Dates are in the correct order within the set of records for a given Supervisor. However, the Supervisor fields do not appear to be in alphabetical order, either

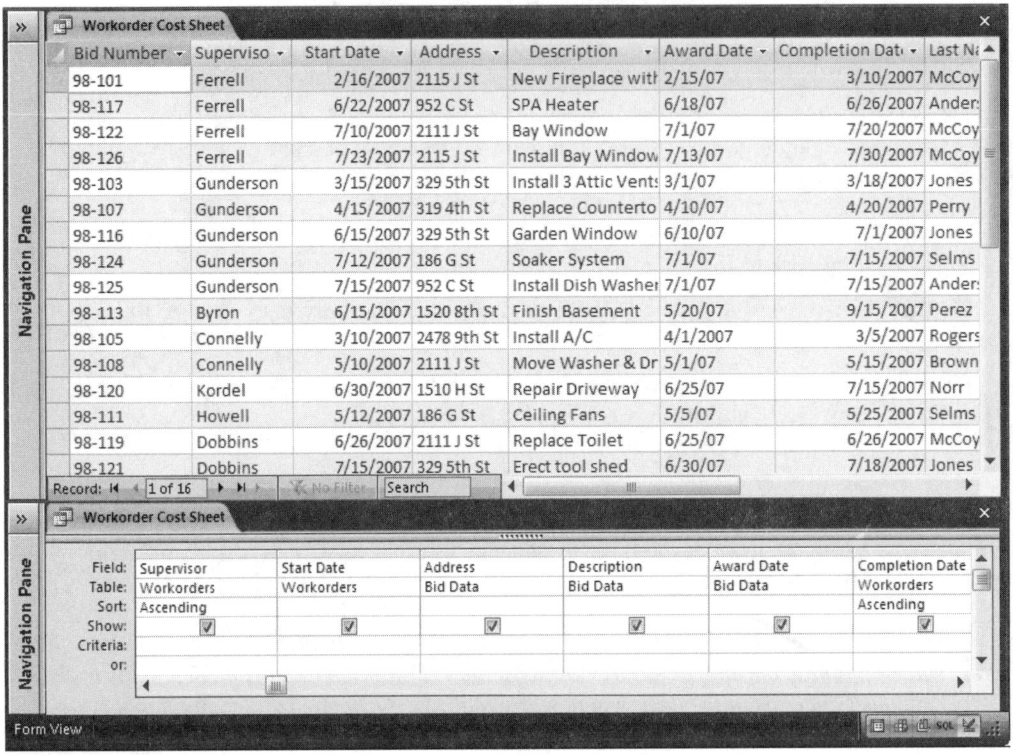

FIGURE 7-8 Sorting on a Lookup field.

ascending or descending. When you specify a sort in the query grid, Access sorts on the stored value, which in this case is the Employee ID number, not the employee name. If you want the records sorted by the displayed value, sort in the Datasheet view, which has access to the related lookup list values.

As you saw earlier, with a sort order, you can apply a filter to the query results instead of making it a part of the query design. This will have the same effect as adding the criteria to the design, but the filter will not be saved with the query.

Show Highest or Lowest Values

Limiting the results to the few highest or lowest values in a field can be handy for isolating the more labor-intensive jobs or finding the employees who could use a raise. For example, you can ask Access to display only the records with the 15 highest or lowest values in a field or the records with the highest or lowest 15 percent of values.

In the query Design view, use the Return command in the Query Setup group to specify how many or what percentage of the records to include in the results. The Return list includes 5, 25, and 100 records and 5 percent and 25 percent of the values to choose from as well as All. You can also type any percentage or number of values you want directly in the box.

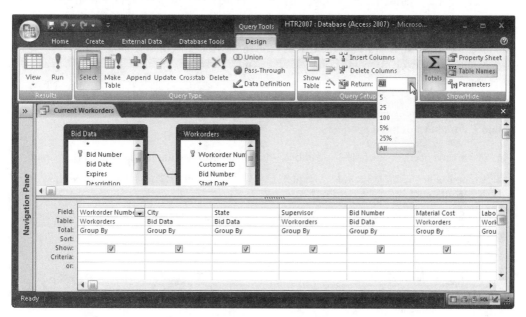

Access selects the records starting from the top of the list, so before you select the Return setting, you must sort (descending) on the field you want to display the highest values. If you want the lowest values, sort in ascending order. If you have specified a sort on any other field in the query, make sure that field (or fields) is to the right of the top values field so it will be subordinate to the Return list.

Add Selection Criteria

The selection criteria in queries are expressions that define a condition that must be met for the record to be included in the subset. An *expression* is a combination of symbols, values, identifiers, and operators that are used for many purposes, many of which you have already seen. Others will be discussed in later chapters, including the following:

- ■ **Symbols**   Quotation marks, colons, asterisks, and other special characters that are used in expressions
- ■ **Values**   Literal values, constants, results of a function, or identifiers
- ■ **Identifiers**   The values of a field, controls in a form or report, or properties
- ■ **Operators**   Symbols or words that indicate an operation that is to be performed on one or more elements in the expression

Use Wildcards and Operators

If you want to set a criterion for a text field and you want to match only part of the field, you can use the same wildcards that you used in filters, for example **?** to represent a single character and ***** to represent any number of characters. So, to find all Bid Data records for jobs on J Street, you would enter the expression ***J St*** in the Criteria cell in the Address column and press ENTER. Access examines the expression and completes the syntax by adding special characters such as Like "*J St*".

Operators are the key to more flexible expressions. Access has several classes of operators: *arithmetic, comparison, concatenation,* and *logical.*

Here's a rundown of these operators:

- Arithmetic operators include + (addition), − (subtraction), * (multiplication), and / (division).

- Comparison operators include = (Equals), > (Greater Than), < (Less Than), Is Null, Is Not Null, and Like.

- The concatenation operator usually is the & (ampersand) symbol.

- Logical operators include And, Or, and Not.

Use a Single Criterion

Imagine you want see information from the Workorder Cost Sheet for only those jobs that are supervised by Gunderson:

1. Open the Workorder Cost Sheet query in Design view and enter **12** (the Employee ID number for Gunderson) in the Criteria cell of the Supervisor column. Then, press ENTER. Access adds quotation marks around 12 because the field is a text data type.

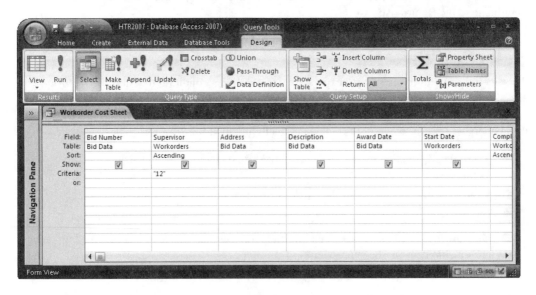

2. Switch to Datasheet view to display the five records for Gunderson's jobs.

3. Now you'll want to see the records for all jobs that were started before July 1, 2007 without regard to the supervisor. Return to Design view and delete the Supervisor criteria by selecting the expression and pressing DEL.

4. Enter **<7/1/2007** in the Start Date Criteria cell and press ENTER. Access adds the # date delimiters.

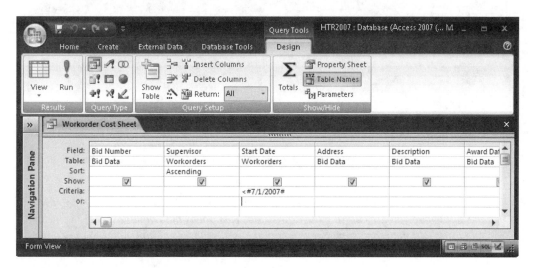

5. Run the query to see the records for jobs started before July 1, 2007.

Use Multiple Criteria

To apply more than one selection criterion, combine them with the AND or OR operators, using the same logic as with filters:

- Use AND to require that both criteria be met to include the record in the query result.
- Use OR to extract records that satisfy either expression.

NOTE *If you want to select records based on field values, the field must be in the design grid even if you don't show it in the results.*

Where you enter the expressions in the design grid depends on how you want them applied:

- In a single field using OR, enter one expression in the Criteria row and the second expression in the OR row.

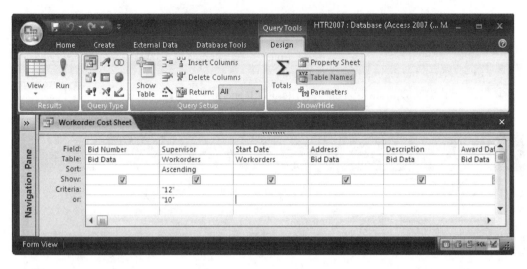

■ In a single field using AND, enter both expressions in the Criteria row combined with the AND operator.

TIP *If the expression is wider than the input area, press SHIFT-F2 with the insertion point in the cell where you are entering the expression. This opens the Zoom box where you can enter and edit the expression. Even though the text wraps to multiple lines in the Zoom box, the expression is only one line.*

■ In two fields using OR, enter one expression in the Criteria row of one column and the other expression in the OR row of the other column. It doesn't matter which is which.

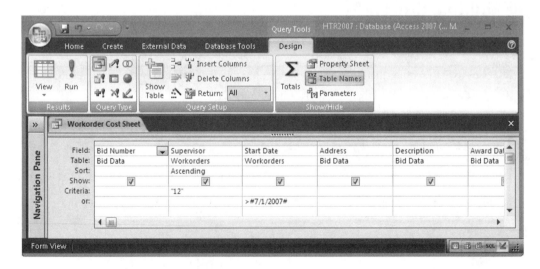

■ In two fields using AND, enter both expressions in the Criteria row.

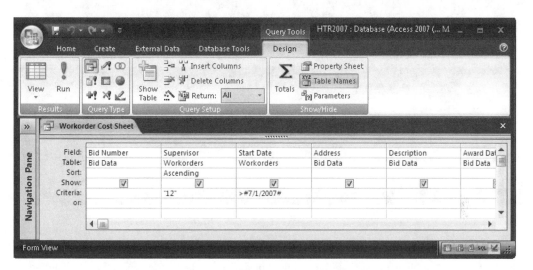

■ In three fields using both AND and OR, enter one pair of AND expressions in the Criteria row and the other pair in the OR row.

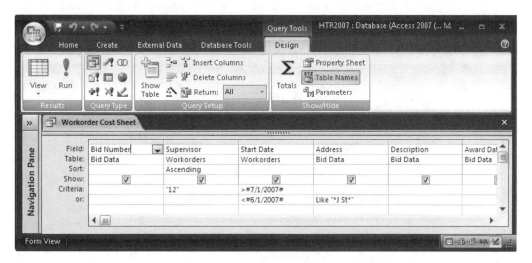

The results of this query are sorted by Supervisor (actually by Employee ID), and show all workorders by Gunderson (12) that started before July 1, 2007, and other workorders on J Street that started before June 1, 2007.

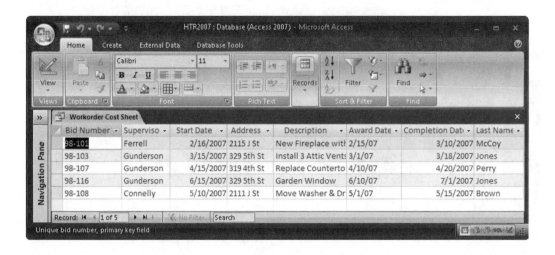

Get Help from the Expression Builder

When entering a complicated expression in a query design as a selection criterion for constructing a calculated field, you can call upon the Expression Builder for help. To open the Expression Builder, click in the cell where you want to enter an expression, and then on the Design tab in the Query Setup group, click the Build command. You can also right-click in the cell where the expression will go and choose Build from the shortcut menu. If the cell already contains an expression, it is copied to the Expression Builder. For example, the Builder shows a Date criterion left over from an earlier query. Notice the Workorder Cost Sheet folder is open and a list of fields is displayed in the center of the lower section.

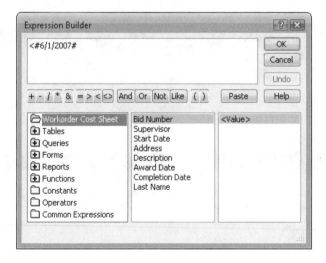

The upper pane of the Expression Builder is where you enter the expression. The lower pane consists of expression elements divided into three levels. The leftmost panel contains all the groups of elements that you can include in an expression. When you open a folder in this panel, the contents of the selected item are listed in the middle panel.

Selecting an item in the center panel opens a list of individual elements in the right panel. You can add one of these to the expression by double-clicking the name or selecting it and clicking Paste. The row of buttons between the upper and lower panes gives you a quick way of adding many of the commonly used operators and symbols.

For example, suppose you want to use the Month() function to define a selection criterion on the Start Date field in the Workorder Cost Sheet query, so that it will display only records for jobs started in June. To accomplish this, do the following:

1. In the Query Design view, right-click in the Criteria cell of the Start Date column and choose Build from the shortcut menu. Delete any expression already in the upper pane.

2. Double-click the Functions folder to open two subfolders: Built-In Functions and HTR2007, the name of the current database.

3. Open the Built-In Functions folder. A list of function categories appears in the center panel.

4. Choose Date/Time. The right panel shows a list of all the date- or time-related built-in functions.

5. Scroll down the list and select Month, then choose Paste. The Month() function is copied to the upper pane with the correct syntax.

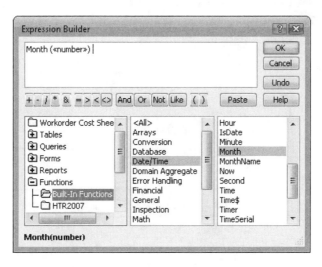

6. The Month() function requires an argument, a number, to tell Access which month you want to specify in the expression. Click to highlight <<number>> in the parentheses and enter **6** (for June).

7. Click OK. Month(6) now shows in the Criteria cell of the Start Date column.

You will see more of the Expression Builder in Chapter 15 when you add condition expressions to macros.

Set Query Properties

Like all other database objects, a query has a set of properties that control its appearance and behavior. To open the Query Properties dialog box (see Figure 7-9), place the insertion point in the table pane and do one of the following:

- On the Design tab in the Show/Hide group, click the Property Sheet command.

- Right-click anywhere in the design window outside the field lists, and then choose Properties from the shortcut menu.

- Click in the table pane and press ALT-ENTER.

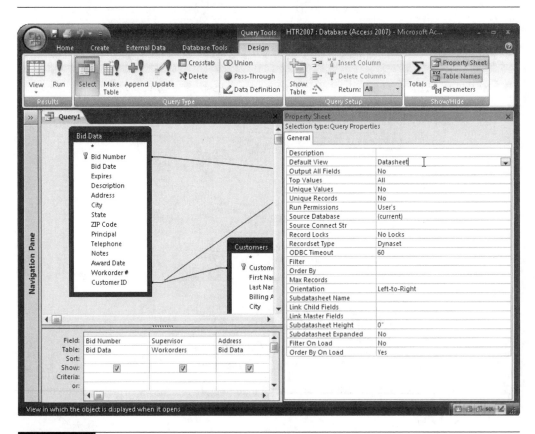

FIGURE 7-9   Set query properties in the Query Properties list.

To see a description of a property, place the insertion point in the property box and read the description in the status bar. You can also press F1 to open the corresponding Help topic.

Modify a Query

You can add or delete a field, rearrange the columns, show or hide any of the fields, change the resulting records sort order, and add one or more selection criteria. To open a query for modifying the design, right-click the query name in the Navigation Pane and choose Design View in the shortcut menu. If you want to view the results of the query first, choose Datasheet View, then switch to Design view later.

Insert a Field and Change the Field Order

If you want to add another field to the grid, drag the field name to the Field row of the column where you want the field. The field is inserted and the other columns move to make room.

> TIP   *If you double-click the field name, Access puts it at the end of the line in the first empty column.*

Moving a field in the design grid works the same as in a datasheet. Select the field by clicking the column selector (the mouse pointer changes to a down arrow). Release the mouse button and click again when it changes to a left upward arrow. Now drag the column to a new position.

When you see the dark vertical line where you want the column's left margin to appear, release the mouse button. The column moves and the other columns slide over to oblige.

Change Field Properties

The fields that appear in the query results inherit the properties from the table design. However, you might want the field to look different or show a different name in the query results, especially if you are going to use the results as the basis for a custom form or report. You cannot change all of a field's properties, only those that appear in the field's property sheet in the query.

Now you'll rename a field in the query design:

1. Place the insertion point left of the first letter of the name in the grid.

2. Type the new name followed by a colon (:). If you are replacing Expr1 or another Access-assigned name, replace only the name, not the expression following the colon.

3. Press ENTER.

> TIP   *If you want to keep the name in the grid but show a different name in the datasheet, change the field's Caption property in the property sheet.*

To change other field properties, click in the field on the grid and in the Show/Hide group, click the Property Sheet command or press ALT-ENTER. You can also right-click the field name and choose Properties in the shortcut menu. Entries in the field property sheets are blank; they do not contain the settings defined in the table design. Any entries you make in the Query Design window will override the preset properties.

The field property sheet has two tabs: General and Lookup. The General tab shows several properties that you can change in the query design, as follows:

■ **Description** Presents the text that is displayed in the status bar when you click the field in the Datasheet view. Any text entered here replaces the Description entered in the table definition. You can enter up to 255 characters.

■ **Format** Shows a list of applicable formats for the field. A Text field has no list but you can enter a custom format.

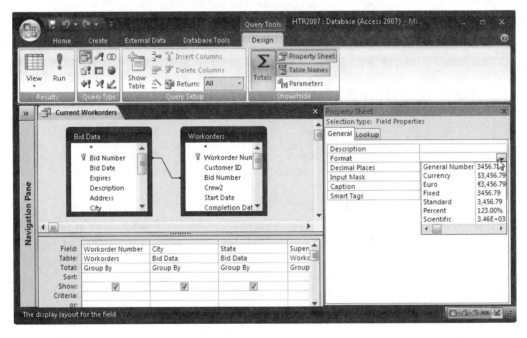

■ **Input Mask** Creates a data entry skeleton. You can either type the mask in the box or click Build to start the Input Mask Wizard.

■ **Caption** Specifies the column header for a datasheet, form, or report in place of the field name.

■ **Smart Tags** Specifies which available Smart Tags are attached to the field.

■ **Text Format** Offers a choice between Plain Text and Rich Text.

■ **Decimal Places** Appears in the property sheet if the field is a Number field and specifies the number of digits right of the decimal point.

If the field is a Lookup field, the Lookup tab has one option that can change the display control to a text box, list box, or combo box. The other properties on the Lookup tab are the same as those in the table design. If the field is not a Lookup field, this tab is blank. Changing field properties in a query design has no effect on the underlying table design.

> TIP
>
> *If you want to change properties of several fields or even a query property, keep the property sheet open and the options will change when you click another object in the query design.*

Perform Calculations in a Query

You can perform many types of calculations in a query that are recomputed each time the query is run so data is always current. The results of the calculations are not stored in the table. In a query, there are two types of calculations: aggregate calculations and calculated fields.

The *aggregate calculations* are predefined operations that are performed on groups of records and provide totals, counts, averages, and other information about field values in all records or in groups of records. Think of these aggregate calculations as vertical computations. For example, you can add up the number of jobs on J Street or calculate the average labor cost for all jobs.

The *calculated fields* actually create new fields in a record by combining the values in other fields in the record, producing a horizontal computation. You can create new numeric, date, or text fields for each record using custom calculations. For example, use the expression:

```
[Completion Date]-[Start Date]
```

to create a new field named Job Time. After creating a calculated field, you can use the aggregate calculations to further analyze the data. For example, after finding the Job Time for each job, you can compute the average time over all jobs or even add a selection criterion to limit the records to jobs in a specific area or supervised by a specific employee.

Add a Calculated Field

To add a new field that displays the results of a calculation based on other fields in the grid, click in the Field row of an empty column and enter an expression. The field names in the expression must be enclosed in brackets so Access recognizes them as fields.

For example, add a calculated field to a query of the Home Tech Repair Workorders table that shows the total cost of each current job:

1. In the Query Design view, drag the fields you want to see in the result to the grid, including Material Cost and Labor Cost.

2. Click in the Field cell on the first empty column and enter the expression **[Material Cost]+[Labor Cost]**, then press ENTER.

3. Move the insertion point to the left in the Field cell and replace Expr1 with **Total Cost**, keeping the colon.

4. Right-click the query document tab and choose Datasheet view in the shortcut menu. Figure 7-10 shows the results of the new calculated field.

If you want to see the total cost of each job, including a 15 percent markup for overhead expenses, add another calculated field using the expression:

```
[Total Cost]*1.15
```

If you misspell a field name in an expression when running the query, Access assumes it is a parameter needed by the query and asks you to enter the value. Click Cancel to close the Enter Parameter Value dialog box and return to the grid to correct the field name. See Chapter 8 for information about query parameters.

You are not limited to Number and Currency fields in calculated fields. Text fields are easily combined with the concatenation operator (&). For example, to create a new field showing employees' complete names in one field, use the following expression as the Field in the query grid:

```
Full Name:[First Name]&" "&[Last Name]
```

Supervisor	Material Cost	Labor Cost	Description	Address	Bid Number	Principal	Total Cost
Ferrell	$1,045.93	$520.93	New Fireplace with t	2115 J St	98-101	McCoy, John	$1,566.86
Gunderson	$1,212.75	$882.00	Install 3 Attic Vents	329 5th St	98-103	Jones, David	$2,094.75
Connelly	$937.68	$138.92	Inst 100g Heater	2478 9th St	98-105	Rogers, Ohykki	$1,076.59
Gunderson	$127.34	$347.29	Repl Countertops	319 4th St	98-107	Perry, Oliver	$474.63
Connelly	$275.63	$264.60	Move Washer & Drye	2111 J St	98-108	McCoy, John	$540.23
Howell	$826.88	$882.00	Ceiling Fans	186 G St	98-111	Brown, Agnes	$1,708.88
Byron	$2,625.00	$7,560.00	Finish Basement	1520 8th St	98-113	Selms, Harry	$10,185.00
Gunderson	$420.00	$787.50	Garden Window	329 5th St	98-116	Jones, David	$1,207.50
Ferrell	$1,155.00	$472.50	SPA Heater	952 C St	98-117	Anders, Bob	$1,627.50
Dobbins	$175.00	$100.00	Repl Toilet	2111 J St	98-119	McCoy, John	$275.00
Kordel	$300.00	$1,300.00	Rpr Driveway	1510 H St	98-120	Norr, James	$1,600.00
Dobbins	$280.00	$480.00	Erect Tool Shed	329 5th St	98-121	Jones, David	$760.00
Ferrell	$420.00	$1,155.00	Bay Window	2111 J St	98-122	McCoy, John	$1,575.00
Gunderson	$78.75	$315.00	Soaker System	186 G St	98-124	Brown, Agnes	$393.75
Gunderson	$441.00	$105.00	Install Dishwasher	952 C St	98-125	Anders, Bob	$546.00
Ferrell	$262.50	$131.25	Install Bay Window	2115 J St	98-126	McCoy, John	$393.75

FIGURE 7-10 Displaying the new Total Cost field.

The quotation marks between the field names add a space between the names.

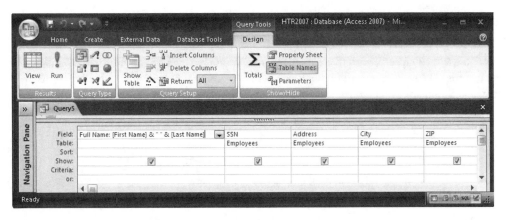

To include only the employees' initials and add some text to the display, you can use an expression such as the following:

```
"Supervised by: " & Left([First Name],1) & Left([Last Name],1)
```

The Left function extracts characters from the left of the field value. The integer argument in the function indicates how many of these characters you want to see—only one in this case. The result of this calculated field looks like this:

7

If you need help with a more complex expression, click Build to open the Expression Builder as described earlier.

Summarize with the Wizard

When you use the Query Wizard to create a new query, you have an option to summarize data in the records. The second wizard dialog box offers two choices: Detail, in which all records are shown, and Summary. Next, you'll see how to include a summary:

1. In the second Wizard dialog box, choose Summary and click the Summary Options button (see Figure 7-11).

2. Choose Sum in both the Material Cost and Labor Cost rows.

3. Choose Avg in both the Material Cost and Labor Cost rows.

4. Click the Count Records in Workorders check box in the Summary Options dialog box.

5. Click OK, then click Finish.

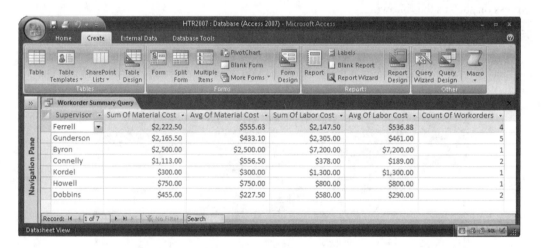

Summarize with Aggregate Functions

The summaries work with values in a field from multiple records, whether from all records in the result or a group of records based on a specific field value. A summarizing query produces a snapshot instead of a dynaset, and none of the fields in the result can be edited.

Summarize All Records

To summarize field values in a query, start with a select query, add the field you want to summarize, then specify the way you want the fields summarized. For example, to find the total and average Material Cost for current work orders, do the following:

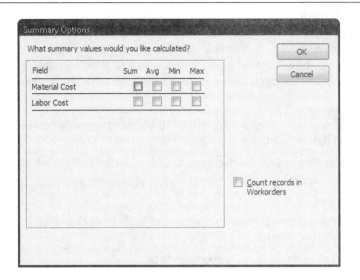

FIGURE 7-11 The Summary Options dialog box.

1. Start a new select query of the Workorders table and drag the Material Cost field to the grid.

2. On the Design tab in the Show/Hide group, click the Totals command (the sigma symbol) to add the Total row to the grid. You can also right-click in the grid and choose Totals from the shortcut menu.

3. Click the Total cell in the Material Cost column in the design grid and choose Sum from the drop-down option list.

4. To summarize on the same field in two ways, drag another copy of the Material Cost field to the next empty column and choose Avg from the Total list.

5. Switch to Datasheet view to see the results. This example is summarized over all the records in the table.

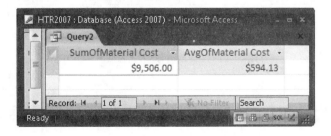

Summarize by Group

When you add fields to the grid with the Total row visible, the default entry is Group By. To group records with the same value in that field, leave the Group By option in the Total cell. Otherwise, change the Total cell to the desired summary function. For example, to count the number of work orders and calculate the average Workorder costs under control of each supervisor:

1. Start a new select query with the Workorders table and drag the Supervisor, Workorder Number, and Labor Cost fields to the grid.

2. Change the Workorder Number Total cell to Count and the Labor Cost Total cell to Avg.

3. In the next empty Field column enter the expression **Avg([Labor Cost]+[Material Cost])** and press ENTER.

4. The Total cell in the new column still holds the Group By option. Change this to **Expression** and press ENTER.

5. Change the default Expr1 name to **Average Total**.

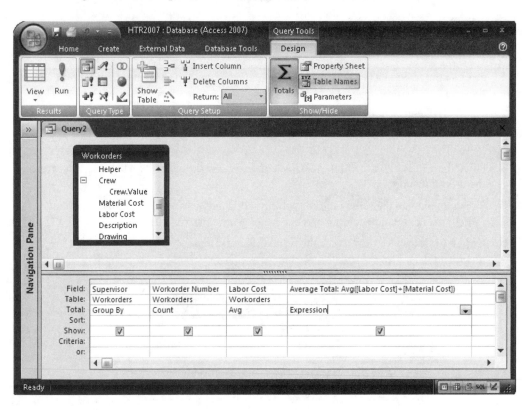

6. Run the query.

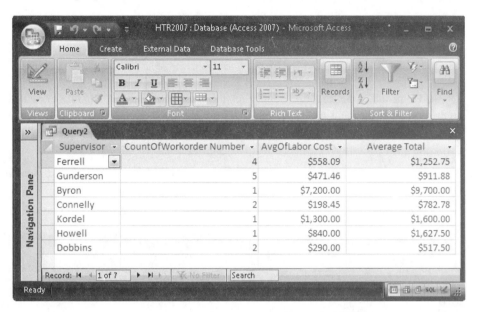

NOTE   *You can also sort the groups by the values computed in the summaries. For example, you could reorder the preceding records in descending order of the average total cost of the work orders assigned to each supervisor.*

Add Criteria

You can add selection criteria to summary queries to limit the result in three ways:

- To limit the records before they are included in the group and before the group calculations are performed, add the field whose records you want to limit, and then enter the criterion. For example, you could include in the Supervisor's group only those work orders whose labor costs exceed $500. If you are calculating any totals in the same query, change the Total cell in that column to Where.

- To limit the groupings after the records are included in the group but before the group calculations are performed, enter the criterion in the Group By field. For example, you could include a summary for specific Supervisors.

- To limit the results of the group summaries, enter the criterion in the field that contains the calculation. For example, you could display results only for Supervisor groups whose average total cost exceeds $1,000.

Summarizing in Datasheet View

New with Access 2007 is the ability to add a Total row to the query results in Datasheet view that summarizes values in a column. For example, you can summarize the data in the query built in the previous section:

1. Open the query in Datasheet view.

2. On the Home tab in the Records group, click the Totals command. A Total row is added to the bottom of the datasheet.

3. Click in the Total row below the Count of Workorder Number and choose Count in the drop-down list.

4. Move to the Total row below AvgOfLabor Cost and choose Maximum in the drop-down list.

5. Move to the Total row below Average Total and choose Minimum in the drop-down list.

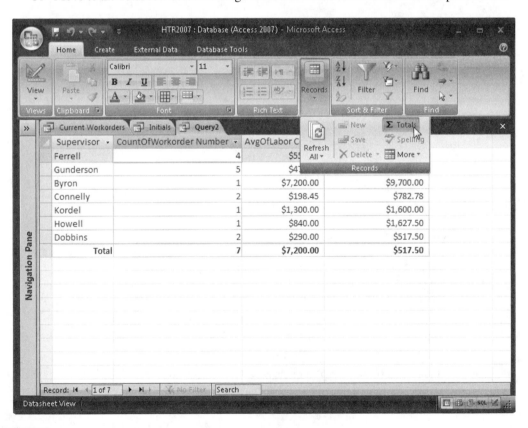

NOTE   *You have different choices depending on the field data type.*

To clear the Total row from a single column, click the down arrow in its Total row and select None from the drop-down list. To hide the entire row, on the Home tab in the Records group, click Totals in the context menu.

Create Special Queries with the Query Wizard

As you saw in the New Query dialog box, there are more Query Wizards than the Simple Select Wizard. The list includes wizards that create crosstab queries, queries that find duplicate records, and queries that find unmatched records in related tables.

Create a Find Duplicates Query

A Find Duplicates query locates and displays records in which the specified field has the same values. To display all the bids that were made on jobs at a particular address:

1. On the Create tab in the Other group, click the Query Wizard command.

2. Select Find Duplicates Query Wizard in the New Query dialog box and click OK.

3. Choose Bid Data and click Next.

4. In the next dialog box (see Figure 7-12), double-click Address in the Available Fields list to add it to the Duplicate-value fields list, then click Next.

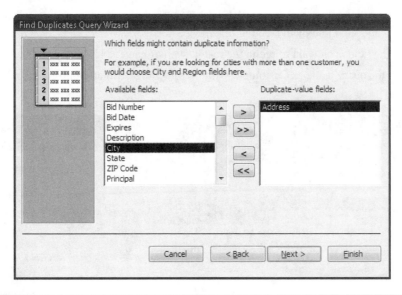

FIGURE 7-12   Choosing the duplicate value field.

5. Select all the fields you want to display in addition to the field in which duplicates might occur—for example, Bid Number, Bid Date, Description, and Principal. Click Next.

6. In the last dialog box, enter **Duplicate Addresses** as the name for the query and click Finish.

The query result shows only those records that have duplicate address fields.

If you want to sort the results or modify the query in some other way, choose to modify the query in the last wizard dialog box rather than view the results.

Create a Find Unmatched Query

With the Find Unmatched Query Wizard, you can locate and display records in one table that have no match in a related table. For example, you can find customers who have no current work orders so you can send them a letter reminding them of your services.

To create a Find Unmatched query:

1. Start a new query with the Find Unmatched Query Wizard.

2. In the first dialog box, choose Customers as the table whose records you want to display and click Next.

3. In the next dialog box, click Queries and choose Current Workorders as the recordset you want to match with the Customers table. If there are any customers with no corresponding work orders, the Customer record is included in the result. Click Next.

4. In the next dialog box, specify the joining field. Choose the field from each list and click the <=> button to join them (see Figure 7-13). Click Next.

5. Select the fields you want to see in the result, such as name, address, and phone number.

6. Accept the query name as Customers Without Matching Current Workorders and click Finish.

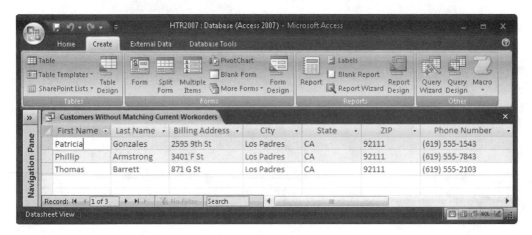

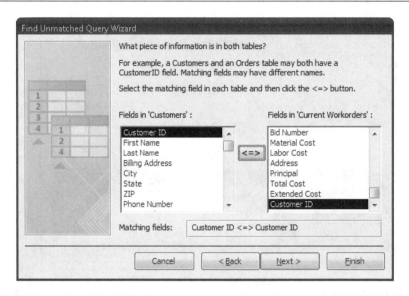

Specifying the joining field.

Create a Crosstab Query

A *crosstab query* is a special type of summary query that correlates summary values between two or more sets of field values, such as sales of types of products within certain sales regions or categories of work order costs correlated with the active supervisor. One set of facts is listed vertically as row headings at the left of the crosstab; the other is listed as column headings across the top. The summarized values—whether sums, averages, or counts—are contained in the body of the crosstab.

To create a crosstab, you need at least three output fields: row headings, column headings, and values. You can create a crosstab query from scratch or with the help of the Crosstab Query Wizard. The result of running a crosstab query is a snapshot, and none of the data in the results is editable.

As an example of creating a crosstab query, use the table named Workorder Crosstab, which has all the costs in one field and a field that indicates the category of the cost: labor or material. Next, use the Crosstab Query Wizard to correlate the category of cost with the job supervisor:

1. On the Create tab in the Other group, click the Query Wizard command and choose Crosstab Query Wizard from the New Query dialog box. Then click OK.

2. In the first dialog box (see Figure 7-14), choose the Workorder Crosstab table as the basis for the query and click Next. (This is just an example; the table name needn't include the word "Crosstab.")

3. In the next dialog box, double-click Supervisor as the field to use as the row heading (see Figure 7-15) and click Next.

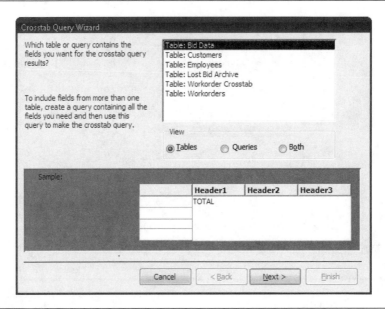

FIGURE 7-14 The first Crosstab Query dialog box.

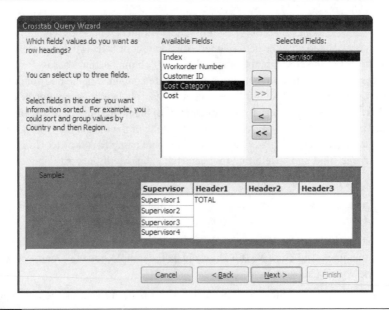

FIGURE 7-15 Choosing the row heading.

4. In the next dialog box, choose Cost Category as the column heading and click Next.

5. In the next dialog box, select Cost in the Fields list as the value field and Sum in the Function list. Clear the check mark next to "Yes, include row sums," if you don't want to see a Total of Costs column (see Figure 7-16). The sample pane shows how the fields will be arranged in the crosstab. Click Back to return to a previous dialog box to make changes or click Next to finish the query.

6. Enter the query name, Workorder Costs by Category and Supervisor, in the final dialog box and click Finish.

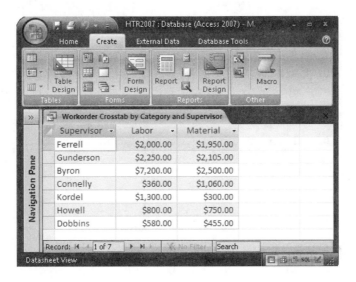

 The icon that accompanies the query name in the Navigation Pane indicates that it is a crosstab query.

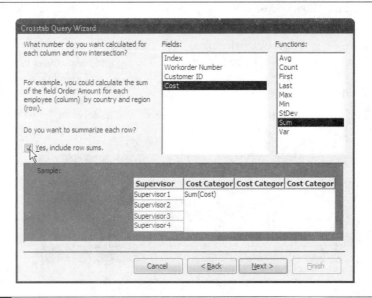

FIGURE 7-16 Choosing the values for the crosstab.

Chapter 8

Create Advanced Queries

How to...

- Create a parameter query that requests user input
- Create an AutoLookup query that fills in table data
- Create an action query
- Create a SQL query
- Create a subquery for an existing query

Queries are the primary means of retrieving information stored in an Access database. In addition to providing the popular select query discussed in the previous chapter, Access offers more flexible ways to retrieve data such as permitting the user to specify which records to extract at run time and automatically filling in field data during data entry. Queries can also perform data management operations such as adding, updating, or deleting data.

Create Special Purpose Queries

When you want to specify quickly which group of data you want, use a *parameter query*. This is much the same as a common select query except that Access prompts for one or more of the selection criteria before running the query. You can use a parameter in any field in which you can type text in the Criteria row.

Another special query, the AutoLookup query, can save data entry time by looking up the value you enter in the matching field and then automatically entering the corresponding information into fields in the related tables.

Parameter Queries

To create a parameter query, start with a normal select query and instead of entering the criteria in the Criteria cell, enter the text for the prompt enclosed in brackets ([ ]). The text you enter becomes the prompt in a dialog box, so be sure it is informative enough for the user to know how to respond. You cannot use the field name as the prompt but you can include it in the prompt text.

To create a parameter query that allows the user to specify which customer's work orders you want to see, complete the following steps:

1. On the Create tab in the Other group, click the Query Design command.

2. In the Show Tables dialog box, hold down CTRL and choose the Work orders, Bid Data, and Customers tables. Click Add, and then click Close.

3. Drag the Supervisor, Description, and Start Date from the Workorders table, as well as the Address field from the Bid Data table to the design grid. Add the customer's Last Name field, which is the parameter the user will enter.

4. Type **[Enter customer's last name]** in the Criteria row of the Last Name column.

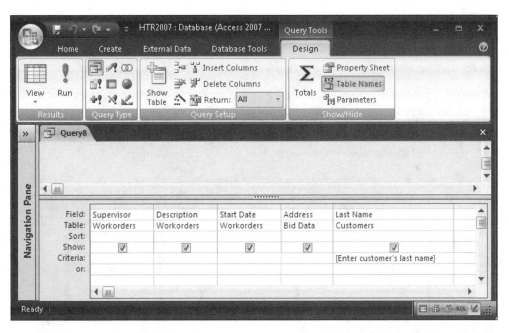

5. In the Results group, click Run. The Enter Parameter Value dialog box will appear.

6. Enter the desired Last Name (**McCoy** in this example) and click OK.

7. Run the query. The result shows four current work orders for customer McCoy.

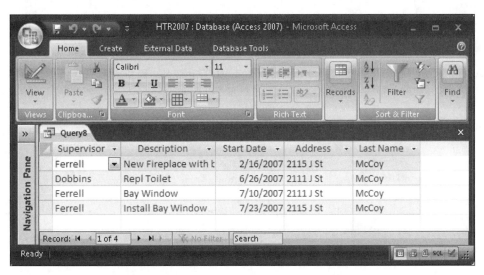

You also can use a parameter query to find records that have a range of values, such as a time period. For example, you can show all the work orders that were started in the month of June. To do this, include parameters in a Between...AND expression in the Criteria row. Access will prompt for each parameter in a separate dialog box.

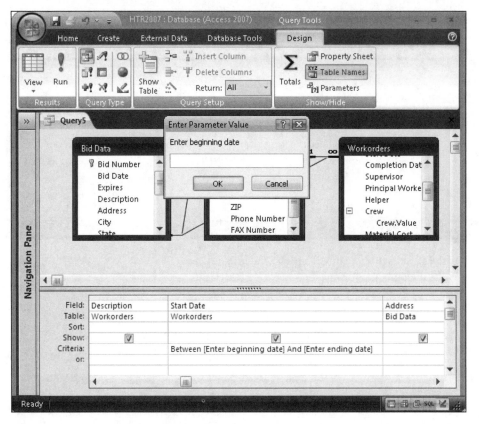

After entering 6/1/07 in the first prompt box and 7/1/07 in the second, Access runs the query and displays records for the five work orders that began in June.

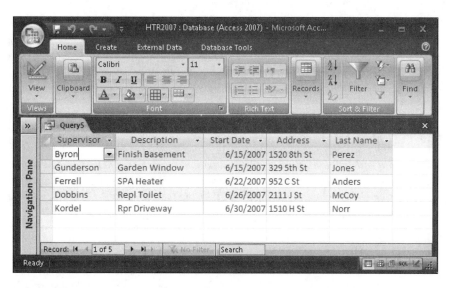

By default, the data type of a parameter is Text but you can specify a different data type by opening the Query Parameters dialog box while in the Query Design view:

1. On the Design tab in the Show/Hide group, click the Parameters command or right-click in the table pane and choose Parameters from the shortcut menu.

2. In the Query Parameters dialog box, enter the parameter text exactly as it appears in the Criteria row (without the brackets).

3. Choose the data type from the Data Type drop-down list.

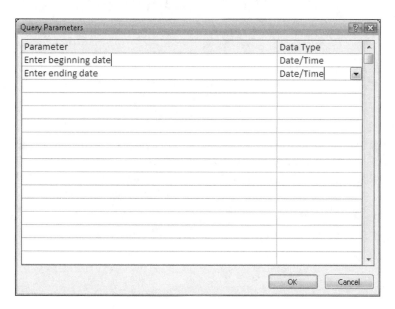

8

4. Repeat steps 2 and 3 for each parameter for which you want to specify a data type.

5. Click OK.

 Sometimes Access prompts for a parameter in a field you have not designated as a parameter. This can be caused by misspelling the field name or by changing the name in the table, but not changing it in other database objects. If you have checked the Name AutoCorrect option, field name changes are projected to all objects that include that field.

*If you would rather see all the records without creating a new query, you can return all records with a parameter query by not entering a parameter value. Place the parameter prompt in the Criteria cell in the query grid for the field used as the parameter. Next, move to the Or cell and enter the same parameter prompt followed by **Is Null**.*

AutoLookup Queries

The AutoLookup query was invented to save time during data entry by pulling field values from the parent table into the form or datasheet. For example, when you enter a valid Customer ID, the query will fill in all the rest of the customer information in the datasheet or form. An AutoLookup query is actually a special-purpose select query containing data from related tables.

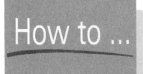 **Display the Parameter in the Results**

If you want to display the entered parameter value itself in the query result so you can use it in a form or report, add a calculated field with the parameter's name. For example, if you want to see the beginning date in the result of the previous query, enter the following expression in the Field row of an empty column: **Job Start:[Enter beginning date]**. The value will be the same in all the records in the result.

To show the date in the form or report, you can use the Format function to customize the parameter display. For example, use the expression **Job Start:Format([Enter beginning date],"d mmm yyyy")** to display the date as 1 Jun 2007. Then you can use the expressions in the form or report title: "All jobs started between" & [Job Start] & "and" & [Job End]. The dates will now be formatted correctly.

NOTE   *An AutoLookup query is different from a Lookup field, in that the query automatically fills in the data for you, whereas the Lookup field merely displays a list from which to choose.*

To create an AutoLookup query:

1. Create a new query based on the Customers and Workorders tables.

2. Drag the Workorder Number and Customer ID fields from the Workorders table (the "many" side of the relationship) to the grid.

3. Drag the Last Name, First Name, and Billing Address fields from the Customers table to the grid.

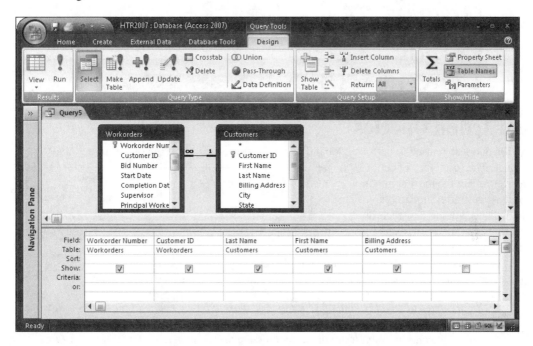

The field on the "many" side that you add to the query grid must not be a primary key or a unique index; the linking field on the "one" side must be a primary key or unique index, but do not add it to the query design. You can add other fields from either table to the query design.

In the query result datasheet, when you add a new record or change the value of the join field on the "many" side, Access automatically looks up and displays the associated values from the table on the "one" side. Here a new record is being entered in which the Customer ID value, 1033, was entered and TAB was pressed. Access filled in the remaining three fields.

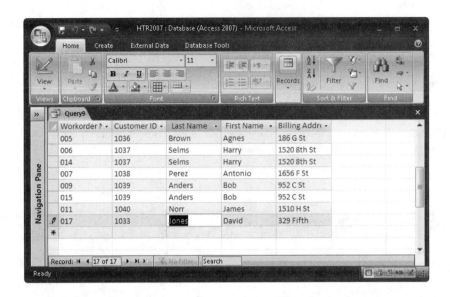

Design Action Queries

Action queries are used to perform global data management operations on one or more tables at once. The four types of action queries reflect the most common database activities: updating field values, adding new records, deleting existing records, and creating new tables.

The results of action queries cannot be used as a record source for forms or reports. However, if you save the result as a table first, you can use the table as a record source.

Before undertaking any kind of action query, make a backup copy of the tables that will be involved. If several tables will be changed, back up the entire database. An additional safety precaution when designing an action query is to switch to Datasheet view to check your progress instead of running the query. Showing the results in Datasheet view does not actually run the query and carry out the intended action, so no data is changed.

Update Query

Update queries are used to change one or more field values in many records at once. You can add criteria that screens the records to be changed or update records in more than one table. Update queries can use most types of expressions to specify the update.

In the Home Tech Repair database, several bids have expired but can be renewed. To renew the bids, the company must increase the costs slightly to reflect inflation and set a new expiration date. For example, renewing bids might involve finding records in the Bid Data table whose Expires date is before August 15, 2007, and making changes to the related Workorders table to increase the Material Cost and Labor Cost values. If there is no corresponding Workorder record, the update query does not change the Expires value because the relationship is defined as an inner join.

To create this update query, start with a new query design with the Bid Data and Workorders tables, and then do the following:

1. On the Design tab in the Query Type group, click the Update Query command. A new row, called Update To, appears in the grid.

2. Drag the Expires field from the Bid Data table to the grid.

3. Drag the Material Cost and Labor Cost fields from the Workorders table to the grid.

4. Enter the expression **<8/15/07** in the Criteria cell in the Expires column to limit the records. Access adds the pound sign (#) date delimiters.

5. Enter the following update expressions in the Update To row:

- **[Expires]+90** in the Expires column

- **[Material Cost]*1.05** in the Material Cost column

- **[Labor Cost]*1.05** in the Labor Cost column

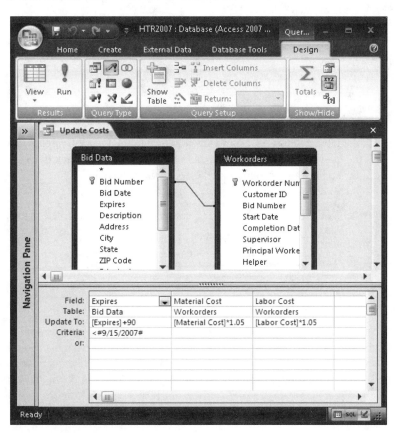

6. Right-click the query tab and then choose Datasheet View in the shortcut menu to see which records will be affected by the update query. If the selection is not correct, right-click the tab again to return to the Design view and make changes.

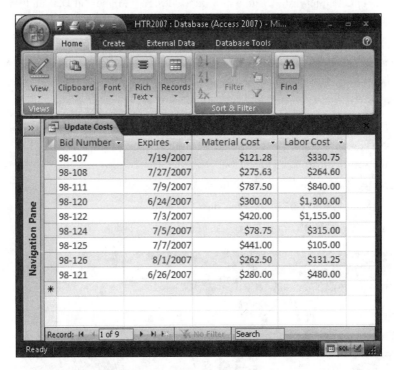

7. Right-click the tab and choose Design view to return to the Query Design window. Once there, save the query as **Update Costs**, then in the Results group, click the Run command Access displays a message warning that the update is irreversible.

8. Choose Yes to update the records or No to abandon the process.

Figure 8-1 shows a comparison of the updated Bid Data records with the backup copy. The four of the nine updated records that appeared in the datasheet of the update query show the Expires Date updated in the left table. You can see the others if you scroll down the datasheet.

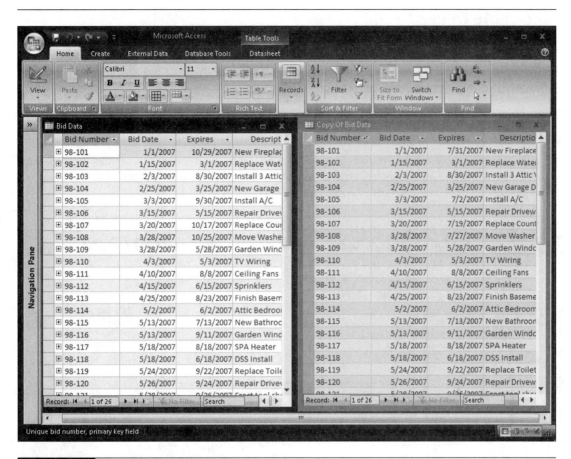

FIGURE 8-1   Comparing updated and backup tables.

NOTE   *You can see in the figure that there are still several records in the Bid Data table, for example numbers 98-102 and 98-104, whose Expires date is prior to August 15, 2007. This might seem confusing or like an error; however, as mentioned earlier, they are not updated because there is no matching record in the Workorders record and because the join is an inner join, which includes in the result only those records that have matching values in the join field. If you have enforced referential integrity between related tables in the database and checked the Cascade Update Related Records option on the "one" side, Access will apply the updates to the matching fields on the "many" side even if they are not included in the query.*

Make-Table Query

The make-table query does just what it advertises: it makes a new table out of records from one or more existing tables or queries. For example, you might need to combine information from the Bid Data, Workorders, and Customers tables into a single table to be used as a basis for reports to be distributed at the general meeting of partners.

 *Make-table queries copy the data to the target table. The source tables and queries are unaffected.*

To build a make-table query, create the new select query with the tables and queries that have the information you need, including any criteria you need. Then on the Design tab in the Query Type group, click the Make-Table Query command and do the following:

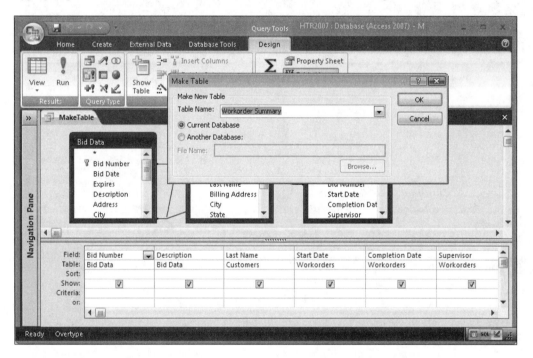

- If the target table is new and you want it in the same database, enter the table name and click OK.

- If the target table is an existing table, choose the table name from the drop-down list. Be aware that the query will replace the records in the existing table.

- If you want the new table in a different database, select Another Database and type in the full path and filename of the database, and then enter the table name and click OK. If the target is not an Access database, follow the database name with the name of the application, such as **Paradox**. You can also click Browse to navigate to the other database.

Before running the query, switch to Datasheet view to preview the records that will be included in the new table. Then return to the Design window and in the Results group, click the Run command. If you are replacing records in an existing table, Access asks for permission to delete the existing records before proceeding. Respond Yes or No to the final confirmation box that completes the make-table query and pastes the records to the table.

Although you cannot undo an action query (including the make-table query), remember that if the new table isn't what you want, you can delete it and start over.

> NOTE *The only field properties that are inherited by the table created with a make-table query are the field size and data type. All other properties (including the primary key, format, default values, and input masks) are not inherited and must be reset in the new table or in the form or report that uses the new table as a record source.*

Make-table queries create snapshots of the data as it was at the time it was run—and as such cannot be updated manually. If the data in the source tables changes, run the query again to update the values.

Append Query

When you want to add records from one or more source tables to other tables, you first must decide the fields that you want to append, then locate the target table, and, finally,determine the fields in the target table that correspond to the fields from the source. The field values are only copied to the target table, however, not moved.

> NOTE *To be matched, fields don't need to have the same names, but they do need to be of the same data type. Also, the target table doesn't need to have exactly the same structure as the source table.*

For example, the Home Tech Repair Bid Data table will become large and cumbersome if none of the outdated records are removed. The bids that have been lost are no longer needed in the current table, but they might be useful in an archive history of past bidding. Before you can archive the records, though, you must create a new table with the same design as the Bid Data table to hold the records. You can do this by using the following steps:

1. Right-click the Bid Data table name in the Navigation Pane and choose Copy.

2. Right-click on the Tables group in the Navigation Pane and choose Paste.

3. In the Paste Table As dialog box, name the new table **Lost Bid Archive**, choose Structure Only, and then click OK.

Now create the append query:

1. Start a new query, adding only the Bid Data table.

2. In the Query Type group, click the Append Query command.

3. In the Append dialog box, enter the table name, **Lost Bid Archive**, in the Table Name box, choose Current Database, and then click OK.

4. Drag the asterisk (*) from the Bid Data field list to the grid. If you do not want all the fields appended, drag the fields to the grid individually.

5. To add the Lost criteria, drag the Award Date field to the grid and enter **"Lost"** in the Criteria cell.

6. Remove the field name from the Append To cell of the Award Date column so that you won't append two copies of the Award Date field.

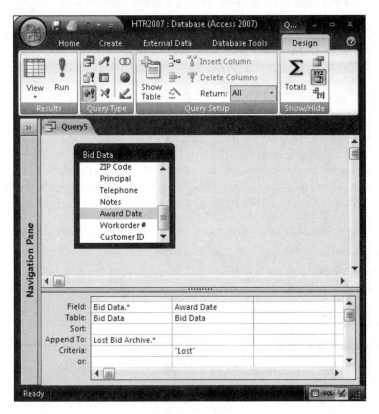

7. Switch to Datasheet view and then check for Lost in the Award Date field to make sure the right records will be appended, switch back to Design view and then save the query as **Add to Archive.**

8. In the Results group, click the Run command. Access now displays a message asking for confirmation to append six records.

9. Choose Yes to complete the addition or No to cancel the operation.

10. Once you have copied the Lost Bid data records to the archive, the next step is to remove them from the original table.

Delete Query

The delete query might be the most dangerous action query of all. No action queries can be reversed, but deletion seems to be the most drastic of them—all the more reason to make a backup copy of all the tables before you begin a delete query.

A delete query removes entire records from the table, not just the specified fields. You can remove records from a single table, multiple tables related one-to-one, or multiple tables related one-to-many.

Delete from a Single Table

Deleting records from a single table or from several one-to-one tables is straightforward: add the tables to the query design and specify the criteria for deleting the record—for example, if the account is paid in full, the work order is completed, or the house has been sold.

To delete records from a single table with a Delete query, do the following:

1. Start a new query with the table that you want to delete records from, such as a copy of the Bid Data table.

2. In the Query Type group, click the Delete Query command or right-click in the table pane and point to Query Type and choose Delete Query in the context menu.

3. Drag the asterisk from the field list to the grid; the Delete row now shows From.

4. Drag the field containing the value that indicates the record is to be deleted (for example, the value Lost in the Award Date field) and enter the criteria expression in the Criteria row.

8

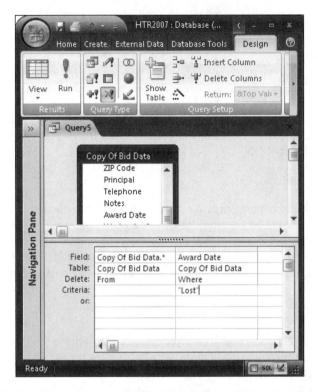

5. Switch to Datasheet view to preview the records that will be deleted and make any necessary changes in the query design.

6. Return to Design view and run the query. You will be warned that you will modify data in your table. Respond Yes to proceed or No to cancel the operation.

Delete from Related Tables

If you have Cascade Delete Related Records enabled for the relationship, all matching records on the "many" side are deleted with the records on the "one" side. If that option is not selected, you must run two delete queries to accomplish the job. First, delete the records from the tables on the "many" side, and then go after the records on the "one" side.

For example, a customer has left town and you need to remove the record from the Customers table as well as all records from the Bid Data table that involved that customer. To delete records from multiple related tables, start a new select query with both the tables, and then do the following:

1. On the Design tab In the Query Type group, click the Delete Query command.

2. Drag the Customer ID field to the grid to use as the criterion.

3. Drag the asterisk (*) from the field lists of the Bid Data table (on the "many" side of the relationship) to the grid. If more tables are on the "many" side, drag them to the grid as well. Do not drag the "one" table to the grid yet.

4. Switch to Datasheet view to preview the records that will be deleted.

5. Return to Design view and click the Run command. You are warned that you are about to delete records. Click Yes.

6. Back in the query design, right-click the Bid Data table and choose Remove Table in the shortcut menu. Remove any other "many" side tables also from the Query window.

7. Drag the asterisk (*) from the Customer table to the grid and run the same query again to delete the records from that table. Click Yes again in response to the warning.

Look at Structured Query Language (SQL)

SQL is the language Access uses behind the scenes to program query operations. It is composed of statements, each complying with specific language syntax and conventions. To view or edit SQL statements while working on a query, switch from Design view to SQL view by right-clicking in the table pane and choosing SQL View in the shortcut menu. Or on the Design tab in the Results group, click the View command and choose SQL View in the context menu.

    You can enter a SQL statement in most places where you would enter a table, query, or field name such as the record source for a form or report. If you use a wizard to create a form or report, the record source is a SQL statement created by Access.

Review SQL Statements

Without going too far into the details of the language, look at some simple examples of SQL statements. The SELECT statement is the most common statement in SQL and the most important. All select queries start with the SELECT statement. For example, if you create a query that retrieves all of the fields in records from the Bid Data table with "Lost" in the Award Date field, the SQL version would look like this:

```
SELECT *
FROM [Bid Data]
WHERE [Award Date]="Lost";
```

- The SELECT * command means to include all the fields, as does SELECT ALL.

- The FROM clause names the table that contains the records to retrieve.

- The WHERE clause specifies the selection criteria. This is the same value you entered in the Criteria row of the Award Date column. Include the WHERE clause only if you have used the complete FROM clause.

    SQL statements always end with a semicolon (;). All the queries result in SQL statements, which can be viewed by switching to SQL view. Choose SQL view from either the View button or the View menu. Figure 8-2 shows the SQL views of a few of the queries in the Home Tech Repair database including the action queries from the previous section.

8

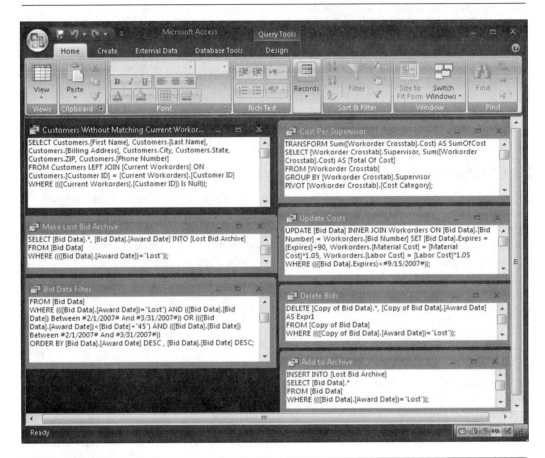

FIGURE 8-2   SQL views of existing queries.

Take a look at the Customers Without Matching Current Workorders (shown in the upper-left corner in Figure 8-2). This query was created to locate records in the Customers table that had no matching records in the Workorders table. The entire SQL statement is shown here:

```
SELECT Customers.[First Name], Customers.[Last Name],
Customers.[Billing Address], Customers.City, Customers.State,
Customers.ZIP, Customers.[Phone Number]
FROM Customers LEFT JOIN [Current Workorders] ON Customers.[Customer ID] =
[Current Workorders].[Customer ID]
WHERE ((([Current Workorders].[Customer ID]) Is Null));
```

This statement has two clauses in addition to the SELECT command: FROM and WHERE. Each clause begins on a separate line for readability; Access treats the entire statement as a single line.

- **SELECT** Determines which fields are included in the query result. Because there are two tables involved in the query, field names must be qualified with the table name separated by a period (.). If the field name contains a space, be sure to enclose it in square brackets [].

- **FROM** Shows the table name and specifies the join type that relates the Customers table with the Workorders table using the Customer ID as the matching field.

- **WHERE** Sets the criteria that limit the result to Customer records with no matching records in the Workorders table. That is, the Customer ID field has a Null value because there is no matching record.

Like all programming languages, SQL has strict conventions and grammatical syntax. The more sophisticated the language, the more complex the rules and procedures become. For the complete details of the SQL language, refer to the many Help topics that Access provides.

Create a Subquery

Subqueries are select queries within other select or action queries. You can use a subquery to specify a criterion for selecting records from the main query or to define a new field to be included in the main query. Using subqueries is like layering filters to close in on the data you need, except that the subquery runs first and results in a single criterion value that is used in the main query.

Define a Criterion

To define a criterion, you can enter the SELECT statement directly in the Criteria cell in the query design grid or in a SQL statement, in place of an expression in a WHERE clause.

For example, suppose you want to see fields from the Workorders table for all the jobs run by supervisors who have at least one job incurring more than $1,000 in material costs. Start a new query and add the Workorders table, and then place the Workorder Number, the Bid Number, Supervisor, and Material Cost fields in the grid.

To place this subquery in the query grid, type **IN (SELECT Supervisor FROM Workorders WHERE [Material Cost]>1000)** into the Supervisor field Criteria cell. Be sure to enclose the SQL statement in parentheses. If you switch to SQL view, you can see both the main query and the subquery that were created from the criteria:

```
SELECT Workorders.[Workorder Number], Workorders.[Bid Number],
Workorders.Supervisor, Workorders.[Material Cost]
FROM Workorders
WHERE (((Workorders.Supervisor) In (SELECT Supervisor FROM Workorders
WHERE [Material Cost]>1000)));
```

Supervisor Ferrell has four jobs listed, one of which has Material Cost over $1,000. Gunderson has five jobs, only one of which has Material Cost over $1,000; Byron has only one. You can compare the results of this query/subquery to the full Workorders table to see how it works.

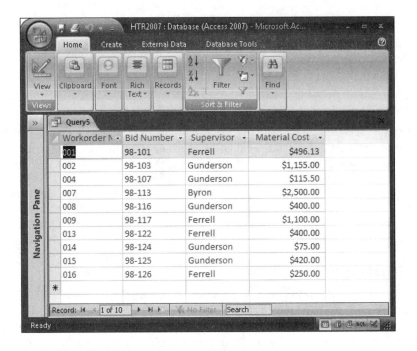

Define a New Field

To use a subquery for defining a new field, type the statement in the Field cell of an empty column. For example, the following subquery adds the field Address from the Bid Data table to the grid.

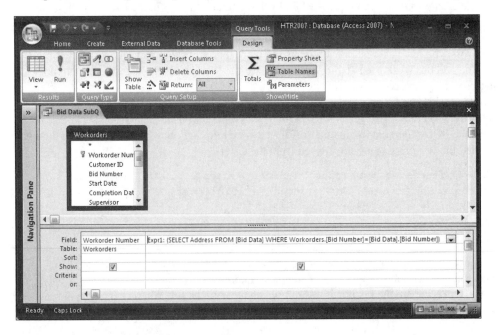

You can return to the Field cell and change the Expr1: default field name to a more informative one, such as Workorder Locations:. Be sure to keep the colon (:), however.

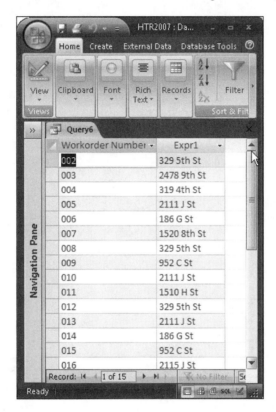

Although this is a simple example, you can see that using subqueries to define fields based on values found in other tables can reduce the number of tables you need in a query. In this case, we don't have to add the related Bid Data table to the query design to include the job address.

NOTE   *You cannot calculate totals with, or group records by, fields defined with subqueries.*

Chapter 9

Understand Form Report Design Basics

How to...

- Use the Simple Form and Simple Report tools
- Look at form and report design elements
- Work in the form or report Design window
- Add controls to a form or report design
- Modify or delete controls
- Modify form or report properties

Now that you have seen how you can store data efficiently in a relational database and retrieve the information in the arrangement that will be most helpful to you, it is time to learn how to present the information. Information can be displayed on the screen in forms suitable for viewing, editing, or entering data accurately.

If you need to print the information (such as for an annual report or form letter) or simply wish to transport the information to the outside world, Access offers a variety of reporting features.

Use Simple Form and Simple Report Tools

When you select the Create tab, you can choose to build a Simple Form and a Simple Report without having to specify any format or style options.

A Simple Report creates a quick report of all the data in a table or query. A Simple Form produces a columnar arrangement of data from a single table or query. If there is a subdatasheet that goes with the table, the Simple Form also includes a subform. You can see this at the bottom of the Workorders form in the Home Tech Repair database.

The report isn't fancy but it is useful for checking and verifying the data in your table. No customized style is applied, and no page numbers or dates are included. Figure 9-1 shows the default Simple Report and Simple Form for the Workorders table.

To create a new Simple Form, in the Navigation Pane click the table or query that has the data you want to see in the form or report. Then on the Create tab in the Forms group, click the

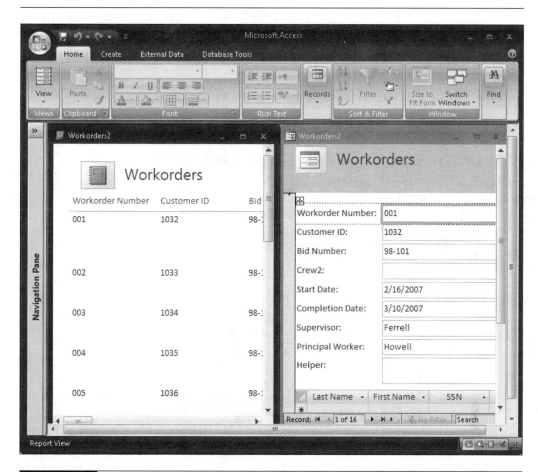

FIGURE 9-1 The default Simple Report and Simple Form.

Form command. The new form appears in Layout view, where you can make changes at the same time as you are viewing the data. Or you can right-click in the form tab and choose Design View in the shortcut menu.

To create a Simple Report, after selecting the table or query you need on the Create tab in the Reports group, click the Report command. As with the new form, the new report appears in

Layout view. After creating the Simple Report, you can print it as it appears or switch to Design view and make changes.

The Report and Form tools are so quick and easy, that unless you plan to use the form or report quite often, don't bother to name and save the object you just created. To close the form or report without saving the design, choose right-click the document tab and choose Close in the shortcut menu. Or you can simply click the Close button in the upper right corner of the tabbed document. Respond No when you are asked if you want to save the changes.

Common Form and Report Design Elements

The design elements that are common to forms and reports include the record source that contains the data and the graphic objects that are added to the design. The Record Source is where you find the data you want in the form or report. It can be a table, a query, or a SQL statement. The individual fields in the underlying tables and queries become elements in the design. Many of the properties set to control the appearance and behavior of the form or report and their components are also common to both.

Understand Controls

A *control* is a graphical object that you place on a form or report to display data, perform an action or enhance the appearance of the form or report. Controls come in three basic types, depending on their relationship to values in the tables:

- **Bound control** Gets its value from a field in the table or query and as the data changes, the value of the bound control changes with it. The data fields you add to a form design are examples of bound controls.

- **Unbound control** Has no tie to the underlying table data and retains the parameters you used to create it. Examples of unbound controls are lines, rectangles, labels, and images.

- **Calculated control** Gets its value from values in the table and actually is an expression that produces a result. Expressions contain functions, operators, and fields. The value shown in a calculated control changes as the values in the underlying fields change, but you cannot directly edit a calculated control.

Here are some examples of the many typical controls you will add to your form and report designs. The option group contains a set of option buttons but in this case they could also be check boxes or toggle buttons. The combo box is shown expanded to display the value list. All controls are accessible from the Controls group on the Design tab which is displayed during the form or report design process.

In Chapter 10, you will learn about more special controls you can add to forms, including hyperlinks.

Work in the Design Window

Similarities also exist in the form and report Design windows. The ribbon tabs and groups are nearly identical and the design surface looks the same. The only difference between them shows up at the beginning of a new design. The report Design window shows the page header and footer sections by default, but in the form Design window, only the detail section is shown at the outset. You can add the headers and footers to the form design if needed.

Start a New Design

Because the two Design windows are so similar, the following paragraphs will focus on the form Design window and point out any significant differences in the report Design window. To start a new form, select the Workorders table in the Tables group in the Navigation Pane, and then click the Create tab. Next, in the Forms group, do one of the following:

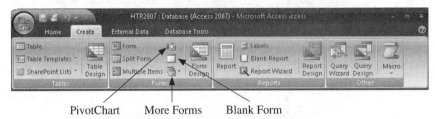

PivotChart   More Forms   Blank Form

- Click the Form command. This creates a simple form in Layout View. You must have already selected a table or query as the basis for the form.

- Click the Split Form command. This creates a form based on the selected table or query and displays it in Layout view along with a datasheet view of the underlying data source. You can use the form to enter data into the record selected in the datasheet.

- Click the Multiple Items command. The form resembles a datasheet with data arranged in rows and columns. Must have selected a table or query as the basis.

- Click the PivotChart command. This starts a form with a blank chart for presenting data in a PivotChart format based on data in the selected table or query.

- Click the Blank Form command. This opens a blank form design in Layout view that isn't based on any existing table or query.

- Click the More Forms command. Choose Form Wizard in the gallery to start the Form Wizard. Other options are Datasheet, Modal Dialog, and PivotTable. You will see how to create dialog boxes in Chapter 17.

- Click the Form Design command. This starts a new form object in Design view not based on a table or query.

Let's start a new form design by building a data entry form for Home Tech Repair to enter new workorder data. To start the new form, select the Workorders table in the Tables group in the Navigation Pane, and then do the following:

1. On the Create tab in the Forms group, click the Form Design command. The blank form now appears in Design view and the ribbon changes to the Design tab.

2. In the Tools group, click the Add Existing Fields command or press ALT+F8. The Field List pane opens at the right side of the screen.

3. Keep the form design open (see Figure 9-2) for adding fields and other controls.

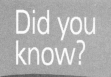

About Form and Report Sections

A new form consists only of the detail section, where most of the information will be displayed. If you want to display some text or other information in a form header or footer, add the section by choosing Form Header/Footer in the Show/Hide group on the Arrange tab. You also can right-click in the form design and choose Form Header/Footer from the shortcut menu; both sections are added to the design.

If you want a header or footer, but not both, you can shrink the unwanted section to nothing. Report designs automatically include page headers and footers in addition to the detail section. You can add report headers and footers by choosing Report Header/Footer in the Show/Hide group on the Arrange tab.

You also can add page headers and footers to forms. In a form, the information placed in the page header and footer appears only when the form is previewed or printed, not when it is open in Form view. Choose Page Header/Footer in the Show/Hide group or the shortcut menu to add a form page header and footer.

9

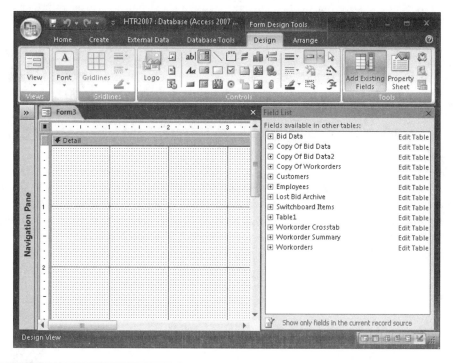

FIGURE 9-2   The form design with the Field List pane.

*If the Field List shows no tables or queries, click the message in the Field List pane,
"Click to shows all tables."*

Tour the Design Window

As you see in Figure 9-2, the form Design window has many new commands on the Design
tab. The Design tab provides five groups for adding fields and controls, formatting, changing
properties, switching object views, and other tools. The Report Design tab has an additional
group with commands to group and summarize data.

*If you rest the mouse pointer over the button, a ScreenTip appears displaying the name
of the button.*

The Arrange tab has six groups with commands to align and group controls and further
improve the design arrangement.

The Controls Group

With a new blank form, the next step is to add controls to the design. The Controls group in the
Design tab is divided into four sections, the largest of which contains commands for adding
21 different kinds of controls to the form design. Rest the mouse pointer on the icon to see the
name of the control.

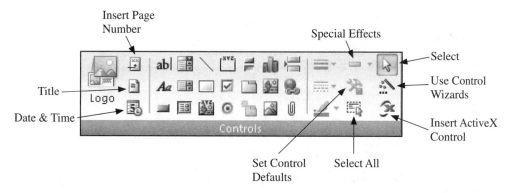

To add a control, click on the desired command and then click on the place in the design where you want the control to go. For some controls, you can draw an outline to specify the size of the control.

The first section in the Controls group provides special controls for form and report header sections, such as a logo, title, page numbers, and the current date/time.

The second section contains the tools for adding controls to the form or report designs.

The third section is used for formatting controls by line thickness, type, and color as well as for adding special effects such as flat, raised, or sunken type. One command allows you to change the default properties for specific control types. Another command selects all the controls in the form or report at once so you can make changes to them all at the same time.

The fourth section contains three special commands. When the Select command is pressed, you can click one of the control object commands to add the control to the design. The second command is the Control Wizards command, which automatically invokes one of the Control Wizards when you add its control to the design. Wizards are available for adding List boxes, Combo boxes, option groups, command buttons, subforms, and subreports. If the button is deactivated, a wizard won't appear when you add one of those controls. The Insert ActiveX command opens a dialog box where you can select one of the ActiveX controls from a list.

You can't actually turn off the Select Objects button, but when you want to add several controls of the same type, you can lock down that control button by double-clicking it. This deactivates the Select Objects button until you click it again or press ESC to unlock the control button.

The Tools Group

You can use the commands in the Tools group to open the Field List pane and Property Sheets for selected controls or sections. Three other commands open the Visual Basic window, which allow you to view any code attached to the form or report; display the first 10 records in a report preview so you can check the layout; or open the subform or subreport in a separate window so that you can make changes to the design.

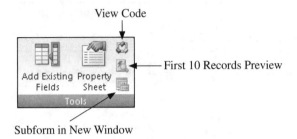

Subform in New Window

The Font Group

The Font group has all the standard font commands for style, size, color, and alignment as well as the Format Painter and conditional formatting options.

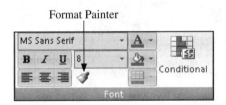

The Gridlines Group

If your controls are contained in a stacked or tabular layout, you can add gridlines with the commands in the Gridlines group to provide more visual separation between the controls. You have a choice in the Gridlines gallery of using both horizontal and vertical, only one or the other, Cross Hatch, Top, Bottom, Outline, or None. The other three commands set the line thickness, style, and color.

The Property Sheets

Property sheets list all of the properties that pertain to the form or to the selected form section or control. The properties are grouped by category into four tabs, with a fifth tab showing the entire list. The categories are Format, Data, Event, and Other.

Use the property sheets to view the properties that are set for the controls and to make any necessary changes. Some properties have drop-down lists of valid settings, while others include the Build option.

If you have selected more than one control, the property sheet shows only those properties that the group has in common. If the selected controls have no properties in common, the sheet will be blank.

The Field List

The field list resembles the list that you saw in the Relationships window and in a query design, but without the asterisk. Use the field list to add fields to a design by dragging the name to the design grid. A text box control in the design displays the field value, and an attached label shows the field caption, which might be different than the field name.

The Alignment Tools

The horizontal and vertical rulers help you place controls accurately in the design. The rulers are optional and you can either show or hide them by right-clicking anywhere in the form design and then choosing Ruler in the shortcut menu. The single command, Ruler, applies to both the vertical and horizontal rulers.

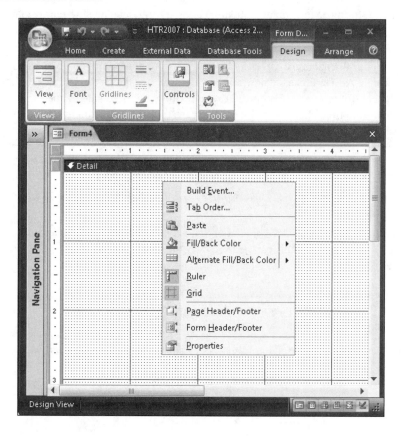

The grid shows as faint dots and lines in the design background. One of the settings you can choose from the Control Layout group is Snap To Grid. With this setting selected, Access automatically aligns the controls to the nearest grid mark.

Add Controls

You can add all types of controls to the design with the commands in the Control group, but it is easier to use the field list to add text box controls for the table fields. In the following paragraphs, you will learn how to add fields from the Workorders table, how to add a form title and subtitle, and also how to include some calculated fields. When you are adding controls to a form design, you have a choice of two automatic arrangements you can use instead of manually adding each control:

- Tabular layout places controls in rows and columns, like a datasheet with the labels at the top.
- Stacked layout arranges controls in a vertical list with the labels at the left.

See Chapter 10 for more information about creating a form design using the special layout.

From the Field List

The field list contains the names of all the fields in the record source. When you add a field from the list to the design, Access creates a new text box control that shows field values in the Form view. A text box control has two parts: the edit region where the field value appears and the label that visually shows the field name. There are three ways to add fields from the list to the design:

- Drag a field name from the list to the design. Dragging the field name to the design works much like dragging a field name to the query grid. When you drop the button, the control appears showing the new control with its attached label.
- Double-click the field name. The text boxes and attached labels appear in a tight column in the form design.
- Use the standard CTRL-click to select contiguous or dispersed field names, and then drag the group to the design. This can be used only on fields listed in the Fields available for this view group.

The field list remains open until you click the Close button or click the Add Existing Fields command again. To get back to the Home Tech Repair data entry form and add fields from the Workorders table, do the following:

1. Click on the Workorder Number field in the field list and then drag the button to the design at about the 1½ -inch mark on the horizontal ruler.

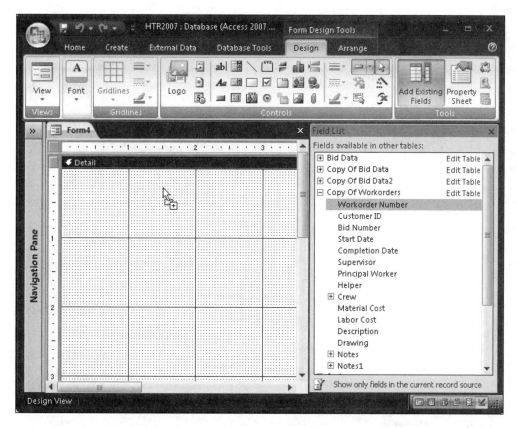

2. To make room for more fields, drag the form's right border to the 6-inch horizontal mark and the lower border to the 5-inch vertical mark.

3. Drag the other fields from the field list to positions in the design resembling Figure 9-3.

Once you have all the fields you want in the design, close the field list to make more room on the screen. Next, add a form header and use the Label control command to add a title and subtitle to the header.

From the Control Group

To add a control, click the appropriate command and then draw the control outline in the design. What happens next depends on the type of control you are adding. To add a title in the Workorders form header, do the following:

1. Right-click in the form design and choose Form Header/Footer in the shortcut menu.

2. Move the mouse pointer to the dividing line between the Form Header and Detail sections. When it changes shape to a double vertical arrow, click and drag the line down ½ inch on the vertical ruler.

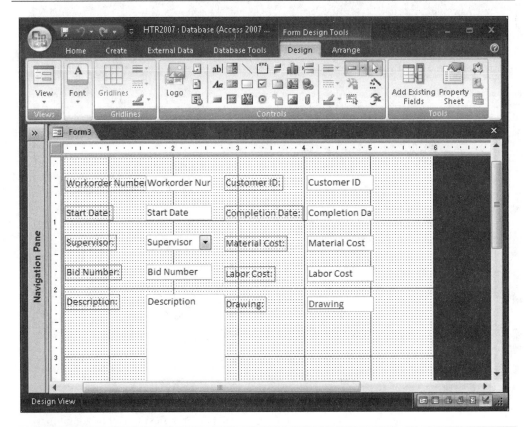

FIGURE 9-3   Other Workorder fields are added

3. In the Controls group, click the Label command and then draw an outline in the Form Header across the form. The outline will now appear with the insertion point at the left.

4. Type **Home Tech Repair** and press ENTER or click outside the label box. If you press Enter, the control remains selected. Otherwise select the label control again.

5. Use the Font group to change the font size to 18 points, italic, and centered. Figure 9-4 shows the form design with the new header.

6. Click the Label command again and draw a box beneath the title, then type **Data Entry Form—Workorders** in the label control. You may need to drag the Detail section bar down to make room in the Header section.

7. Use the Font group to customize this text so that it is bold and the font is size 10.

8. Right-click the document tab and then switch to Form view to see how the design looks now (see Figure 9-5).

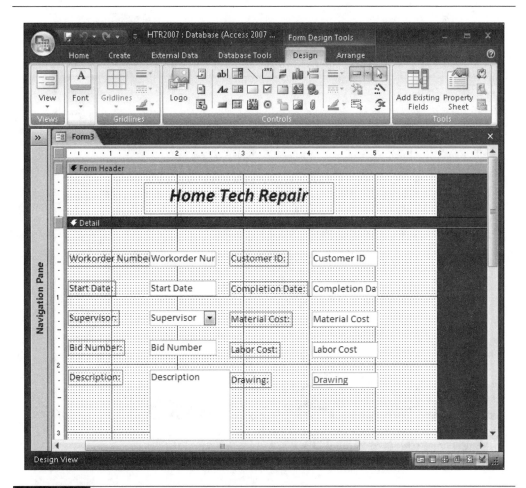

FIGURE 9-4   Adding a title in the form header.

Add Calculated Controls

A calculated control contains values from multiple text, number, currency, or date fields in the record source. For example, in Chapter 7 you saw how to combine text values from first and last name fields into a single, whole name field.

You also can combine currency or date fields; for example:

- **[Birthday]-Date()**   Displays the number of days you have to wait until your next birthday.

- **[Price]*1.07+[Shipping&Handling]**   Computes and displays the sales price plus seven percent tax and adds in the shipping and handling charges.

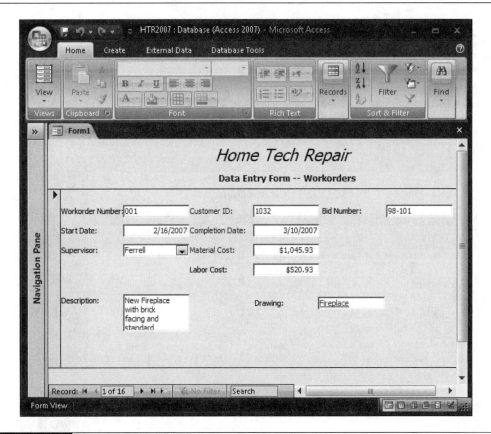

FIGURE 9-5   The Workorders Data Entry Form in Form view.

You can also add two calculated fields to the Workorders data entry form that will display the total cost of the job and the number of days estimated to complete the work:

1. Switch back to Design view and on the Design tab in the Controls group, click the Text Box command and then click in the area to the right of the Material Cost field. Access adds an unbound text box control.

2. Double-click the new control or click the Property Sheet command in the Tools group to open the property sheet for the new unbound text box. You can also right-click on a control and then choose Properties from the shortcut menu.

3. Click the Data tab and then enter the following expression in the Control Source property box: **=[Material Cost]+[Labor Cost]**. Notice that you must start the expression with an equal sign (=) or Access assumes the expression is a field name.

4. Double-click the attached label that shows Text*n* where *n* is the sequentially numbered label, and then type **Total Cost**.

5. Repeat steps 1 through 4 to add another calculated field to show estimated work time with the expression **=[Completion Date]-[Start Date]** and label it **Work Time (days)**.

6. Switch to Form view to see the design with the new calculated fields.

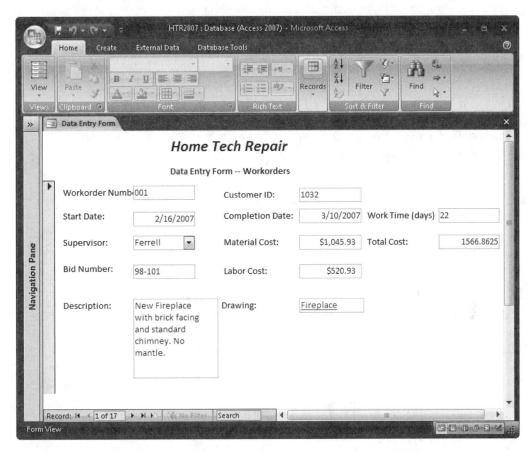

You can see that although the two cost fields retain the currency format with the dollar sign and two decimal places, the Total Cost field does not. In addition, the Work Time control is left-aligned, although it is a Number field. A later section in this chapter, called Use Property Sheets, discusses how to correct this problem.

If you draw a rectangle around other controls and then add a background color, you might obscure the other controls. To keep this from happening, select the rectangle and choose Format | Send To Back to place it behind the others.

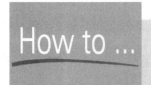

Dress Up Forms and Reports with Lines and Rectangles

While they aren't essential, lines can be useful in forms and reports for creating a visual separation between parts of the design. For example, a heavy line can help focus attention on a specific area. You can draw a line anywhere in a form or report section.

To draw a line, click the Line toolbox button and then either click where you want the line or drag the pointer to draw the line. If you only click within the design, Access draws a solid horizontal line, 1-inch long and 1-point thick. When you drag to draw the line, you can drag it in any direction and any length. To make sure the line is horizontal or vertical when you draw it, hold down SHIFT while you draw.

Rectangles come in handy as boxes that group related data or as a means to emphasize another control. For example, in a form, you can draw a box around a set of command buttons to set them off from the rest of the design.

To draw a rectangle, click the Rectangle command in the Controls group and draw the box in the design. After drawing the line or rectangle, you can use the Font commands and Controls to change the line or border thickness, choose colors, and add a special effect. You can also use the property sheet to change the line or rectangle border style to a dashed or dotted line, for example.

Starting a New Form in Layout View

You don't have to start a new form in Design view. You can also use the Layout view, which is a feature that is new in Access 2007. The Layout view looks nearly the same as Form view but you can make changes to the form design in Layout view and then see how they will look in Form view without switching to Form view. Figure 9-6 shows the beginning of a new form in Layout view.

In addition to adding the fields you want, you can add some other controls. The Controls group in the Formatting tab includes Logo, Title, Page Numbers, Date/Time, and options for setting the line thickness, style, and color. No other controls can be added in Layout view but you can still do all the font, formatting, and gridline modifications to change the appearance and usability of the form.

Modify Controls

You can customize the controls you add to a form or report design so that they present information in just the right way. Controls can be moved about in the design or resized, and any of the properties can be changed to create the appropriate effect. To change any control, you must first select the control, so that Access is focused on the target control.

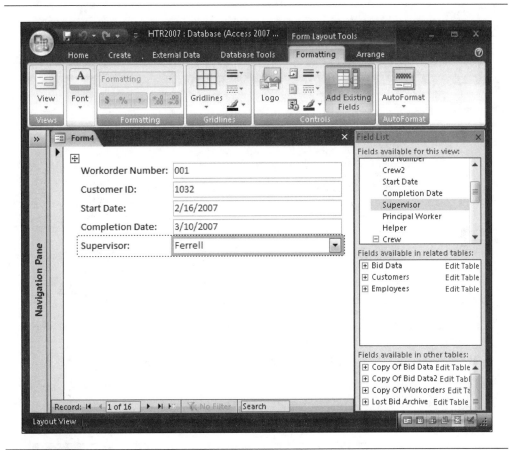

FIGURE 9-6   Starting a new form in Layout view.

Select Controls and Other Objects

There are many ways of selecting the form or report design, a specific design section, or one or more controls. What you want to work with dictates the way you need to select it.

Select the Form or a Form Section

Once the form or form section is selected, you can view and change any of the properties, including the record source, in the form or report property sheet. You can select the form itself in the following ways:

- If the rulers are displayed, click the form selector (the small square in the upper-left corner where the horizontal and vertical rulers meet).

Form selector

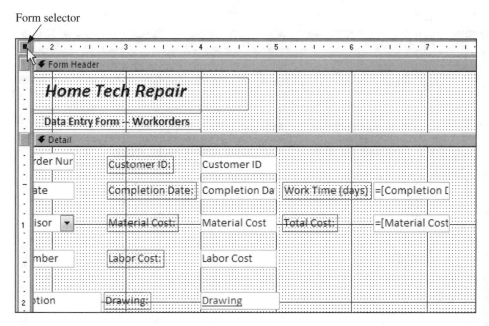

■ Click anywhere in the plain gray background—within the window, but outside the form design.

To select a form or report section, you should do one of the following:

■ Click the section selector (the small box in the vertical ruler opposite the section bar)

Section selector   Section bar

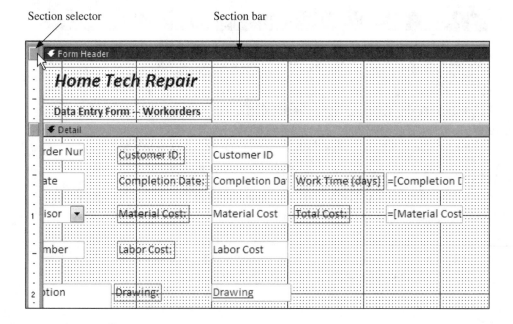

- Click in the section bar
- Click anywhere in the gray background of the section

When a section is selected, the section bar (the horizontal divider that contains the section title), appears shaded.

Select Controls

That just leaves the selection of the controls themselves. To select one control, you can simply click on the control. When you select a control, a set of small dark squares called *handles* appear around the control. You use these handles to move and resize the controls. The larger squares are the *move handles* and the smaller ones are the *sizing handles*. You'll learn more about moving and resizing later in this chapter.

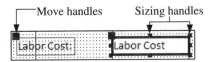

If you want to make the same change to several controls at once in the form design, you can select more than one of them in one of the following ways:

- Hold down SHIFT as you click each control.
- To select a column of controls, click the selection arrow in the horizontal ruler above the controls.
- To select a row of controls, click the selection arrow in the vertical ruler to the left of the controls.
- To select a block of controls, click the selection arrow in one of the rulers and drag to draw a rectangle around the controls. This selects all the controls that are inside or partially within the rectangle.
- To select a block of controls within the design but not a complete column or row, click in the design outside of any control and draw a rectangle around the controls.
- To select all the controls in the design, press CTRL-A.

To remove the selection, click anywhere outside the selected objects. To remove only a few controls from a group of selected controls, hold down SHIFT and click each of the controls that you want to exclude.

A text box control is a special case because it contains two parts that can be treated either together or separately. The attached label is usually the field name, and the edit region displays the field value. If you click the edit region to select a text box control, you can change the text box properties. If you click the attached label, only the label is selected and you can change its properties. Either way you can move them together or separately.

You can tell by the size and number of handles that appear around the control whether you have selected them both or only the label. Two text box controls are shown here, and as you can see, the edit region of the Labor Cost control is selected, while the label of the Material Cost control is also selected.

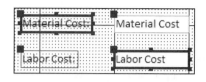

Once you have selected the controls you want to work with, you can move, resize, align, or space them equally or change any of their properties.

Group Controls

If you have several controls that you want to look and behave alike, you can define them as a single group and format them all at the same time. To create the control group, select all the controls you want to include, including the labels for the text box controls, and on the Arrange tab in the Control Layout group, click the Group command. A frame appears around the set of controls but does not show up in Form view.

The new form, shown next, contains the cost and date fields in a single group. To remove the group designation, click the Ungroup command in the Control Layout group.

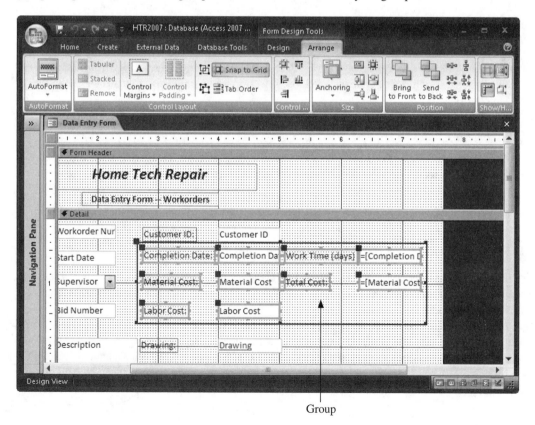

Group

Move and Resize Controls

One reason to select a control is to change its size or move it to a different position in the design. As mentioned earlier, when you select a control, handles appear around the control. These handles are used to move and resize a control or a selected group of controls.

Move Controls

To move a control in the design, move the mouse pointer to the move handle (the larger square in the upper-left corner of a selected control). When the pointer changes shape to four-headed arrow with an up-left pointer, click and drag the control to the desired position. You can drag it over other controls to place it where you want it.

Again, the text box control is a special case because it has two move handles. If the pointer is directly on the move handle of the edit region, you can move the edit region by itself. If the pointer is elsewhere in the edit region, the control and its label move together. When you move the pointer to the move handle of the attached label, you can move the label by itself. You can't move both parts with the move handle in the label unless you have selected both the label and the edit region.

> **TIP** *Even though you have Snap To Grid selected, dragging a control by its move handle can be inaccurate, so if you want to move a control a smaller or more precise distance, hold down CTRL, and then press the appropriate arrow key. Each key press moves the control one-fourth of a grid unit in the direction of the arrow. Holding down CTRL while you drag a control temporarily turns off the Snap To Grid feature.*

9

If you have selected more than one control, you can drag any one of them and all will move together.

Resize Controls

A selected control has seven sizing handles, one on each side and one at each corner (except the move handle corner). Dragging one of the side handles changes the width or height, whereas dragging a corner handle can change both height and width at once.

If you have selected several controls, all will change size the same when you drag the sizing handle of one of them.

> **TIP** *If you need to make more precise adjustments in the size of the selected control, hold down SHIFT while you click the appropriate arrow key. Each keypress increases or decreases the size of the control by one grid unit.*

The Control Layout group on the Arrange tab as well as the shortcut menus have options that help you size one control or a group of controls, so that they match in length or width. First select the controls you want to resize. Next, on the Arrange tab in the Size group, click one of the same six commands or right-click and point to Size in the shortcut menu.

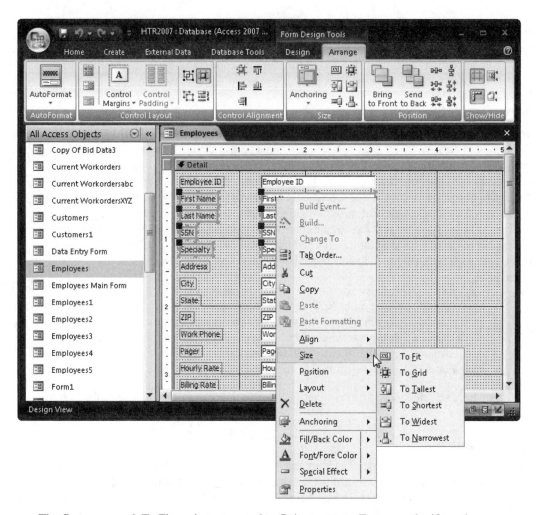

The first command, To Fit, resizes a control to fit its contents. For example, if you have drawn a long label control, but entered short text on the label, choose the To Fit command to reduce the size of the control to fit the entered text. The second command, To Grid, automatically adjusts the size of the control so that all four corners fall on the nearest grid points.

TIP

Double-clicking one of the sizing handles automatically resizes a label control to fit the contents.

The remaining four commands adjust the size of each control in a group of controls relative to the tallest, the shortest, the widest, or the narrowest of the group.

Align and Space Controls

Lining up the controls in a form gives the form or report a more professional look. To align a group of controls, select them first, and then on the Arrange tab in the Control Alignment group, click the Tabular or Stacked command. Tabular arranges all the controls like a datasheet while Stacked puts them in a vertical list. To remove this arrangement, select a member of the group and click the Remove command in the Control Layout group. You can also right-click the group and point to Align in the Shortcut menu.

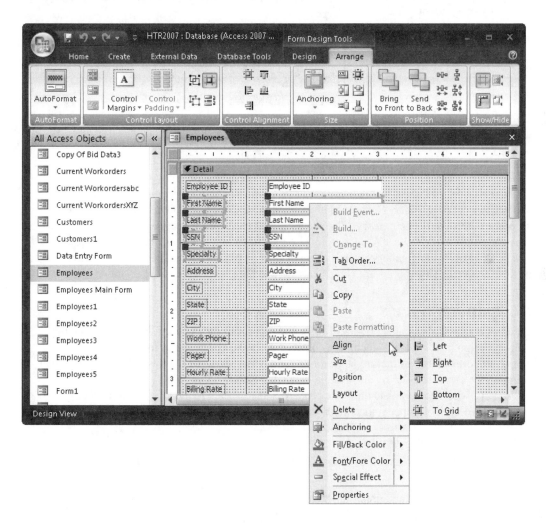

When aligning controls, be sure to select only those in the same row or same column. If you have controls in the group from a different area of the form, they will be aligned with the rest, creating a confused appearance.

When you have a row or column of controls that you want uniformly spaced across or down the form or report, you can use the Horizontal Spacing or Vertical Spacing commands in the Position group on the Arrange tab. These commands also are used to increase or decrease the spaces evenly between the controls. Each time you choose Increase or Decrease, the spacing is changed by one grid interval.

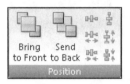

If the controls are grouped together by the Tabular or Stacked command, you need to click the Remove command before the spacing commands will apply.

Two more control positioning options are available in the Control Layout group: Control Margins and Control Padding. When you click the Control Margins command, you see a gallery from which to choose: None, Narrow, Medium, and Wide. The None option limits the vertical size of the control to fit the font size. The other options increase the empty space above the text in the control. If you choose a Wide margin, you may have to increase the height of the controls.

The Control Padding gallery includes similar options to specify the space between columns in a tabular layout. The options are None, Narrow, Medium, and Wide.

Use Property Sheets

Properties establish the characteristics of form and report design elements. Everything in a form or report design has properties, including controls, sections, and even the form or report itself. Control properties set the structure, appearance, and behavior of the controls. Properties also can determine the characteristics of the text and data contained in a control.

Property sheets contain lists of all the properties that pertain to the selected control or group of controls. To open a property sheet for a control, do one of the following:

- Double-click the control
- Select the control and on the Design tab in the Tools group, click the Property Sheet command
- Select the control and press ALT-ENTER
- Right-click the control and choose Properties from the shortcut menu

The list of properties that you see will depend on the current selection. The property sheet's All tab for the Workorder Number text box control lists all the control's properties. As you can tell by the scroll bar, there are more properties in the list. The properties are grouped in the sheet by type: Format, Data, Event, Other, and All. Click on the tab that will show the properties you want to change, or stay with All to see the entire list.

To change a property, click the property in the list, and then do one of the following:

- Type the desired setting in the property box.

- If an arrow appears in the property box, select the desired setting from the list.

- If a Build button (...) appears, click it to display a builder or a dialog box with a choice of builders, depending on the type of control.

> **TIP** *When you click a property in the property sheet, you can see a description of the property in the status bar. If you need more information about the property or how to use it, press F1.*

The calculated field, Total Cost, which you added to the Workorders data entry form earlier, needs to show currency symbols. To set the format property, do the following:

1. In the form Design window, double-click the edit region of the Total Cost text box control.

2. Click the arrow in the Format property box and choose Currency from the list.

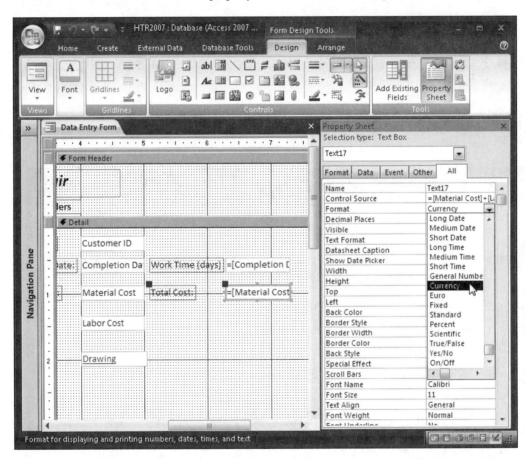

To apply the same property settings to a group of controls of the same type, select them all, and then open the property sheet. Only those properties common to all members of the group are visible in the sheet.

Once you open a property sheet, it remains on the screen until you close it. To set properties of a different object in the design, select the object from the drop-down list at the top of the property sheet or select the control in the design.

Assign a Default Value

When you assign a default value to a bound control in a form or report design, the value you enter overrides any default value set in the underlying table design. The default value you assign is stored in the field when a new record is entered in the form unless you enter a different one. For example, if you are entering new bid data and one of the fields in the form is the date, you can assign the current date as the default value. This automatically stores the current system date in the new record. To assign the current date as the default value, type **=Date()** in the control's Default Value property box.

Change Default Control Properties

Access provides a default set of properties for each type of control. The set specifies the general appearance and behavior of that type of control. For example, the default properties for a text box control determine the font size and alignment of text within the attached label. Another default text box property automatically includes the field name as an attached label. This set of properties is called the *default control style* for that control type.

If you find that you are making the same changes to most of the controls of a certain type, you can change the default property setting. For example, if you usually want a larger font size in your text boxes, change the Font Size from the default size of 8 to a larger size. Or, if you don't want the attached labels for every text box, change the Auto Label property on the Format tab to No.

TIP *When you change a default setting to the one you use most, you save space. Access doesn't need to store both the default and the custom settings.*

To change a default property setting:

1. Click the tool in the Controls group for the desired control type.

2. In the Tools group, click the Property Sheet command. The property sheet for that control type opens, but the title bar indicates that these are the default settings instead of the settings for a particular control in the design.

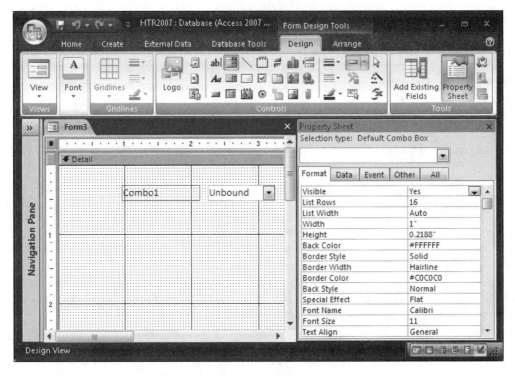

3. Change the setting in the default property sheet.

The changes you make affect only the new controls of that type that you add to the design; the existing controls aren't changed. The changes remain in effect for the current design until you change them again.

If you have already made changes to a control and like what you see, there is a quick way to copy the changes to the control type's default style. Any new controls now will use the properties from the existing control as a default control style. Select the control that has the characteristics you want as defaults for subsequent controls, and then in the Controls group, click the Set Control Defaults command.

Use the Font Group

The Font group of commands provides a quick way to change the appearance of the text in selected controls. The group has eight commands for formatting text in the design. These eight commands change the font name, size, and style, and they align the text within the control boundaries. Other commands give you a quick way to change the color and style of many elements in the design.

The three color commands each display a color palette you can use to change the color of the background, the font/foreground, or the Alternate Fill/Back Color described earlier. The Format Painter command can be used to copy the format settings of a selected control and apply them to other controls.

If you want to apply the same formatting property changes to a group of similar controls, select them all, then change the common property.

Format Conditionally

You can use conditional formatting with text boxes and combo boxes to specify a default format for the control. You can also use up to three additional formats to be applied under special conditions: the current value of the field, when the field gets focus, or when an expression evaluates to True. The expression can refer to the values in other fields in the same record. For example, if the date in a field is more than 30 days ago, display the value in this field underlined and in red on a light green background.

To activate conditional formatting, select the control you want to apply it to and then in the Font group, click the Conditional command. The Conditional Formatting dialog box shows two areas: one for setting the default format and one for specifying a conditional format to be applied under specific conditions.

The formatting choices include bold, italic, and underline as well as text and background colors. The button on the right end of the condition box enables or disables the control. When a control is enabled, you can reach it by pressing TAB. If it is disabled, it is skipped in the tab order. The box in the middle displays an example of how the chosen formatting will look.

To set conditional formatting, set the default format, then move to Condition 1. In the first box, you have a choice of conditions:

- **Field Value Is**   Defines the value or range of values for which to apply the format settings
- **Expression Is**   Applies the formatting if the expression you enter evaluates to True
- **Field Has Focus**   Applies the formatting to the field as soon as it gets focus

Depending on which selection you make in the first condition box, other specifications can be made in the other boxes. If you choose Field Value Is in the first box, you have a choice of several comparison operators.

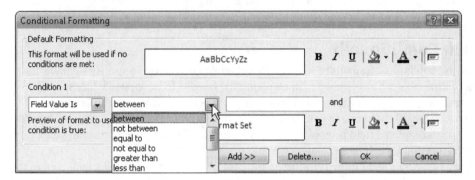

If you choose Expression Is, you have only one box in which to enter the expression. Field Has Focus requires no additional criteria.

After defining the condition, use the formatting buttons to set the format you want to apply if the condition is met. Choose Add to add another condition. You can specify up to three conditional formatting scenarios for each text box or combo box control. The conditions are ranked with the first one taking precedence. If the first condition is not met, the second is evaluated, and so on. Figure 9-7 shows the Conditional Formatting dialog box with settings for the Total Cost text box control. The three conditions are listed next:

- If the Total Cost exceeds $5,000
- If the Total Cost is less than $1,000
- If the Labor Cost is greater than the Material Cost

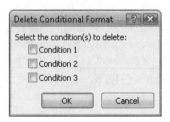

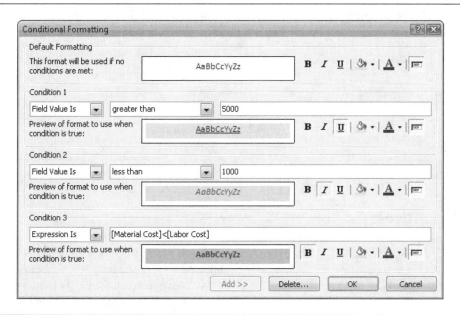

FIGURE 9-7   Conditionally formatting a text box control.

If you want to remove a condition, choose Conditional again and click Delete in the dialog box. The Delete Conditional Format dialog box opens. In this dialog box, you can check the conditions you want to delete. Then click OK.

Change a Control Type

When you change your mind about what type of control you want in the form or report, Access lets you change the control type dynamically. Not all types can be converted and you are limited to the types you can convert to, depending on the original control type.

If you want to change a control type, right-click the control and then point to Change To in the shortcut menu. A list appears displaying the list of controls to which the selected control can be changed. Click on the new type of control. If a control type is dimmed in the list, you cannot change the selected control to that type. Table 9-1 describes the types of conversions permitted by Access.

When you change to another type of control, the applicable properties are copied from the original control to the new control. If the original control has property settings that don't exist for the new control, they are ignored. If the new control has properties that were not used in the original control, Access assigns the default settings for the new control.

Original Control	Permitted Conversions
Label	Text box
Text box	Label, list box, combo box
List box	Text box, combo box
Combo box	Text box, list box
Check box	Toggle button, option button
Toggle button	Check box, option button
Option button	Check box, toggle button

TABLE 9-1 Permitted Control Conversions

Delete Controls

To delete a control, select it and then press DEL. You can also right-click the control and choose Delete from the shortcut menu. If you change your mind, you can restore the control by clicking Undo on the Quick Access toolbar. You can delete more than one control by selecting them all, then pressing DEL. With the stacked Undo/Redo, you don't have to act immediately to reverse an action. You can select the action to undo from the Undo drop-down list next to the Undo button on the Quick Access toolbar. If you choose to undo an action other than the most recent, you will undo all the actions performed after it as well.

Modify Form or Report Properties

Forms and reports have many properties in common such as Record Source, Filter, Order By, Width, and several event properties. Each of these can be changed in the object's property sheet; some can also be changed in Layout view.

Change the Record Source

When you have created a useful form or report design using one set of data, you can easily reuse the design with other data by changing the Record Source property to the new data. To change a form or report record source, you should do the following:

1. In the form or report Design view, click the form or report selector, then in the Tools group, click the Property Sheet command or right-click the selector and choose Properties in the shortcut menu.

2. Click the Data tab and then click the down arrow in the Record Source property.

3. Choose the new record source from the drop-down list of all tables and queries in the current database.

You can also click the Build button to the right of the Record Source property box to start the Query Builder where you can create a new query to use as the record source.

When you change the record source, some of the bound text boxes no longer represent fields in the underlying record source. You will immediately see a marker in the upper-left corner of the text box edit region.

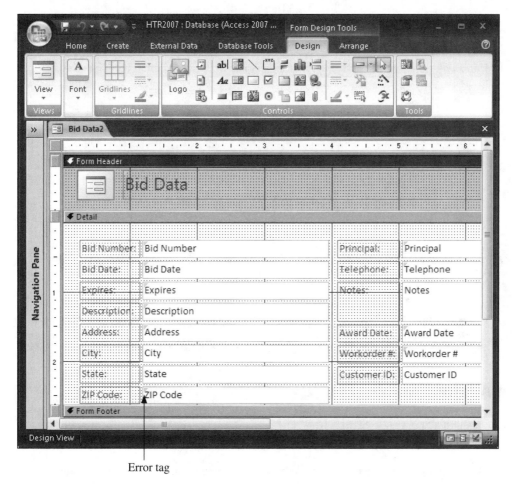

Error tag

Click the marker and then rest the pointer on the tag, if you want to see the reason for the marker. To see how to fix it, click the tag and choose from the drop-down list. This is a big improvement over earlier versions of Access that simply displayed #Name? or #Error? with no clue as to what was wrong. If you are in Form or Report view, you may still see those error messages. Switch to Design view to take advantage of the error tags.

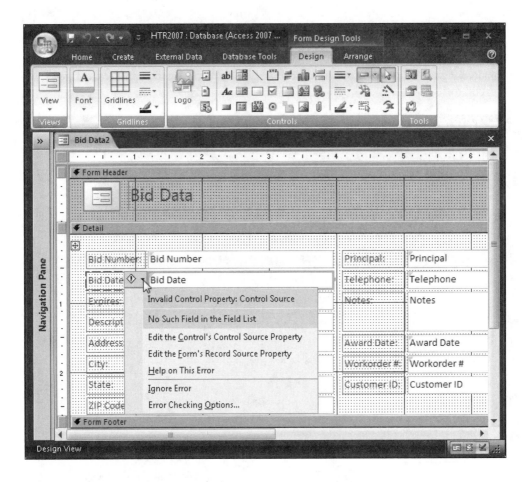

Apply Filters and Sort Orders

When you create a form or report based on a table or query with a filter or a specified sort order, both are included in the object's properties. The sort order is automatically applied but the filter may or may not be, depending on how you created the form or report:

- If you created the form or report from a table not open in Datasheet view, the filter and sort order are inherited but not applied. You must apply them when you need them.

- If you created the form or report from a table that is open in Datasheet view and contains filtered data, the filter is applied every time you open the report but only the first time you view the form in Form view. After you save and close the form, the next time you open the form, you will have to apply the filter yourself by clicking Apply Filter.

Use AutoFormat

Access has provided several attractive formats for forms and reports that add style to the design. To apply the style to a form or report under construction or already completed:

1. Open the object in Design view and click the form or report selector.

2. On the Arrange tab in the QuickFormat group, click the AutoFormat command and choose AutoFormat Wizard at the bottom of the gallery.

3. In the AutoFormat dialog box, you can select from a list of formats. Click Options to see how you can apply the font, color and border attributes selectively. When you are satisfied with the format, click OK.

CAUTION *If you customize one of the pre-designed AutoFormat, the changes are permanent.*

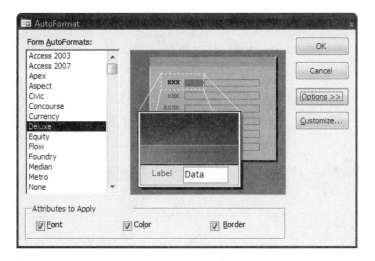

9

NOTE *If you want to apply AutoFormat to just one section in the form or report design, click the section selector before opening the AutoFormat dialog box. You can also use AutoFormat for a single control.*

Chapter 10

Create Custom Forms and Subforms

How to...

- Create a new form design
- Modify the form
- Use the form for data entry
- Create a multiple-page form
- Add calculated and special fields
- Create a hierarchical form
- Add custom user guidance
- Control data entry

Create a New Form Design

Access forms usually are used for viewing and entering data. It is important to design a form that will make data entry as foolproof as possible and present the data so that it is easily understood. For example, you will want to arrange the data in a logical sequence in the form or group related information together on the screen.

Although the Access Form Wizard will do most of the work for you, it does only what you ask; so it pays to plan ahead. Design the form on paper before invoking the wizard. If a manual data entry form has already proved efficient, the design can be repeated in an Access form.

You can start a new form, using one of the Forms group of commands on the Create tab, where you can chose the type of form that best suits your needs. Most of the form tools require that the table or query you use as the base be open in Datasheet view or at least selected in the Navigation Pane. The exception is the Blank form which opens an empty form in Layout view.

Before we get started with the Form Wizard, let's take a quick look at the other pre-designed forms that are available in the Forms group of commands on the Create tab. When you start a new form, you have several choices for the form structure.

The More Forms command displays a context menu of options: Form Wizard, Datasheet, Modal Dialog, and PivotTable. Let's use the Form Wizard now and find out more about the other forms later in this chapter.

Use the Form Wizard

When you choose Form Wizard from the More Forms command, the first wizard dialog box opens where you choose the fields to add to the form. If you haven't selected a table or query in the Navigation Pane, you can do that here too.

Here's how to start a new form design based on the Current Workorders query:

1. Select the Current Workorders query in the Queries group of the Navigation Pane.

2. On the Create tab in the Forms group, click the More Forms command and then choose Form Wizard in the context menu. The first Form Wizard dialog box opens (see Figure 10-1).

The Current Workorders query name shows in the Tables/Queries box and the Available Fields list shows all the fields in the query, including the calculated fields. The fields appear in the same order as in the query design grid. You can place any or all of the fields in the form design in the desired order. Add them all at once or one at a time in the sequence you want them to appear in the form.

To continue with the Current Workorders form:

1. Click the double right chevrons (>>) to add all the fields from the Current Workorders query to the Selected Fields list.

2. Click Next. The Form Wizard's second dialog box opens. If you select fields from more than one table or query, the Form Wizard will create a main form with one or more subforms. The Create a Hierarchical Form section discusses this subject in more detail. The second Form Wizard dialog box offers a choice of four form layouts: Columnar, Tabular, Datasheet, and Justified (see Figure 10-2).

10

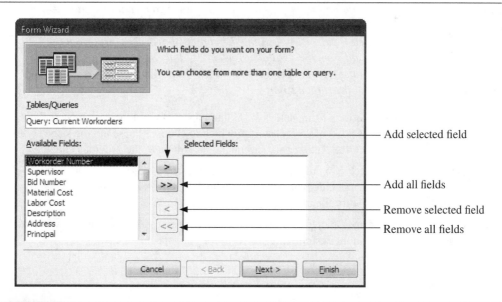

FIGURE 10-1   Choosing fields for the form.

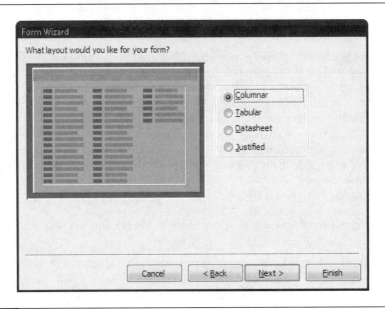

FIGURE 10-2   Choose the form layout.

TIP   *If the fields in the Available Fields list are not in the order you want to see in the form, choose the fields one at a time in the order you want them to appear. To insert a field name into the Selected Fields list, select the field name above where you want the new one, select the field from the Available Fields list, and click the right chevron. By selecting the fields in the right order in the Form Wizard dialog box, you avoid moving the controls around in the form design.*

3. For the Current Workorders form, select the Columnar layout and then click Next. The next dialog box shows a list of 25 styles from which to choose. These are the same styles you see when you click the AutoFormat command, as shown in the previous chapter.

4. Choose a style and click Next to reach the final Form Wizard dialog box, where you name the form and then decide whether to view the data in the new form or go directly to the Design view to modify the design.

5. After entering the form name, click Finish to save and open the form. Once the wizard is finished, you can go about customizing the form for your special needs.

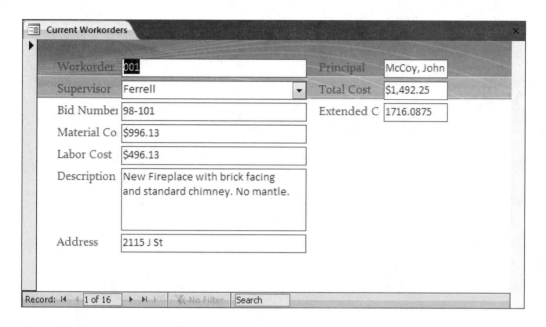

Create a Form Without the Wizard

You don't need the help of a wizard to create your form. To start one of the automatic form layouts, go to the Create tab in the Forms group, and click one of the commands. All the automatic form tools arrange the fields in the same order as in the table structure or the query design grid. The table or query name appears in the form document tab and the form adopts the most recently used style.

The automatic form tools create the following types of forms:

- The Simple form tool creates a stacked form with the data from the selected table or query.
- The Split form tool offers the data in two views at once: the form Layout and Datasheet views.
- The Multiple Items form displays several records in the Layout view.
- The PivotChart form tool helps to create a graphical analysis of the data in the table or query.
- The Blank form tool opens a blank form in Layout view with the Field List pane open at the right.
- The Form Design tool opens a blank form in Design view.

If you have selected a table or query in the New Form dialog box to use as the basis for the form, you can display the field list and drag the fields into the form design. If you have not already selected the basis for the form, you can define it in Design view by opening the form's

10

Property Sheet and selecting the table or query from the form's Record Source property list; then you can add other controls and set properties as before.

Modify the Form Design

Although the Form Wizard does a good job of creating a form, there are a lot of things you can do to improve the result. For example, you can do any of the following:

- Add a form header with a title
- Resize the form
- Move, resize, or reformat controls
- Add special controls such as the current date, a calendar, or an AutoDialer
- Change the text of attached labels
- Add lines and rectangles for emphasis
- Change the progression of the cursor through the controls when TAB is pressed (the tab order)

Add Form Header and Footer Sections

By default, a form created by the wizard from a single table or query has a detail section as well as form header and footer sections in which the user can specify information that will appear at the top and bottom of the form. This information remains on the screen as you scroll through records in the detail section. You also can add page header and footer sections to hold information such as a title, graphics, or column headings. Page sections appear only when you preview or print the form, not in Form view.

To add the form header and footer sections, right-click in the form in Design view and choose Form Header/Footer in the shortcut menu. The thin form header section appears above the detail section. If you scroll down the form design, you will also see the footer section. Both sections are shrunken, but appear in the form design. To increase the size of the form header section, move the mouse pointer to the detail section bar; when the pointer changes to a black plus sign with up and down arrows, click and drag the bar down.

To add a title to the form design, do the following:

1. On the Design tab in the Controls group, click the Title command. The form header automatically expands and then the form name is added.

2. Using the Font group of commands on the Design tab, you can change the appearance of the title.

Figure 10-3 shows the Current Workorders form design with a title in the new header section.

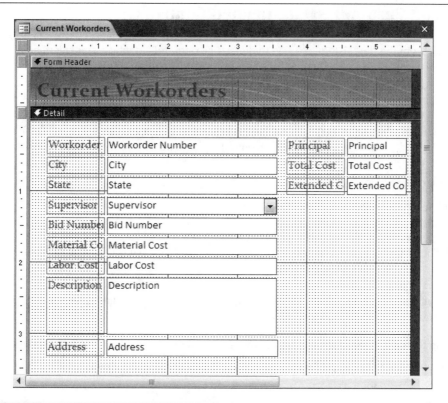

FIGURE 10-3   Adding a title to the form header section.

TIP

When you choose Form Header/Footer in the shortcut menu, both sections are added to the form design. If you have no information to put in the footer and don't want the section to take up room in the form, you can drag the bottom form border up to reduce the footer section space to zero.

All the sections in a form have the same properties. Double-click one of the section selectors to open the property sheet for the section. Form sections have fewer properties than the form itself. Most of the section properties apply to formatting.

For example, the Can Shrink and Can Grow properties resize the section to fit the data within it. The Force New Page property can start printing the form section on a new page rather than on the current page, either before or after printing the current section.

10

Place and Customize Data-Related Controls

In the last chapter, you saw how to add bound text box controls to a form design by dragging the field names from the field list. In addition to the text box controls in which you enter and edit data, list and combo boxes enable you to choose from a list of values.

List boxes limit your choice to values in the list but combo boxes usually let you type entries as well as choose from the list. Either of these can be bound or unbound. If the control is bound, the selected or entered value is stored in the field to which it is bound. If it is unbound, the value is not stored in a table but can be used by another control or as a search criterion.

First, let's take a look at how Access can automatically arrange the controls in a form.

Build a Control Layout

A control layout is a specified arrangement of controls—either laid out horizontally or stacked vertically. Using these layouts helps give your form a uniform appearance without having to adjust the location of each control individually.

The tabular layout places controls in rows and columns like a datasheet, with the control labels at the top. The stacked layout arranges controls in a vertical list with the labels at the left. You can mix layouts in a form.

You can create your own layouts by selecting all the controls you want in the same layout and then doing one of the following:

- On the Layout tab in the Control Layout group, click the Tabular or Stacked command.
- Right-click in the selection and point to Layout in the shortcut menu and choose Tabular or Stacked.

You can switch from one layout to the other by clicking the orange layout selector in the top left corner of the group and repeating one of the previous steps. You can also move controls around in the layout, move a control to another layout of the same type, and add controls to or remove controls from the layout.

Add New Text Box Controls

Let's say that the Current Workorders query does not have all the fields you would like to see in the Current Workorders form. To add more bound text box controls, change the query that is the form's Record Source property and include the additional fields. If you are using a table as the record source, you may need to create a query that includes the fields from the original table plus the additional fields from related tables.

To add more fields from the related tables that are used in the query, open the form in Design view and do the following:

1. If the Property Sheet is already visible, click the form selector or select Form from the drop-down list in the Property Sheet. If not, right-click the form and choose Properties in the shortcut menu.

2. Click in the Record Source property box on the Data tab, and then click the Build button. This starts the Query Builder, which looks much like the query design grid except that the words "Query Builder" appear in the title bar.

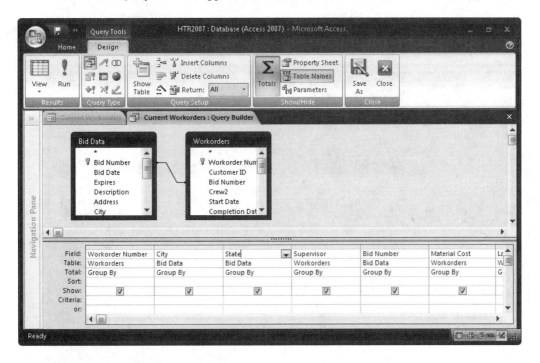

3. Hold down CTRL while you select the City and State fields in the Bid Data field list and drag the group to the grid. The position in the grid is unimportant right now.

4. Right-click the Query Builder tab and choose Save in the shortcut menu, then right-click again and choose Close button to return to the form design.

The additional fields now are available to the form and the field list is displayed. Follow the next steps to complete the addition of the City and State fields:

1. Select Bid Number in the field list and drag it close to the 5½-inch mark on the horizontal ruler.

2. Select the City field in the field list and drag it to a position in the design below the Bid Number field, and then drag the State field next to the City field.

3. Resize the City and State labels to fit the text, and then resize the State text box because it contains only two characters. Move the State text box next to its attached label.

4. To make the three address fields the same height, click in the vertical ruler level with the row of text boxes to select all three, then right-click the group and point to Size in the shortcut menu. Choose To Tallest.

5. To align the boxes, right-click the group again and point to Align in the shortcut menu and choose Top.

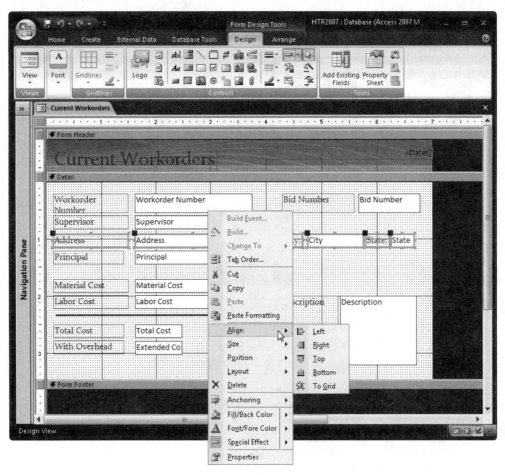

You can also add a line to separate the material and labor cost from the calculated fields that show the total and extended costs. First, move the two calculated fields down a little to make room for the line. Then, in the Controls group, click the Line command and draw a line across under the Labor Cost text box. You can change the line thickness, style, and color by selecting from the Lines properties lists in the Controls group on the Design tab.

The last control to add to the Current Workorders form is the current date, which will appear in the form header section. To add the date, do the following:

1. On the Design tab in the Controls group, click the Date & Time command. The Date and Time dialog box appears (see Figure 10-4).

2. Check Include Date (if it is not already checked) and select the middle date format (Medium Date), which displays dates as *dd-mm-yy*.

3. Clear the Include Time check box and click OK. The expression = *Date( )* appears in the upper-right corner of the form header section.

Figure 10-5 shows the completed Current Workorders form in Form view.

Create List and Combo Boxes

It often is quicker and safer to select a value from a list than to try to remember the correct value to type. List boxes and combo boxes consist of rows of data with one or more columns that can

10

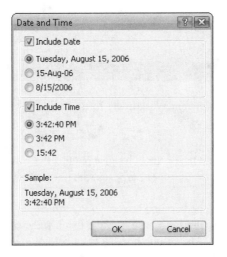

FIGURE 10-4 Setting Date and Time properties.

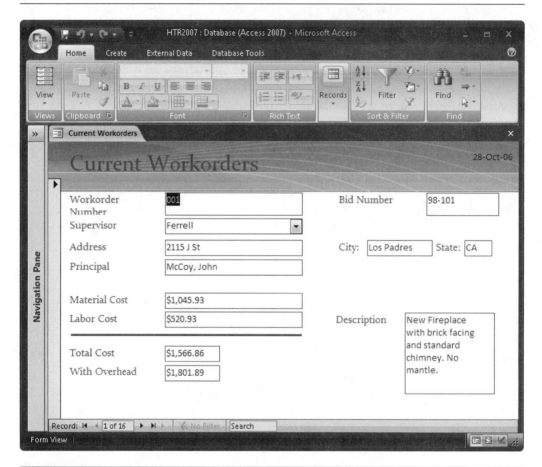

FIGURE 10-5   The completed Current Workorders form.

appear with or without headings. One of the columns contains the values you want to store in the field (the bound control) or use for other purposes (the unbound control); the other columns contain explanatory information.

When you compare text, list, and combo boxes, you see that the list box is always open but is limited to the size you draw in the form design. If the list is wider or longer than the space allowed, Access adds scroll bars. The combo box list is by default the same width as the control in the design, but you can change the width to fit the list. Scroll bars also are added to combo boxes when necessary.

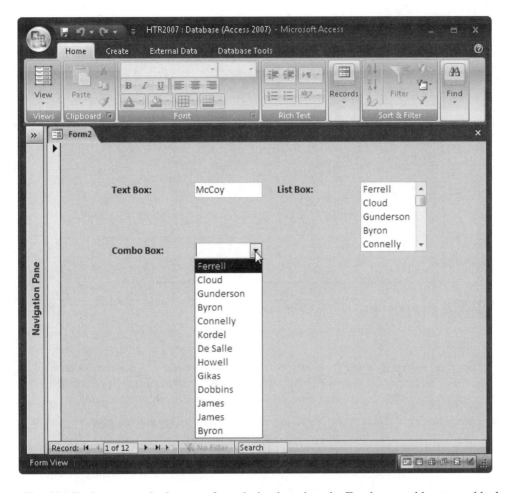

To add a list box or combo box to a form design based on the Employees table, open a blank form in Design view and do the following:

1. Make sure the Use Control Wizards command is pressed, then click the List Box or Combo Box command in the Controls group.

2. Click in the form design or draw an outline where you want the control to appear. The wizard's first dialog box opens (see Figure 10-6). For both the List Box Wizard and the Combo Box Wizard, the first dialog boxes are nearly identical.

3. Choose one of the following options (both wizards offer the same options):

   ■ **I want the combo (or list) box to look up the values in a table or query.**   If you choose this option, the box displays field values from the table or query you choose.

   ■ **I will type in the values that I want.**   If you choose this option, the list contains values you type into the next dialog box.

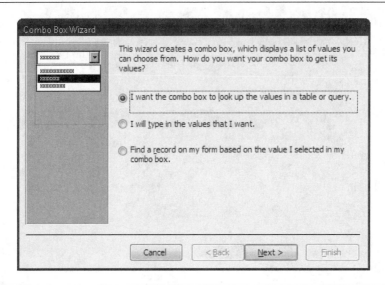

FIGURE 10-6   The first Combo Box Wizard dialog box.

■ **Find a record on my form based on the value I selected in my combo box.**   This
option is used to create a combo box that acts as a search string to find a specific
record and display it in the form. This option creates an unbound control.

4. After making a choice in the first dialog box, click Next. Depending on your choice in
step 3, do one of the following:

■ If you chose the first option, select the table or query that contains the values the box
will display. Click Next, select the fields you want to see in the list, and click Next
again.

■ If you chose to type in the values, enter the number of columns you want to see and
the values to display. Choosing this option skips the next dialog box.

*If you are typing in the values, press TAB to move to the next row in the list of values. If
you press ENTER, you will advance to the next wizard dialog box. In that case, click Back
to return to the value list dialog box.*

■ If you chose the third option, choose the field whose values you want to see. The
value you choose in Form view acts as a search value. Click Next.

5. In the next dialog box, adjust the column widths to show the values and decide to show
or hide the primary key field. Click Next.

6. Unless you chose the third options in step 3, the next dialog box asks what you want
Access to do with the value you select in the list box or combo box:

- **Remember the value for later use**   Saves the value for use by a macro or procedure. When you close the form, the value is erased.

- **Store that value in this field**   With this option, you select the field in which you want to store the selected value.

7. If you want a label attached to the box, type it in the last dialog box and click Finish.

Create Unbound List and Combo Boxes

An unbound list or combo box can display either a set of fixed values that you enter when you create the box or specific values from a table or query. The value chosen from the control list is not stored in a field in the underlying table. You can use the value for other purposes, such as looking up a record with that value in a field.

To add a combo box to an Employee form that will display the record for a selected employee:

1. Start a new form based on the Employee table and then add the desired fields to the form.

2. Start the Combo Box (or List Box) Wizard as before and in the first dialog box, choose the third option, "Find a record on my form based on the value I selected in my combo box." Click Next.

3. Choose Last Name as the field value to show in the list and click Next.

10

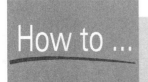

Decide Between a List Box and a Combo Box

Because list and combo boxes are similar, how do you decide which type of control to use in the form?

- The values in a list box are always visible and you are limited to the values in the list. To choose from the list, click the entry and press ENTER or TAB. You also can choose one of the values by typing the first letter of the value and pressing ENTER or TAB. (If you have more than one value starting with the same letter, the first one is selected.) You cannot enter a value that is not on the list. List boxes are best when you are limited to just a few values; otherwise the list box takes up valuable viewing space.

- The values in a combo box are not displayed until you click the arrow to open it, so it takes up less room on the screen than a list box. As with the list box, you can select one of the values by clicking it or by typing the first few characters of the value into the text box area of the combo box. You also can type in values that are not in the list unless you have set the Limit To List property to Yes.

4. Choose Hide key column (recommended) and click Next.

5. In the final dialog box, enter **Show record for:** as the control label and then click Finish.

When you use the combo box in Form view, select a value from the list and Access will move to the first record with that value in the corresponding field. This option offers a quick way to move to a specific record in Form view.

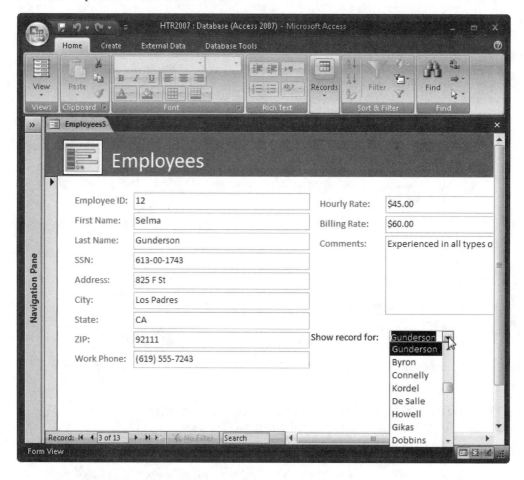

Set List and Combo Box Properties

If your form contains a bound list box or combo box, the control inherits most of its properties from the field properties you set in the table design. When you use a wizard to create such a control, Access sets certain other properties for you. You can modify these properties by changing the settings in the property sheet to make them work just the way you want.

For example, Auto Expand automatically fills in the remaining characters with a value in a combo box when you type the first few characters of the value. Limit To List prevents entering values that are not in the list. The Row Source is another important property. If the Row Source

Type property is set to Table/Query or Field List, Row Source specifies the name of the table or query or a SQL statement. If the Row Source Type property is set to Value List, the Row Source property displays a list of items separated by semicolons. If the Row Source Type is a user-defined function, this property is blank. See the related Help topics for complete descriptions of the control properties.

Add Yes/No Controls

Three different types of controls can be used to view or enter a Yes/No value in the underlying table or query. They are check boxes, option buttons, and toggle buttons. When you have a limited number of alternative choices in one field, you can also group the controls together in an option group. The grouped options work as a single control; only one can be selected. The option group can display the list of choices as any of the three types of Yes/No controls.

When you select or clear a check box, option button, or toggle button, Access displays the value in the table or query according to the format property set in the table design (Yes/No, True/False, or On/Off). Here's how the various Yes/No controls appear when the values are Yes and No.

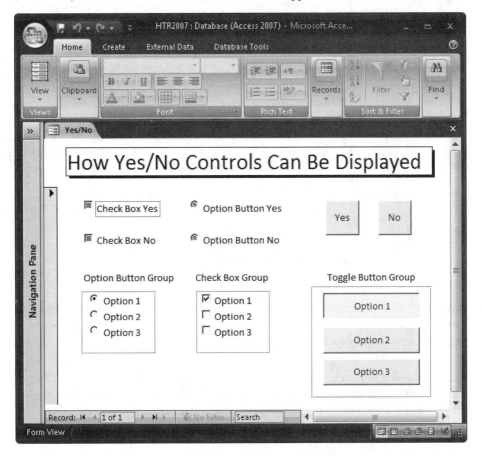

Option groups are a little different. An option group offers a limited set of mutually exclusive alternatives, usually four or less. The option group control consists of a frame around a set of check boxes, option buttons, or toggle buttons.

If the option group is bound to a field, the frame itself is the bound object, not the individual controls in the group. When you create an option group, you specify the values of the options in terms of numbers that are meaningful to the underlying field. When you select an option in the group, that value is stored in the field. If the group is not bound to a field, Access uses the value of the option you choose to carry out one of a list of actions, such as to print the report you choose or open another form.

Although you can create an option group without the help of the wizard, it is a lot easier to take advantage of the wizard. To create an option group, make sure the Use Control Wizards command is pressed in on the Controls group, and then do the following:

1. Click the Option Group command and then click in the form design where you want the upper-left corner of the group to appear. The wizard draws a 1-inch square box. Click Next.

2. In the first wizard dialog box, enter the text you want to see as choices in the group.

3. Press TAB to move to the next row. After entering all the values, click Next.

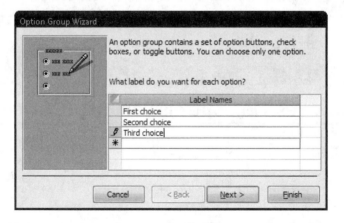

4. In the second dialog box, set the default option (if desired) and click Next.

5. Specify the Option Value property for each of the options in the group. This property must always be a number. This is the value that is passed to the field when the option is selected. By default, the values are consecutive integers: option 1 has the value 1, option 2 has the value 2, and so on. Click Next.

6. The next dialog box asks in which field you want to store the value (bound) or if you want Access to save the value for later (unbound). If the form does not have a record source, the wizard skips this dialog box.

7. Choose the type of control and the style you want to see in the option group and click Next.

8. In the final wizard dialog box, enter the name you want as the label for the group. This text will appear in the group frame. Click Finish.

About Events and Event Properties

10

Access is an object-oriented, event-driven application. Nothing happens until the user tells it what to do by pressing a key or clicking the mouse button. An *event* is an occurrence that is recognized by an Access object. You can define a response to events by setting the object's or control's event property.

Here are some examples of events:

- Pressing or releasing a key
- Opening or closing a form
- Moving the cursor to or away from a control
- Applying a filter to records in a form
- Changing or deleting the value in a control

The action Access takes depends on the event property that has been specified. For example, double-clicking an object in the Navigation Pane opens the object (the response). When you move to another record after entering or editing data, the event causes Access to automatically check any validation rules and, if there is no violation, save the record. The system triggers these actions based on the build-in event properties.

The action Access takes depends on the event property that has been specified. For example, clicking the Open command button (the event) in the Navigation Pane opens the selected object (the response). When you move to another record after entering or editing data, the event causes Access to automatically check any validation rules and, if there is no violation, save the record. This system triggers these actions based on the built-in event properties.

Add User-Interactive Controls

Because a form is often used to enter data, the user is constantly interacting with the form and the controls it contains. Some of the controls are directly associated with table data such as text boxes, list boxes, and combo boxes; others accept user actions.

The most common control unrelated to data is the command button, which is used in Form view to perform an action. When the user clicks a command button, Access recognizes this event and carries out the response you have specified for the event.

Add Command Buttons

The Command Button Wizard is on hand to help create more than 30 different types of command buttons that accomplish tasks ranging from moving to the next record to closing the form. The wizard helps you select the category of action you want and the specific procedure to execute. It also enables you to identify the button with text or a picture.

To add a command button to the Current Workorders form that then prints the current record, do the following:

1. Make sure the Use Control Wizards command is pressed in, then click the Command Button command and click in the form design. The first Command Button Wizard dialog box now appears (see Figure 10-7).

2. Select the Record Operations category, select the Print Record action, and then click Next.

3. The next wizard dialog box lets you choose between text and a picture for the button. Accept the default picture and click Next.

4. Enter a name for the button or accept the default name. Click Finish.

Figure 10-8 shows the Current Workorders form with the new Print Record command button. When the Command Button Wizard builds the button for you, it writes an event procedure containing Visual Basic code to store with the form.

Add Hyperlinks

In Chapter 5, you saw how to add a hyperlink field to a table and how to insert a hyperlink address in the field. A hyperlink in a table can jump to a different address for each record. For example, the hyperlink field Drawing in the Home Tech Repair Workorders table contains addresses of files containing scanned engineering drawings. If you don't need to tie the hyperlink

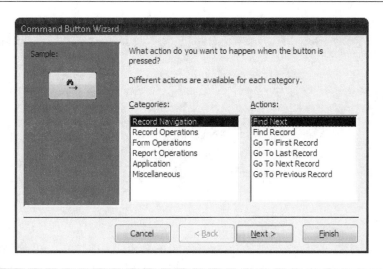

FIGURE 10-7 Choose the type of command button.

address to a record, you can add it to the form in Design view as an unbound label or an image control.

To add a hyperlink as a label control to the Home Tech Repair Roster form that will jump to the Employees table:

1. With the form open in Design view, on the Create tab in the Controls group, click the Hyperlink command. The Insert Hyperlink dialog box opens.

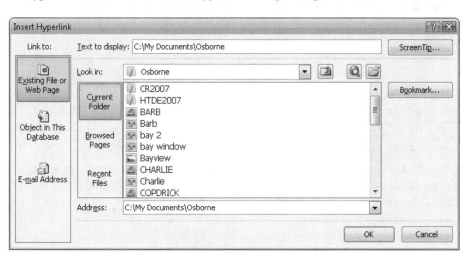

10

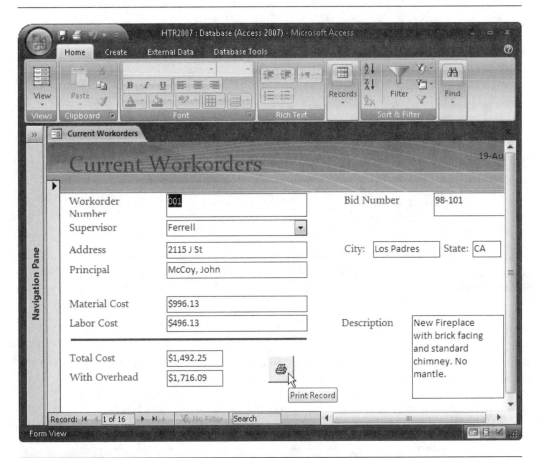

FIGURE 10-8 A Print Record command button added to a form.

2. Click the Existing File or Web Page and the Current Folder buttons, if not already checked. If the database you want is in another folder, click Browse for File to locate it.

3. Select HTR2007 in the list of databases in the current folder. The complete address appears in the Address box.

4. Click the Bookmark button to open the Select Place in Document dialog box where you can specify the object to which you want to jump, the Employees table in this case.

5. Click the plus sign next to Tables and select Employees from the list of tables in the database. Click OK.

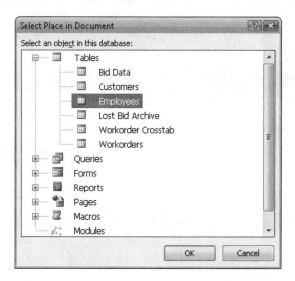

6. Enter **Lookup Employees** in the Text To Display box to see it in the hyperlink instead of the address.

7. Click ScreenTip and enter **Display Employees table** in the Set Hyperlink ScreenTip dialog box, and then click OK. The default is the complete hyperlink address.

8. Click OK to close the Insert Hyperlink dialog box. Access creates the hyperlink in the upper-left corner of the form.

9. Drag the hyperlink control to the position you want in the form design.

You can test the new hyperlink in the form design by right-clicking the control and pointing to Hyperlink in the shortcut menu and choosing Open Hyperlink from the shortcut menu. When you switch to Form view, the hyperlink appears as an underlined label. Rest the mouse pointer on the hyperlink to see the ScreenTip. Click on it to open the Employees table in Datasheet view.

10

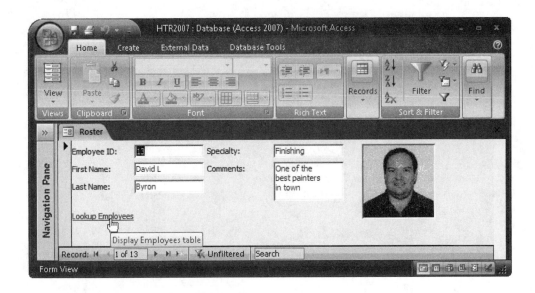

Use the Form for Data Entry

Forms are the principal user interface for the database information. The user can view all the data, search for specific records, enter new records, and edit existing records. To accomplish these tasks efficiently, the user must know how to get around in the form and how to move through the records in Form view.

To open a form in Form view, where you can view and edit data, double-click the form name in the Forms group in the Navigation Pane or right-click the form name and choose Open in the shortcut menu. In Form view, you can add a new record by clicking the New Record button in the record navigation bar to show a blank form. You also can edit existing records using the navigation bar or the Find group of commands.

Navigate in the Form

As with datasheets, you can operate in two different modes in a form: navigation and editing. In navigation mode, the cursor moves to other fields; in editing mode, it moves among characters in a field. The keypresses have different consequences depending on the current mode. For example, in editing mode, pressing RIGHT ARROW moves the insertion point one character to the right. In navigation mode, it moves the cursor to the next field and usually selects the value.

To change modes, do the following:

- To switch from editing mode to navigation mode, press F2 or click in a field label. You also can press TAB or SHIFT-TAB to leave editing mode and move to another field.

- To switch from navigation mode to editing mode for the currently selected field, press F2 or click in the text box.

Clicking the navigation buttons at the bottom of the form moves the cursor to the first, previous, next, or last record. You can enter a specific record number in the record navigation bar and press ENTER to move to that record. On the Home tab in the Find group, clicking the Go To command also moves the cursor to the first, previous, next, or last record. These methods move the cursor to the same field in another record.

Change the Tab Order

Each time you press TAB in Form view, the cursor moves to another field. The progression of the cursor through the fields in the form is called the *tab order*. Each text box control is assigned a tab index number indicating its position in the sequence. The first control in the order has 0 as the tab index number; the second, 1; and so on. Access sets the tab order to match the order in which the fields were added to the design.

Here's what you should do to change the tab order so that the cursor moves more logically through the records:

1. Open the form in Design view and then click in the detail section selector.

2. On the Arrange tab in the Control Layout group, click the Tab Order command. The Tab Order dialog box opens showing a list of all the text box controls in the detail section.

10

3. To reposition a control in the tab order, move the mouse pointer to the row selector (the shaded box at the left end of the row) and drag the row to a new position. You can also select a group of rows and reposition them as a group.

4. Repeat step 3 until you have the order the way you want it, and then click OK.

 *Clicking the Auto Order button in the Tab Order dialog box rearranges the controls in the order they appear in the form, from left to right and top to bottom. If this is the way you want the cursor to move through the fields, click Auto Order instead of moving the controls by hand.*

Locate Records

Searching for specific records by examining the value in one or more fields is just the same in a form as in a datasheet. Use the same Find dialog box to specify the search string and the scope of the match, whether you want to search all of the field or only part of it.

To display a specific record in the form in Form or Layout view, place the insertion point in the field that has the value you are looking for and on the Home tab in the Find group, click the Find command. If you want to replace the current field value with another, click the Replace command. Refer to Chapter 5 for more information about using Find and Replace.

Sort and Filter Data in a Form

Once you are viewing data in the form, you can filter the records just as in a datasheet: in the Sort & Filter group, use Filter By Selection, Filter By Form, or Advanced Filter/Sort. To sort records in the form, place the cursor in the field you want to sort on and then click one of the Sort commands. You can also enter filter and sort expressions in the form's property sheet.

If the form is based on a table or query that already has a sort order or filter saved with it, the form inherits both properties. A sort order is automatically applied to the records in the form. Whether the filter is automatically applied to the records in the form depends on the status of the table or query when you created the form.

■ If the table or query was open and the filter was applied when you created the form, the filter is automatically applied to the records in the form. The word "(Filtered)" will appear to the right of the navigation buttons at the bottom of the form and "Filtered" also appears in the status bar to remind you of the filter. To remove the filter, click the Remove Filter command in the Sort & Filter group, which appears pressed in when a filter is applied.

The filter is not saved with the form. Therefore, if you close and reopen the form, you see all the records.

■ If the table or query was closed and saved with the filter, the filter is inherited by the form but is not automatically applied. Click the Apply Filter command in the Sort & Filter group.

To disable all filtering of records in the form, set the Allow Filters property to No. This disables the Filter By Selection, Filter By Form, Filter For Input, and Advanced Filter/Sort.

View Multiple Records

If you want to see more than one record on the screen, you can change the form's Default View property from Single Form to Continuous Forms. Then when you choose Form View from the View command, the form appears with as many records as will fit on the screen. Home Tech Repair uses a form named Roster as a quick way to look up employees. When the Roster form is set to Single Form, only one record appears on the screen, as shown in the following illustration.

Figure 10-9 shows the same Roster form with the Default View set to Continuous Forms.

Create a Multiple-Page Form

Access offers two ways to create a multiple-page form: inserting a page break control or adding a tab control. A page break separates the form horizontally into two or more pages, which are separate controls. To move sequentially among the pages, press PGUP or PGDN. Tab controls produce multiple-page forms that combine all the pages into a single control. To move between pages in a tab control, click the desired tab.

Add a Page Break

To insert a page break, click the Page Break Control tool in the toolbox, and then click in the form where you want the split. Access shows a short dotted line at the left border where the break occurs.

Pages are not necessarily full-screen height. If you want every page to be the same size and show only one page at a time, design the form with evenly spaced page breaks. Use the vertical ruler to help place the page breaks evenly.

After placing the page break, change some of the form properties as follows:

- ■ Change the Cycle property on the Other tab from the current default All Records to Current Page, which keeps you from moving to the next page when you press TAB at the last control in the tab order on one page.

- ■ Change the Scroll Bars property on the Format tab from Both to Horizontal Only to remove the vertical scroll bar. This prevents scrolling to a different page. If the form is not wider than the screen, you can set the property to Neither and remove both scroll bars.

Switch to Form view and press PGDN and PGUP to see if the page breaks are properly placed.

10

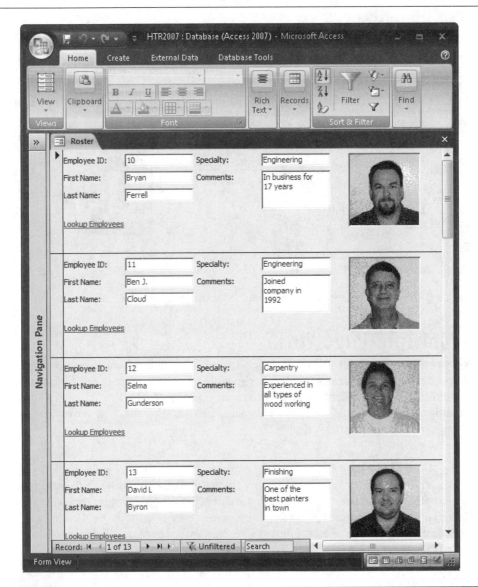

FIGURE 10-9 Showing the Roster in continuous form.

Add a Tab Control

Tab controls are easier and more efficient than page breaks because all the pages in the form belong to a single control. Tab controls are useful for presenting groups of information that can be assembled by category. They are also widely used in dialog boxes.

Here's how to add a tab control to the Roster form:

1. Open the Roster form in Design view and drag the lower form border down to make room for the tab control.

2. On the Design tab in the Controls group, click the Tab Control command and draw a tab control frame in the lower half of the form design across the width (see Figure 10-10).

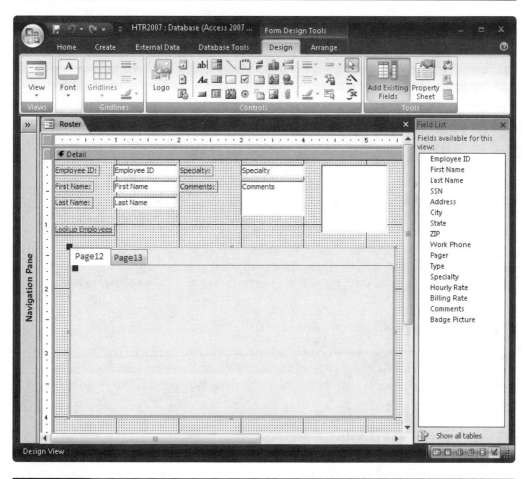

FIGURE 10-10   A new tab control.

3. Press SHIFT and select the Employee ID, First Name, Last Name, Specialty, and Picture fields in the Roster form. Then right-click in the group and choose click Copy in the shortcut menu.

4. Right-click in the tab control and choose Paste from the shortcut menu. The controls from the Roster form appear in the first page of the tab control.

5. Click the Field List command if the list is not already showing, drag Work Phone and Pager fields to the first page, then click the tab for the second page in the tab control and drag the SSN, Hourly Rate, and Billing Rate, Address, City, State and Zip fields from the field list.

6. Copy the Last Name and Comments fields from the form to the second page.

7. Double-click in a page to open the property sheet and change the Caption property to read Employee Info, then click in the other page and change its caption to read Rates and Comments.

8. Select the Picture control and change the Size Mode property to Zoom.

9. Delete the controls from the upper half of the form and reduce the form height to show just the tab control, then switch to Form view. Figure 10-11 shows two copies of the form so you can see both pages.

To add another tab or delete a tab, right-click the tab control border and choose Insert Page or Delete Page. When you delete a page this way, the last page to be inserted is deleted.

Customize a Tab Control

Two property sheets are used to customize a tab control: the tab control property sheet and the page property sheet. To customize the tab control as a whole, double-click the control border outside of a page to open the property sheet. For example, you can change the style to show tabs or buttons and specify multiple rows of tabs. To set individual page properties, double-click in the page tab. You can enter the text you want to show on the tab or even add a graphic to it.

Add Special Controls

In addition to images, unbound option groups, lines, and rectangles, there are other special controls that you can add to a form design to enhance its appearance or provide additional information. Calculated controls can combine data from more than one field into processed or summary information.

Add Calculated Controls

It often is helpful to include a calculated field in a form or report. For example, in the last chapter, we used a query to add two calculated fields to the Current Workorders form. You can also add a calculated field to a form directly without using a query.

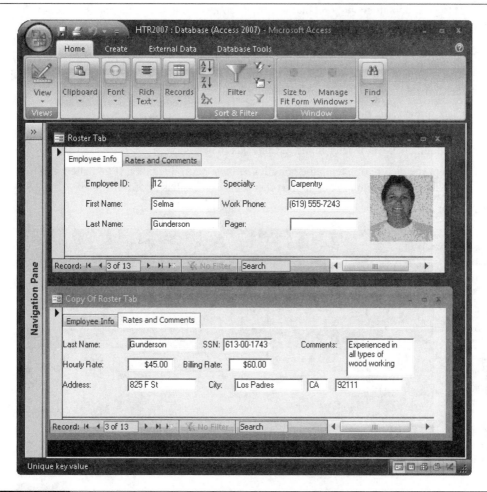

FIGURE 10-11   A two-page tab control.

An unbound text box control usually is used for a calculated field but you can use any control that has a Control Source property, which tells Access where to get the information to display. Combo boxes, list boxes, bound and unbound object frames, toggle buttons, option buttons, and check boxes all have a Control Source property.

After adding the control to the form design, enter the expression in the Control Source property box. You can also type the expression directly into the calculated control box. Be sure to precede the expression with an equal sign in both cases.

Add an AutoDialer Control

You can use the Command Button Wizard to create a command button that you can click to dial a selected phone number automatically. To use the AutoDialer, you need to have a dial-up modem connected to your computer and a regular telephone connected to the same line. Here's how to add this special control:

1. Open the form in Design view.

2. Make sure the Use Control Wizards command in the Controls group is pressed in, then in the Controls group, click the Button command.

3. Click in the form where you want the button.

4. In the first Command Button Wizard dialog box, click Miscellaneous in the Category box, then click AutoDialer in the Actions box. Click Next.

5. Accept the picture of a telephone or click Browse to find another. If you choose Show All Pictures, you can look at all the other icons Access has to offer.

6. Enter a name for the new control and click Finish.

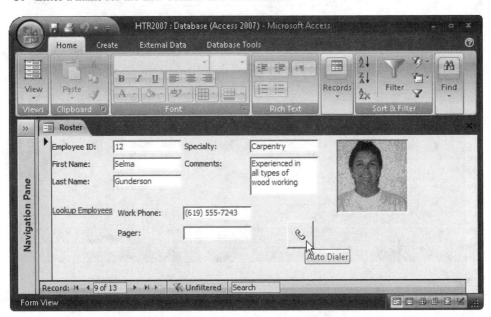

When you click the button in Form view, the AutoDialer dialog box opens. If you have moved the cursor to a telephone number field before clicking the button, the number appears in the box. If not, you can enter a number in the empty Number box. Choose OK to dial the number.

Create a Hierarchical Form

A hierarchical form usually consists of a main form and one or more subforms. The main form shows data from records on the "one" side of a one-to-many relationship; the subforms show related data from records on the "many" side. You can use the Form Wizard to help you create the form and subform at the same time or, if you already have the subform designed separately, you can simply add it to the main form design.

Use the Form Wizard

You can create a form and a subform at the same time using the Form Wizard by choosing fields from related tables. For example, to create a hierarchical form showing the list of work orders currently active for each customer, choose fields from both tables. The Form Wizard will figure out how the tables are related, and decide which data goes in the main form and which in the subform.

To create the Workorders By Customer hierarchical form, do the following:

1. Start the Form Wizard with the Customers table and in the first dialog box choose the Customer ID, First Name, Last Name, and Billing Address from the Customers table.

2. Choose the Workorders table in the Tables/Queries list and then add the Workorder Number, Bid Number, Start Date, Completion Date, Supervisor, Material Cost, and Labor Cost fields. Click Next.

3. The second dialog box (see Figure 10-12) asks how you want to view the data—in other words, which records should go in the main form and which in the subform. Access has assumed that the Workorders data (on the "many" side of the relationship) goes in the subform. The other two options in the dialog box let you specify whether the data is to be arranged as a single form with a subform or as two separate forms linked by a common field value.

10

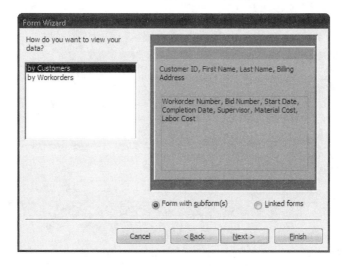

FIGURE 10-12   Creating a form with a subform.

4. Accept the default options and click Next. The next dialog box offers two layouts for the subform: Tabular or Datasheet. Choose Datasheet and click Next.

5. Choose the style for the form in the next dialog box.

6. Enter the name **Workorders by Customer** for the main form, leave the default name for the subform, then click Finish.

Figure 10-13 shows the completed hierarchical form with a few modifications such as a title in the form header. The columns in the subform also have been resized to fit the screen. You can

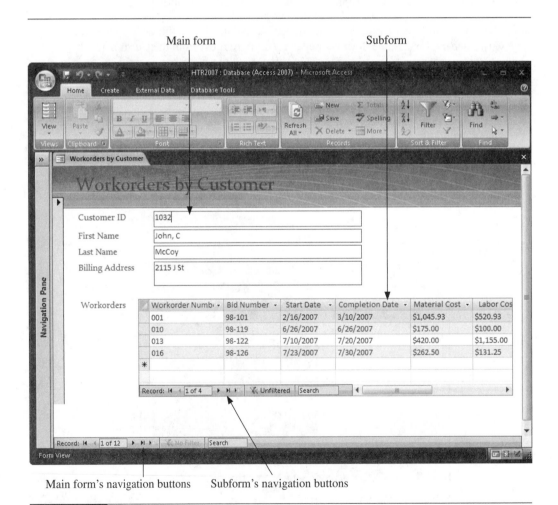

FIGURE 10-13   The completed hierarchical form.

modify the subform in place. To modify the subform design, open the main form in Design view and click the subform selector or any of the controls in the subform. Modify the subform and its controls the same as in the main form.

Use the Subform Wizard

You can use the Subform Wizard to create and insert either a new subform or an existing subform into a main form. To use the wizard to add the Workorders Subform to a form based on the Employees table, do the following:

1. Create a new form named Workorders by Supervisor based on the Employees table.

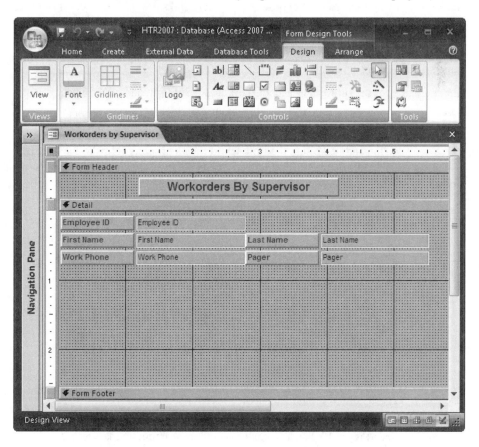

2. Make sure the Control Wizards command is pressed in and in the Controls group, click the Subform/Subreport command.

3. Click in the form design and draw an outline where you want the subform. Usually you will want the subform to span the width of the detail section in the form below the information in the main form. Once the wizard starts, do one of the following:

■ If you are creating a new subform, click "Using existing tables and queries" and click Next. Then choose from the Tables/Queries list and fields lists just as when creating a regular form with the Form Wizard. Click Next.

■ If you have already created and saved the form you want to insert, choose Use an existing form and select Workorders Subform from the drop-down list, then click Next.

4. In the next dialog box, you can choose from a list of links provided by Access or define your own. If you choose to define your own, the dialog box includes boxes where you can choose the fields that link the main form to the subform. Choose the Employee ID field from the Workorder by Supervisor form and Supervisor from the Workorders Subform, then click Next.

5. Enter a name for the subform or accept Workorders Subform and click Finish.

6. Open the property sheet and click the subform border (not the label), if not already selected.

7. Click the Data tab and make sure the Link Child Fields property refers to the foreign key in the subform and the Link Master Fields property refers to the linking field in the main form.

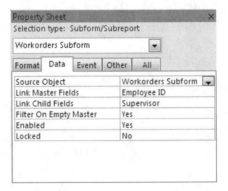

8. Delete Supervisor from the subform and move the other controls to fill the space.

9. Switch to Form view and double-click the column dividers in the subform to resize the columns (see Figure 10-14). You can also drag the column dividers to get the size you want.

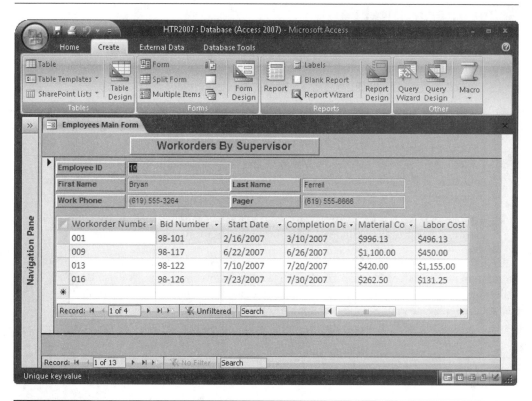

FIGURE 10-14 The Workorders by Supervisor form with a subform.

How to ... Add a Subform Without the Wizard

If you have already created and saved the form you want to insert into the main form as a subform, the easiest way to insert it is to drag it to the form design from the Navigation Pane. To do this, open the main form in Design view and select the subform in the Navigation Pane and drag it to the lower part detail section in the main form. As you drag the form name, it becomes a subform icon. After placing the subform, check the Source Object and linking properties as before.

Use the Hierarchical Form

To move from the main form to the subform in Form view, click in the subform, usually in a record selector or an editable area. To return to the main form, click an editable control or its label in the main form. When you are working in Navigation mode, special key combinations move the cursor from the subform back to the main form; for example:

- **CTRL-TAB**   Moves the cursor through the sequence of editable controls in the main form, then moves to the first record in the subform. Pressing the combination again moves to the first control of the next record in the main form.

- **CTRL-SHIFT-TAB**   Moves the cursor to the previous control in the main form or, if anywhere in the subform, it moves the cursor to the last control in the tab order of the main form.

- **CTRL-SHIFT-HOME**   Moves the cursor to the first editable field in the main form even if it was pressed while the cursor was in the subform.

Each form has its own set of navigation buttons that you can use to move among the records. The subform also has a vertical scroll bar to move other records into view. You can add new records, or edit or delete existing records in either the main form or the subform using the standard data entry techniques. You can also sort records and set filters to limit records in either the main form or the subform using standard sorting and filtering methods.

Make sure the cursor is in the right place—in the main form or the subform—before you try to add or delete records.

Modify a Subform

The complete subform design is included with the main form design. You can make changes to it in place. Select the control in the subform that you want to change and change as usual. If you want to work on the subform in its own window, select the subform control and on the Design tab in the Tools group, click Subform in New Window to work on the subform in a larger environment. You can also right-click the subform control and choose Subform in New Window in the Shortcut menu.

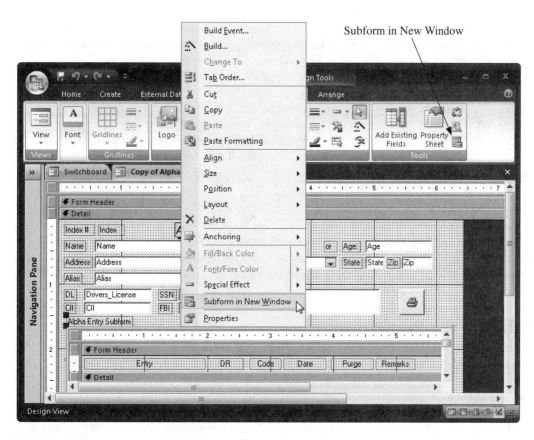

Subform in New Window

The subform control in the main form is a separate control and has different properties than the subform object itself. To select the subform control, click on one of the subform boundaries. To select the subform object for making changes in the subform itself, click the form selector for the subform.

Add Custom User Guidance

You have already seen some of the ways you can get help from Access. When you move the mouse pointer over a ribbon command, a ControlTip then pops up displaying the name of the command—often with additional information. The status bar displays messages related to the current activity or object, including the description you entered for the fields in your table design. When you design your own application, there might be times when a quick reminder can help with entering data, creating a filter, or printing a report. Access lets you create your own custom tips and status bar messages as properties of a form or report.

The ControlTip Text property specifies the message that appears when you rest the mouse pointer over a control in the form. Short tips are best but you can enter up to 255 characters. To create a ControlTip, select the control and type the message in the ControlTip Text property box on the Other tab.

A status bar message is a good way to display instructions for entering data in a control or explaining the options in an option group. Status Bar Text is a control property for any control on a form that you select. The message displays when the control gets focus. To specify a message to display in the status bar, type the text in the Status Bar Text property box on the Other tab. Again you can enter up to 255 characters but the amount of text displayed is limited by the space across the status bar.

Add Data Validation

Access offers several ways to validate or restrict data that is entered in forms. You can create controls such as check boxes that limit the data to Yes/No values or a list box that requires a value be picked from the list. You can also set certain form and control properties that will do the job.

Validate with Properties

When you designed your tables, you set field properties that would help ensure valid data. You created input masks, entered validation rules, and specified default values for some of the fields. This is the preferred way to validate data because you must do it only once. Any bound control that you add to a form inherits the properties you set in the table design. If you wait and add the validations and restrictions to a form, you must do it for every form that refers to that data.

However, there might be times when you want to superimpose more validation in the form. For example, you might want to display different error messages when the data is invalid or prevent entering data in a field altogether. If you want to validate unbound controls, you must do it in the form design because they have no ties to a table. The validation rules for controls in a form are created just the same as for a field in table design.

You can combine property settings to accomplish specific purposes. For example, if you want the form to be read-only, set Allow Edits, Allow Additions, and Allow Deletions to No.

NOTE   *If you have set one of these properties in the table design and set the same property to a different value in the form design, the bound control property in the form overrides the field property.*

The Enabled property determines whether a control can have focus. The Locked property determines whether data can be changed in Form view. Combining the two settings for a control can create custom results as shown in Table 10-1.

Enabled Setting	Locked Setting	Results
Yes	Yes	Control can receive focus. The data is displayed normally and can be copied but not edited.
Yes	No	Control can receive focus. Use this combination to allow editing of objects in unbound object frames. The data is displayed normally and can be copied or edited.
No	Yes	Control cannot receive focus. Data is displayed normally but cannot be copied or edited.
No	No	Control cannot receive focus. Control and data both appear dimmed and are disabled.

TABLE 10-1   Combining Enabled and Locked Properties

You can also combine the Enabled and Tab Stop properties. If you set Enabled to Yes and Tab Stop to No, users cannot select the control by pressing TAB but can still select it by clicking the control or its label.

Validate with Events

Attaching macros or event procedures to form and control event properties can give you additional flexibility and power over data entry. For example, you can require that at least two of three fields must be filled in before you can save the record. You would also use an event procedure if the validation refers to controls on other forms or if the control contains a function.

If you want to validate the data before the whole record is updated, add the procedure to a form event. To validate the data before moving to the next control, add the procedure to a control event. Table 10-2 shows a few of the form and control events that can be used for data validation.

See Chapter 15 for more information about events and the sequence of their occurrence. You will also see how to create the macros that will validate the data.

Event	Description
Before Update (form)	Rule enforced before saving new or changed data in a record
On Delete (form)	Rule enforced before deleting a record
Before Update (control)	Rule enforced before saving new or changed data in a control
On Exit (control)	Rule enforced before leaving the control

TABLE 10-2   Data Validation Events

Chapter 11

Create and Customize Reports and Subreports

How to…

■ Create and save a new report design

■ Preview and print the report

■ Modify the report design

■ Sort and group records in the report

■ Add a subreport

■ Design a multiple-column report

■ Print mailing labels

In this chapter I introduce you to the Police database, a sample database that might be used 24 hours a day by a local police department. It is a user-interactive system that tracks incidents and maintains records of all persons who report or who are involved in activities that require police attention. The database consists of four tables:

■ **Alpha Card**   Maintains a list of all persons who have filed a report, called in an incident, or might be a suspect in an incident.

■ **Alpha Entry**   Contains details of all the reports and is related to records in the Alpha Card table.

■ **Explanations**   Contains a more detailed version of the police shorthand Entry descriptions.

■ **Penal Codes**   Provides a lookup list and contains the Penal code numbers with their descriptions.

The Police database example provides the opportunity to see how to create simple and more complex reports. It is important to the department to be able to summarize crimes and maintain records of the incidents. So let's get right to work creating reports that are useful for the Bayview City Police Department.

Start a New Report

Although you create Access reports using many of the same techniques you use for forms, the design concepts of forms are different from that of reports. Forms deal with data and the processes of data management such as data entry, validation, and retrieval. Reports, on the other hand, deal with information derived from the data and are more widely distributed, often to people who might never have seen a computer. Therefore, reports must be self-explanatory and focus on the purpose of the report in plain language.

The Access Report Wizards help you prepare many types of reports, from simple ones that contain complete information gathered from one or more tables to reports that calculate and summarize lots of information and present it in a variety of visual representations, including charts and graphs. You can also create multiple column reports to be used for printing mailing labels of all kinds or use Access tables for mail merge applications.

As with most Access activities, there are several ways to start a new report design. Depending on the type of report you need, the Reports group on the Create tab has many tools to start a new report:

- Use the simple Report tool to build a report based all the fields in the selected table or query. The new report is displayed in Layout view.

- Use the Report Wizard to help create your report.

- Create your own design with the Report Design command based on the table or query selected in the Navigation Pane. The report opens in Design view.

- Create a report for printing labels. This command launches the Label Wizard that we will look at later in this chapter.

- Click Blank Report to start with a new report. This opens a blank report in Layout view with the Field List pane at the right:

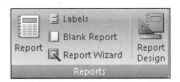

The next step is to choose the method you want to use from the Reports group and then select a table or query as the basis for the report, if desired. When you use the Report tool, Access uses the most recently selected table or query as the basis for the report. If you choose the wizard without first selecting a table or query as the basis, you can select one from the first wizard dialog box.

Use the Report Tool

The Report Tool creates a quick report of all the data in a table or query and displays it in Layout view. The report isn't fancy, but it is useful for checking and verifying the data in your table or query. When you print the report, the data appears in a tabular layout resembling the datasheet itself.

In Layout view, you can make some changes to the report design. For example, you can adjust column widths, rearrange columns, and even add grouping levels and totals. You can also add fields to the report design and set properties for the report and its controls.

After creating the report, you can either print it as it appears or switch to Design view and make further changes. To close the report without saving the design, right-click the document tab and choose Close in the shortcut menu. Respond No when asked if you want to save the changes.

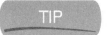

If you have converted a database from an earlier version of Access, Layout view is not available for the reports. To change that, open the report in Design view and change the Allow Layout property to Yes.

Use the Report Wizard

The Report Wizard behaves much like the Form Wizard. It presents you with a series of dialog boxes that guide you through the design process. Most of the dialog boxes present the same kinds of options, but the Report Wizard includes a couple of new ones that let you choose the sorting, grouping, and summarizing features.

In your first example, use the Report Wizard to create a report based on the Alpha Entry by Code Query, which limits the data in the Alpha Entry table of the Police database to only those with a numeric incident code. This screens out any employment fingerprint and traffic collision reports that do not involve a crime and therefore don't have an incident code.

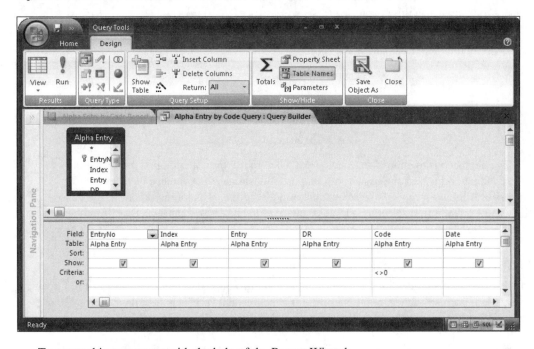

To create this new report with the help of the Report Wizard:

1. Select the Alpha Entry by Code Query in the query group in the Navigation Pane. Then, on the Create tab in the Reports group, click the Report Wizard command.

2. In the first dialog box, choose the fields you want to include in the report from the tables and queries in the database. Select all the fields in the Alpha Entry by Code Query and click Next.

Add grouping field   Clear grouping field

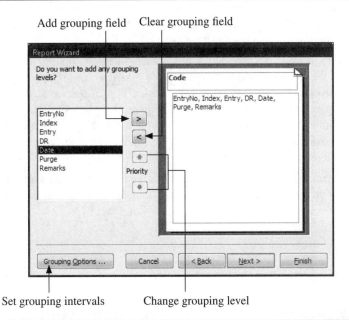

Set grouping intervals   Change grouping level

FIGURE 11-1   Choosing code as the grouping level.

3. In the second dialog box, the wizard asks if you want to group the records by any of the field values. Select Code as the name of the field by which you want to group and click the right arrow (>), as shown in Figure 11-1.

■ If you change your mind, select the field name and click the left arrow (<) to remove the group designation. The up and down arrows near Priority change the grouping order level.

■ If you are grouping on a field with numeric values, you can group by an interval such as 50 or 100. Click Grouping Options and choose from the drop-down list in the Grouping Intervals dialog box.

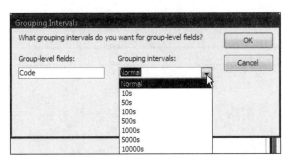

■ If one of the fields you are grouping on is a number or currency field, the Summary Options button becomes available in the next dialog box. You'll learn more about adding summaries in a later section.

4. Click Next to move to the next dialog box, which, like the grouping level dialog box, is unique to the Report Wizard. This dialog box asks if you want to sort your records within the groups in other than primary key order. The groups are automatically sorted in ascending order by the group field value. Figure 11-2 shows a sort specified by date in ascending order. You can sort on up to four fields by clicking the arrow next to the sort box and choosing the field from the list. If you want the sort in descending order, click the Ascending button to the right of the sort box. When you are done, click Next.

5. In the next dialog box (see Figure 11-3), select the layout that you want for the report and for the print orientation. Choose a format and look at the sample in the left pane. For this example, select Stepped and Portrait and then click Next.

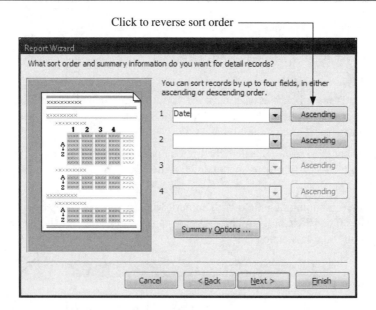

FIGURE 11-2 Specifying the record sort order.

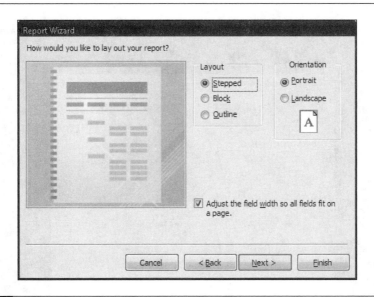

FIGURE 11-3   Choosing the report layout and orientation.

If you have selected a lot of fields, you might want to change the print orientation to landscape.

11

6. The next wizard dialog box offers 25 different styles from which to choose.

7. In the final dialog box, enter **Alpha Entry by Code Report** as the report name and click Finish.

Figure 11-4 shows a Print Preview of the Alpha Entry by Code Report generated by the Report Wizard. If some of the fields in the report seem incomplete, you can switch to the report Design view and resize them to fit the contents.

If you also want to see an interpretation of the code with the code number in the group header, add the Description field from the Penal Codes table to the original query. Then with the report in Design view, add a new text box control with the Description field as the control source.

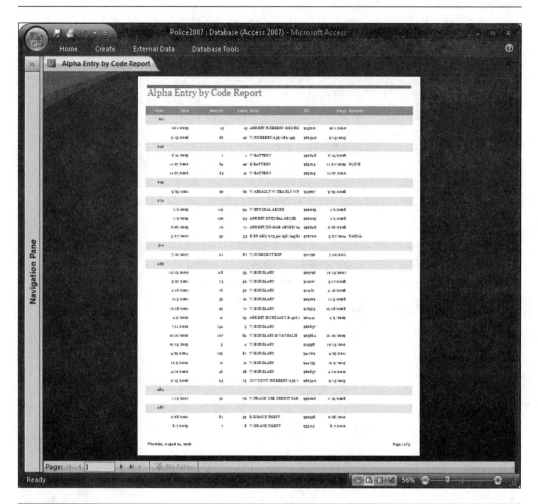

FIGURE 11-4 The Alpha Entry by Code Report in Print Preview.

Preview and Print the Report

When the Report Wizard has finished creating the report design, you can go directly to the Report Design view to make changes or preview the report as it will be printed. If you have not used the Report Wizard or you just want to preview an existing report, right-click the desired report name in the Reports group in the Navigation Pane and choose Print Preview in the shortcut menu.

If the report is already open in some view, right-click the document tab and choose Print Preview in the shortcut menu.

Work in the Print Preview Window

The Access Print Preview window (refer to Figure 11-4) offers all kinds of ways to view the report including moving around, within, and among pages, looking at several pages at once, and changing the magnification so that you can see the details more clearly.

The horizontal and vertical scroll bars enable you to move about on the current page. The page navigation buttons at the bottom of the Print Preview window let you move among pages in the report. Click one of the buttons to move to the first, previous, next, or last page of the report. You can also enter the page number in the page number box and press ENTER to move to a specific page.

To close the Print Preview window, do one of the following:

- On the Print Preview tab in the Close Preview group, click Close Print Preview.
- Press C or ESC.
- Right-click the document tab and choose Close in the shortcut menu.

View Multiple Pages

Previewing several pages at once can help you find pages that have too much white space or another format error. Using the Print Preview commands, you can view one or two pages adjusted to fit the screen or up to 12 pages arranged in three rows of four pages each.

To view one complete page at a time, do one of the following:

- On the Print Preview tab in the Preview group, click the One Page command.
- Right-click and choose One Page from the shortcut menu.

To view two or more complete pages adjusted to fit the screen, right-click in the preview, click Zoom and choose Fit in the drop-down list and then on the Print Preview tab in the Preview group, do one of the following:

- Click the Two Pages command.
- Click the More Pages command and drag the mouse pointer over the grid to select the number of pages and the arrangement you want. You have a choice of 4, 8, or 12 pages.

You can also right-click in the Print Preview and choose Multiple Pages from the shortcut menu, then drag the mouse pointer over the grid to select the number of pages and the arrangement you want to see.

11

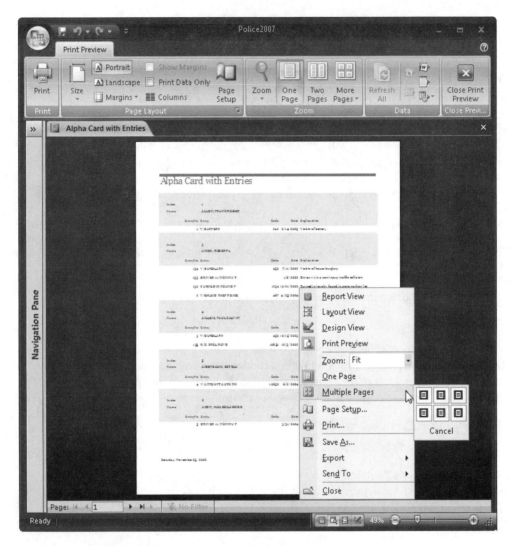

To return to previewing a single page, click the One Page command in the Preview group.

Change the Magnification

When you first open the Print Preview window, the report is automatically displayed to fit a single page vertically on the screen. You can increase or decrease this degree of magnification to almost any value or ask Access to adjust the report to fit on the screen. To change the magnification, click the arrow under the Zoom command and choose a percentage between 10 percent and 1000 percent from the list, or enter a value and press ENTER. You can also right-click in the print preview and click the Zoom to toggle between Fit and the most recent magnification you set.

NOTE   *You can also drag the Zoom control at the right end of the status bar to get just the right magnification.*

NOTE   *The number of pages you choose to preview at once determines the degree of magnification when you choose Fit.*

When the mouse pointer passes over the report preview, it changes to a magnifying glass with a plus sign (+), which you can click to zoom in and out in a particular area in the report. This alternates the preview between Fit and the last percentage you have chosen. When the glass shows a minus sign (−), clicking zooms out, making the preview less magnified; clicking the magnifying glass with a plus sign (+) zooms in on the area where the pointer was when you clicked it.

Print the Report

You can print the report from any view of the report, including Design view, and without even opening the report.

To print the report from the Print Preview, do one of the following:

- On the Print Preview tab click the Print command.
- Right-click in the report and choose Print from the shortcut menu.
- Click the Microsoft Office button and choose Print in the context menu.
- Press CTRL-P.

All these methods open the Print dialog box where you can change some of the print options, such as the margins, or choose to print the data only without the titles and other features.

If the report is not open in Print Preview, right-click the report name in the Navigation Pane and choose Print in the shortcut menu. This method sends the report directly to the printer.

If you want to change any of the page options such as the margins, the page layout, the printer selection, the number of columns on the page, or the page size, use the commands in the Page Layout group on the Page Setup tab. You can make these changes from Layout or Design view. The Page Layout group offers common settings for margins and paper size while in the Page Setup dialog box, you can specify custom settings. After setting the page specifications, you can choose the print options such as number of copies and the range of pages to print.

Change Page Settings

When you switch to Print Preview, the Print Preview tab is active with several Page Layout commands. You can change many of the settings from other views but if you use Print Preview, you can see how the changes affect the report. You can scroll through the pages to make sure the changes are appropriate.

Some of the Page Layout commands you can use to change the report layout include the following:

- ▪ Size that displays a gallery of letter and envelope sizes from which to choose.
- ▪ Portrait and Landscape change the orientation.
- ▪ Margins offers a gallery of preset vertical and horizontal margin settings including Normal, Wide, and Narrow as well as the last custom setting.
- ▪ Show Margins shows or hides the margin spacing in Design or Layout view.
- ▪ Print Data Only leaves out the labels and other unbound controls.
- ▪ Columns opens the Columns tab in the Page Setup dialog box where you can specify a columnar report. This is used mostly for printing mailing labels that come in predesigned sheets. Access offers ready made layouts for most of the commercially available label sheets. More about columns in reports in section, Design a Multiple-Column Report.
- ▪ Page Setup opens a Page Setup dialog box.

The page layout settings are stored with the report; they need to be set only once to be in effect every time you print the report.

You can also use the Page Setup dialog box to make changes in the report page settings. You must be in Print preview to open the Page Setup from the report. Click the Page Setup command in the Page layout group or right-click in the report and choose Page Setup in the shortcut menu. The Page Setup dialog box has three tabs: Print Options, Page, and Columns.

- ▪ Click the Print Options tab to set the width of each of the four page margins and choose whether to print only the data, without any of the labels or other unbound objects.

■ Click the Page tab to set the orientation of the print on the page (portrait or landscape), select the paper size and source, and select a different printer if you have more than one in your system. The choice of paper sources depends on the printer you are using.

If you want to print using a printer other than the default printer, click Use Specific Printer, then click the Printer button. This opens a dialog box that displays a list of the printers currently installed in the system. Select a different printer and click OK to return to the Page Setup dialog box.

After you have made all the desired changes to the page setup, click OK to return to the previous view of the report or the Database window.

You can also open the Page Setup dialog box from the Print dialog box but there are only two tabs in that version: Print Options and Columns.

The Column tab options are explained in the section Design a Multiple-Column Report, found later in this chapter.

Modify the Report Design

Working in the report Design view is almost identical to working in the form Design view; the Design ribbon is the same, except for a new group of commands in the Grouping & Sorting group. You use the same control commands, select the controls the same way, and set the control properties with the same property sheets. The method you use to open a report in Design view depends on where you start:

■ If the report is not open, right-click the report name in the Navigation Pane and choose Design View from the shortcut menu.

■ If the report is open, right-click the document tab and choose Design View in the shortcut menu.

■ If the report is open, you can also click the View command on the Home tab and choose Design View in the context menu.

Examine the Report Sections

The wizard automatically adds page header and footer sections when it creates a report. The Page Header section contains information that is to be printed at the top of each page, such as the field names used as column headings. The Page Footer section contains information to be printed at the bottom of each page, such as the current date and the page number. To toggle the header and footer sections in and out of the design, right-click in the report and choose Page Header/Footer in the shortcut menu.

The Report Header and Footer sections contain information to be printed only once at the beginning or the end of the report. The Detail section contains the bulk of the data in the report. Add report headers and footers the same way you would add page sections: right-click in the report and choose Report Header/Footer in the shortcut menu. Choose again to delete both the sections. If there are any controls in one of the sections you try to delete, Access displays a message asking if you want to delete all the controls in the sections. Click Yes to delete them or No to abandon the deletion.

The group header and footer sections, which are optional, contain information to be printed at the top and bottom of each group of records. These sections are used when you group the records by the values in a specific field, such as by Code in the Alpha Entry by Code Query shown earlier.

You select a section in a report design the same way as in a form design by using one of the following methods:

■ Click the section selector at the left of the section label line.

■ Click anywhere in the section label line.

■ Click anywhere in the section, outside of any control.

To change the size of a report section, select the section and drag the lower boundary up or down. The report and page sections both come in pairs, so if you want to remove one, just reduce its height to zero; the section must be empty before you can do that. When you add a group, you don't need to use both the header and footer. You can choose whether you want a group header or footer, or both, by setting the group properties.

Set Report and Section Properties

Property sheets are opened and used in a report design the same as in a form design, and many of the properties are also the same. Some additional properties that relate to the printed report do not apply to forms. Some of the special properties are listed next.

- When you create a report with a special title page and you don't want to print the page header or footer information on the page, set the report's Page Header and Page Footer properties to Not With Rpt Hdr. Then, select the report header section and set its Force New Page property to After Section in order to continue printing the rest of the report on a new page.

- If you want the report footer information printed on a separate page at the end of the report, set both the Page Header and Page Footer properties to Not With Rpt Hdr/Ftr and then set the report footer Force New Page property to Before Section.

- When you create a report based on a table or query that was saved with a sort order or a filter, the report inherits both properties. If you look at the report properties, you can see the Filter and Order By expressions that were saved with the table. In addition, the Order By On Load property is set to Yes and the records are sorted by the inherited sort order. The inherited filter is not applied. To change the report or section filter and sort properties, do the following:

  - To apply the filter, set the Filter On Load property to Yes.

  - To remove both the filter and the sort, change the Filter On Load and the Order By On Load property settings to No.

  - To change the filter or sort order, type a new expression in the Filter or Order By property box and then set both the Filter On Load and Order By On Load properties to Yes.

  - To suppress printing a section that contains information, set the section's Visible property to No.

Each of the report sections also has a list of properties that you can set to get just the appearance and behavior you want. For example, you can set a different color or add a special effect.

Page headers and footers have no additional properties but the remaining sections—report header and footer, group header and footer, and detail sections—share several other properties. For example, Force New Page specifies whether the section is to be printed on a separate page rather than the current page. To print a complete section all on one page, set the Keep Together property to Yes. To allow a section to expand or shrink vertically to fit the data, set Can Grow and Can Shrink to Yes.

The group header section has one more property that is unique to that section: Repeat Section, which is used to specify whether a group header is repeated on the next page or column when a group spans more than one page or column. The default setting is No. If the group header contains column headings and other relevant information, you might want to change it to Yes so that it will print at the top of each page or column.

Change the Report Style

When you use the Report Wizard to create a new report, the fifth dialog box offers a list of styles to choose from.

If you find you don't like the style you selected, you can change it with the report in Design view. Click the report selector if you want to reformat the entire report or one of the sections to reformat only that section. Then on the Arrange tab in the AutoFormat group, click the AutoFormat command and choose AutoFormat Wizard from the gallery. Click the Options button to apply the font, color, and border formatting selectively. By default, all three options are checked. If you clear them one at a time, you can see the difference in the displayed sample.

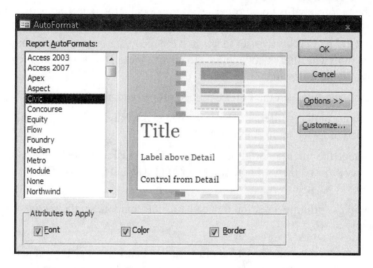

Add Page Numbers and Date/Time Controls

The Report Wizard automatically adds page numbers and the current date/time to the Page Footer section of the Alpha Card with Entries report. The page number is an unbound text box control that you can add to a report design and format in several ways. The date/time field is also an unbound control and is based on your current system's date/time settings.

Add a Page Number

If you have not used the Report Wizard, but want to add a page number to your report, do the following:

1. On the Design tab in the Controls group, click the Insert Page Numbers command to open the Page Numbers dialog box.

2. Choose Page N to show only the page number. Or choose Page N of M, where N is the current page number and M is the total number of pages.

3. Choose to see the page number at the top or bottom of the page.

4. Choose the Alignment from the drop-down list: left, center, or right. If the report prints on both sides of the page, you can also choose Inside or Outside.

5. Clear Show Number on First Page box to prevent printing the page number on the title page. Then click Ok.

Add a Date/Time Control

To add the current date and time to the report, on the Design tab in the Controls group, click the Date & Time command and then choose the format you want from the Date and Time dialog box, the same as with forms. Refer to Chapter 10 for more details.

Add Page Breaks

If left to its own devices, Access starts a new page when a page fills up. But you can add a page break control within a section to tell Access where you want a new page to begin. For example, imagine that a report title and an abstract of the report's contents are all in the Report Header section, but you want them printed on separate pages. To accomplish this, on the Design tab in the Controls group, click the Page Break command and place the control in the report header section between the controls you want on the first page and those you want on the second page. Access displays the position of the page break as a short dotted line at the left edge in the report design.

Save the Report Design

When you create a report with the help of the Report Wizard, the report is saved for you with the name you entered in the final wizard dialog box. If you don't use the wizard, you should make a practice of saving the report design frequently as you refine it. This guards against catastrophe and gives you a recent starting point if something goes wrong.

11

To save the report design, do one of the following:

- Right-click the report document tab and choose Save in the shortcut menu.
- Click Save on the Quick Access toolbar.
- Press CTRL-S.
- Click the Microsoft Office button and click Save.

If this is the first time you have saved the report, you are prompted to enter a name for it in the Save As dialog box.

There are two other options on the Microsoft Office button menu when saving a report design with the Microsoft Office button:

- **Save As**   Opens the same Save As dialog box, where you can choose to save the report design to the current database with the same name or a new name.
- **E-mail**   Opens the Send Object To dialog box where you locate the folder in which you want to save the report and enter a report name. See Chapter 18 for more information about exporting Access reports and other objects.

To close the report, right-click the report document tab and choose Close in the shortcut menu.

Filter, Sort, and Group Records in Layout View

One of the most useful features of Access reports is the ability to sort and group records based on the value in one or more of the fields. After doing so, you can summarize the information in many ways to illustrate trends and draw conclusions.

If you have a report based on a query that sets criteria for the records, you can use that filter or set a new one later in Layout view. You can apply the filter by setting the report's Filter On Load property to Yes while in Design view. But you can also filter the records while you are viewing the report in Report or Layout view.

You can also change the sort order that the report has inherited from the underlying record source. Records can be grouped on Text, Number, Date/Time, Currency, or AutoNumber field types, or expressions containing those field values. Access will nest up to ten group levels, each group subordinate to the previous group.

Depending on the data type of the group-on field, there are different ways to group the records. For example, if the field is a Text field, you can group the entire value or the first few characters of the value. Date/Time values can be grouped by each value or any time increment of the value: year, day, hour, minute, and so on.

Filter Records in Layout View

To filter on the value in a single field, right-click the value and choose from the shortcut menu. For example, filter the Alpha Card Report to show only reports from the selected city. Right-click the City field that contains that name and then choose Equals from the shortcut menu. If you want all of the reports except those from the selected city, choose Does Not Equal in the shortcut menu. If you filter on a number or date field, you will see other options for criteria. These are the same choices you saw in Chapter 6 when filtering table.

You can create a more detailed filter by using the Text Filters command in the drop-down menu. Rest the mouse pointer on Text Filters to see a list of options, each of which opens a dialog box where you can specify the filter criteria. These are the same options you see if you right-click the field and choose Text (or Date or Number) Filters in the shortcut menu.

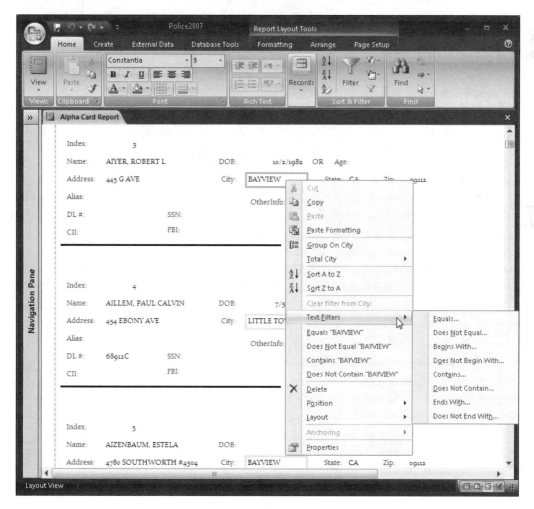

If you want to filter on the values in more than one field in the report, you need to use the Filter tool as follows:

1. Select one of the text box controls in the report layout and then on the Home tab in the Sort & Filter group, click the Filter command. A drop-down menu appears listing all the values in the selected field in the report, including blanks, with check marks indicating they will all appear in the report.

2. Click the Select All button to clear the check marks from all the values. Then check the boxes for the values you want in the report and click OK. This menu also gives you a choice of sorting on the value in the field by which you are filtering.

To remove the filter, select one of the filtered fields and click the Filter command again. In the drop-down menu, click the Clear filter from *field name* button. You can also simply right-click the field and choose the same command in the shortcut menu. If you want to change the filter select the filtered field again and click the Filter command and make the changes in the drop-down menu.

Change the Sort Order

You can remove or reapply the sort order the report has inherited from the record source by setting the report's Order By On property. Choose No to remove the sort order or Yes to reapply it. If you want to use the inherited sort order, you must also set the Filter On property to No.

You can also change the sort order in Report or Layout view to a different field or to more than one field.

Work in Layout View

To sort by field values while in Layout view, right-click any value in the field and choose the Sort option in the shortcut menu. If the field contains text, your options are Sort A to Z or Sort Z to A. A date field has the options to Sort Oldest to Newest or Sort Newest to Oldest. Numbers can be sorted Smallest to Largest or Largest to Smallest.

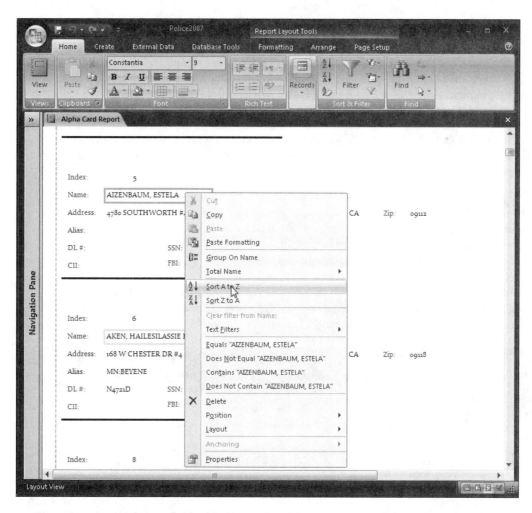

You can sort on only one field with this method. If you want to sort on more that one field, use the Order By property or the Group, Sort and Total pane as described in section "Adding Group Sections."

Set the Report Sort Property

To sort the records in the report in a different order than the underlying table or query, set the report's Order By On property to Yes and its Order By property as follows:

■   To sort the records by values in one field in ascending order, type the field name enclosed in brackets followed by **ASC**; for example, **[Code] ASC**.

■ To sort the records by values in one field in descending order, type the field name enclosed in brackets followed by **DESC**; for example, **[LastName] DESC**.

■ To sort the records by values in more than one field in ascending or descending order, type each field name enclosed in brackets followed by **ASC** or **DESC** and separated by commas. For example, the setting **[Code] ASC, [Date] DESC** sorts first by the Code field in ascending order, then by the Last Name field in descending order.

If you don't specify ASC or DESC, Access automatically sorts in ascending order. The new setting overrides the inherited sort order without affecting the data source. Be sure to set the Order By On property to Yes to effect the new sort order.

Add Group Sections

To illustrate grouping records in a report, create a new report based on a query that extracts only those records from the Alpha Entry table with a value in the Code field. This eliminates Alpha Entry records not related to a potentially criminal offense.

The Alpha Entry by Code query contains the expression <>0 in the Criteria row of the Code column in the grid. Create a new report based on this query in Design view and after dragging the field names from the list to the detail section of the new Entries by Year report, you can proceed to group the records by the year the incident was reported.

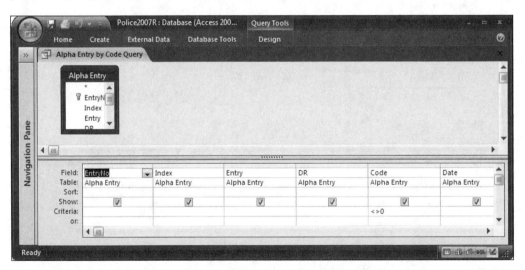

To add a group section to this report, open the report in Layout view. Then on the Formatting tab in the Grouping & Totals group, click the Group & Sort command. This opens the Group,

Sort, and Total pane below the report layout, which you can use to set the sort order and to choose the field or expression on which you want to group. You can also specify totals with this pane.

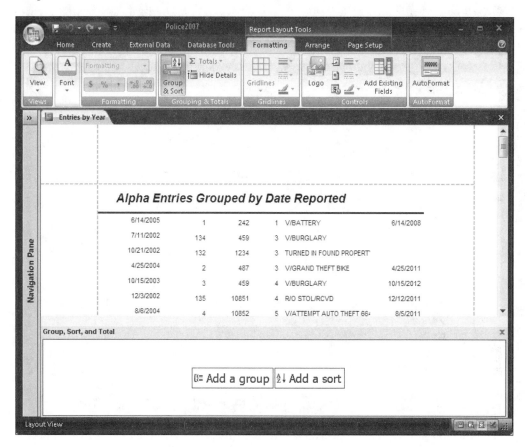

To group the records, do the following:

1. Click the Add a Group button to add a new list to the pane that can display a list of available fields.

2. Select Date in the drop-down menu of fields to group by.

3. Click the "from oldest to newest" button and then click More.

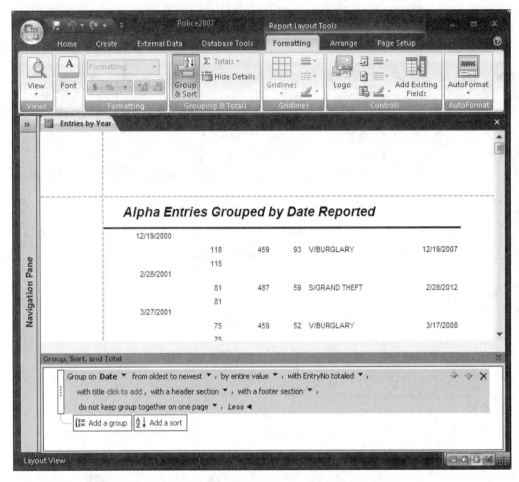

4. To set the grouping interval, click the by entire value down arrow and check by year in the drop-down list and click in an empty area in the Group, Sort and Total pane to close the list.

5. Click the **with no totals** down arrow and select EntryNo in the Total On drop-down list and accept Count Records as the Type. Then check the Show Grand Total and Show in Group Footer options. The Grand Total appears in the report footer and totals all the values from all the groups. The Show in Group Footer places the group total in the group footer.

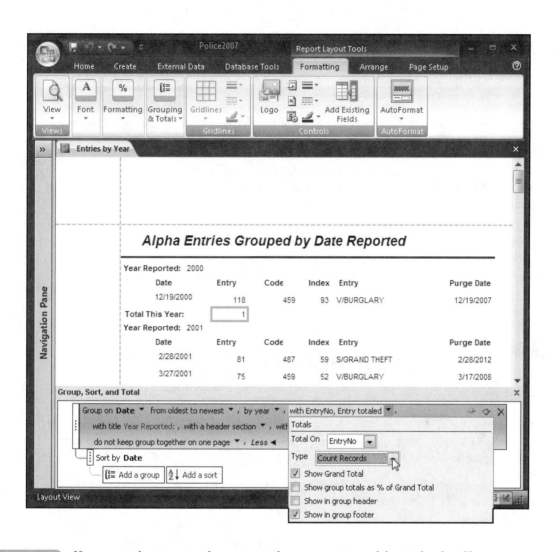

11

NOTE *If you want the group totals represented as a percentage of the total, select Show group totals as % of Grand Total.*

6. To add a special title for the field being summarized, click the blue text, "click to add" following the "with title" option and enter Year Reported: in the Zoom box and click OK.

7. Choose to include a group header and group footer, and then click Less to shrink the pane.

8. To sort the records within the group, click the Add a sort button, choose Date in the drop-down list, and keep the from oldest to newest sort order.

9. Click the Close button in the Group, Sort, and Total pane to return to the report Layout view to see the results of the grouping.

 If you want to delete the selected group level, click the Delete (X) button in the Group on pane.

Use the Label control to add the field labels to the page header section. Then set the font for these field labels to Bold. Figure 11-5 shows the completed report in Report view. You can also change the report title in the report header section.

Modify and Add Groups

To change the sort order of the records in an ungrouped report or of the groups in a grouped report, on the Formatting tab in the Sorting & Grouping group, click Sort Order command.

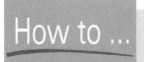 **Number Items in a Report**

Sometimes it is handy to have the items in a report numbered so you can reference each one uniquely by number; for example, in a teleconference, you would need to be sure everyone is talking about the same item. To number the items:

1. Add a calculated text box control to the detail section in a prominent position at the left of the record data.

2. Remove the new text box label.

3. Double-click the new control to open its property sheet and change the Control Source property to the expression **=1**.

4. Set the Running Sum property to Over All, which increments the calculated text box value by 1 for each record in the detail section.

This works for grouped records as well. To number the records in each group separately, add the calculated control to the detail section as previously, but set the Running Sum property to Over Group instead of Over All.

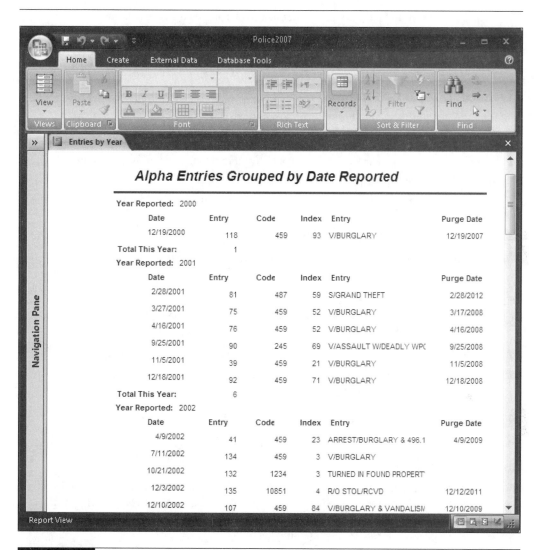

FIGURE 11-5 The Entries by Year report in Print Preview.

If you want to change the grouping levels of existing groups, click the row selector (the four vertical dots) at the right of the group you want to move. Click it again and drag the row to the desired position in the list of groupings. If the groups you move have headers or footers, Access moves them and all the controls they contain to the new positions in the report design. The controls might need some adjustment after repositioning.

To change the group-on field or expression, click the Group on down arrow and choose another field from the drop-down list or enter a different expression. If you want to add another grouping level, click the Add a group button. You can also insert a new grouping level above an existing one by clicking the row selector and dragging it up above the other level.

Add a Second Level Grouping

As an example of adding a second group level, group the Entries by Year Report by quarter within the year group by doing the following:

1. Open the Entries by Year Report in Layout view and on the Formatting tab in the Grouping & Totals group, click the Group & Sort command.

2. On the Group, Sort, and Total pane, click the Add a group and choose Date field in the drop-down list.

3. Click by Quarter and choose to group by quarter and leave the group interval at 1.

4. Click More and choose to show the group header but not the group footer.

5. Close the Group, Sort, and Total pane.

6. Switch to Design view and add an unbound text box at the left end of the detail section. Delete the new text box label then open the Property Sheet and enter the expression = **"Qtr: "& DatePart("q",[Date])** in its Control Source property box.

7. On the Format property tab, change the text box's Hide Duplicates property to Yes.

8. Save the report as Entries by Quarter and switch to Print Preview to see the changed report.

Figure 11-6 shows a preview of the report that now groups the Alpha Entry records by the year the entry was reported, and then by quarter. You could also edit the report title accordingly.

Change the Group Level

You can rearrange the property of the grouping and sorting levels with the Group, Sort, and Total pane. To move a group level up, on the Formatting tab in the Grouping and Totals group, click the Grouping command. In the Group, Sort, and Total pane, click the row you want to move then click the up arrow or down arrow in the pane title bar.

To remove the grouping level, click the row you want to delete and click the Delete (X) button at the right end of the row header.

TIP *If you want to see only the group summary data in the report, open the report in Design view. Then on the Design tab in the Grouping and Totals group, click the Hide Details command.*

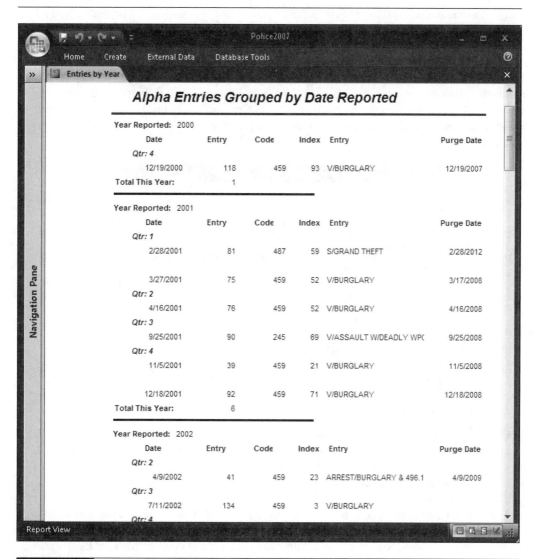

FIGURE 11-6   Previewing the Entries by Quarter report.

Create a Summary Report with the Report Wizard

The Report Wizard's summarizing capabilities are very useful when creating reports involving numeric or monetary information. When you choose to group records, the wizard makes summarizing options available with which you can compute the total value; determine the average, minimum, and maximum of the group of values. The Wizard might not create exactly the report you want to see, but it can save you a lot of time with the arithmetic.

For this example, let's return to the Home Tech Repair database, which has some currency fields that can demonstrate the summary options. Select the Workorders table in the Navigation pane and on the Create tab in the Reports group, click the Report Wizard. When you choose to group the Workorder records by Supervisor, the next dialog box in which you set the sort order now has the Summary Options button available. Clicking this button opens the Summary Options dialog box, which shows the names of all the fields in the report that contain number or currency data.

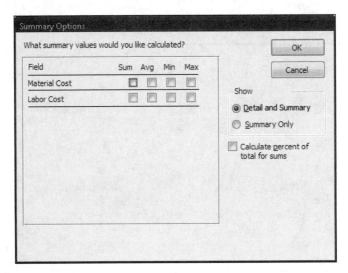

Click the check boxes for all the summary values you want the wizard to calculate for you. In the Show option group, you can choose to include the detail records with the summaries or show only the summary values. The other option, "Calculate percent of total for sums," includes the relative size of each group sum compared to the grand total, which is calculated and printed at the end of the report.

The wizard finished the report in Print Preview. Right-click the document tab and look at the report in Layout view (see Figure 11-7). The report groups the Home Tech Repair workorders by supervisor and computes the sum, average, minimum, and maximum of the Material Costs and Labor Costs for each group of workorders.

You can see that some small changes need to be made in the report. For example, you might want to format the summary values to show currency symbols and also widen some of the controls to show the entire name or value.

Incomplete labels ——————————————————— Unformatted currency fields

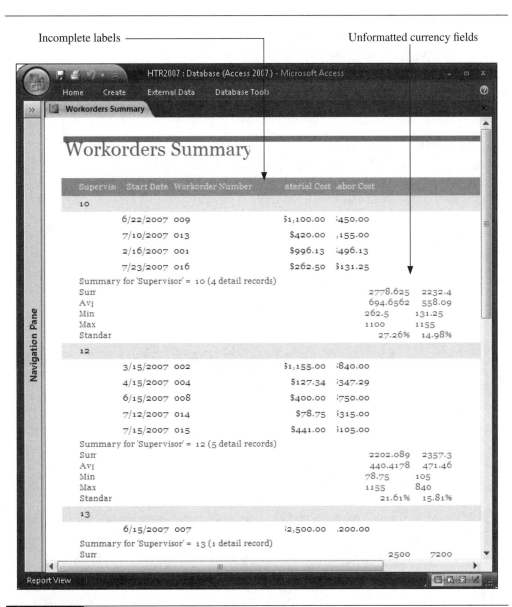

FIGURE 11-7   Summarizing Workorder costs by supervisor.

The Report Wizard also automatically counts the number of detail records in each group and displays it at the top of the summary section. The group header has a different background color to separate one supervisor's work orders from the next visually.

>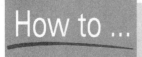
> *You might also want to replace the Supervisor ID field with the LastName field to make the report more understandable to outsiders.*

Print an Alphabetic Index

By combining the Group On and Group Interval settings, you can create an alphabetic list of items grouped by the leading character. For example, let's get back to the Police database and create a list such as that shown in Figure 11-8, do the following:

1. Select the Member List table in the Navigation Pane and on the Create tab in the Reports group, click the Blank Report command. The new report appears in Layout view.

2. Drag the LastName field from the Field List.

How to ... Hide Duplicates and Other Tips

Duplicate values appearing in the detail section can clutter up a report. For example, a report grouping the Alpha Entry records by code would show multiple records with the same code value. There are two ways to solve the problem—you can move the Code field to the group header section, where it will be printed only once, or leave it in the detail section and change a control property:

- To move the control, drag it from the detail section to the desired position in the group header.

- To leave the control in the detail section and avoid printing duplicate values, open the control property sheet and set the Hide Duplicates format property to Yes.

Two other properties are useful when printing reports containing memo fields that might contain a varying amount of data or possibly none at all. Changing the Can Shrink property to Yes will prevent blank lines when there is no value in the field. Changing Can Grow to Yes lets the field value expand as necessary.

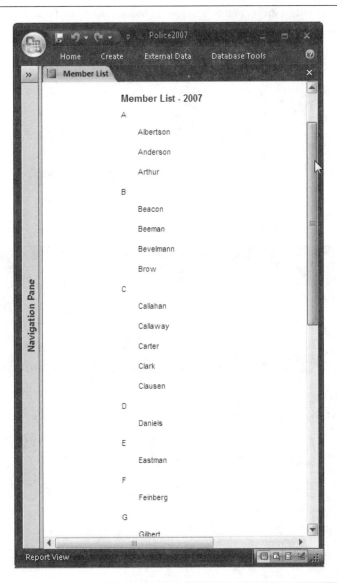

FIGURE 11-8   The Alphabetic Member list.

3. On the Formatting tab in the Grouping & Totals group, click the Group & Sort command.

4. In the Group, Sort, and Total pane, click the Add a sort button and select **LastName** as the field to group on, and choose **with A on top** in the next group setting.

5. Then click the Add a group button and again choose LastName from the drop-down list then choose following group settings:

   - ■ With A on top
   - ■ By first character
   - ■ With a header section
   - ■ Without a footer section

6. To place the initial character in the group header, add a text box control to the group header and then delete the attached label.

7. Set the new text box Control Source property to **=Left([LastName],1)**. Figure 11-9 shows the completed report design and as well as the Sorting and Grouping pane.

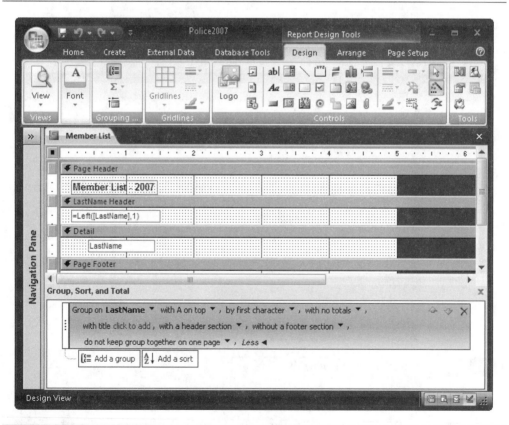

FIGURE 11-9   The Member List report in Design view.

TIP
Be careful to avoid using the word "Name" as a field name. Access reserves that word as the name of the current object. If you use the expression =Left([Name],1) in the group header, you will see "M" (the first letter of the report name) in every group header. There are many more reserved words in the Access language.

Add a Subreport

A subreport, a complete report in its own right, is inserted into another report, called the main report. A main report can be either bound or unbound. A bound main report is based on a table or query, and its subreports contain related information. For example, the main report could contain details about the year's business, while the subreport could show charts and graphs summarizing and illustrating the numbers in the main report.

An unbound main report is not based on a table or query but can serve as a container for one or more subreports. For example, you may produce an annual report with a title page containing some introductory information. This constitutes the unbound main report. The one or more subreports contain parallel information unrelated to each other but nevertheless important to the business during the previous year.

A main report can include as many subreports as necessary. You can also add up to two levels of nested subreports. A first-level subreport can contain another subreport or a subform. If the first level is a subform, it can contain only another subform, not a subreport, as the second level.

Create a Subreport with the Report Wizard

11

When you use the Report Wizard to create a report based on two or more tables or queries, you can specify which table contains the main data and which contains the subordinate data. In the example in this section, the Alpha Card table is specified as the parent table and the Alpha Entry table as the related child table. The Entry Explanation table, which is related one-to-one to the Alpha Entry table, also is included. The resulting report will show multiple Alpha Entry records for a single Alpha Card record.

To create both the report and subreport, do the following:

1. Select the Alpha Card table in the Navigation Pane and then on the Create tab in the Report group, click the Report Wizard button.

2. In the first dialog box, choose the Index and Name fields from the Alpha Card table; the EntryNo, Entry, Code, and Date fields from the Alpha Entry table; and the Explanation field from the Entry Explanation table. Click Next.

3. In the second dialog box, the wizard asks how you want to view the data. Access assumes that the parent table of the relationship is to appear as the main report. Accept the choice and click Next.

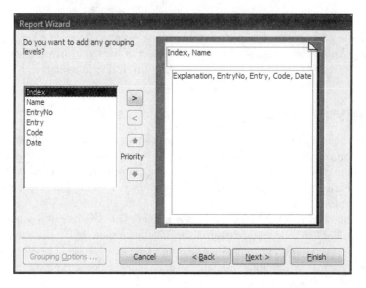

4. Click Next twice to skip this and then go to the Sort Options dialog box to reach the Layout dialog box, in which you select a layout.

5. Choose the Stepped layout and the Portrait orientation, then click Next.

6. Choose a style, such as Civic, from the list and click Next.

7. In the last dialog box, name the report **Alpha Card with Entries** and then click Finish.

Figure 11-10 shows the new Alpha Card with Entries report in Report view. As you navigate through the pages, you will see that there are several improvements to be made. For example, you might want to truncate the title in order to widen the label control. You might also want to add a line to better separate the groups of records.

Create a Subreport Control

As an example of creating a new subreport without the help of the Report Wizard, let's add the Alpha Entry information to the Alpha Card report, relating the two reports by the Index field. Just to be safe, save the Alpha Card report with a different name before adding the subreport as follows:

1. Select the Alpha Card report in the Navigation Pane.

2. Click the Microsoft Office button and point to Save As. In the Save Database Object As group, click the Save Object As button.

3. Enter the new name, **Alpha Card with Subreport**, in the Save As dialog box and click OK.

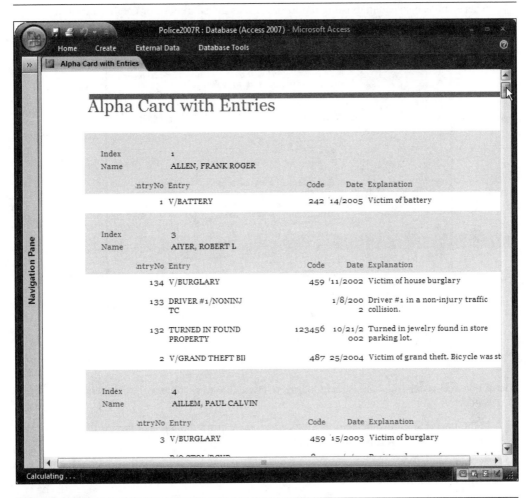

FIGURE 11-10 Previewing the report with the new subreport.

4. Open the Alpha Card with Subreport report in Design view and increase the height of the detail section and move the line to the bottom to make room for the subreport in between.

5. On the Design tab in the Controls group, click the Subform/Subreport tool and click in the report design between the last row of controls and the line at the bottom of the detail section. Access draws a square frame in the report design and opens the first dialog box

where you can select an existing report or form as the subreport, or create a new one based on a table or query.

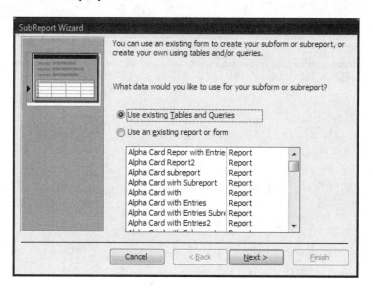

You can also draw a custom subreport frame to the desired size before releasing the mouse button and starting the wizard.

6. Choose Use existing Tables and Queries to create the new subreport, and then click Next.

7. In the next dialog box, select the Alpha Entry table from the Tables/Queries drop-down list, then click >> to select all the fields and click Next.

8. Accept the link the wizard suggests, which links the report and subreport by the Index field. Then click Next.

9. Accept the default name for the report name or enter a different name, such as **Alpha Entries**, and then click Finish to return to the main report Design view.

10. You can delete the subreport label if it is in the way, then move and resize the subreport control as appropriate.

The style of your subreport might be different than that of the example. As you can see in the preview, there are several refinements you can make in the subreport to improve its appearance. For example, you could hide the Index field and spread out the remaining controls to make room for the Entry information. Additionally, the Code field doesn't need so much space because it contains no more than six characters, so you can reduce the width of that control.

Insert an Existing Subreport

To use an existing report as a subreport, make sure the underlying tables or queries are properly related to those used by the main report, then open the Subreport Wizard as described previously. Instead of choosing Use existing Tables and Queries in the first wizard dialog box, choose Use an existing report or form, and then select the desired report or form from the drop-down list of all the reports and forms in the current database. Follow the instructions in the remaining wizard dialog boxes.

TIP   *You can also just drag the name of the report you want to use as a subreport from the Navigation Pane window onto the Design view of the main report.*

Link the Report and Subreport

If you insert the subreport in a bound report, the underlying tables must be linked so both reports will contain corresponding data. You must set the links in the Relationships window before trying to insert the subreport.

When you use the wizard to create a subreport or drag an existing report or datasheet from the Database window, Access automatically links the main report and subreport if one of the following conditions is met:

- The reports are based on related tables.

- The main report has a primary key and the table in the subreport contains a field with the same name and of the same or compatible data type.

- Both reports are based on queries whose underlying tables meet either of those same conditions.

The linking fields must be included in the underlying record sources, but you don't have to show them in either report. The wizard automatically includes linking fields even if you don't select them with the field picker.

If for some reason the wizard hasn't linked the tables properly, you can set the properties yourself by doing the following:

1. Open the main report in Design view.

2. Select the subreport control and open the property sheet.

3. Enter the name of the linking field (not the control) in the subreport in the Link Child Fields property box and enter the name of the linking field in the main report in the Link Master Fields property box.

11

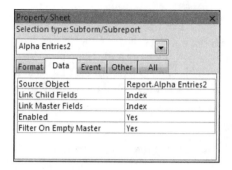

If you aren't sure about the field names, select the Build button (...) next to one of the Link properties and choose them with the help of the Subreport Field Linker dialog box.

You can link on more than one field by entering the field names in the property sheet, separated by semicolons, or by selecting them in the Subreport Field Linker dialog box.

Modify a Subreport Control

The first thing you might want to do with a new subreport control is to edit or delete the attached control label in the main report Design view. Make changes in the subreport design to match the style and arrangement of the controls in the main report. Subreport controls share many of the properties with other types of controls, for example, the position and size properties as well as the Special Effect and border properties. By default, the Can Grow property is set to Yes and the Can Shrink property to No. In addition to the link field properties, the subreport has a Name property which is set to the name you saved the file with or the name you entered in the Subform/ Subreport Wizard dialog box.

Design a Multiple-Column Report

Another way to arrange information in a report is in columns. When information is arranged in a tabular layout, it is easy to scan down a column of data and compare values in different records. Arranging the information in columns makes it easier to focus on individual records because all the data for one record is grouped together.

The Report Wizard gives you a choice of tabular or columnar layout in one of the dialog boxes. Choosing Columnar creates a report with the fields arranged in a single column on the page. Using Page Setup, you can change the layout to include as many columns as will fit across the page. Figure 11-11 compares the columnar report created by the Report Wizard with the same data in a newspaper column report.

To create this three-column report, do the following:

1. Open the Name List report in Print Preview and in the Page Layout group, click the Columns command. The three-tab Page Setup dialog box now opens.

2. Click the Columns tab and change the Number of Columns to **3**.

3. Leave the Column Spacing at the default, **.25"**. If you have left some space between the bottom control in the detail section and the lower boundary of the section, you can also leave the Row Spacing at **0**.

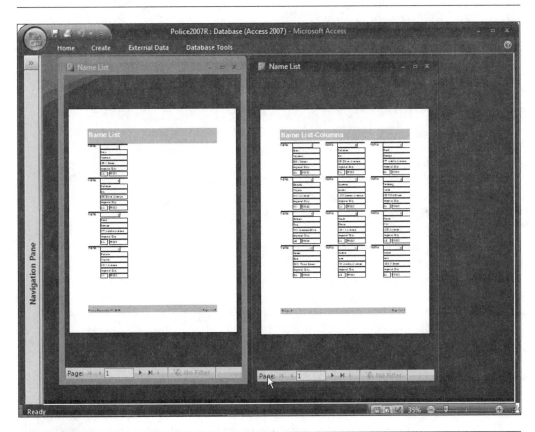

FIGURE 11-11   Comparing a single-column with a three-column report.

4. In the Column Size group, set the Width to **2"**. You can also set the Height here or use the height drawn in Design view.

5. Choose OK. If you are in Print Preview, the report shows the new layout. If not, switch to Print Preview to see how the report looks.

 Make sure the total of the width of the columns and the margins plus the spaces between the columns does not exceed the page width.

Another setting in the Columns dialog box is the Column Layout option group. This option group determines the order in which the records are laid out on the page. The default is Down, then Across, which places records down the page in the first column to the bottom of the page, then moves to the second column, and so on. The alternative choice is Across, then Down, which places the records across the first row to the right margin of the page, then moves to the second row, and so on.

Print Mailing Labels

Labels are used for many purposes: mailing addresses, name tags, disk labels, and book-plates. Because labels usually are smaller than a sheet of paper, you can print many of them on one page. This leads to a multiple-column-per-page report layout such as the one in the previous section.

Label printing is so common that Access has provided a special Label Wizard to help with the layout. After you create the label design, you can use it to print addresses on envelopes as well with a few changes to the page layout. Through the Label Wizard, you can create your own custom label size and layout and save it to use again.

Use the Label Wizard

The Label Wizard helps with every stage of the label design, including choosing the layout, changing the text appearance, adding field data to a prototype label, and even offering to sort the labels for you before printing. As an example of printing mailing labels, the local police department keeps the names and addresses of the Retired Senior Volunteer Program (RSVP) members in the Name List table in the department's Access database so that the program can mail monthly notices to the members.

To create mailing labels for the volunteers, do the following:

1. Select the Name List in the Navigation Pane and then on the Create tab in the Reports group, click the Labels tool.

2. In the first dialog box, set the following options:

   ■ Select the desired Unit of Measure: English or Metric.

   ■ Select the Label Type: Sheet feed or Continuous.

   ■ Choose the brand of label from the "Filter by manufacturer" drop-down list.

   ■ Choose the desired label size from the Product Number list. The dimensions are specified as height times width.

   ■ If you want to create a custom label size, click the Customize button.

   ■ If you have already created some custom label sizes, you can choose Show custom label sizes to see that list.

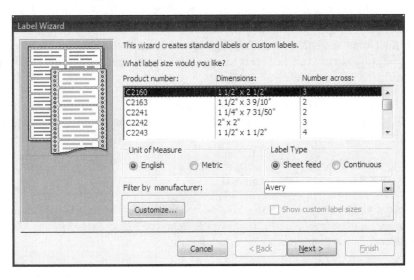

3. Click Next to open the second dialog box, where you can select the font name, size, and weight, and text colors. Italics and underlining also are options here.

4. Click Next to continue. The next Label Wizard dialog box displays a blank label prototype where you arrange the data. Double-click the field name to move it to the prototype label. Be sure to enter a space between fields. Press ENTER to move to the next line in the label.

5. Access automatically concatenates the values in the fields and trims the spaces from the names and addresses. Notice the spaces entered between the field names and the comma entered between the City and State fields.

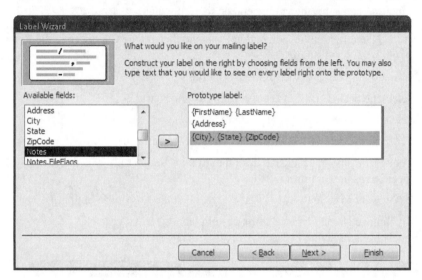

6. Click Next to move to the next dialog box, where you can choose to sort the records before printing the labels. Click Next to move to the last Label Wizard dialog box, where you enter a name for the label design.

It is a good idea to print one page of the new labels on plain paper and compare it with your label stock before committing to print many pages of labels on expensive label sheets.

Figure 11-12 shows a preview of the new labels for the Name List, using the Avery 5160 label size. The labels are sorted by Last Name.

You can use the same report design you created for printing the labels to print the addresses on envelopes. All you need to do is change the Page Setup options to reflect the different size and arrangement of the controls.

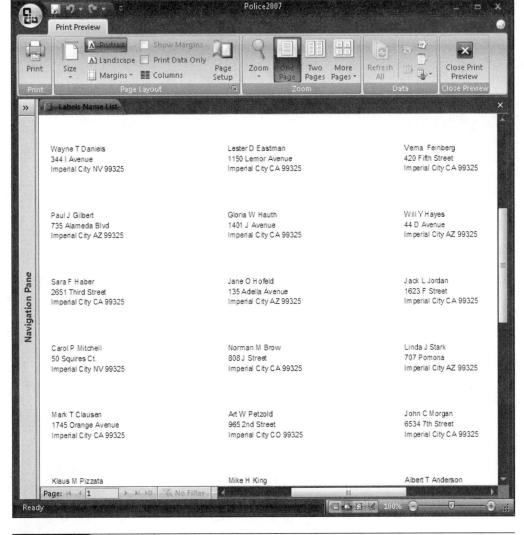

FIGURE 11-12   Previewing the first page of new labels.

Chapter 12

Create Charts and Graphs

How to…

- Choose the appropriate type of chart
- Create a new chart with the Chart Wizard
- Create a new chart without the Chart Wizard
- Add an existing chart to a form or report
- Modify the chart

Charts and graphs enhance data presented in forms and reports by summarizing and illustrating information in easily understood ways. With these tools, the reader can analyze trends and make comparisons. Access offers a wide variety of chart types including column, bar, line, pie, XY scatter, area, and many others. If you want the chart to reflect the values in the currently displayed record, you can also link the chart to a field in the underlying table or query.

Choose a Chart Type

When you decide to add a chart to a form or report, you must first understand the purpose of the chart. Do you want to point out trends over a period of time or compare the relative values summarized by groups? Figure 12-1 shows a typical column chart based on data from the Northwind sample database that came with Access. This chart compares the sales of six product categories during 2006.

Many other types of charts can show comparisons among data groups. For example, Figure 12-2 shows the same Northwind sales data displayed in an exploding pie chart. Each slice of the pie represents a product category.

Another reason to include charts in a form or report is to show trends over a period of time. Figure 12-3, which uses data from the Police database, shows a line chart that tracks the number of crimes that were reported over a four-year period. The crimes are grouped as violent or non-violent and a legend is included, which identifies the lines.

Create a New Chart with the Chart Wizard

The way you create a new chart depends on the type of chart you want. Do you want a stand-alone chart in its own form or report design, or a chart embedded in an existing form or report? In either case, you'll use the Chart Wizard to create it. The chart exists in a chart control in the form or report.

Select the Data for the Chart

Once you decide on what the chart is intended to accomplish, you can locate the data the chart will require. If the data is all contained in one table, you can use the table as the basis for the chart. If not, you can create a select or crosstab query that will group and summarize the data for the chart. With a select query, you can combine data and add calculated fields such as an extended price, and add totals that summarize field values.

Value axis title   Value (Y) axis   Chart title   Gridline

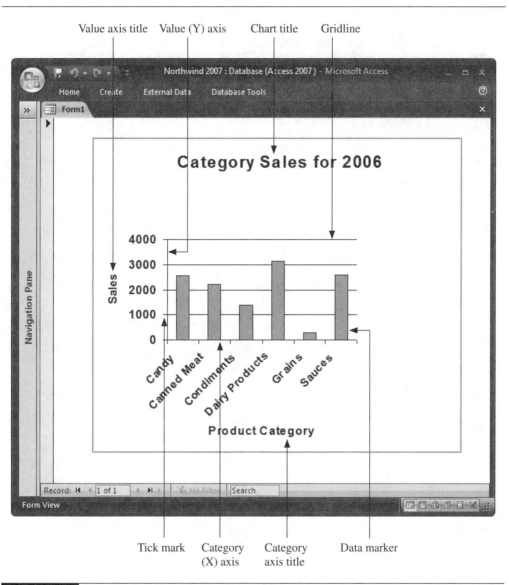

Tick mark   Category   Category   Data marker
(X) axis   axis title

FIGURE 12-1   A typical Access column chart.

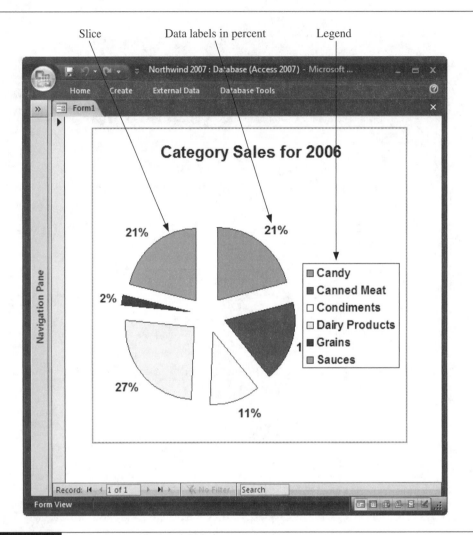

FIGURE 12-2 A pie chart with data labels in percent.

You can use up to six fields of any data type except OLE, Memo, and Attachment. There are only two requirements:

- You must include at least one field for categorizing data, such as the year the crime was reported or the area of the city where it occurred.

- You must include a field or a calculated field that you can add up, average, or count, such as the number of violent crimes or the sales during the third quarter of 2005.

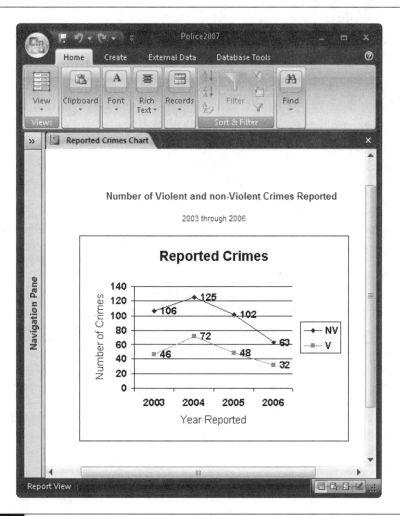

FIGURE 12-3 A line chart showing a trend over time.

A simple chart can contain only two fields: one as the category and the other as the data or value that corresponds to the category. For example, in Figure 12-1 there are only two fields: Product Category, which is used as the category, and Sales, which was summed to form the value.

Use the Microsoft Chart Wizard

The easiest way to create a new chart is to invoke the Chart Wizard. You can start the Chart Wizard in one of the following ways:

- If you are creating a free-standing chart, start a new blank form or report in Design view and on the Design tab in the Controls group click the Insert Chart command.

- If you want to insert a new chart in an existing form or report, open the form or report in Design view and click the Insert Chart command as you did previously.

Then, click in the design where you want to place the chart. You can also draw a box for the chart control. The Chart Wizard opens and the first dialog box asks you to select the table or query to use as the basis for the chart.

Once you have specified the underlying record source, follow the instructions in the wizard dialog boxes as follows (this example uses the Crimes by Beat Number table in the Police database):

1. Choose the fields you want to use in the chart; for example, Year, Crime Type, and Number of Crimes. Click Next.

2. Select the type of chart you want to create (see Figure 12-4) and then click Next. You can click each type of chart and read a description in the right pane.

The next dialog box (shown in Figure 12-5) shows you the arrangement of the fields in the layout of the sample chart.

Click the Preview Chart button to see how this arrangement would look. The preview does not show what the chart is meant to present: the number of crimes by type that were reported in each year. It shows the number of years in which violent and non-violent crimes were reported.

To change this layout, close the Preview window and do the following: Drag the SumOfYear label to the area below the chart to replace Crime Type. The label changes to Year because it represents a category on the X axis rather than a numeric value on the Y axis.

Next, complete the following steps:

1. Drag the Number of Crimes field button to the Data area below the Preview Chart. The label changes to SumOfNumber of Crimes.

NOTE *When you drag a field to the Data area in the sample chart, the Chart Wizard assumes you want to use the Sum aggregate function to create the value, but you can change to another function by double-clicking the "SumOf<nnn>" field, choosing the function from the Summarize dialog box, and clicking OK.*

2. Drag the Crime Type field button to the Series area.

3. To remove a field from the Preview Chart, drag it off the chart. The field name is replaced by Series, Data, or Axis, depending on the chart area.

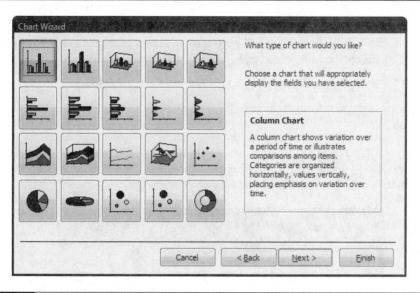

FIGURE 12-4 Selecting the type of chart.

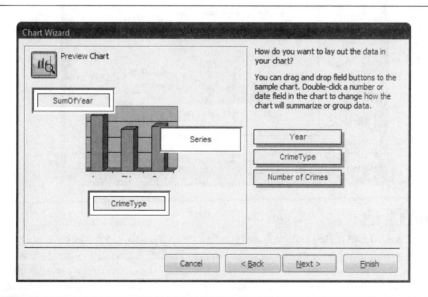

FIGURE 12-5 The Chart Wizard's layout dialog box.

4. Click the Preview Chart button again to see the effects of the changes. Figure 12-6 shows the new layout.

5. In the final Chart Wizard dialog box, enter a name for the chart, such as "Crimes by Year Chart," or accept the name of the table or query you used as the basis.

6. Choose to display a legend explaining the series data and then click Finish.

The chart appears in the new form. You might have to resize the form or the chart to get the appearance you want.

NOTE *When you first create a chart, it shows sample data rather than the data you asked it to process. Don't worry, the chart will show the real data the first time you view the form in Form view or the report in Report view or Print Preview.*

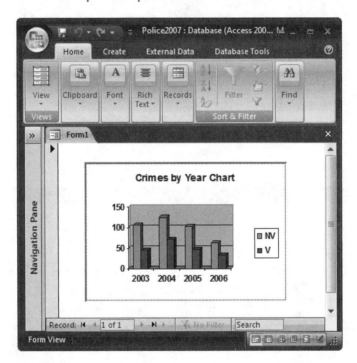

Save the Chart

In the final Chart Wizard dialog box, you assigned a title to the new chart, but have not yet named the host form or report, as you can see from the "Form1" name still in the document tab. If you want to name and save the form or report that contains the chart, first right-click the tab and choose Save in the shortcut menu, and then enter the desired file name. The new name is added to the Navigation Pane. When you reopen the form or report containing the chart, it will contain the current data from the underlying record source.

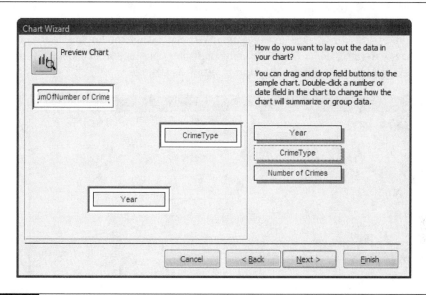

FIGURE 12-6   Chart layout after modification.

Link the Chart to Record Data

When you start a new chart from within a form or report design, Access assumes you want to link the chart to one of the fields in the underlying record source so that a different chart displays with each record. To do this, first create the host form or report, and then insert the new or an existing chart. For example, you can create a columnar form based on the City Beats table that contains only two fields: the beat number and a brief description of the territory, then switch to Design view and create a new chart by doing the following:

1. On the Design tab in the Controls group, click the Insert Chart command and then click in the design just below the text box controls in the form. Be sure that you have made room in the section for the embedded chart.

2. In the first Chart Wizard dialog box, choose the Crimes by Beat Number table as the basis for the chart and click Next.

3. In the second dialog box, select the fields you want in the chart. For this chart, choose Year, BeatNo, Crime Type, and Number of Crimes from the field list, and then click Next.

4. In the next dialog box, choose a simple column chart and click Next.

5. In the layout dialog box, drag the Year field to the Axis area, the Number of Crimes to the Data area, and the Crime Type to the Series area. Click Next.

12

6. In the next dialog box, the wizard suggests BeatNo as the linking fields in both the form and chart because they have the same name. If there are no matching names between the tables, the wizard makes no suggestion. You can change the linking field names or choose not to link the chart to the form by choosing <No Field>. Click Next to move to the final dialog box and name the form "City Beats Crimes."

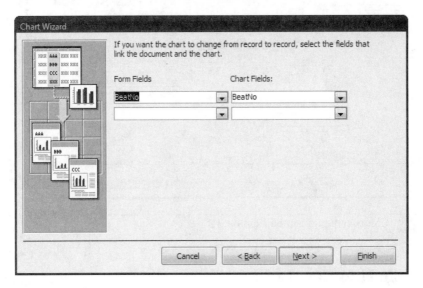

 *The linking fields need not have the same names, but they must have the same kind of data and be of the same or compatible data types.*

Switch to Form view to see the finished form with the linked chart (see Figure 12-7). As you move through the records, the heights of the data column markers change to reflect the number of crimes that were reported in that beat area.

It might take a few seconds to reconstruct the chart when you move to the next record— be patient.

Add an Existing Chart to a Form or Report

You can insert an existing chart into a form or report whether it is created within the current database or in another Access database. You can drag or copy the chart from one form or report to the other. To use drag-and-drop to insert the chart from another database, you must have two instances of Access running: one as the source and one as the destination.

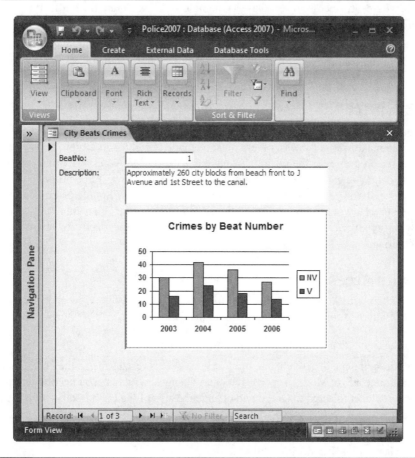

FIGURE 12-7   Viewing the new form with a linked chart.

Microsoft Graph is an applet you can use within Access to edit the charts you have created with the Chart Wizard. When you activate Microsoft Graph, use the special toolbars that appear in the Access window to edit the chart in place.

NOTE   *Access 2007 still uses Microsoft Graph 2003. This may change later.*

To insert a new chart created with Microsoft Graph in another Office program, open the form or report in Design view and do the following:

1. On the Design tab in the Controls group, click the Unbound Object Frame command and click where you want the chart. You can also draw the frame in the design.

2. In the Microsoft Access (Insert Object) dialog box, click Create from File, then enter the path to the file or click Browse to locate the file if you don't know the path.

3. If you want to link the chart to the form or report, select Link. If you want the chart to appear as an icon instead of the full chart, select Display as Icon. Click OK.

Modify the Chart

The tools you use to modify a chart depend on what kind of changes you want to make. Some changes you can make within Access, others must be made in Microsoft Graph. If you want to change any of the properties or the position of the control, do so in Access. If you want to change the underlying data, you can create a new query and change the Row Source property of the chart within Access. You can also edit the SQL statement in the Row Source property rather than create a new query. However, if you want to change any of the chart's elements, such as the axis titles or the chart type, or change the appearance of the chart, you must activate Microsoft Graph for in-place editing.

Modify with Access

To modify the chart with Access, open the host form or report in Design view and select the chart control frame. With the frame selected, you can do the following:

- Drag the frame to a different position in the form or report.
- Drag the sizing handles to change the frame size. This resizes the frame and, depending on the frame's Size Mode property, the chart changes to match. You need to double-click the chart object to activate Graph and change the size of the chart itself within the frame.
- Open the chart's Property Sheet and then change any of the control properties including frame's fill color, border color and width, and special effects as well as the Row Source, Link Master Fields, and Link Child Fields.

Save Disk Space

If disk space is a concern, you can save space by converting the unbound object control to an image control. Right-click the chart control in the form or report Design view and choose Change To in the shortcut menu. Then select Image, the only option available to an unbound OLE Object control. The data shown in the chart will not be updated with changes in the underlying record source. Use caution with the transformation because it can't be undone.

For example, to unlink the Crimes by Beat Number chart from the form:

1. Open the City Beats Crimes form in Design view.

2. Select the chart control and open the Property Sheet.

3. Delete the BeatNo field names from the Link Master Fields and Link Child Fields properties.

When you return to Form view and move through the records, you can see that the chart no longer changes with each record. Instead, it always shows the total crimes for all beats when you navigate through the records.

Edit the Row Source Property

If you created the chart in Access with the Chart Wizard, it creates a query whose SQL statement becomes the row source for the chart. You can modify the row source by using the query grid or by editing the SQL statement itself.

To change the row source, do the following:

1. Open the Sum Crimes report in Design view and open the Property Sheet for the chart control.

2. Click the Build button (...) next to the Row Source property to open the Query Builder dialog box with the Sum Crimes query.

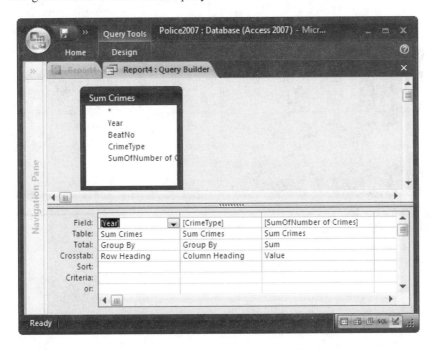

3. To limit the chart to crimes occurring in specific years, enter **Between 2003 And 2005** in the Criteria row of the Year column.

4. Close the Query Builder dialog box and respond Yes to save the changes, then switch to Report view. You now see only three sets of columns.

Edit the Chart Legend

When you add a series to the chart layout that summarizes data within the category, as shown in Figure 12-8, the legend is not always as informative as it should be. The two charts illustrate the same data and are based on tables that contain the same data but use different table structures.

The chart on the left is based on the Crimes by Beat Number table. From this table, the Chart Wizard created a crosstab query that totals the number of both types of crimes reported for each beat.

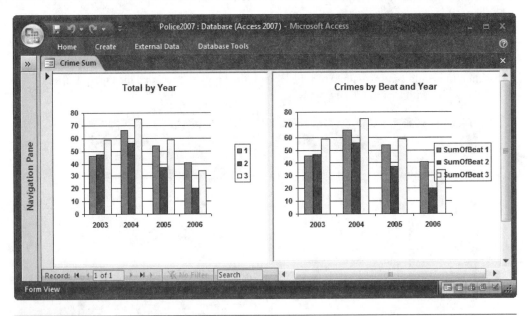

Two charts illustrating the same data.

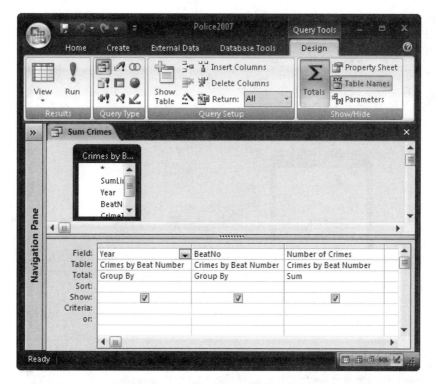

The legend in the chart on the left takes its values from the field whose Crosstab row shows Column Heading, which is BeatNo (1, 2, and 3). The legend would be more informative if you edited it to read Beat 1, Beat 2, and Beat 3. There are two ways to do this after opening the Query Builder for the Row Source property:

■ Change the BeatNo field in the query grid to the expression **"Beat "&[BeatNo]**. Be sure to include a space after **Beat** within the quotation marks to separate it from the number in the result.

12

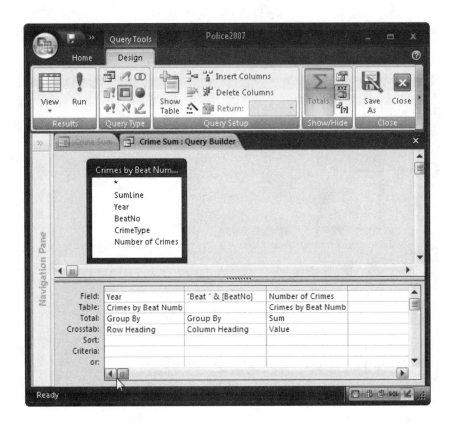

■ Right-click the document tab and choose SQL View then change the PIVOT clause from

```
PIVOT [Crimes by Beat Number].[BeatNo];
```

to

```
PIVOT "Beat "&[Crimes by Beat Number].[BeatNo];
```

When you save the design, close the Query Builder dialog box and switch to Form view. You can see the change in the legend. The chart on the right in Figure 12-8 is based on the more compact Crimes by Beat and Year table.

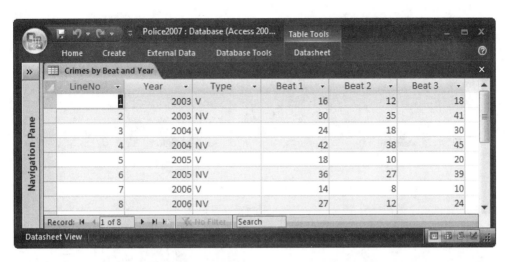

For this chart, the Chart Wizard has created a select query that sums the value in each of the Beat*n* fields by year. The legend shows SumOfBeat 1, SumOfBeat 2, and SumOfBeat 3. You can use the same method to change the legend text: add expressions to the Field row of the query grid or edit the SQL statement.

Open the form in Design view and start the Query Builder as before. This time, edit the SQL statement. Switch to SQL view and edit the AS clauses by deleting SumOf from each clause.

CAUTION *Be sure to leave the brackets around the field names because they contain spaces.*

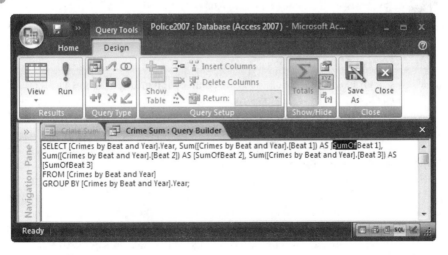

Save the changes and switch to Form view. Figure 12-9 shows the two charts with their new legends.

12

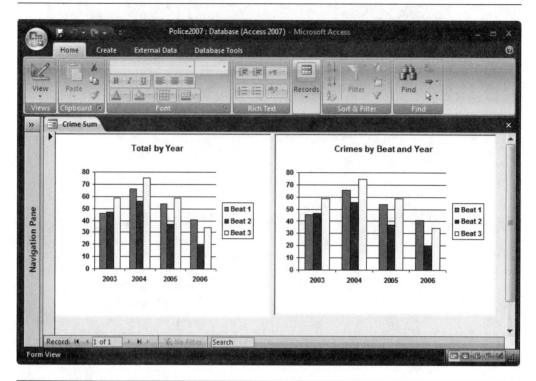

FIGURE 12-9 The charts with legends edited in Access.

Edit with Microsoft Graph

To activate Microsoft Graph, double-click the chart control in the form or report Design view. Figure 12-10 shows the Crimes by Year Chart form when Microsoft Graph is active. In addition to the form window containing the chart, a Datasheet window appears below the chart which contains the related data. Notice the cross-hatched border around the chart, which indicates that Microsoft Graph is currently running. The title you entered in the Chart Wizard dialog box appears as the chart title in Graph.

To show or hide the datasheet, choose View in the menu bar and then click Datasheet, which toggles the Datasheet window in and out of focus. You can also right-click the Chart window and choose Datasheet from the shortcut menu. To close the Datasheet, click the Close button. To leave the Microsoft Graph window and return to the Access form or report Design view, click anywhere outside the chart object. The changes you made to the chart in Microsoft Graph are shown in the Access chart. You must save the form or report design to save the changes.

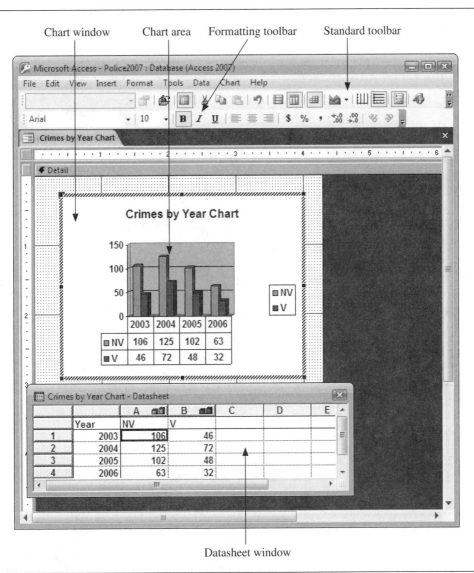

Chart window   Chart area   Formatting toolbar   Standard toolbar

FIGURE 12-10 A typical Microsoft Graph window.

Datasheet window

Look at the Graph Toolbars

The Microsoft Graph window normally has two toolbars: Standard and Formatting. The Drawing, Picture, and WordArt toolbars, which can be used to add special objects to the chart, are available upon demand. To add a toolbar, right-click in any toolbar and select the one you want to add from the drop-down list. You can also choose from the View | Toolbars menu. To see what the toolbar button does, rest the mouse pointer on the button and read the ScreenTip. All the buttons have menu equivalents.

Change the Chart Appearance

You have a lot of ways to change the appearance of the chart. For example, you can change the size of the chart control itself or change any of the text elements in the chart. To change the size of the chart, select the chart control and drag the sizing handles until it reaches the proper size.

Format Text Elements   The same options are available to you when you format most of the text elements in the chart. Select the element and choose Format | Selected *object* to open the Format dialog box or press CTRL-1. The dialog box has three tabs: Patterns, Font, and Alignment.

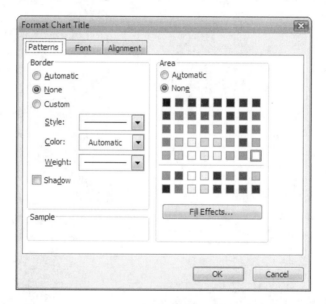

NOTE   *Select Fill Effects in the Format dialog box to open another dialog box where you can choose gradients, fill textures, or patterns and even select a picture to use as a background.*

The Font tab contains the standard font name, size, weight, colors, and effects such as underline, strikethrough, superscript, and subscript. When you select the chart title or one of the axis titles and choose Format | Selected, the Alignment tab appears, in which you can choose the text alignment plus the orientation. You can display the text vertically or at a specific angle by clicking on the arc in the Orientation area.

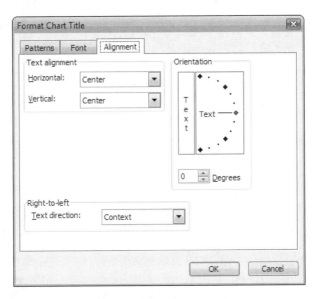

If you select the legend and choose Format | Selected Legend, the Alignment tab is replaced by the Placement tab. In the Placement tab you can choose to display the legend at the bottom, corner, top, right, or left of the plot area.

Format Other Chart Elements   When you select one of the axes and choose Format | Selected, the Format Axis dialog box shows five tabs: Patterns, Scale, Font, Number, and Alignment. The Patterns, Font, and Alignment tabs are the same as for text elements. The other tabs offer the following options:

■ The options in the Scale tab depend on which axis you have selected. If you select the Value (Y) axis, you can choose to set manually the minimum and maximum values for the axis as well as the major and minor units for the gridlines and tick marks. The alternative is to let Microsoft Graph set these values automatically. You can also specify where the Category (X) axis is to cross the Value axis and whether to arrange the values in reverse order.

12

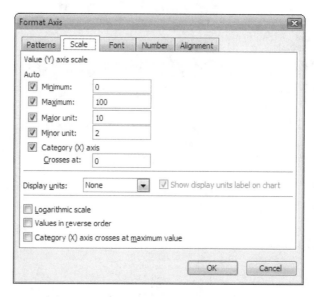

- The Number tab gives you a selection of number categories and specific formats for the values on the Value (Y) axis. There is also a check box that links the values to the source data. Clear this check box to create a snapshot chart that does not update with changes to the underlying data.

- When you select the Category (X) axis, the formatting options are slightly different. The Scale tab contains options that relate to data categories instead of values.

When you format the data series by clicking one of the columns, bars, or other representations of the data, the Format (data series) dialog box appears with four or five tabs, depending on the type of data series. For example, the column and line series Format dialog box contains five tabs: Patterns, Axis, Y Error Bars, Data Labels, and Options. The 3-D and pie series Format dialog boxes show four tabs.

The Patterns tab offers the same color, border, and fill options as before. The other tabs offer the following options:

- **Axis tab** Specifies whether to plot the series on the primary or secondary axis. A sample chart illustrates the current choice.

- **Y Error Bars tab** Offers the option of displaying the statistical error estimation or the standard deviation in the values either as values or percentages. This option is handy for presenting the results of a statistical survey for which you need to express the validity.

- **Data Labels tab** Enables you to display the data values and labels with the data series. You can display the values as percentages or in the unit of the value itself.

■ **Options tab**   For a column data series, this tab enables you to overlap the series and set the amount of overlap, and also specify the amount of space between the sets of data series. Options vary with different types of data series.

A 3-D column data series Format dialog box includes the Shape tab that offers different configurations including cones, pyramids, and cylinders.

Change Chart Type   When you are creating charts to analyze the data in your database, you may want to try out different representations. You may want to show trends with a line chart or comparative values with a pie chart. There are two ways to change the chart type:

■ Click the Chart Type toolbar button and choose from the palette containing 18 chart types.

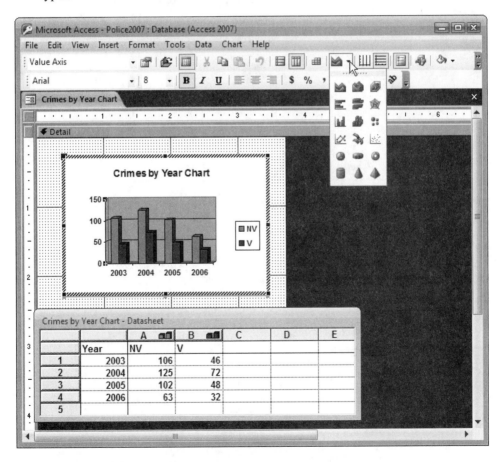

■ Choose Chart | Chart Type and choose from the Chart Type dialog box. The Standard Types include 14 types with many subtypes for each. In the Standard Types tab, press and hold the button below the Chart subtype pane to see a sample of the selected chart. The Custom Type tab shows an additional 20 chart types from the built-in list of charts; if you have created any custom chart types, they are displayed when you choose Select from User-Defined.

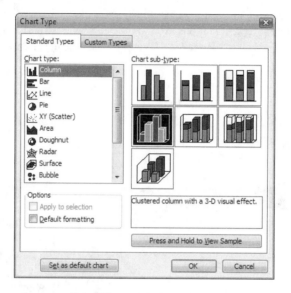

After making your selection, click OK to apply it to the current chart. You can also specify a chart type as the default chart.

Set Chart Options   You can adjust many additional chart features to achieve the appearance you want. When you choose Chart | Chart Options, the Chart Options dialog box opens with six tabs: Titles, Axes, Gridlines, Legend, Data Labels, and Data Table.

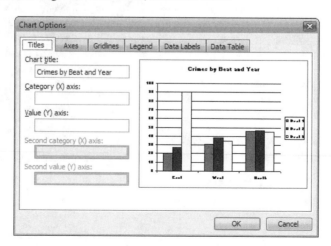

Troubleshoot Charts

Sometimes the changes you make in Microsoft Graph fail to show up in the chart when you switch to Form view or Print Preview even though they appear in Design view. For example, you can change the column headings in the Microsoft Graph datasheet to display the text you want in the legend. When you return to Access, the new labels appear in the design but not in Form view or Print Preview.

The reason for this seeming inconsistency is that you have several places in which to specify the chart information and Access must set an order of precedence to decide which values to use. The order is as follows:

- First, the data in the underlying table or query; for example, the field names or the expressions in the Field row of the query grid.
- Second, the contents of the Row Source property.
- Last, the data entered in Microsoft Graph.

If you set the legend text in Microsoft Graph but the underlying query column headings are different, they will override the Microsoft Graph settings. If the columns don't appear in the order you want in the chart, open the Query Builder and rearrange the fields, left to right; then choose the sort order for each.

The tabs offer the following options:

- In the Titles tab, you enter the text you want to display as the chart title and the axes titles. You can specify a primary and secondary title for each axis but only one for the chart itself. If the chart is 3-D, you won't see secondary title boxes.
- In the Axes tab, you specify whether to display the axes and choose the method by which to display the Category (X) axis.

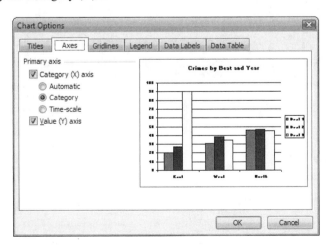

- In the Gridlines tab, you specify whether to display the gridlines on one or both of the axes. You can choose to display both major and minor gridlines on each axis.

- In the Legend tab, you choose whether to display the legend with the chart. The Legend tab offers these options for placing the legend: Bottom, Corner, Top, Right, or Left.

- The Data Labels tab includes the same options as the Data Labels tab in the Format Data Series dialog box.

- In the Data Table tab you can choose to display the data in the underlying data source in a grid attached to the bottom of the chart. When you choose to display the data table, you can also display the legend keys. Figure 12-11 shows the Total by Year chart with the corresponding data table. The Data Table option is not available for some of the chart types.

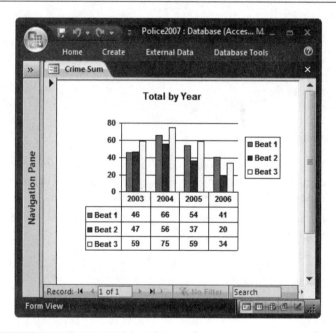

FIGURE 12-11   The data table added to the chart.

Part III

Improve the Access 2007 Workplace

Chapter 13

Customize the Workplace

How to...

- Personalize your workplace
- Work with objects in the Navigation Pane
- Set Access options
- Customize the status bar

Some of the features discussed in this chapter have been briefly mentioned in previous chapters; and some are covered in detail later. However, I have brought them all together in one place for easy reference. Using the many Access and Windows options, you can change the default appearance and behavior of many aspects of your workplace. In addition to making changes that affect the current Access database, you can change many Access startup options such as displaying a startup form; opening a specific database; and changing language settings.

Personalize the Workplace

You don't have to bow down to the layout and behavior of the Access environment as it is when first installed. The Access developers have designed a workplace that is appropriate for most users, but if there are some aspects you would like to change, it is easy to change them. For example, if you have a large screen, you might want to see a larger font size. Of course, you can change each of these factors every time you work with Access, but you can also change the default settings once and for all.

Work with Objects in the Navigation Pane

You don't even have to accept the way the Navigation Pane lists the database objects. You can choose a specific sort order for the list of Access objects in the Navigation Pane. You can also change the appearance of the object names. If you don't want an object type to appear in the list, you can choose to hide that group. To set these options, right-click any of the group title bars and choose from the shortcut menu.

Sort Objects

To begin, in the shortcut menu, point to Sort to see the Sort options. You can choose Sort Ascending or Sort Descending and choose the means of sorting. By Type is the default, but you can choose to sort by name, the date it was created or the date it was last modified.

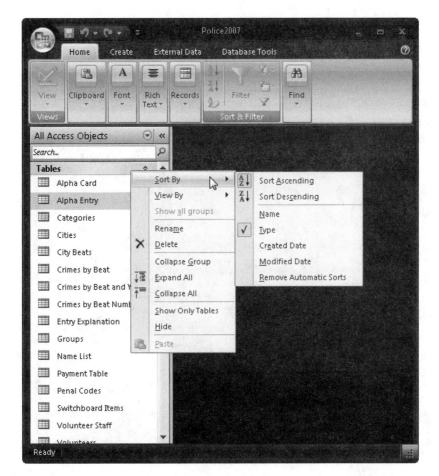

The final choice removes the automatic sorts so that you can move the objects' names in the order you want. This clears the check marks from the other choices. To return to an automatic sort, check one of the other sort options.

Change the Object Appearance

You can include detail information about objects within the names in the Navigation Pane or add a larger object icon. To see the options, in the shortcut menu, point to View By and choose from the list:

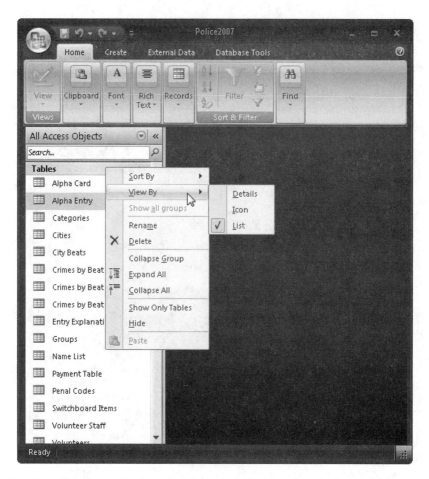

The Details option shows the date of creation and the date of the latest modification as well as the object type name.

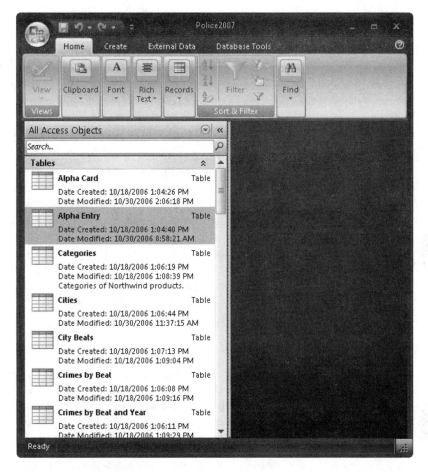

The Icon option adds a larger object type icon to the names in the lists. The **List** option, which is the default, displays the names as a list with smaller icons.

Other Navigation Pane Options

Several more options are available in the object header shortcut menu.

The Expand Group option applies to the selected group and shows all objects in that group. This is the same as clicking the down arrow in the group header. It becomes Collapse Group in the group in already expanded. The Expand All option opens the lists of all object groups. Collapse All leaves only the group headers with no object lists in any of the groups.

The Show Only option leaves the object list displayed in the selected group but closes all other object lists, leaving only the group headers. Hide removes all the objects of that type along with the group header. To restore the objects, right-click the Navigation Pane title bar and choose Navigation Options. In the Navigation Options dialog box, check the object group you have hidden and click OK.

Using the Ribbon

As you have probably noticed while working with Access 2007, the ribbon changes its content depending on the current activity. The ribbon also changes configuration based on the size of the current window. With the window maximized, the ribbon appears with two rows of commands with all their labels. With the window resized and narrowed, the ribbon can change to three rows of commands, which then lose many of their labels.

When the window is very narrow, the ribbon removes the right-most commands and adds a right arrow that you can click to scroll through the ribbon. If the window is even narrower, for example, if it shows only the Navigation Pane, the ribbon is removed from view.

If you want more room to work on your database, you can hide the ribbon by pressing CTRL-F1. To restore the ribbon press CTRL-F1 again.

Create a Shortcut

If you use an Access object regularly, you can create a shortcut that launches Access and opens the database object directly from the Windows desktop. The easiest way is to drag the object from the Navigation Pane to the Windows desktop. You must first resize the Access window so you can see the area on the desktop where you want to place the shortcut icon. When you double-click the shortcut, Access opens the database that contains the object and displays the object.

To delete a shortcut, click it and press del. This does not delete the object itself; only the shortcut.

NOTE   *If you have moved the database that is the destination of a shortcut, remove the shortcut and create a new one with the new path.*

Set Access Options

Access is installed with certain characteristics set as defaults. For example, the width of the print margins, default database folder, color of hyperlinks, gridlines, and font styles in a datasheet are set by default. If you find yourself changing specific default values when you work with a database, you can reset the default value to the one you use the most. All default values can be overridden later, if necessary.

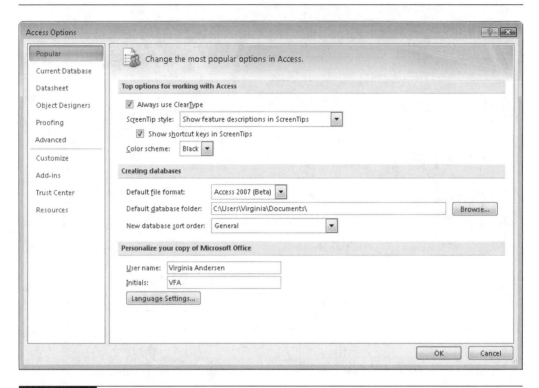

Open the Access Options dialog box.

To make changes in the default settings, click the Microsoft Office button and choose Access Options. In the left pane of the Access Options dialog box there are 10 categories of options you can change (see Figure 13-1). Many of the options in them relate to settings for all Microsoft Office programs, not just Access.

This chapter won't cover every option on every page of the Access Options dialog box so if you want to know more about any of the settings, click the Help button (?) in the upper right corner. The Help window opens with descriptions of all the options in the current dialog box.

Popular Options

These options relate to the basic characteristics applied when you start Access.

Set Top Options

You can use the ScreenTip Style to show enhanced screentips (the default) or don't show enhanced screentips. You can also check Don't show any screentips.

Clear the Show shortcut keys in ScreenTips check box if you don't want to see them when you rest the mouse pointer on the command. In the Color Scheme setting you can choose between Blue, Silver, and Black.

Creating Database Options

In the Default file format option, you can choose between Access 2007, 2002–2003, or 2000. Enter the folder name in Default database folder or click Browse and locate the folder you want to use.

In the New database sort order setting, you can choose from a list of 33 language settings that change the default alphabetic sort order for new databases. The General setting applies to English, French, German, Italian, Portuguese, and modern Spanish. To change the sort order for an existing database, select the language, and then compact the database.

You must close and reopen the database for these options to take effect.

Personalize Office

In the Personalize your copy of Office group, enter your user name and initials and then choose the appropriate Language Settings.

To change the Language Settings, click the button to open the Microsoft Office Language Settings 2007, where you can choose from the list of Available editing languages. Scroll down the list and select the language you want to use and click Add. You can choose more than one language, but when you choose other than English, you see a warning message that the language has limited support in Microsoft Office and will require additional support.

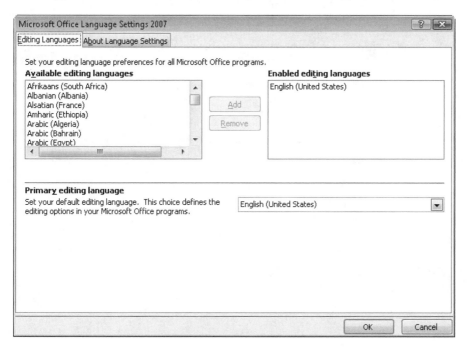

Set Options for the Current Database

There are many options available for the current database, including Application, Navigation, Toolbar, Name Autocorrect, and filter lookup limitations (see Figure 13-2). All of these are applied only to the current database. For most of these options to take effect, you need to close and reopen the database. To use them for other databases you need to open them and choose the settings again.

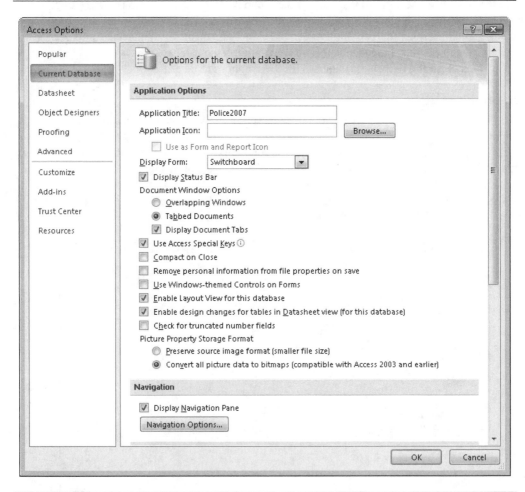

FIGURE 13-2 Setting options for the current database.

Application Options

Most of the changes in the Application Options group take effect the next time you open the database. Only the Application Title and Application Icon options take effect as soon as you close the dialog box.

Use Application Title and Application Icon to display a custom title and icon in the Windows title bar. Enter the text you want to display in the Application Title box. To add a custom icon to the title bar in place of the default Access icon in the Windows title bar, type the name of the bitmap (.bmp) or icon (.ico) file in the Application Icon box or click the Browse button to use the Icon Browser to locate the file. If you want the application icon to appear in the tabs above the form and report documents, check Use as Form and Report Icon.

TIP   *If you're creating an application to be distributed to multiple users, you should place the icon file in the same folder as the host application.*

Many applications display a special form when opening—either as a welcoming screen or as a switchboard with a list of choices of actions to take next, such as enter/edit data or preview a report. After you create the special form and save it in the current database, you can use it as the startup form. To choose a form for display at startup, click the drop-down arrow in the Display Form box and choose the form from the list of forms in the current database.

Clear the Display Status Bar option if you don't want to see the status bar at the bottom of the window.

The Document Window Options are new to Access 2007. They allow you to change the structure of the document window. Overlapping Windows allows you to open and view more than one Access object at a time. If you hide the Navigation Pane and use this option, it looks like earlier versions of Access. The Tabbed Documents option is the default in this set, which applies the single-document interface to display only one object at a time. The Display Document Tabs shows and hides the tabs that appear above the documents. The default setting is to show them.

If you choose to show overlapping windows with no tabs, a new group of commands appears on the Home tab. The Windows group includes two commands:

- Size to Fit Form, which reduces the window to fit the currently displayed form.
- Switch Windows, which offers a list of the currently open objects to choose from. You also have the option of tiling or cascading the objects in the window.

13

When you select Use Access Special Keys, you can use the special key combinations that display the Navigation Pane or the Immediate window, open the Module window, or interrupt a server. The special keys are as follows:

- F11, which shows or hides the Navigation Pane
- CTRL-G, which displays the Immediate window in the Visual Basic Editor
- ALT-F11, which starts the Visual Basic Editor
- CTRL-BREAK, which, in a project, stops Access from retrieving records from the server

The Layout view for forms and reports is new with Access 2007. The Enable Layout View for this database option shows or hides the Layout View option in the status bar and in the shortcut menus that appear when you right-click the object tab. You may need to set the Allow Layout View property to Yes to make it available.

If you have not chosen the Enable design changes for tables in Datasheet view (for this database) option, you must be in table Design view to make design changes.

Another helpful setting in this group is Check for truncated number fields. If the control in a form or report is not wide enough to show the complete number value, ##### appears in the control. If this option is not checked, you will see only part of the number and not realize the number is incomplete.

The final setting in this group is Picture Property Storage Format where you can choose Preserve source image format to store images in their original format or Convert all picture data to bitmaps which creates a copy of the original image file in Windows Bitmap or Device Independent Bitmap format. With the second option, you can view images in databases from Access 2003 and earlier.

Navigation Options

The Display Navigation Pane option shows or hides the Navigation Pane. You can also press the special key F11 to show or hide the pane. The other option is the Navigation Options button that you can use to create custom categories for listing the objects in the Navigation Pane. See Chapter 17 for more information about customizing the grouping in the Navigation Pane.

Ribbon and Toolbar Options

Scroll down the Current Database window to see more options. For these options to take effect, you need to close and reopen the database.

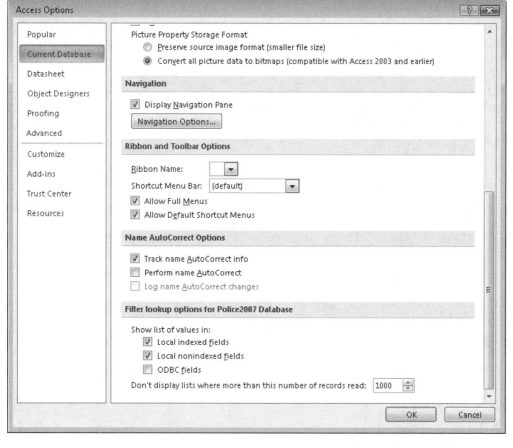

If you want a special ribbon or shortcut menu instead of the standard ones, click Ribbon Name or Shortcut Menu Bar down arrow and select the name from the drop-down list.

The Allow Full Menus setting expands the menu list to include all commands. If you clear this option, Access hides certain menus that give the user the power to open an object in Design view and make changes.

Leave the Allow Default Shortcut Menus checked to allow access to the built-in shortcut menus that appear when you right-click a database object, or a control in a form or a report. Clear the option to disable all shortcut menus.

13

Name AutoCorrect Options

The Name AutoCorrect group of options helps Access propagate name changes to objects that refer to the renamed object. The group offers three options that help fix common side effects that occur when you make changes in an object via a user interface. Access stores the identifier for each object and tracks naming information. When Access notices an object has been changed since the last Name AutoCorrect action, it runs it again for all items in that object. For example, if you added a text box to a form that is bound to the Alpha Card table and you change the Alpha Card table name to Alpha Card Plus, Access can track down all the items from the original Alpha Card and change their names to match the new table name.

Filter Lookup Options

The Filter Lookup options group limits or extends the size of the value list displayed in the Filter By Form window and sets the maximum number of records to read in order to build a value list for a given field. The more fields you include in the filter operation, the longer it takes. This group also specifies whether to display values for indexed or non-indexed fields and for a linked table in an external file. These settings apply only to the current database:

- **Local indexed fields**   Limits the value list to the indexed fields in the current database.
- **Local nonindexed fields**   Includes the fields in the current database that aren't indexed.
- **ODBC fields**   Includes fields in a linked table in an external source.

Enter a number in the Don't display lists where more than this number of records read box to set the maximum number of records you want to build the list of unique values for the field. If the number of records exceeds this amount, no values at all are displayed for the field in the Filter By Form window. Instead you will have a choice between Is Null and Is Not Null. The default number of values is 1000.

Set Datasheet Options

The Datasheet category of options (see Figure 13-3) includes settings for the visual properties of a datasheet. The default colors, fonts, gridlines, and cell special effects are all set in this group.

Set Object Designers Options

The groups of options in this set (see Figure 13-4) specify many default settings for creating Access objects. One group offers several methods of checking for many types of data entry and keyboard errors.

Table Design Options

The Table Design group includes default field size and type choices, as well as specifying prefixes to use for automatically indexing fields. The AutoIndex on Import/Create setting is very useful when you import a table from an external source or create a new table in Design view.

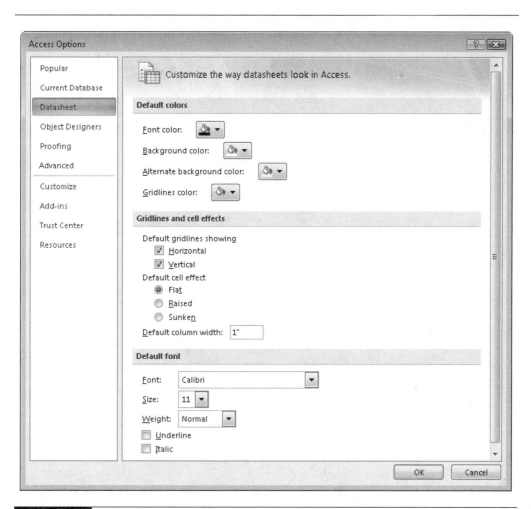

FIGURE 13-3 Setting options for datasheets.

This setting tells Access to index on all fields automatically that begin or end with the characters you type in the box. Multiple entries are separated by semicolons. For example, the entries in the AutoIndex box instruct Access to create an index on all fields whose names begin or end with the characters ID, key, code, or num.

The Show Property Update Options buttons, when checked, gives you the option of propagating property changes you made in a table or query to controls bound to that field.

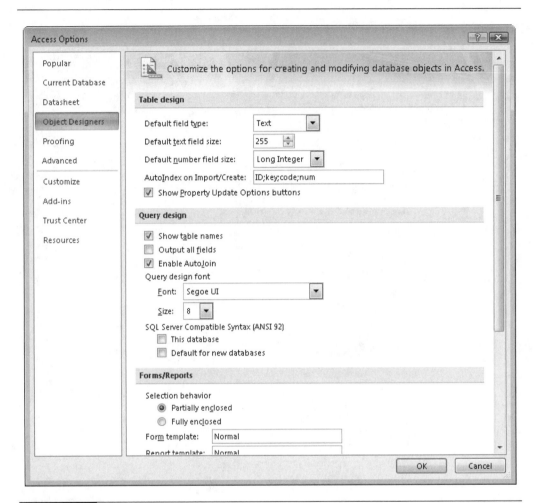

Setting options for object designers.

Query Design Options

In the Query Design options group, checking Show table names displays the table names in the Table row of the query grid. This helps to keep track of the field source when multiple tables are used in a query. If you want all the fields in the tables used in the query design to appear in the query result without bothering to add them all to the design grid, check Output all fields. The fields aren't added to the query grid, only to the resulting datasheet. When you select this option, only the new queries are affected.

The Enable AutoJoin option automatically creates an inner joint between two tables in the query grid. For two tables to be autojoined, they must have fields with the same name and of the same data type, and one of the fields must be the primary key field for that table. If you want to define the relationships yourself, clear the option.

In the SQL Server Compatible Syntax (ANSI 92) option group, you can choose to format queries for only the current database or for all new databases exclusively in ANSI 92 standard syntax. This setting ensures SQL server compatibility.

You can also change the default query font type and size.

Form and Report Options

The settings in the Forms/Reports group in the Object Designers window all relate to working in a form or report Design view.

The Selection behavior group specifies the results of drawing a rectangle in the design to select controls. Partially enclosed, the default, selects all controls with any part within the drawn rectangle, while Fully enclosed selects only those controls that are totally within the drawn rectangle.

- The Form template and Report template settings allow you to specify an existing form or report as the template for new designs. Type the name of the form or report you want to use as the default template.

- The Always use event procedures setting, when selected, takes you directly to the VB Editor window when you click the Build button in a property sheet, bypassing the Choose Builder dialog box which usually offers the choice of Expression Builder, Macro Builder, or Code Builder.

Error Checking Options

Automatic error checking identifies errors in form and report designs, and offers suggestions for correcting them. You can choose to apply automatic error checking to five general types of errors. You set these rules in the Error Checking group of Object Designer options.

To request error checking, check the Enable error checking box. Then choose a color for the error indicator button, the small triangle that appears in the upper-left corner of the control that caused the error.

The categories of rules you can specify include the following:

- An unassociated label and control error occurs when you select a label and a control not associated with each other.

- The new unassociated labels error occurs when you add a label to a form or report that is not associated with another control.

- The keyboard shortcut error occurs when you select a control on a form that shows an invalid shortcut key (the underlined character you can use with ALT to move focus to the control), for example, an unassociated label, a duplicate shortcut key, or a space used as the shortcut key.

- The invalid control properties error occurs when you select a control with invalid values in one or more properties.

- The common report errors occur when the report has an invalid sorting and grouping definition. Can also occur when the report width exceeds the paper width.

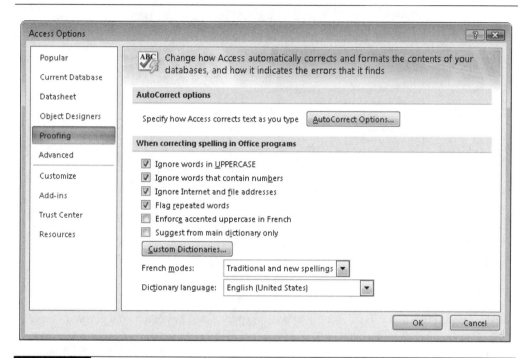

FIGURE 13-5 Choosing options for document proofing.

Set Proofing Options

The Proofing options (see Figure 13-5) set the way Access automatically detects and corrects errors in the database. You can also use these options to choose a custom dictionary that includes special words and terms related to your workplace. The proofing option settings are shared with other Office users.

AutoCorrect Options

You can choose the method Access uses to correct typos and commonly misspelled words as you enter the data. Click the AutoCorrect Options button to see the choices.

In the AutoCorrect dialog box, you can choose to apply AutoCorrect to certain types of errors as well as specify certain replacement text or characters for other misspellings. If there are some combinations of text or abbreviations that would normally be caught by the AutoCorrect tool, you can click Exceptions and make some changes.

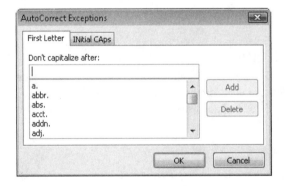

Spelling Corrections

The correct spelling options in the When correcting spelling in Office programs group, as shown earlier, offer choices of which misspellings to ignore. You can also choose to underline words that are repeated in case they aren't intended to be.

Set Advanced Options

The Advanced Options set of options (see Figure 13-6) includes editing, display, printing, and some general and advanced settings.

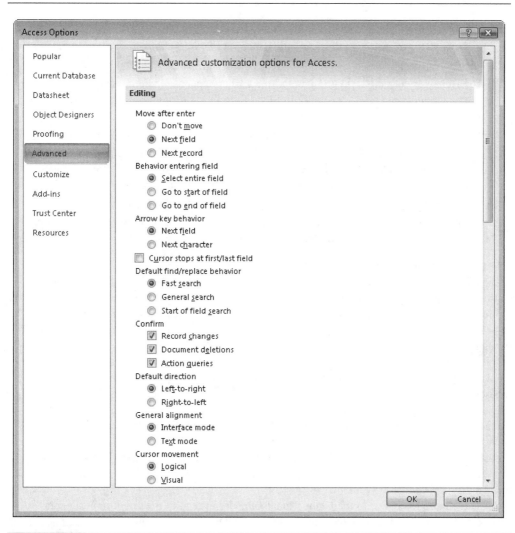

FIGURE 13-6 Choosing Advanced options.

Editing

The large group of Editing options includes both setting keyboard behavior and the edit and find options. There are also some international options that specify the direction and alignment of text as well as the cursor movement.

The first set of options determine the consequences of pressing certain keys such as ENTER, TAB, RIGHT ARROW, and LEFT ARROW.

- The Move after enter group of options determines the behavior of the insertion point (cursor) after pressing ENTER. It can either stay put, move to the next field, or to the next record.

- The Behavior entering field group determines what happens when the insertion point enters a field. It can select the entire field, or go to the start or end of the field without selecting any characters.

- The Arrow key behavior settings specify what occurs when you press RIGHT ARROW and LEFT ARROW. Choosing Next field moves the insertion point to the next or previous field when you press RIGHT ARROW or LEFT ARROW whereas choosing Next character moves the insertion point to the next or previous character in the current field instead.

- The Cursor stops at first/last field setting locks the insertion point within the current record and prevents the RIGHT ARROW and LEFT ARROW keys from moving the insertion point to the next or previous record.

The second set of Editing options set the Find and Replace features.

The Default find/replace behavior setting determines the extent of the search. These options are also available on an immediate basis in the Find and Replace dialog box. Fast search searches the current field only and matches the entire field. General search searches all the fields and matches any part of the field. Start of field search searches the current field and matches only the beginning characters in the field.

The Confirm group requires Access to display a message requiring a confirmation of the current operation under specific conditions, such as when a record changes, when you delete a database object, or when you run an action query.

The final set of Editing options deal with the direction and alignment of text and the movement of the cursor through the data. If you are building a database for Middle Eastern language users, change the Default direction to right-to-left and set the General alignment to Interface mode, which sets the text alignment consistent with the user interface language. For example, if the language reads right-to-left, the text is aligned to the right. Also accept the Logical option for Cursor Movement.

You can choose to change to the Islamic lunar calendar instead of the Gregorian calendar by checking Use Hijri Calendar. Checking the Datasheet IME control option sets the East Asian IME Mode to No Control when entering data in a table datasheet.

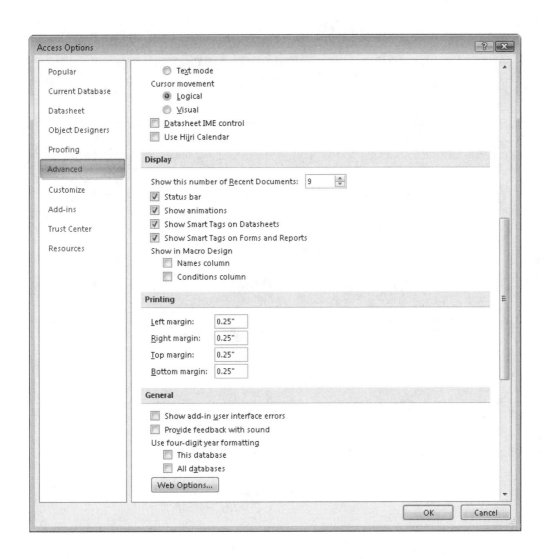

Display Options

The Display options all relate to what you see at startup, while working in the Database window, or when creating a macro.

In the Display group, you can choose to show or hide the following items:

- **Show the number of Recent Documents**   Sets the number of file names that appear in the Open Recent Database pane on the Getting Started page.

- **Status bar**   Displays the status bar at the bottom of the Access window.

 **Design for Multiple Languages**

When you have a database that involves two languages, one left-to-right and the other right-to-left, you can specify how the cursor decides which way to move as you enter text or when to click the RIGHT ARROW or LEFT ARROW keys. In the Cursor movement group, you have a choice between Logical and Visual.

- If you choose Logical, the cursor moves within bidirectional text, according to the direction of the language it's encountering. For example, if you have English and Arabic words in the same sentence, the insertion point moves left-to-right in the English text, and then starts at the rightmost character of the Arabic word and continues to move in a right-to-left direction.

- If you choose Visual, the cursor moves within bidirectional text by moving to the next adjacent character. For example, if you have English and Arabic text in the same sentence, the insertion point moves left-to-right through the English text, and then continues at the leftmost character of the Arabic word and continues in the left-to-right direction.

- **Show animations**   When checked, this shows movement in the datasheet. For example, when you insert or delete a column, the other columns can be seen to slide over.

- **Show Smart Tags on Datasheets**   When checked, displays the Smart Tag Action button when you move to a field that has a Smart Tag attached.

- **Show Smart Tags on Forms and Reports**   Accomplishes the same thing with forms and reports.

When you start a new macro, by default the Macro Name and Condition columns are not displayed. If you need them most of the time, you can use the Show in Macro Design group to show one or both when you start the macro. If you don't need them, you can clear them after opening the macro design window.

See Chapter 15 for more information about creating macros.

Printing Options

You can set the default margin sizes for all four margins. You can enter any number in the Print margins group that's compatible with your printer and paper size, ranging from 0 to the height or width of the printed page. The default setting for all margins is .25˝. You can override the default settings established here by running Page Setup before printing a form or report.

General

One of the options in this group adds sound to the workplace. If you select the Provide feedback with sound option, you activate sounds to accompany such tasks as a print job completion or an alert notification. You can customize sounds for this option through the Sounds dialog box in the Windows Control Panel.

CAUTION   *The sound option affects all Office programs.*

The Use four-digit year formatting applies the format to the current database or to all databases, even if the Format property of the field or control is set to show a two-digit year.

Customize Your Hyperlinks

If you are fussy about the looks of the hyperlinks in your Access documents, click the Web Options button in the General group of Advanced Options. Choose the colors you want for the hyperlinks before and after jumping to them. You can also remove the underline that shows up when you move the mouse pointer to the hyperlink.

13

Web Options

General

Appearance

Hyperlink color: Followed hyperlink color:
Blue   Violet

☑ Underline hyperlinks

OK   Cancel

Advanced

The last group of settings in the Advanced page apply to the performance of the database and restricting time spent interfacing with outside sources:

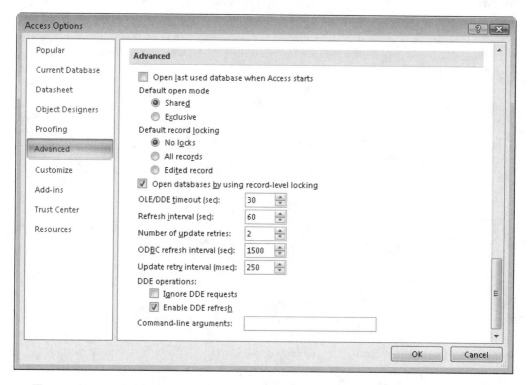

- ■ Open last used database when Access starts opens the most recently used database instead of the Getting Started page.

- ■ In the Default open mode group, you have a choice between Shared, which allows others to open the database at the same time you have it open, and Exclusive, which gives you sole access to the database. See Chapter 20 for more information about running Access in a shared environment.

- ■ You can set the Default record locking option to No locks, which doesn't lock records while they're being edited; All records, which locks all the records in a form or datasheet (and the underlying tables) as long as the form or datasheet is open; or Edited record, which locks only the record currently being edited.

- ■ The next option in the Advanced group is Open databases by using record-level locking, which makes record level locking the default for the open database. When you check this option, only one row or record is locked at a time instead of locking an entire page that might include several records.

The next group of selections in the Advanced group deals with shared databases and interactions with external sources. For example, enter a number between 0 and 300 seconds in the OLE/DDE timeout (sec) option to set the period of time Access should wait to re-attempt a failed OLE or DDE operation. The Number of update retries refers to the number of times Access tries to save a changed record locked by another user. Enter a number between 0 and 10.

Customize the Toolbar

The Customize options page (see Figure 13-7) is used to add buttons to the Quick Access toolbar that will perform specific actions. You can click one of the buttons from the list of Popular Commands and click Add.

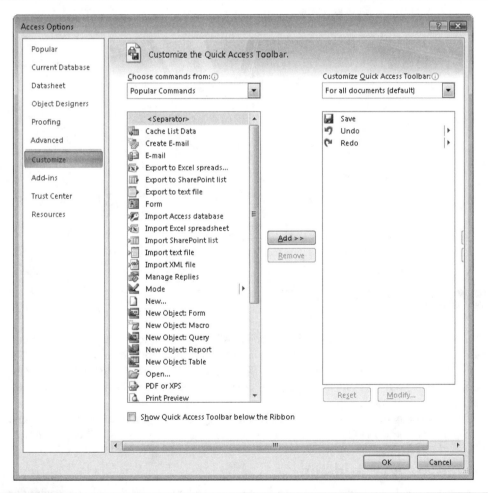

FIGURE 13-7   Adding actions to the Quick Access toolbar.

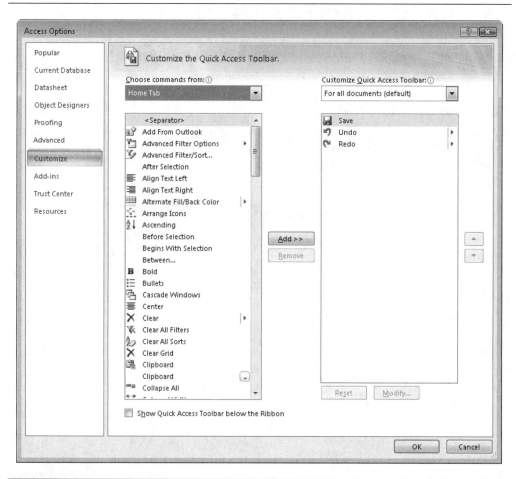

FIGURE 13-8   Looking at Home tab commands.

To see the list of commands on specific ribbon tabs and groups, click the Choose commands from down arrow and select the group that contains the commands you want to add. Figure 13-8 shows the list of commands that are available in the Home tab. You can choose the actions from the list and click Add. If the toolbar is hard to see above the ribbon, you can also choose to move the toolbar below the ribbon.

You can also drag a command from the ribbon to the Quick Access toolbar without using the Access Options window. See Chapter 17 for examples of customizing the Quick Access toolbar.

View and Manage Add-Ins

Add-ins are described as applications extensions because they go beyond the built-in capabilities of the Access program. For example, customized templates, smart tags, and XML Schemas are add-ins. The Add-ins page (see Figure 13-9) shows the name, location, and type of add-in in four groups:

- Active Application Add-ins are currently registered and running in Access.

- Inactive Application Add-ins are registered but not currently loaded. Document Related Add-ins are template files currently referenced by open documents.

- Disabled Application Add-ins are automatically disabled because they caused programs to crash.

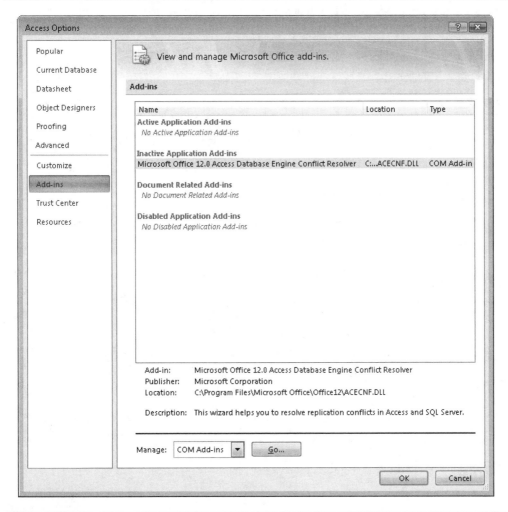

FIGURE 13-9   Viewing and managing add-ins.

There are no currently active add-ins in this database.

To pick more add-ins, click the Manage down arrow and choose from the list of available add-ins. Then click Go and choose the options you want.

Choose Trust Center Options

The Microsoft Office Trust Center (see Figure 13-10) was designed to protect against hackers that can do harm with add-ins. Microsoft has designed specific criteria that add-ins must meet to be accepted. Click the hyperlinks to see more information about the criteria.

To change any of the Trust Center Settings, click the button and click one of the options in the left pane. The Message Bar is the security message you see when you open a database that includes macros, VBA code, or add-ins that are not certified. You'll learn more about database security in Chapter 21.

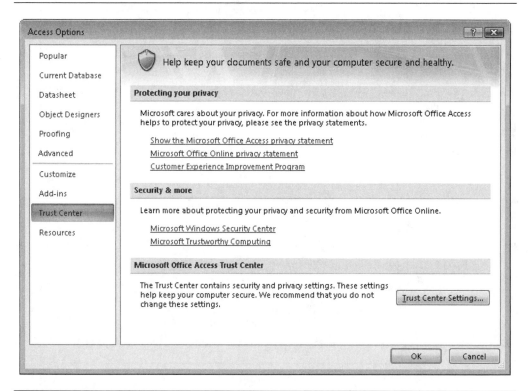

FIGURE 13-10 Finding security information.

Search Additional Resources

The Resources page in Access Options (see Figure 13-11) provides many ways to keep up to date with the latest improvements and get help with problems. You can use this page to activate Microsoft Office and register for online services.

FIGURE 13-11 Using additional resources.

Customize the Status Bar

The Access status bar at the bottom of the screen displays many indicators of current activities. For example, when the Caps Lock or Num Lock keys are pressed, their names appear in the status bar. It also shows Filtered when the current object contains filtered data. To change these settings, right-click in the status bar and check or uncheck the options.

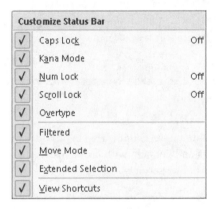

Now that you have seen the many ways you can create your own personalized workplace, let's move on to improving your database performance.

Chapter 14

Speed Up Your Database

How to...

- Optimize your database
- Optimize the tables and queries
- Optimize the forms, reports, and their controls
- Back up and restore the database
- Compact and repair the database

Unless you have a system that runs at 15 gazillion megahertz, you probably are interested in improving your database performance and speeding things up. Optimization is the ultimate goal, and stacking up performance improvements can help you get there. Access offers many ways to create an efficient database, including the Analyzer tools, which can examine the organization of your database, suggest ways to improve the distribution of information among the tables, and speed up overall database performance. For the purpose of security and reliability, there also are tools to back up and restore databases in case of emergency. Other tools compact the database to consume less disk space and repair databases that have become damaged.

Optimize a Database

Access provides two analytical tools that can save you a lot of time and help you optimize the structure of a new database. You can optimize the performance of a database without using the Analyzers by focusing on each of the elements that comprise the database—for example, the efficient distribution of data among the tables, the features of the database including the filters and indexes, and the objects themselves.

Use the Analyzer Wizards

The Table Analyzer Wizard examines the distribution of data among the tables and presents suggestions and ideas for further improvement. Another tool, the Performance Analyzer, looks at any or all of the objects in the database and makes suggestions to improve their performance. It also can examine the relationships you have established in the database and the set of Visual Basic code modules in the database, including both class and standard modules.

Table Analyzer

When you design a new database, you try to reduce the redundancy of data by creating a set of related tables. The Access Table Analyzer can look at the data distribution and make suggestions for additional optimization, including adding more indexes and further normalization to reduce data redundancy.

To start the Table Analyzer, do the following:

1. On the Database Tools tab in the Analyze group, click the Analyze Table command (see Figure 14-1).

NOTE *The first two dialog boxes offer a good description of the process of table optimization by first describing the problem, then showing possible solutions to the problem. Each dialog box also offers a look at examples of the problems and the solutions.*

2. Click Next. The second Table Analyzer dialog box shows how it plans to solve the problem by splitting tables so that each piece of data is stored only once.

3. Click Next. The third Table Analyzer dialog box shows a list of tables in the current database (see Figure 14-2).

TIP *If you expect to use the Table Analyzer often and don't want to see the two introductory dialog boxes each time, clear the check mark next to Show introductory pages, in the dialog box showing the list of tables. If you want them back, the next time you start the Analyzer, check the box again, click Cancel and then restart the Analyzer.*

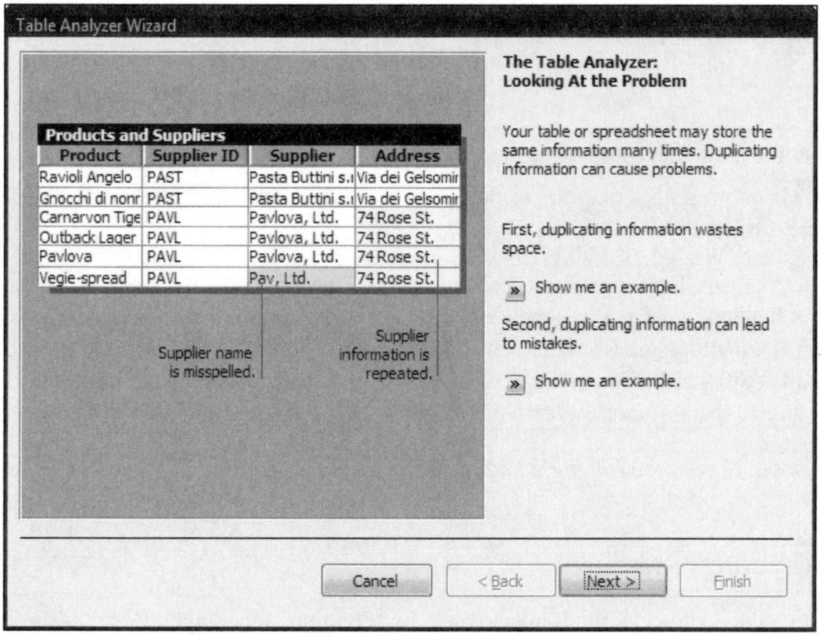

FIGURE 14-1   Starting the Table Analyzer.

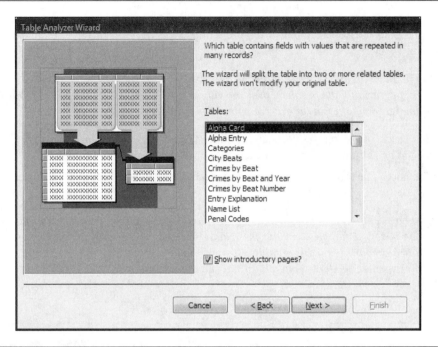

Selecting the table to analyze.

4. Select the table that contains repeated data and click Next.

5. The wizard presents a diagram of the suggested redistribution of information (see Figure 14-3).

The Table Analyzer has found that the values in the ZipCode and City fields are repeated many times in the Police database Name List table. It has suggested that you create a lookup table for each field with a link from the new Table2 to the original Name List table (now called Table1) and an additional link from the new Table3 back to Table2. Notice that the wizard has not changed any table names; changing table names is only a suggestion.

Click the Tips button (the light bulb icon) to get instructions about how to handle the wizard's suggestions.

To change the Table3 name:

1. Select Table3 and click the Rename Table button in the upper-right corner of the dialog box.

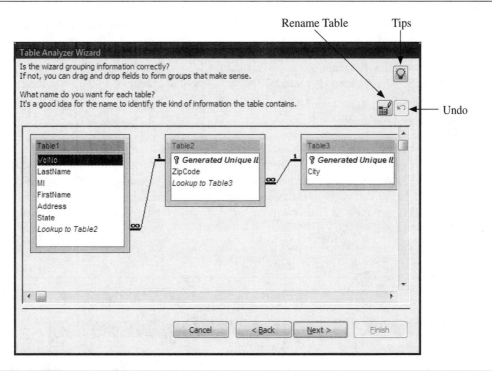

FIGURE 14-3   The Table Analyzer has some suggestions.

2. Enter a new name in the Table Name text box. When you change the name of the related table, the wizard changes the table name in the linked field in the primary table (Table2, in this case) to match. If you change your mind about the new name you entered for a table, click the Undo button next to the Rename Table button.

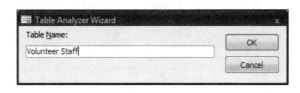

> You can also drag the field names from one table to the other to change the way the fields are grouped if it doesn't make sense to you.

3. Click Next to move to the dialog box in which you verify that the primary key fields are correct. The wizard has, by default, added a unique field to each new table and created the corresponding linking fields.

Access always recommends that tables have primary key fields assigned. Each of the new tables has been renamed and assigned a designated primary key field, but Table1 (VolunteerStaff) has no primary key field, you can specify a primary key for Table1 in one of two ways:

- Select an existing field that you know has unique values—for example, VolNo—and click the Set Unique Identifier button. The key symbol appears next to the field name.

- Select the table and click the Add Generated Key button. A new Generated Unique ID field is added to Table1.

Figure 14-4 shows the tables with the new primary keys.

After adding key fields, click Next. In the final dialog box, the wizard offers to create a query that uses the same name and looks like the original table. Allowing the wizard to do this enables you to work with the data all in one place and guarantees that all the forms and reports you have created using the original table as a basis will continue to work properly. You can also choose to create this query yourself.

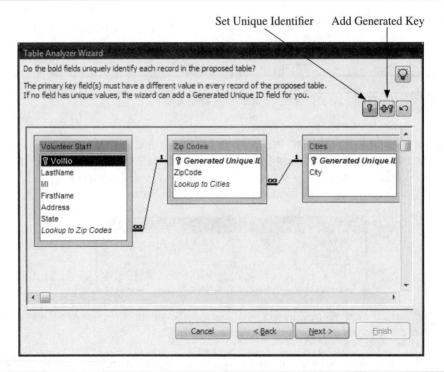

FIGURE 14-4   Verifying the primary key fields.

If you chose to decide which fields to place in which tables (refer to Figure 14-3), the next dialog box shows only the original table without the new, intermediate Table2. You can create the new table by dragging a field name from the list in Table1. You can also rename the tables and define the primary key field for the new table using the buttons in the dialog box. After you click Next, the wizard offers to create a query for you as before.

Using the Performance Analyzer

The Performance Analyzer looks at the objects in the database and suggests ways to improve the application's performance. When you finish with the Performance Analyzer, many of the suggestions can be implemented automatically.

To start the Performance Analyzer, do the following:

1. On the Database Tools tab in the Analyze group, click the Analyze Performance command. The first dialog box includes a tab for each type of database object. Each tab contains the names of all those objects in the current database. The Current Database tab contains the Relationships and VBA Project options. If you click the All Object Types tab, you can see all the names in one place.

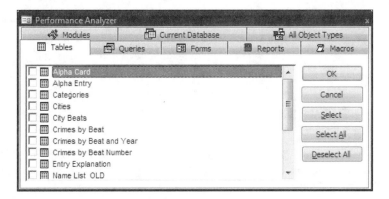

2. Select the appropriate tab and select the names individually or click Select All to choose all the objects.

3. If you want to analyze the entire database, click the All Object Types tab and choose Select All.

4. After selecting the items you want analyzed, click OK.

A message box informs you about the progress of the analysis and when all the objects have been inspected; the wizard displays a dialog box with a list of recommendations, suggestions, and ideas (see Figure 14-5). Any problems that have been fixed are also denoted. The Analysis Notes pane describes the general overall findings. When you select one of the items in the list, additional explanations are displayed in the Analysis Notes pane.

14

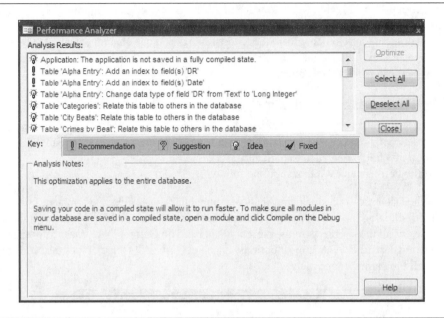

FIGURE 14-5 The findings of the Performance Analyzer

If you include queries in the objects to analyze, be sure to have enough data in the tables to give the query a good workout.

The Analyzer has recommended that you add an index to the Date and DR fields of the Alpha Entry table. When you select one of these recommendations, the Analysis Notes show that if you index on this field, it will benefit the Alpha Entry table and your queries will run faster. To implement a recommendation, select it and then click Optimize. After considering all the items in the list, click Close to close the Performance Analyzer.

The Performance Analyzer doesn't always have the whole picture. Accept its recommendations and suggestions carefully. For example, adding indexes might improve query performance but it also increases the disk space needed for the database and could slow down entering and editing data.

Optimize Tables and Queries

After you have done all you can to normalize the database and distribute data efficiently among the tables, there are a few other things you can do to speed up data processing:

- Choose the appropriate data type for each field to save space and improve join operations. Also, if you know the range of values that will be stored in the field, choose the smallest field size that the data type will accept. You have no choice with date/time fields, but you can reduce the default 255-character field size for text fields if the data is, for example, a ZIP code.

- Make sure the fields on either side of a relationship are of the same or a compatible data type.

Optimize with Indexes

In addition to the primary key, which is automatically indexed, you can create indexes on one or more fields to find and sort records faster. Indexes can speed up queries if the fields on both sides of the join are indexed. In a one-to-many relationship, the primary table is already indexed on the primary key field, creating an index for the foreign key field in the related table helps when the query is run. Also, indexing any field used in a criteria rule in the query reduces processing time for it.

For example, in the Police database, the Alpha Entry table has two indexes in addition to the primary key. The Alpha EntryCode index relates the table to the Code field in the Penal Codes table. The Alpha EntryIndex index related the Alpha Entry table to the Index field in the Alpha Card table.

NOTE   *Refer to Chapter 3 for information about creating indexes.*

Multiple-field indexes help distinguish between records that might have more than one record with the same value in the first field. If you are creating a multiple-field index, use only as many fields as necessary.

NOTE   *Although indexes can speed up searches and sorts, as well as queries of related tables, they can also add to the database size. Each index represents a condensed lookup table. Additional problems can occur in a multiple-user environment because indexes can reduce the concurrency of the database, thereby limiting the ability of more than one user to modify data at the same time.*

Optimize Queries

Queries are key for retrieving the right data from your database. There are many things you can do to help speed up running queries. Among the guidelines for optimizing queries are the following:

- Include only the fields you need in the query. If a field is not needed in the result set but you are using it as a criterion, clear the Show check box in the query grid.

- Avoid calculated fields in a query as much as possible. If you need an expression in the result of the query, add a control to the form or report instead and use the expression as the control source.

- Use Between...And... in a criteria expression rather than the > and < operators.

- If you want to count all the records in the recordset, use Count(*) instead of Count([*field name*]).

14

- When grouping records by values in one of the joined fields, be sure to place the Group By aggregate function in the field on the side of the joint containing the values you want to summarize. If you place Group By in the joined field, Access must join all the records and calculate the aggregate using only the necessary fields.

- Use as few Group By aggregates as possible. You might be able to use the First function instead in some cases.

- Try not to use restrictive criteria on non-indexed or calculated fields.

- If you need to place criteria on one of the fields used to join two tables in a one-to-many relationship, you can place it on either field in the grid. Run some tests to see which placement results in a faster query.

- If you are working with fairly static data, consider running a make-table query and using the resulting table instead of the query as the basis for forms and reports. You can always run the make-table query again if the data changes. Be sure to add indexes to the resulting table.

- When you create a crosstab query, try to use fixed column headings to save the time it takes to update them.

Optimize Filter By Form

The Filter By Form defaults in the filter lookup options for the current database can improve the performance of all tables and queries, and all text box controls that use the Database Default setting in the Filter Lookup property. As discussed in Chapter 13, the Filter lookup group of options can limit the displayed list of values to indexed fields only or include local indexed and non-indexed fields. You can also set a limit on the number of records that must be read to come up with the list of unique values to display in the drop-down list in the grid.

If the list of field values takes too long to display, you can optimize the Filter By Form for a single text box control on a form by setting the control's Filter Lookup property (on the Data tab) to Never. This suppresses displaying the field values on the drop-down list in the Filter By Form window.

Optimize Forms and Reports

Most of the optimization strategies can be used on forms, reports, subforms, and subreports. There are also techniques that you can apply to individual text box and combo box controls to improve their performance in forms and reports.

The following tips apply to both forms and reports:

- Base the subform or subreport on a saved query that includes only the required fields and that has a filter that results in only the required set of records.

- If the record order is not important, you can save time by not sorting records in an underlying query, especially if the query uses fields from multiple tables.

■ Try not to sort or group on expressions.

■ Make sure the underlying query is optimized before loading the form or report.

■ Index on the fields you use for sorting or grouping.

■ Don't overdo the design with bitmaps and graphic objects. However, when you need to add graphics, convert the unbound object frame controls to image controls, which take less time to load.

■ You can save a lot of disk space by using black-and-white bitmaps rather than color.

■ Don't overlap controls unless absolutely necessary. Access must draw the controls in the form or report window twice to place overlapping controls.

■ Use subforms and subreports sparingly; they occupy as much space as the main form or report. Base all subforms and subreports on queries instead of tables and include only the necessary fields.

■ Index all fields in a subform or subreport that are linked to the main form or report. In addition, index all fields used in the criteria.

■ If the form or report has no event procedures associated with it, make sure the form or report Has Module property (on the Other tab) is set to No. The form or report will load faster and take less disk space without taking up the reserved class module space.

A few more strategies apply only to forms:

■ Don't leave a form open if you aren't using it. Access still must take time to refresh the window whether you are working in it or not.

■ Design a form with as few controls as possible. Having a large number of controls reduces the efficiency of the form. If you need a lot of controls, consider adding a tab control to create a multiple-page form with controls grouped logically on the pages.

■ If the underlying record source contains a lot of records and you are planning to use the form primarily for data entry, change the form's Data Entry property to Yes. When the form opens, it automatically moves to the end of the recordset and displays a blank record in the form. If you open the form with records showing, Access must read every record before it can display a blank new record.

■ If you don't expect to edit the records in a subform, you can save time by setting the subform's Allow Edits, Allow Additions, and Allow Deletions properties all to No. An alternative is to set the Recordset Type to Snapshot instead of to the default Dynaset. These are all properties of the subform object itself, not the subform control on the main form.

■ Use a hyperlink instead of a command button to open a form. Command buttons added with the help of the Command Button Wizard result in an event procedure written in Visual Basic code; avoiding the use of such command buttons will eliminate the class module and save space and time.

14

Optimize Controls

List box, combo box, and drop-down list box controls all show field values from which you can choose. They are bound to a field in the underlying record source. When you use a wizard to create the list box or combo box control, it automatically constructs a SQL statement and assigns it to the control's Record Source property. You can save time by basing the control on a saved query instead of the SQL statement, which must be evaluated each time you activate the control.

To convert the wizard's SQL statement to a saved query:

1. Open the control's property sheet and click the Build button next to the Row Source property. The SQL statement appears in the Query Builder window.

2. On the Design tab in the Close group, click the Save Object As command and enter a name for the query in the Save As dialog box.

3. When you close the Query Builder window, Access asks if you want to save the query with that name and update the property with the query name. Respond Yes.

There are several more ways to optimize the behavior of these controls:

- Be sure to index on the first field displayed in the combo box or list box and on the bound field in the underlying table, if they are different fields.

- Set the AutoExpand property of the combo box control to No if you don't require the fill-in-as-you-type feature.

- If you do use the fill-in-as-you-type feature by setting the AutoExpand property to Yes, be sure the first field in the displayed list is a Text data type rather than a Number data type. Access converts the numeric value to text to find a match for completing the entry. Using text in the first field eliminates the need for this conversion.

- Use the default format and property settings for the controls. Access saves only the exceptions to the default settings with the form. If you find you are changing the same property frequently, you can change the default setting for the control and avoid having to store both.

Back Up and Restore a Database

To reduce the risk of losing data, it is a good idea to have a backup copy of your database. The database must be closed before you can back it up. If you are working in a multiple-user environment, make sure all the users have closed the database before you start the backup process. There are several ways to make a backup copy:

You Can Back Up Just Part of Your Database

You can back up individual objects of your database without copying the entire file. To do this, create a new, blank database and import the objects into it from the original database. See Chapter 18 for information about importing database objects.

■ In Windows, locate the folder that contains your database. Drag the filename in the Windows Explorer list from the hard disk to another disk drive.

■ Right-click the filename or database shortcut and point to Send To in the shortcut menu, then click the drive to which you want to copy.

You can also use Access to create a backup database. This creates a regular copy to the database with no compression or other reformatting. To restore the database, simply copy it back to where you want to use it. To back up the database with Access, do the following:

1. Click the Microsoft Office button and point to Manage. Once there, choose Backup Database.

2. In the Save As dialog box, enter the name and locations for the backup copy. Click Save.

To restore the database from a copy, use the recover feature of the same method you used to make the backup copy. If you used Windows, drag the filename from the list to the database folder on the hard drive.

 If the backup copy and the existing database in the database folder have the same name, you can replace the existing database when you restore the backup copy. If you want to save the original database, rename it before restoring from the backup copy.

14

Compact and Repair a Database

Access provides some other useful tools for managing databases. One of them converts databases to or from previous versions of Access. Another creates an ACCDE file from the current database. An ACCDE file contains compiled versions of all the code in the database with none of the original source code. ACCDE databases run faster but the user cannot access the source code for viewing or editing.

NOTE *See Appendix A for information about converting databases to and from Access 2007.*

Another utility repairs and compacts a database. As you delete tables and queries and create new ones, your database can become scattered about on the disk with useless small blocks of space between. Compacting the database makes a copy of the database and rearranges the file so that the disk space is used more efficiently. You can compact an open database in place by clicking the Microsoft Office button, pointing to Manage and choosing Compact and Repair Database. Access takes only a few moments to compact the database, showing progress in the status bar.

If a database becomes damaged in some way, Access usually detects this when you try to open the database or if you try to compact, encrypt, or decrypt it. When damage is found, Access offers the option to repair the database at once. However, if your database begins to act strangely but Access has not noticed any damage, you can use the Compact and Repair Database utility manually.

To compact and repair a closed database:

1. Close all databases. Then, from the Getting Started window, click the Microsoft Office button, point to Manage and click Compact and Repair Database.

2. In the Database to Compact From dialog box which looks just like the Open dialog box, select the name of the database you want to compact and click Compact.

3. In the Compact Database Into dialog box, specify the drive and folder for the compacted database and enter a name for the copy or choose a name from the list.

4. Click Save. If you choose the same name as the original database, Access asks for confirmation before replacing the file.

TIP *You can stop the process at any time by pressing ESC or CTRL-BREAK.*

If the compaction is successful and you choose to use the same name and path for the compacted file, Access replaces the original database file with the compacted version. If Access is not successful in compacting a database, one of the following reasons might be to blame:

■ Another user has the database open.

■ Your disk does not have enough free space for both the original copy and the compacted copy of the database. To remedy this, delete as many unnecessary files as you can and try compacting the database again.

■ You do not have permission to copy all the tables in the database. You need both Open Run and Open Exclusive permissions in order to make copies of the data. If you are not the owner of this database, find the owner and try to obtain permission. If you are the owner, update the permissions for all the tables.

■ The database is on a read-only network or the file attribute is set to read-only.

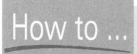

You can save time by specifying that the database is automatically compacted when you close it, if the file size would be reduced by more than 256KB. Check the Compact on Close option on the General tab of the Options dialog box. If another user has the database open, Access will not compact it until the last user closes it.

How to ... Document a Database

One of the most important tasks in a database management system is documentation, especially if many people are involved with its development and use. One of the Access analysis tools is the Documenter, which analyzes the current database and prints a report of the details of the entire database or only specified parts.

To run the Documenter:

1. On the Database Tools tab in the Analyze group, click the Documenter command.

2. Select the items on each tab that you want documented or choose Select All on the All Object Types tab to select everything in the database, including the relationships and the database properties.

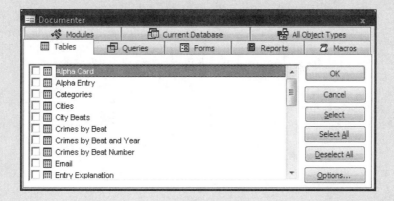

14

(continued)

3. To limit the amount of information to print in the table definitions, click Options and check the desired options in the Print Table Definition dialog box.

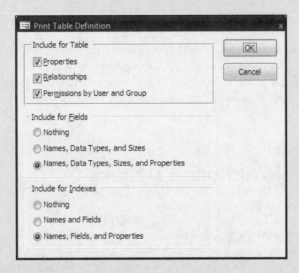

4. To limit the information in another object type, select one of the objects and click Options. Each object has a list of details to select from.

5. After making all your selections, click OK twice to start the Documenter.

You can stop the Documenter any time by pressing CTRL-BREAK.

The status bar shows the progress of the analysis with messages and odometers. When the Documenter is finished, the report is opened in Print Preview.

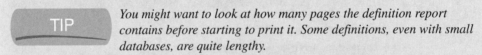

You might want to look at how many pages the definition report contains before starting to print it. Some definitions, even with small databases, are quite lengthy.

If you want to save the report, you can output the definitions to one of several file formats. On the Print Preview tab in the Data group, choose PDF or XPS, Word, Text File, or click More and choose to export to another Access database, an XML file, the Snapshot Viewer, or an HTML file.

Chapter 15

Automate with Macros

How to...

- Create a simple macro
- Test and debug a macro
- Assign a macro to an event property
- Add conditions to the macro
- Create an AutoExec macro that runs when you launch Access
- Create a macro group

A *macro* is an automation tool that can be embedded in a form or report design or available as an individual Access object listed in the Macros group in the Navigation Pane. You can attach a macro to an event property of any object in your database. Macros provide a quick and easy way to program your Access application to do what you want. With macros, you can specify customized responses to user actions such as clicking a button, opening a form, or selecting an option in an options group. Macros can also respond to system conditions such as an empty recordset.

A macro is a list of one or more actions that work together to carry out a particular task in response to an event. Each *action* carries out one particular operation. You create the list of actions in the order in which you want them to execute. In addition to selecting the action to be taken, you specify other details of the action, called *arguments*. These arguments provide additional information such as which form to open or how you want to filter the records to be displayed.

You can also set conditions under which the macro action is to be performed, such as to display a message box if a field contains a certain value or is blank. The macro runs only if the condition evaluates to True. If the condition is False, the action is skipped. If there is another action in the macro, it is executed; if not, the macro stops.

Create a Simple Macro

The first step in creating a macro is to list the actions you want performed when an event occurs. Each action might require specific arguments or need to be performed only under certain conditions. Make sure you choose the right event to which the macro should respond.

You have two ways to start your new macro;

- On the Create tab in the Other group, click the Macro command.
- Go to the Property Sheet of the form, report, section or control that needs the macro and click the Build button in the Event property box. Then choose the Macro Builder in the Choose Builder dialog box.

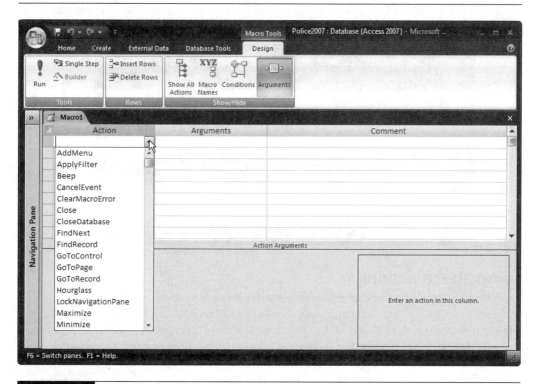

FIGURE 15-1   Working in the Macro window.

The Macro window opens showing a blank macro (see Figure 15-1). The drop-down list in the Action column contains a list of actions from which to choose. The Arguments column displays a list of arguments to select for each macro action. As you enter arguments in the lower pane, they are listed in the Arguments column. Entries in the Comment column are optional but highly recommended as a reminder of what the macro is meant to accomplish.

NOTE   *Comments are especially useful when macros are stored as separate objects, rather than linked with a particular form or report. The comments can explain how the macro is used and to which events it is attached. This can also be important if you rename the macro. You will need to find all the references to it and change the name there, too.*

15

The Macro Tools ribbon has some new groups and commands. You will see how these are used in the next sections.

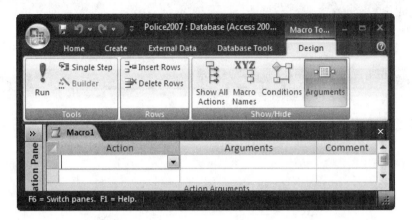

Choose Macro Actions

Access offers actions that cover data management activities such as opening forms and reports, printing reports, filtering data, validating data, moving among records in a form, playing sounds, displaying message boxes, and even exchanging data with other programs. To add an action to a macro, you can either choose from the drop-down list or type the name yourself. Once you select an action from the list, the lower pane displays the associated arguments, some of which are required; others are optional, depending on the action.

As an example, create a stand-alone macro in the Police database that opens the Alpha Card form in read-only mode by doing the following:

1. Open the Macro window using the Create tab.

2. Click the Action drop-down arrow, scroll down the list, and choose OpenForm from the list.

The Action Arguments pane now contains the arguments for the OpenForm action, and the information pane describes the selected OpenForm action. The required arguments are also displayed in the Argument column. The Form Name argument is required. Other required arguments show selections whereas the optional arguments are blank in the pane and skipped in the Arguments column.

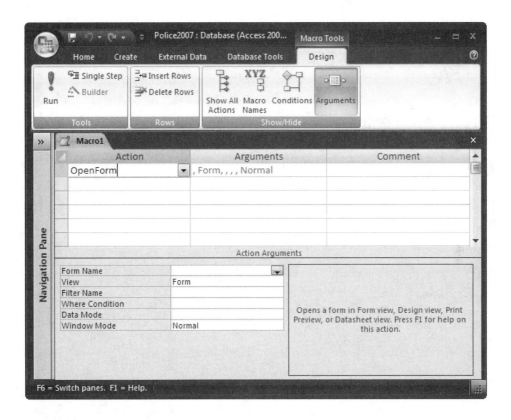

Set Action Arguments

Most macro actions have a list of associated arguments that give Access more information about how you want the action carried out. When you add an action to a macro, the argument list appears in the lower pane and in the Arguments column.

You can usually type the value you want in an argument box but many offer drop-down lists. Some require that if you enter a value it must be one that is in the list. A description of the current argument is displayed in a pane to the right of the argument list. If you need more help, press F1 with the insertion point in the argument box.

To continue with the Alpha Card form example, do the following:

1. Click in the Form Name box in the Action Arguments pane and select Alpha Card from the drop-down list of all the forms in the current database.

15

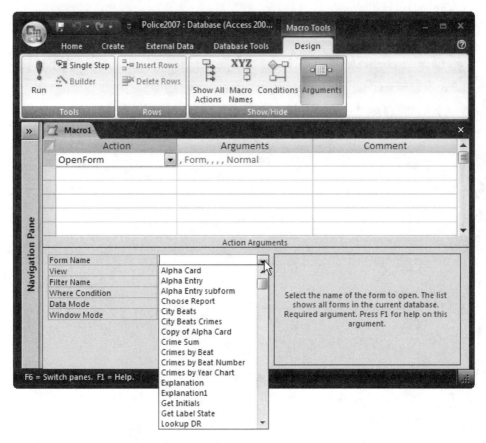

2. Set the other arguments as follows:

- Accept the default Form as the View argument.
- Leave the Filter Name argument blank because we want to see all the records.
- Again, we want all the records so do not add a SQL WHERE clause in the Where Condition argument.
- Choose Read Only from the Data Mode list.
- Leave Window Mode with the default Normal setting.

3. Close the Macro window and enter **Open Alpha Card** as the name for the macro in the Save As dialog box.

4. Click OK. You can now see the name of the new macro in the Macros group in the Navigation Pane.

In some cases, choices for one argument can determine which choices are available for an argument farther down in the list. For this reason, it is best to set the arguments in the order they are listed in the Action Arguments pane.

Instead of selecting from a list or entering a value, you can enter an expression that evaluates to the argument value you want to use. Always precede the expression with an equal sign so Access recognizes it as an expression instead of an identifier. For example, the expression *=[EntryNo]* sets the argument to the value in the EntryNo control. If you would like help from the Expression Builder, click the Build button, which appears at the right of the argument box when you click in an argument that will accept an expression.

Not all arguments accept expressions. For example, you must select from the list for the Object Type argument. If you use an expression where one isn't permitted, you get an error message.

Test and Debug a Macro

Once you complete the macro, you can run it to see if it behaves as planned. You have a choice of running the complete macro at once or stepping through each action one at a time. If an error occurs in the macro or you don't get the results you expect, use the step-through method of running the macro to locate the action that causes the error.

Start the Macro

There are several ways to run a macro after you have finished adding the actions and setting the arguments. While still in the Macro window, you can click the Run button in the Tools group on the Design tab to run the macro in place. After you have named and saved a stand-alone macro, you can run it in place or from the Navigation Pane using one of the following methods:

- Double-click the macro name.
- Right-click the macro name and choose Run from the shortcut menu.

If your macro is embedded in a particular form or report, open it first in Form or Report view.

If an error occurs during the operation, Access displays an error message.

Read the message and then click OK to open the Action Failed dialog box, which tells you which action in the macro failed and the arguments that were being used at the time.

Missing argument

The Arguments box in this case shows that the second argument, Object Name, is required but missing from the GoToRecord action. You can tell by the two commas with no argument between them. It also shows any conditions that were in effect. Your only option in this dialog box is to click Stop All Macros to stop the macro. Before closing the dialog box, note the action name, error number, and other data about where the fault occurred. It is up to you to switch to the Macro window to correct the problem.

Step Through a Macro

If you have created a macro with many actions and it contains an error, you can use the Single Step method to move through the macro one action at a time. You must be in the Macro window to step through the macro actions.

To start stepping through the Open Alpha Card macro:

1. Right-click the macro name in the Navigation Pane and choose Design view.

2. Click the Single Step command in the Tools group.

3. Click Run to carry out the first action. A Macro Single Step dialog box now opens showing the details of the first step in your macro. Notice there is no error number.

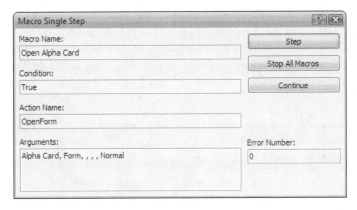

4. Your options in this dialog box are as follows:

    ■ **Step**   Moves to the next action (default).

    ■ **Stop All Macros**   Stops macro execution.

    ■ **Continue**   Quits single stepping and runs the rest of the macro without stopping. If another error occurs, the macro stops and another Action Failed dialog box appears.

    This can get a little confusing when you see steps from other macros in the process. If any other macros run during the running of this macro, you will step through them as well. For example, when the Alpha Card form opens, the ExplainIt macro associated with the Explanation button on the form also runs. Then the maxView macro that restores the form to its full screen view also runs. Finally, you will see the step that causes the error.

    After the macro finishes, click the Single Step command again to turn it off; otherwise, the next macro you run will single step, too.

Modify a Macro

After you see how a macro runs, you might decide to make some changes to it, such as adding an action, changing the order of the actions, adding a condition to the action, adding a Where Condition argument to limit the records, or creating additional macros to include in a macro group.

To open a stand-alone macro for modification, right-click the macro name in the Navigation Pane and choose Design View. If the macro is embedded, do the following:

1. Open the form or report in Design or Layout view.

2. Select the section or control in which the macro is embedded.

3. Open the Property Sheet and click the Build button in the Event property.

4. Choose Macro Builder in the Choose Builder dialog box.

15

Use the Insert Rows and Delete Rows commands in the Rows group or right-click in the macro design and choose from the shortcut menu to add or delete actions. You can also use the standard Cut, Copy, and Paste operations to edit a macro. The Undo button is also available on the Quick Access toolbar to reject any changes. After making the changes to the macro, save it again. If you save it with a different name, be sure to change all references to the macro accordingly.

If the macro operates on important data, make a temporary copy of the data to use during the modification process. This way, if anything goes wrong, you have not destroyed valuable information.

Assign a Macro to an Event Property

If you have not embedded the macro in an event property, you need to decide when you want it to happen. Access responds to all kinds of events that occur when you are working with a form or report including mouse clicks, changes in data, changes in focus, and opening or closing of a form or report. After you decide when you want the macro to run, set the corresponding event property of the form, report, or control to the name of the macro. For example, if you want to run a macro that sounds a beep when a form opens, assign the macro to the On Open property of the form.

See the sidebar "About Events and Event Properties" in Chapter 10 for a brief orientation.

To attach a macro to an event property, do the following:

1. Open the form or report in Design or Layout view and select the form, report, section, or control to which you want to attach the macro.

2. Open the property sheet and click the Event tab to see a list of events that can occur for the selected object.

3. Click the property whose event you want to run the macro and choose the macro name from the drop-down list.

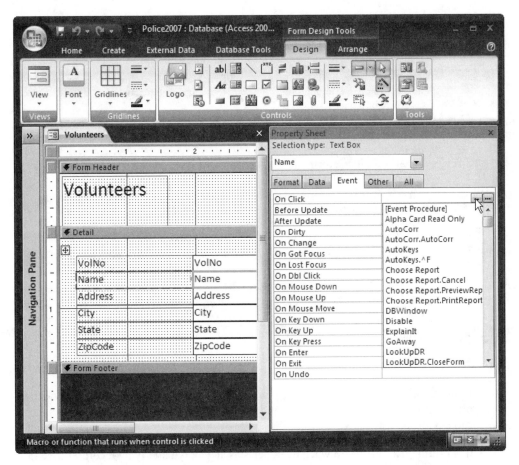

4. Save and close the form or report design.

When the event occurs, the built-in response, if any, occurs first, and then the macro runs. For example, when you click a button, the built-in response occurs and the button appears pressed. If you have attached a macro to the On Click event property, the macro runs next.

Decide Which Event to Use

Although the property sheet shows quite a long list of event properties for forms and controls, there are a few that you will use more often, for example, when a form opens or the data in a control changes. Table 15-1 lists some of the commonly used form and control event properties.

15

Property	Occurs When	Use To
On Open	The form opens before the first record is displayed.	Open, close, or minimize other forms or maximize this form.
On Current	The form is opened and the focus moves to a record, or the form is refreshed or requeried.	Synchronize data among forms or move focus to a specific control.
Before Update	After the focus leaves a record but before the data is saved in the database. Also occurs after a control loses focus but before the control is changed.	Display a message to confirm the change. Validate data entered in a control.
After Update	After the record changes have been saved in the database. Also occurs after a control loses focus and after the control is changed.	Update the data in other controls, forms, or reports. Move focus to a different page, control, or record in the form. Also transmit new data to other applications.
On Click	Press and release the left mouse button over a control.	Carry out commands and command-like actions.
On Enter	Move to a control before it gets focus.	Display information about data to enter in the control or a request for a user password.

TABLE 15-1 Commonly Used Form and Control Event Properties

Reports and report sections have fewer event properties because there is little user interaction with a report. Some of the more common event properties used to attach macros and event procedures to reports are listed next:

- ■ **On No Data** Runs a macro when the report has an empty underlying recordset. Use to cancel the print event.

- ■ **On Open** Runs a macro when the report opens but before printing begins. Use to prompt for a filter for the records to be included in the report.

- ■ **On Page** Runs a macro after the page has been formatted but before printing begins. Use to add a graphic or border design to the report.

Add Conditions to a Macro

When you want a macro to run only under specific circumstances, you can add a condition to any of the macro actions. The macro condition effectively states, "If this condition is true, run this action. If it is not true, go to the next action, if any." You can use conditions to set control values or control properties and even run additional macros. Such test comparisons are not case sensitive.

Some examples of using conditions are listed next:

- If the balance of an account is negative, change the color of the number to red.
- If a student's grades are exemplary, print a congratulatory message.
- If the inventory level of an item is low, display a message to remind the user to reorder.
- If the order exceeds a specific total, calculate the amount due with a volume discount.

NOTE *Do not confuse the macro condition, which determines whether the action takes place, with the Where Condition, which limits the records in the form or report. The macro condition is entered in the Condition column of the macro sheet; the Where Condition is an argument of many macro actions.*

To add the Condition column to the macro sheet, in the Show/Hide group, click the Conditions command. Type the logical expression for the condition in the row with the action you want to carry out if the condition is True. If you want to use the Expression Builder to help with the expression, right-click in the Condition column. and Next, choose Build in the shortcut menu. You can also click the Builder Command in the Tools group.

Normally, a condition applies only to the action on the same row in the macro sheet. If the condition is not met, the next action is executed. To continue the condition to the next action, enter an ellipsis (...) in the Condition column of the next row. You can apply the condition to several sequential actions.

You can also use conditions to create an If...Then...Else structure in a macro. This conditional logic runs one or more actions if the condition is met and a different set if the condition evaluates to False. This structure is very useful for changing the order of execution based on the outcome of the condition. For example, you might want to carry out a calculation if a field has a value but to move to another record if the field is blank. Use the ISNULL function to test for blanks and NOT ISNULL to test for a value.

Create a Macro to Display a Warning

The MsgBox action is one of the most useful macro actions when interacting with the user. You can use it to display warnings, alerts, and other information. The MsgBox action has four arguments: Message, Beep, Type, and Title. One example of using a macro with a condition is the PurgeValid macro, which ensures that certain reports of serious criminal activity in the Police Alpha Entry table are not purged from the database by accident.

The macro is based on a condition that compares the Code value, which identifies the crime, with the value in the Purge field. The Purge field contains the date when the record might be erased from the file. The report of certain crimes is never to be erased. If the Code is in a certain range, there should be no date entered in the Purge field.

An additional condition is combined with the test for the Code value. This condition skips records with blank Purge fields. The reason for this added test is that when the user tabs through the form, the Purge control can get focus whether it has a value or not; you don't want to see the

15

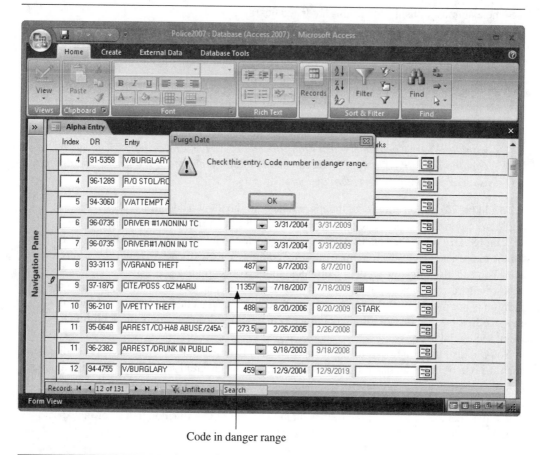

Code in danger range

FIGURE 15-2 A macro helps ensure data validation.

message if you have just skipped through the control. Figure 15-2 shows the result of a macro that checks the code value; if the value is within the danger range (between 11000 and 19999), the macro displays a message when the user tries to enter a date in the Purge field. Since this macro is used only when entering or editing data in the Alpha Entry form, you can embed the macro in the form design.

Here's how to create the PurgeValid macro:

1. Open the Alpha Entry form in Design or Layout view and select the Purge control.

2. Open the Property Sheet and on the Event tab, select the Before Update property and click the Build button.

3. Choose Macro Builder in the Choose Builder dialog box and click OK.

4. In the Macro window, choose MsgBox in the Action list and click the Conditions command in the Show/Hide group.

5. Click the Conditions command and enter the expression **[Forms]![Alpha Entry]![Code] Between 11000 And 19999 And Not IsNull([Forms]![Alpha Entry]![Purge])** in the condition row of the MsgBox action.

6. In the Message argument, enter **Check this entry. Code number in danger range**.

Do not enclose the message in quotations marks unless you also want to display the marks.

7. Set the Beep argument to Yes.

8. Select Warning! as the Type.

9. Enter Purge Date as the message box Title.

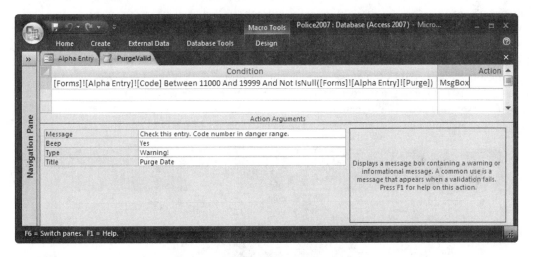

Save and close the Macro window and then test the new macro:

1. Switch to Form view and move to a record with a code number in the danger range.

2. Click in the Purge field, enter a date, and press TAB. The message appears warning you not to enter a date in this record.

Create Other Commonly Used Macros

When you work with a database, Access causes many things to happen in response to your actions. You might not know that you can customize the database with macros to accomplish many similar operations according to your designs. This section discusses some of the more common applications for macros.

15

Set Control Values and Properties

SetValue is a very useful macro action that sets the value of a field, control, or property of a form, a form datasheet, or a report. You can set a value for almost any control, form, and report property in any view with the SetValue action. The action has two arguments, both of which are required: Item and Expression. The Item argument contains the name of the field, control, or property whose value you want to set. The Expression argument contains the value you want to set for the item. Do not precede the expression with an equal sign. Use full syntax complete with all the identifiers when referring to any Access objects in the Item or the Expression argument.

If you don't see SetValue in the list of macro actions, click the Show All Actions command in the Show/Hide group on the Design tab.

Set Control Values

In addition to entering the value itself, you can set the value of a control based on the value of another control in the same or a different form or report. You can also use the result of a calculation or the value returned by an option group to set the value of a control. For example, when you are adding new records to the Alpha Entry recordset in the subform of the Alpha Card form, you can compute the value of the Purge field. Depending on the Code value, the entry can be purged from the person's file after a certain length of time, usually three or seven years. To save data entry time, you can write a macro that examines the Code value and uses the DateAdd function to set the Purge date by adding a specified number of years to the Date field value. Attach or embed the macro to the After Update Event property of the Date control.

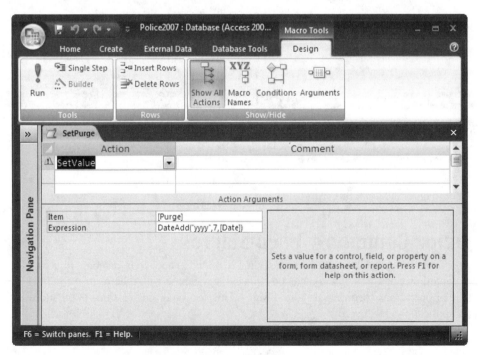

The first argument in the DateAdd function, "yyyy," indicates that the interval you want to increment is the year part of the date value. The second argument is the number to add, while the third names the control that contains the original date.

Set Control Properties

You can set many of the properties of forms, reports, and controls by running a macro. For example, you can hide a control from view on the form or disable it so the user can't enter data in it. You can also change colors, fonts, and other appearance properties.

As an example of setting a property with a macro, disable the Drivers License control if the subject of the Alpha Card report is younger than 16. To do this, set the Enabled property to No. When a control is disabled, it still appears on the screen but is dimmed; you can't reach it by pressing TAB or by clicking it.

To create this embedded macro, do the following:

1. Open the Alpha Card form in Design view and select the Age text box control then open the Property Sheet.

2. On the Event tab, click the Build button in the After Update property.

3. Choose Macro Builder in the Choose Builder dialog box.

4. On the Design tab in the Show/Hide group, click the Conditions command and enter **[Age]<16** as the condition.

5. Choose SetValue in the Action list. (You may have to click the Show All Actions to see it in the list.)

TIP *Make sure the Age field is a Number data type.*

Now you are ready to move to the Action Arguments pane to complete the macro. To ensure that you enter the correct identifier, you can use the Expression Builder in the Macro window. After adding the SetValue action to the macro, click Build (...) next to the Item argument to open the Expression Builder., Next, then do the following:

1. Double-click on the Forms folder, and then double-click on the All Forms folder in the left panel to open the list of forms in the current database.

2. Choose the Alpha Card form. A list of all controls and labels in the form appears in the center panel.

3. Choose Drivers License. A list of all the properties that apply to the Drivers License text box control appears in the right panel.

4. Choose Enabled and click Paste. When you click OK, the expression is placed in the Item argument box.

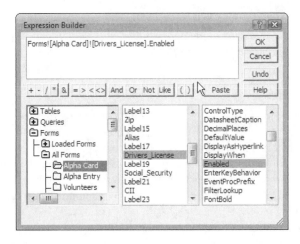

To complete the macro:

1. Enter No in the Expression argument.

2. Add a condition to the SetValue Action row that runs the macro only if the Age value is less than 16.

3. If you were not already working from the Property Sheet to embed the macro, attach the macro to the Age control's After Update event property

TIP *You probably will want to add another macro to reenable the Drivers License when you move to the next record.*

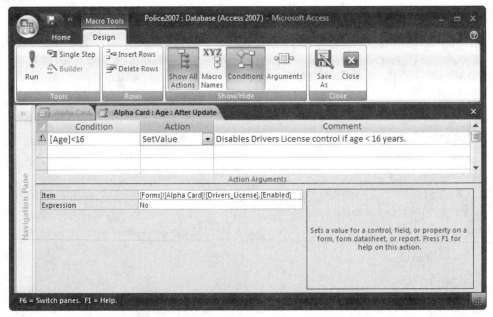

If the property value is a string expression, such as a person's name or a city, enclose it in quotation marks in the Expression argument box. If you want to hide a control, set its Visible property to No.

Change the Flow of Operations

Adding conditions that determine whether a macro action is carried out is one way to control the flow of operations. You can add the MsgBox function to a macro condition to let the user decide which action to carry out. The MsgBox function is similar to the MsgBox action with the exception that the function returns a value, that depends on which button the user clicks in the message box. The MsgBox function displays a dialog box containing the message and waits for the user to click a button indicating the user's choice. Several arrangements of buttons are available in the dialog box.

The MsgBox function has three main arguments and two additional arguments, but only the first one is required:

- **Prompt**   A string expression displayed in the dialog box. You can display up to 1,024 characters, depending on the font size.

- **Button**   A number equal to the sum of three values, which specify the visual characteristics of the message box such as the number and type of buttons, the default button, the icon style, and the modality of the message box.

- **Title**   A string expression that is displayed in the dialog box title bar.

Two additional arguments can specify a Help file and context number in the file where you can find context sensitive help.

You can display seven different buttons in various arrangements, plus a choice of four icons. You also can specify which of the buttons is the default. Each button arrangement and dialog box feature has a numeric value. These values are totaled and placed in the Button argument. The six arrangements of the seven buttons and their values are listed next:

- 0 displays only OK

- 1 displays OK with Cancel

- 2 displays Abort, Retry, and Ignore

- 3 displays Yes, No, and Cancel

- 4 displays Yes and No

- 5 displays Retry and Cancel

Add 16 to the button sum to show the Critical Message icon or 32 for the Warning Query, 48 for the Warning Message, or 64 for the Information Message. Finally, you can add to the sum to specify which button is the default. The default button activates if you press ENTER.

15

For example, to display the Yes, No, and Cancel buttons in that order, add 3 to the Button sum. If you want to display the Warning Query icon, add 32 to the sum. To set the No button as the default, add 256 to the sum. For these features, enter 291 as the Button argument in the MsgBox function. See the Help topic "MsgBox Function" for a complete list of all the button arrangements and dialog box features.

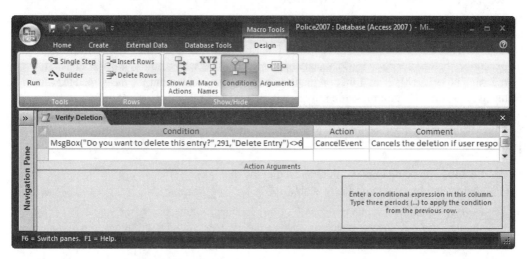

When you use the MsgBox function in a macro condition, you can compare the returned value to a specific number and carry out the action if the comparison is True. For example, you can use the MsgBox function to display a confirmation message before deleting a record. The box contains three buttons: Yes, No, and Cancel.

When the user clicks one of the buttons, the MsgBox function returns a value depending on which button was clicked: 1 for OK, 2 for Cancel, 3 for Abort, 4 for Retry, 5 for Ignore, 6 for Yes, and 7 for No.

For example, if the user clicks the Yes button, the function returns 6; so if any other value is returned, the user did not click Yes. Figure 15-3 shows a macro using the MsgBox function in a condition that evaluates to True if the function returned any value except 6 (Yes). If the value is not 6, the deletion event is canceled. You could add other conditions that carry out actions as a result of the other button selections.

The Button argument in the MsgBox function in Figure 15-3 is 291, which is the sum of the Yes, No, and Cancel button arrangement (3), the Warning Query icon (32), and setting the second button (No) as the default (256).

The Verify Deletion macro should be embedded in or attached to the form's Before Del Confirm event property. The message box displays when you select a record and press DEL. In Figure 15-3, the user selected the Alpha Entry record for Index 24 before pressing DEL. You can see that it has been deleted from the Form view but has not yet been confirmed. If you click No in the box, the record is returned. If you respond by clicking Yes, Access deletes the record.

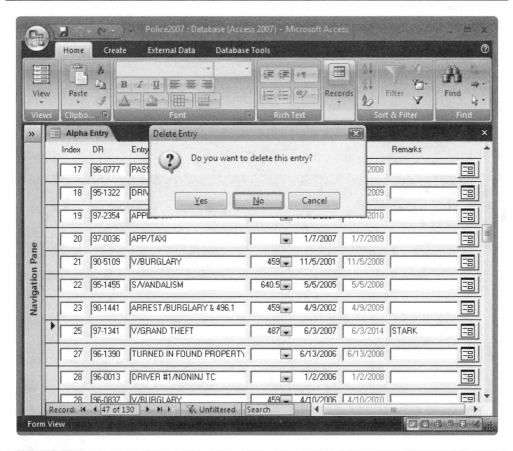

FIGURE 15-3   Using the MsgBox function in a macro.

TIP   *If the deletion will result in cascade deletions of other records or interfere in some other way with the relationships in the database, Access displays another confirmation message.*

Filter Records

You can create a macro to limit the records you want to print by adding a Where Condition to the OpenReport action. For example, suppose that you want to preview the Alpha Entry records for all incidents with a Code in the danger range, 11000 to 19999. Start a new macro with the Macro Builder from an Event property or from the Create tab and do the following:

1. Choose OpenReport in the Action column.

2. In the Report Name argument, select Alpha Entries from the list of available reports.

3. Choose Print Preview as the View argument.

4. Enter **[Alpha Entry]![Code] Between 11000 And 19999** in the Where Condition argument or click the Build button to get help from the Expression Builder.

> **TIP** *Don't use an equal sign in the Where Condition argument.*

5. Save the macro then click Run.

You can see in the Print Preview that only three of the incidents reported fall in the danger range.

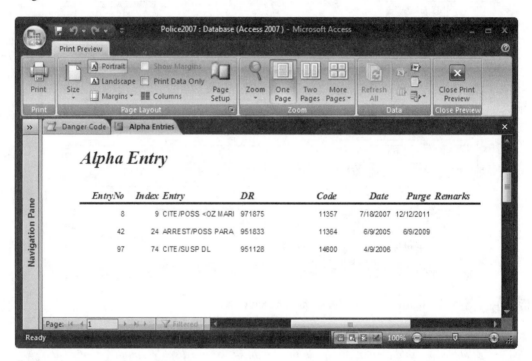

Create an AutoExec Macro

You can create a special macro that runs when you first open a database. The AutoExec macro can carry out such actions as opening a form for data entry, displaying a message box prompting the user to log in, or playing a sound greeting. All you need to do is create the macro with the actions you want carried out at startup and save it with the name AutoExec. A database can have only one macro named AutoExec. Figure 15-4 shows the AutoExec macro for the Northwind Traders database. It chooses which form to open depending on the current project security status.

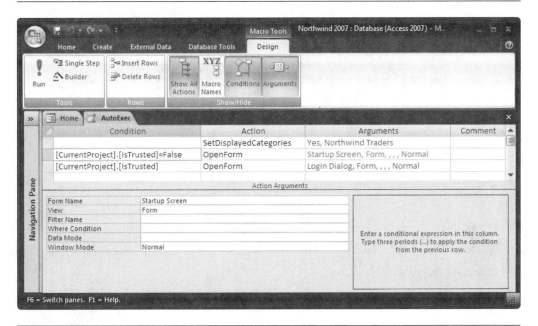

FIGURE 15-4 The Northwind Traders Autoexec macro.

When you open a database, all the startup options you have set in the Current Database group of Access Options take place first. You can see these by clicking the Microsoft Office button and choosing Access Options. Access looks for a macro named AutoExec and executes the actions in it. You can bypass both the startup options and the AutoExec macro by pressing SHIFT when you open the database.

Many of the same options can be set in the AutoExec macro as in the Startup dialog box. Be careful not to include conflicting settings in the macro. See Chapter 13 for information about the startup settings.

Create a Macro Group

If you have created several macros that apply to controls on the same form or report, you can group them together as one file. There are two advantages to using macro groups:

- It reduces the number of macro names in the Navigation Pane.
- You can find all the macros for a single form or report in one place where they are easy to edit.

15

An example of using grouped macros is the Choose Report dialog box that asks you to select the report you are interested in and then decide to print or preview the report. See Chapter 16 for details of this form.

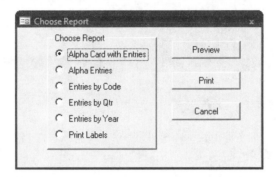

To create a macro group, do the following:

1. Open the macro window as usual.

2. In the Show/Hide group, click the Macro Names command to display the Macro Name column.

3. Add a macro to the sheet and enter a name for it in the Macro Name column of the first row of the macro.

4. Add the rest of the actions to the macro.

5. To add another macro, enter the name in the Macro Name column and add the actions you want to occur. Figure 15-5 shows the completed Choose Report macro group.

6. Save and close the macro window.

When Access runs a macro in a group, it begins with the action in the row that contains the macro name and continues until it finds no more actions or encounters another macro name. After adding all the macros to the group, close and save it as usual with the group name.

 *You will find the macros in a group will be much easier to read if you leave at least one blank row between the groups.*

When you assign macros from a group to an event property, you must use the group name as well as the macro name. In the property sheet for a control, the drop-down list in an event property shows compound names for all the macros in a group and the names of all the single macros. The group name and the macro name both appear separated by a period:

```
macrogroupname.macroname.
```

Now that you have had a glimpse of what macros can do to automate your database, you can put them to work on other forms and reports.

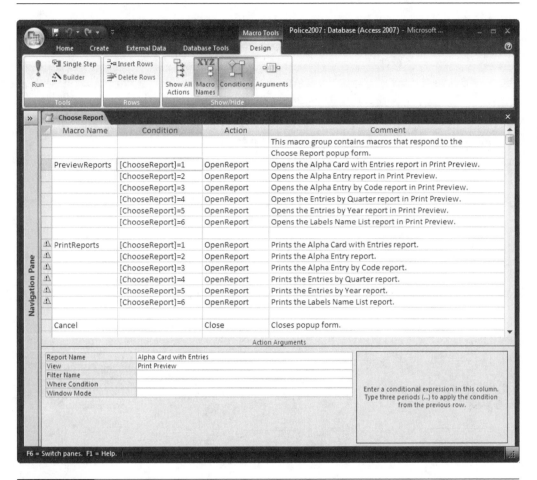

FIGURE 15-5 Grouping macros.

15

Chapter 16

Customize the User Interface

How to...

- Work with the ribbon
- Move the Quick Access Toolbar
- Add commands to the Quick Access Toolbar
- Apply previous startup options
- Create a dialog box

Work with the Ribbon

While you can't customize the commands on the Access 2007 ribbon, you can still manipulate it to fit your needs. The commands shown in the ribbon relate specifically to the current activity but the way they are displayed depends on the current width of your Access window.

Resize the Ribbon

The ribbon is designed to fit the maximized Access window. If you are using Access in a narrower window, the ribbon is resized to fit. When the window is maximized, you see the commands widely spaced with their names displayed.

If you shrink the window width, the commands appear compressed horizontally and many of the command names are removed leaving only the icon. They may show as a stack of three icons instead of in a row, for example, the commands in the Macro and Analyze groups.

Shrinking the window width further reduces the ribbon and eventually hides it altogether. Some groups, for example, the Show/Hide group, are now represented by a single icon with a down-arrow that displays the commands within the group in a context menu.

 If you have created a custom ribbon with XML markup, you can use it with your database. In the Current Database page of the Access Options window, select Ribbon Name in the Toolbar Options and choose the ribbon from the drop-down list.

Hide and Restore the Ribbon

If the ribbon is taking up too much of your work space, you can hide it, either briefly or for the whole session. You have three ways to hide the ribbon:

- Press CTRL-F1.
- Double-click an active ribbon tab.
- On the Quick Access toolbar, click the Customize Quick Access Toolbar button at the right end of the toolbar and then check Minimize the Ribbon in the context menu.

When the ribbon is hidden, the tabs still show, which means you can use the commands by clicking a tab to temporarily restore the ribbon. After you select a command, the ribbon automatically withdraws again. To restore the ribbon to its normal appearance, repeat the action you used to hide it.

Use Keyboard Shortcuts for Ribbon Commands

Access 2007 has a set of KeyTips that provides a way to use any command in the ribbon with only a few key strokes. To see the keys available in the current view, press ALT or F10. The Microsoft Office button shows the KeyTip "F" and the Quick Access toolbar buttons are numbered 1, 2, 3. Each tab also has a KeyTip: the Home tab shows "H", Create is "C", External Data is "X", and Database Tools is "A." When you press one of the tab KeyTips, the commands on that tab show additional tips.

For example, press C to open the Create tab and display the KeyTips for the commands in the tab. The Table command in the Tables group now shows TN and the Forms command in the Forms group shows FN. You can use these KeyTips to carry out complete Access tasks without using the mouse. If a ribbon command is not currently active, the KeyTip is also inactive. To cancel the action you are taking and hide the tips, press ALT or F10 again.

16

 *Access 2007 uses the same key combinations that were used in earlier versions to carry out specific commands. So, if you are used to using key strokes for common actions, you can continue with them. For example, press CTRL-P to open the Print dialog box for the current datasheet, form, or report.*

Customize the Quick Access Toolbar

Unlike the ribbon, the Quick Access toolbar is independent of any current activity and can be customized to fit your requirements. If you like to have the toolbar more accessible or wider, so that it can hold more commands, you can move it below the ribbon. Then you can add frequently used commands to it. For example, if you print reports often, add the Quick Print or Print Preview command to the toolbar.

Move the Quick Access Toolbar

To place the toolbar below the ribbon, click the Customize Quick Access Toolbar button and click Show Below the Ribbon. To restore the toolbar to its original position, clear Show Above the Ribbon from the Customize Quick Access Toolbar context menu.

Add Commands to the Toolbar

The Customize Quick Access Toolbar context menu displays a list of common commands that you can add to the toolbar one at a time. The commands that are already in the toolbar are checked. Check the command you want to add.

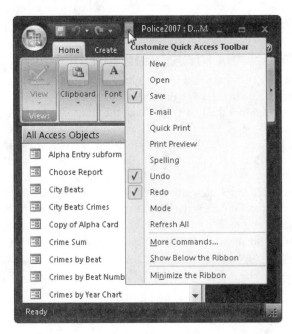

The commands, New, Open, Quick Print, and Print Preview have been added to this toolbar below the ribbon.

If the commands you want to add are not in the short list in the Customize Quick Access Toolbar menu or you want to add several, click More Commands to open the Customize page of the Access Options dialog box. Figure 16-1 shows the list of available commands in the Popular Commands list. The right pane lists the commands already on the toolbar.

To add more commands, select them one at a time and click Add. To remove a command, select it in the right pane and click Remove. The <Separator> command places a vertical line between commands that visibly groups the commands on the toolbar.

The default setting in the Customize page of the Access Options dialog box is for applying the changes in the Quick Access toolbar to all documents. If you want the changes to apply only to the current database, click the "Customize Quick Access Toolbar" down arrow and then choose the database from the drop-down list.

The Choose commands from: drop-down list offers more sources for commands (see Figure 16-2).

Click each of the command categories to see what is available:

- Popular commands are just that - commands that are often used during database management.

- The Commands Not in the Ribbon list includes commands found on the status bar, title bar, and Quick Access Toolbar.

- The All Commands list includes commands from earlier versions of Access as well as all current commands.

- The Macros list includes macros available in the current database.

16

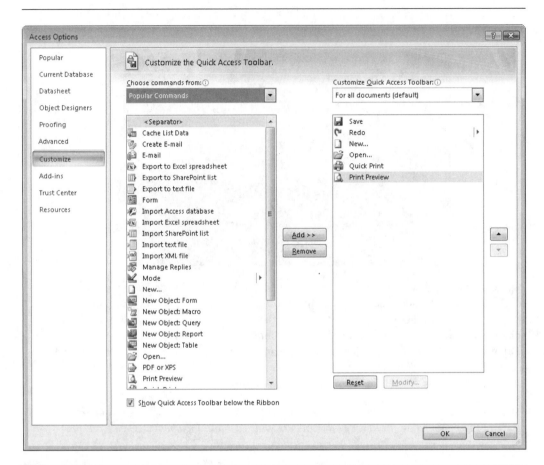

FIGURE 16-1 Choosing commands to place on the Quick Access Toolbar.

- The Office Menu list includes commands to open or close a database, and other database file commands.
- The remaining lists can copy commands from specific ribbon tabs or tab groups.

When you are finished adding the commands to the toolbar, click OK.

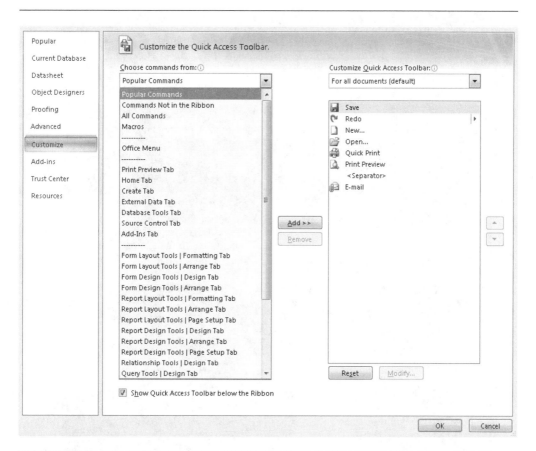

FIGURE 16-2 Other sources of commands.

Add Commands From the Ribbon

Another way to add a command to the Quick Access Toolbar is to bring it directly from the ribbon. Simply right-click the command you want to add and choose Add to Quick Access Toolbar in the shortcut menu.

16

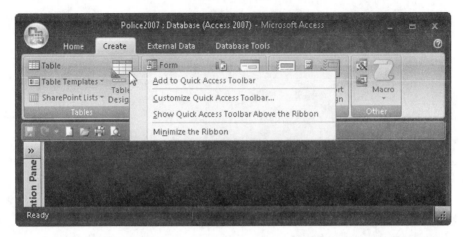

Many of the lists and galleries in the ribbon can also be added to the toolbar. For example, the More Forms and Table Templates commands are added to the toolbar.

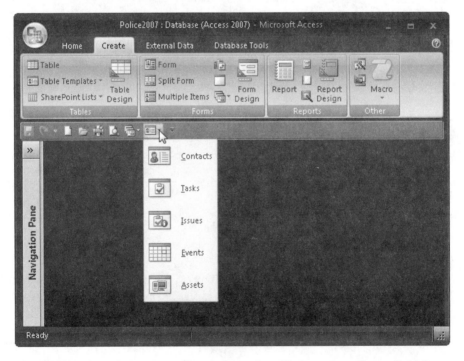

Not all ribbon commands can be added to the toolbar. The contents of some lists, for example, the Data Type and Format on the Datasheet tab are not available. The other commands in the Data Type & Formatting group are available, however.

Remove Commands from the Toolbar

You have two ways to remove a command from the Quick Access Toolbar:

- Right-click the button and choose Remove from Quick Access Toolbar.
- Click the Customize Quick Access Toolbar button and clear the check mark from the command in the list.

To restore the toolbar to its original settings, do the following:

1. Click the Microsoft Office button and choose Access Options.

2. On the Customize page, click the Reset button (see Figure 16-3).

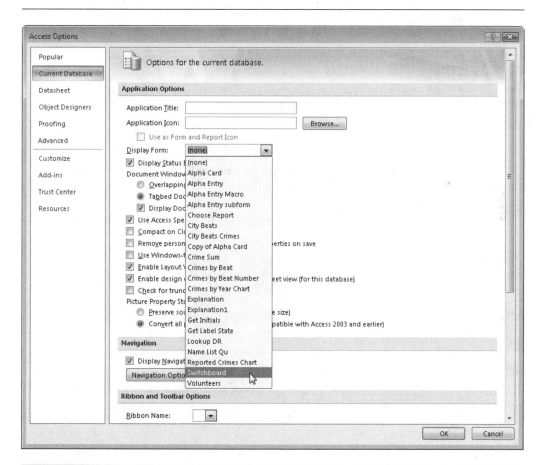

FIGURE 16-3   Choosing the startup form.

3. A message asks if you are sure you want to go back to the default buttons. Click Yes.

4. Click OK to close the Access Options dialog box.

Use Existing Customization

If you are converting from Access 2003, you don't have to give up all your custom settings. For example, you can still have your main switchboard form show at startup. You can also use the custom toolbars and menus you built in Access 2003.

Show Startup Switchboard

If you have a switchboard that appeared at startup in your Access 2003 database, you can use it in Access 2007 as well. All you need to do is change the Current Database option to display the form at startup as follows:

1. Click the Microsoft Office button and choose Access Options.

2. Go to the Current Database page, and choose the name of the form from the Display Form list, which is Switchboard, in this case.

3. Click OK to close the dialog box.

4. Close and restart the database.

Figure 16-4 shows the Police database when it restarts. The switchboard form may need some changes so that it doesn't spread out in the document window. See Chapter 17 for information about creating switchboards for Access 2007.

 *Be sure to remove any unsupported actions such as Open Database Window from the converted switchboard before designating it as the startup form.*

Use Custom menus and toolbars

If you have built some custom menus and toolbars for your Access 2003 database, you can keep them when you work on the database in Access 2007. First, open the database in Access 2003 and do as described next.

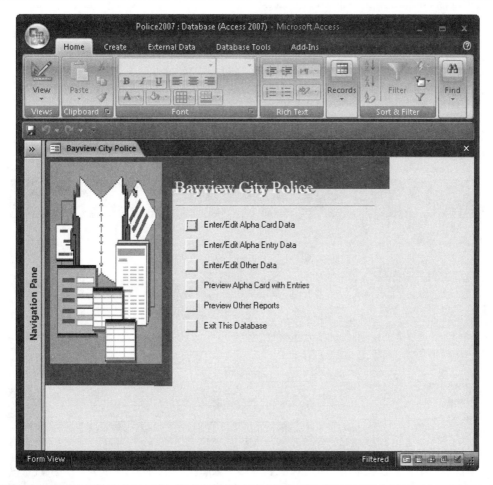

FIGURE 16-4 Starting the Police database with the switchboard.

1. Choose Tools | Startup.
2. In the Startup dialog box, select your custom menu bar from the Menu Bar list.
3. Clear the Allow Built-In Toolbars check box and click OK.
4. Save and close the database.

16

Next, open the Access 2003 database (Access 2007 refers to it as a "legacy" database) with Access 2007 and do the following:

1. Click the Microsoft Office button and click Access Options.

2. Open the Current Database options page.

3. In the Ribbon & Toolbars Options group, clear the Allow Full Menus check box.

4. Click OK.

The custom menus and toolbars from the Access 2003 database appear as groups in the Add-Ins ribbon tab. If your database does not have a custom toolbar, the Add-Ins tab does not appear.

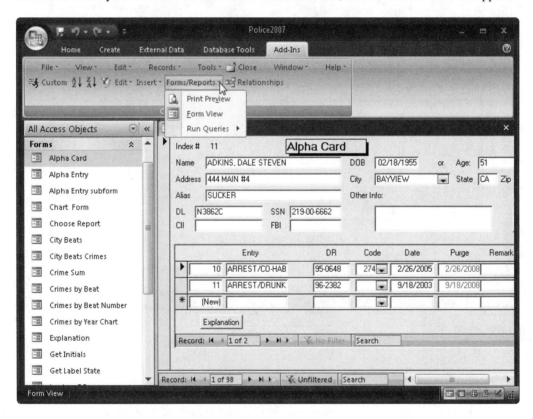

Create a Custom Dialog Box

A dialog box is a special type of window that pops up and stays on the screen until you make a selection, even if it is only to cancel the box. To create a dialog box, you start with a blank, unbound form and add controls that you can select to carry out specific actions. After completing the form, you create macros or event procedures and attach them to the corresponding controls on the form.

Design the Form

In this section, you will see how to create a dialog box that offers a choice of police reports when the user clicks the Print or Preview button on the new dialog box form. There are four major steps in creating this custom dialog box:

- Create the form
- Add an option group control and command buttons
- Create the macros
- Attach the macros to the command buttons

TIP
It may help to open the Navigation Pane to show the report names. Then you don't have to remember the exact wording of the report titles to enter them in the wizard dialog box.

To create the Choose Report dialog box for the Police database:

1. On the Create tab in the Forms group, click the More Forms command and choose Modal Dialog from the context menu. Make sure the Use Control Wizards command is selected.

2. In the Controls group, click the Option Group command and draw a frame in the empty form design to start the Option Group Wizard.

3. In the first wizard dialog box (shown next), enter the report names as the Label Names for the options in the group. After entering a name, press the down arrow or TAB to move to the next line. If you press ENTER, you move to the next dialog box and have to check BACK to continue. After entering all the option labels, click Next.

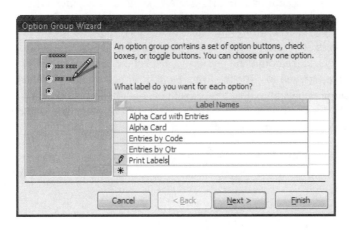

16

4. In the next wizard dialog box, accept the first option as the default returned value and click Next.

5. In the next dialog box, accept the default values and click Next.

6. The next wizard dialog box (shown next) shows a variety of styles for the option group and the options in it. Choose Option Buttons as the type of control and Raised as the frame style, then click Next.

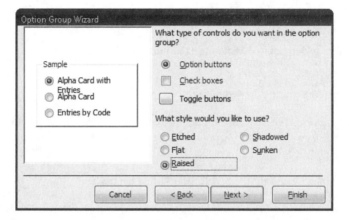

7. In the final wizard dialog box, enter **Choose Report** as the caption for the group that will be displayed at the top of the group frame, then click Finish.

8. Back in the form Design view, select the option group frame, if not already selected, and open the Property Sheet. Choose the Name property on the Other tab and enter **Choose Report** as the name for the option group.

9. Right-click the form tab and choose Save in the shortcut menu.

10. Enter the name Choose Report in the Save As dialog box and click OK.

Table 16-1 lists the property settings that the Modal Dialog Wizard set for the form. This wizard is new to Access 2007. In previous versions, you had to set these properties yourself.

The next step is to add the command buttons to display the selected report in Print Preview, to print the selected report, and to close the form. Do this without the help of the Command Button Wizard because you want to attach macros to the buttons instead of using the default operations offered by the wizard. To add the three command buttons, make sure the Use Control Wizards button in the Controls group is not pressed, and then do the following:

1. In the Controls group, click the Button command and click in the form design. Repeat twice more, spacing the buttons as desired. The buttons will show the default captions as follows: Command*n*.

Property	Setting	Purpose
PopUp	Yes	Form will remain on top of other windows.
Modal	Yes	Form retains focus until it is manually closed.
Caption	Choose Report	Displays the text you enter in the title bar in Form view instead of the form name.
Allow Form View	Yes	Permits the form in Form view.
Allow Datasheet View	No	Prevents switching to Datasheet view.
Allow PivotTable View	No	Prevents switching to PivotTable view.
Allow PivotChart View	No	Prevents switching to PivotChart view.
Scroll Bars	Neither	Removes scroll bars from the form.
Record Selectors	No	Removes record selectors from the form.
Navigation Buttons	No	Removes navigation buttons from the form.
Dividing Lines	No	Removes horizontal lines from the form.
Auto Center	Yes	Centers the form automatically when it opens. If you want the form to appear in a special place, set to No.
Border Style	Dialog	Form has a thick border and includes only a title bar with a control menu box at the left and a Close button at the right.
Control Box	Yes	Displays the control menu box in the title bar in Form view so the user can close the form.
MinMax Buttons	None	Prevents the user from resizing the form in Form view.

TABLE 16-1   Property Settings for a Modal Dialog Form

2. Select the first button, then click in it and type **Preview**. Press ENTER to save the new caption.

3. Repeat step 2 to change the default captions on the other two buttons to **Print** and **Cancel**.

4. If the buttons are not evenly spaced or accurately aligned, select all three and use the Control Alignment commands on the Arrange tab to adjust the buttons.

5. If the buttons are not the same size, use the Size group commands to adjust them.

16

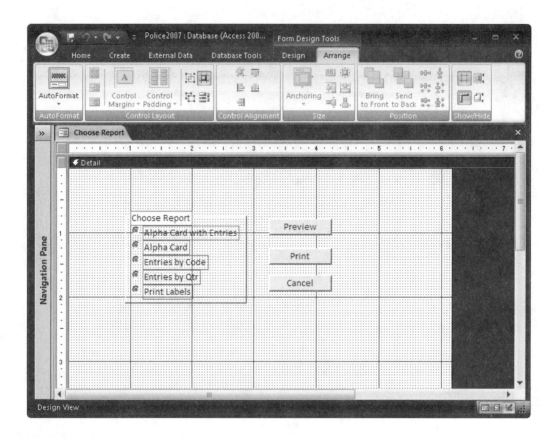

NOTE   *You can also use the sizing handles in the group of controls to size them all at once.*

So far, the controls on the Choose Report form do not carry out an action. You must create the macros that will run and perform the intended action when the user clicks the control.

Create and Attach the Macros

You need a macro for each of the command buttons in the form. In addition, you must convey to the Print and Preview macros which report to open. The macros that you attach to the Preview and Print buttons must distinguish among the reports and open the one chosen in the option group.

The option group returns a value depending on which item in the group was selected. As you saw, the Option Group Wizard set default return values so that if you click the first item the group value is 1, if you click the second item the value is 2, and so on. You can use this value in the macro condition to choose the specific report to preview or print.

Create the Macro Group

The best way to respond to a selection from an option group is to build a set of macros that you can attach to each option in the group. To build a macro for the Preview button:

1. On the Create tab in the Other group, click the Macro command.

2. On the Design tab in the Show/Hide group, click the Macro Names and Condition commands to show the two optional columns. Then click the Arguments command to remove it from the design to save space.

3. Type **PreviewReports** as the name of the first macro and choose OpenReport as the Action.

4. In the Action Arguments pane, choose Alpha Card with Entries from the drop-down list of Report Names and choose Print Preview as the View argument.

5. In the Condition column, enter the condition under which to preview the report: **[Choose Report]=1**. ChooseReport is the name of the option group control, and 1 is the value of the group when you select the first item in the group.

> **TIP** *If you are in doubt about the name of the control, look at the Name property on the Other tab of the control's property sheet.*

6. Move to the next row and repeat steps 4 and 5 to open the Alpha Entry report in Print Preview with the condition that the Choose Report group value is 2.

7. Continue to define macro actions to open the remaining reports in Print Preview. You should have five actions in the PreviewReports macro, with each opening a different report in Print Preview.

> **NOTE** *It is a good idea to add comments in the macro command rows so you will know what it was you wanted it to do.*

8. Then add a final action to the macro that closes the Choose Report form so you can see the Print Preview window without the popup dialog box in the way. Set the following arguments for the Close action:

   - Object Type—Form
   - Object Name—Choose Report
   - Save—No

9. Leave an empty row and create a new macro named PrintReports to print each of the reports using the same conditions. Do not include the Close action with the second macro, so the pop-up dialog box remains on the screen for further selections in case you want to print more reports.

> **TIP** *An easy way to add the conditions to the PrintReports macro is to copy the [Choose Report]= part of the condition and paste it in subsequent lines, then add the values.*

16

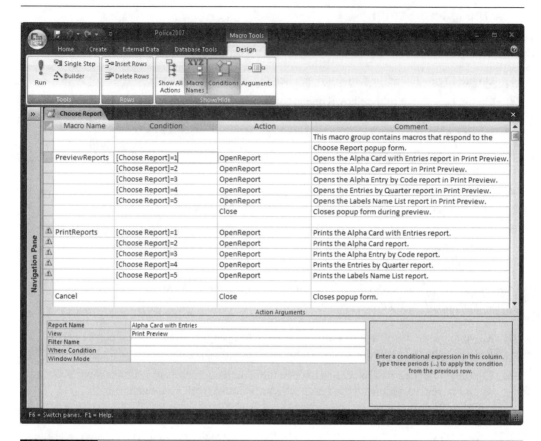

FIGURE 16-5 The macro group for the Choose Report form.

The macro command for the Cancel command button can be simply Close with the Choose Report form name as the argument. Figure 16-5 shows the completed macro group from the Choose Report form.

 *The alarm icons in the left margin of the macro design indicate that the action will not be allowed if the database is not trusted.*

Attach the Macros to Form Controls

Once you have created the macros, the next step is to indicate when they should execute by attaching them to the event properties of the controls. To attach the macros to the command buttons:

1. Return to the form in Design view, select the Preview command button, and then open the Property Sheet.

2. Click the Events tab and choose the macro name from the drop-down list next to the On Click event property. Figure 16-6 shows the PreviewReports macro in the Choose Report macro group as the action to carry out when the button is clicked.

3. Repeat steps 1 and 2 to attach the PrintReports macro to the Print button and the Cancel macro to the Cancel button.

A dialog box created by the wizard is a pop-up modal form. *Pop-up* means that it opens and stays on top of other windows even when it no longer is the active window. *Modal* means that you must hide or close the form before you can work in any other object or menu command. The Form Wizard has set these properties and provided a way for you to close the form by

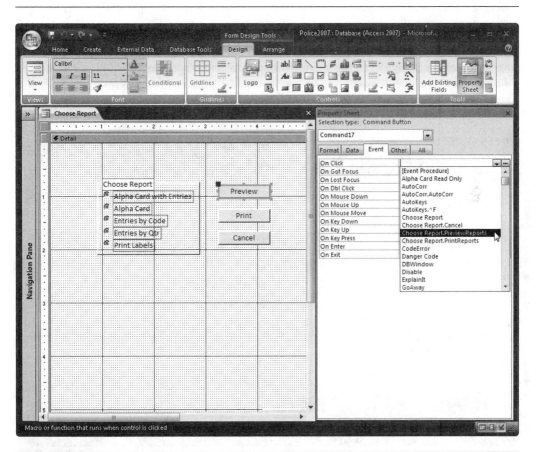

FIGURE 16-6   Attaching a macro to the Preview command button.

adding command buttons. You need to remove two command buttons that were added when the form was created before you can resize the form to fit the contents.

Scroll down the form in Design view and locate the OK and Cancel buttons in the lower right corner. Select them and press Delete. Then resize the form to fit the option group and the command buttons.

NOTE *To switch from Form view to Design view, right-click within the form and choose Design in the shortcut menu. Right-clicking the form tab only closes the form.*

Two additional features that help turn a form into a dialog box are the default and Cancel button properties:

- The command button specified as the default button is pushed automatically when the user presses ENTER.

- The command button specified as the Cancel button is pushed automatically when the user presses ESC.

You can assign any one button in the form as the default button and one other as the Cancel button by setting the Default or Cancel control property to Yes. While you are working with the command button properties, you can add ScreenTips that will appear when you rest the mouse pointer over the button. To add ScreenTips, type the text in the button's ControlTip Text property box on the Other tab of the property sheet.

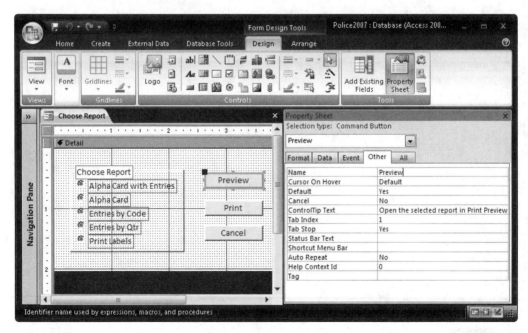

Now switch to Form view and see the new dialog box ready for previewing and printing Police reports.

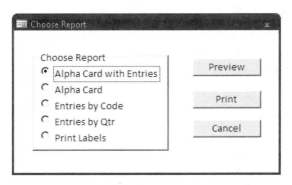

Create a Dialog Box for User Input

In Chapter 8, you saw how to create a parameter query that prompts the user to enter the criteria for the query. You can use a custom dialog box to accomplish the same thing. For example, the dialog box shown in the following illustration prompts the user to enter the DR value of the Alpha Entry records he or she wants to see. It includes instructions to ensure a valid input value.

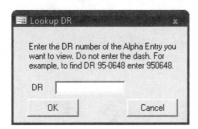

After you enter the DR value and click OK, a parameter query runs using the value as the criteria for the DR field. For this example, make a copy of the Alpha DR Query and name it **Lookup DR.** You can change the criteria of the DR column to get the value from the dialog box instead of a parameter prompt.

Set the Input Form Properties

There are several special features about the Lookup DR form in addition to the properties that make it a dialog box. These include the following:

- The DR box is an unbound text box named FindDR.
- The FindDR text box is first in the tab order with a Tab Index property of 0.

16

- The OK command button Default property is set to Yes so the user can simply press ENTER after typing the DR value to run the query.

- The Cancel command button Cancel property is set to Yes so the user can press ESC to close the dialog box.

Create the Macros

The LookUpDR macro group contains two macros, one for each command button:

- The CloseForm macro attached to the Cancel button closes the Lookup DR form without running the query.

- The Run Query macro attached to the OK button, contains two actions: OpenQuery, which runs the Lookup DR query in Datasheet view in read-only mode, and Close, which closes the Lookup DR form after running the query.

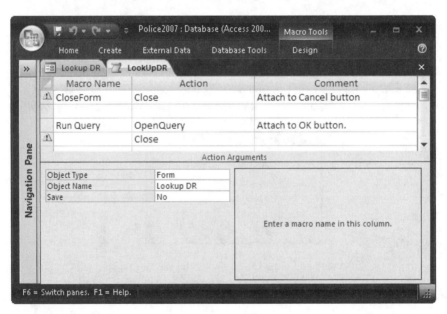

Modify the Query

To pass the DR value from the form to the query, the Criteria must be set to the unbound text box control in the form. To do this, type **[Forms]![Lookup DR]![FindDR]** in the Criteria row of the DR column in the query grid.

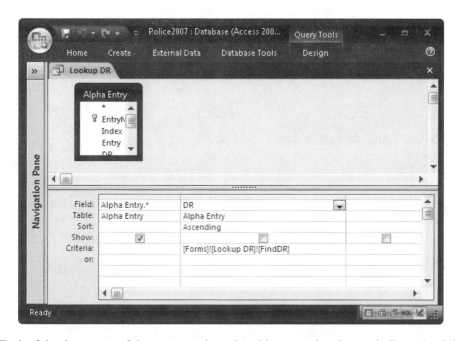

Each of the three parts of the statement is enclosed in square brackets to indicate that it is an identifier that refers to an object or control. The first element defines the object type, Forms; the exclamation point (!) indicates that the element that follows was named by the user. The second element identifies the specific form, Lookup DR, and the third identifies the unbound text box control, FindDR, in the form.

NOTE *Be sure to clear the check box in the Show row of the DR column in the query grid; otherwise, the query results will have two copies of the DR values.*

In the next chapter you will find out how to create custom groups and categories in the Navigation Pane to build the Office 2007 equivalent of a switchboard. If you don't want to customize the Navigation Pane, you can still create a switchboard for the user to choose the desired activities.

16

Chapter 17

Customize the Navigation Pane and Create Switchboards

How to...

- ■ Modify the Navigation Pane
- ■ Create custom categories and groups
- ■ Create a switchboard with the help of the Switchboard Manager
- ■ Modify a switchboard

The Navigation Pane is new to Access 2007. It is the point of entry to your database, which you can use as presented or you can use to create your own custom access to the database objects. The Navigation Pane replaces the Database Window from earlier versions. When you open a database, all the database objects appear in the grouped lists in the Navigation Pane from which you can open an object in a specific view.

The Navigation Pane can also replace the switchboards that were used in earlier versions. The switchboard appeared at startup and offered a choice of actions to perform within the current database. While the Navigation Pane replaces them, you can still use switchboards if you want to. In fact, Access 2007 provides the Switchboard Manager to help you if you want to create and use switchboards instead of customizing the Navigation Pane.

View Objects in the Navigation Pane

You were introduced to the Navigation Pane in earlier chapters, but in this chapter you will see how to make it work for you. By default, the pane displays all the objects in the database in predefined categories and groups. For example, with categories set to Object Type and groups to All Object Types, you can see all the objects in each group by clicking the expand button in the group title bar.

You can open and close the Navigation Pane itself by clicking the Shutter Bar Open/Close button to the right end of the title bar. You can also press F-11 to open and close the pane.

Change Categories and Groups

You have five ways to categorize the database objects (see Figure 17-1):

- ■ **Custom** arranges objects in specially-designed categories and groups that you create for your database.
- ■ **Object Type** (currently selected) groups objects by a specific type or by all types.
- ■ **Tables and Related Views** lists all objects related to the table you choose in the filter group below.
- ■ **Created Date** lists objects created within the time period you choose in the filter group.
- ■ **Modified Date** lists objects modified within the time period you choose.

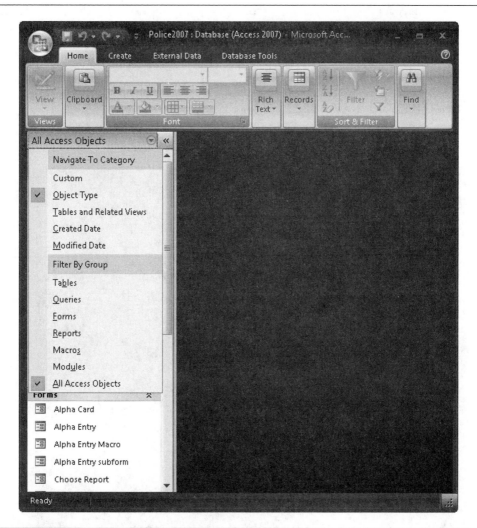

FIGURE 17-1 Choosing a category and group.

The Object Type category is the one you have been working with in this book so far. After deciding how you want to categorize the objects, you can choose how to group them within the category. You will see how to create customized categories and groups in later sections.

Categorize by Tables and Related Views

When you choose the Tables and Related Views category and select a table from the Filter By Group list, you will see the names of all the forms, reports, queries, and other objects that use that table as a source for data. For example, to see all the objects related to the Alpha Entry table, do the following:

1. Click in the Navigation Pane title bar and choose Tables and Related Views in the Navigate to Category list.

2. Click again in the Navigation Pane title bar and choose Alpha Entry from the list of tables in the Filter By Group list (see Figure 17-2).

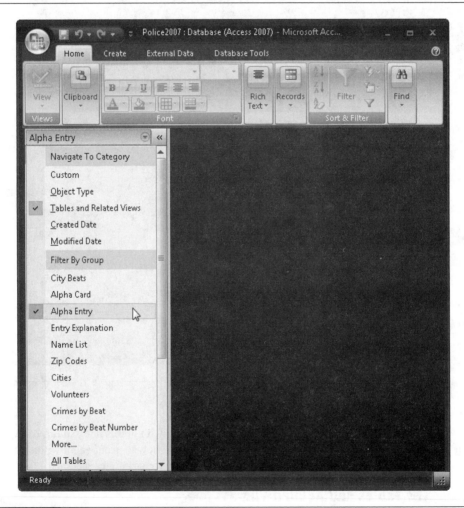

FIGURE 17-2 Choosing to view all objects related to the Alpha Entry table.

NOTE

If you don't see the table you want in the list, click More to open the Filter by Table dialog box where you can choose from the entire list of tables in the current database.

The resulting list of objects includes the Alpha Entry table, with all the queries, forms, and reports related to the table. You can tell by the accompanying icons the types of objects they are. Figure 17-3 shows the list of objects currently related to the Alpha Entry table.

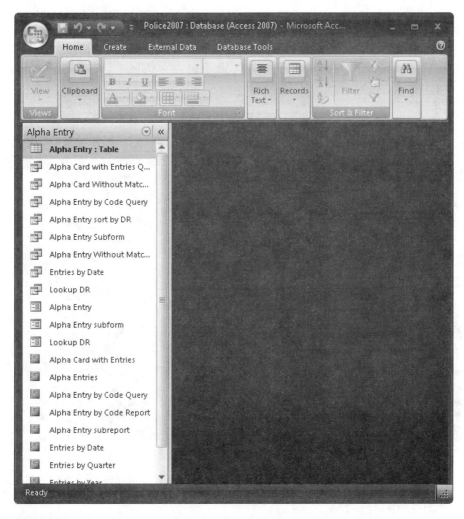

FIGURE 17-3 Viewing the objects related to the Alpha Entry table.

17

If you choose All Tables in the grouping list, you can see the list of all the tables in the database with their related objects. You can shorten the list by hiding some of the repeated objects. For example, if a form uses data from more than one table, the form name will appear in both the table groups. You can right-click the object in the group and choose Hide in This Group in the shortcut menu. The object is not deleted, just hidden from the list.

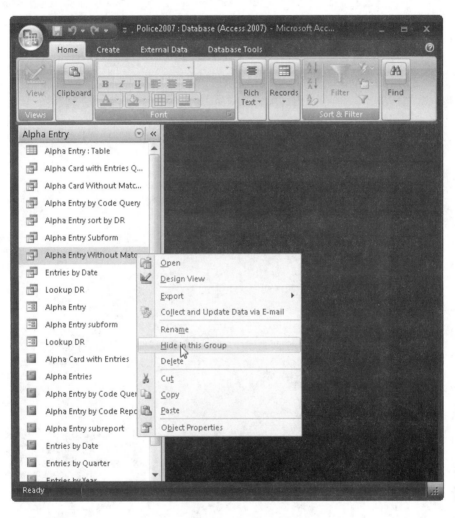

The Navigation Pane Options setting Show Hidden Objects, determines whether "hidden" objects are completely removed from the list or simply displayed as dimmed. See the next section "Hide/Restore Groups and Objects" for information about the difference.

Group by Created or Modified Date

Both date filters offer the same criteria with respect to the time frame. You can choose a specific time frame or choose All Dates.

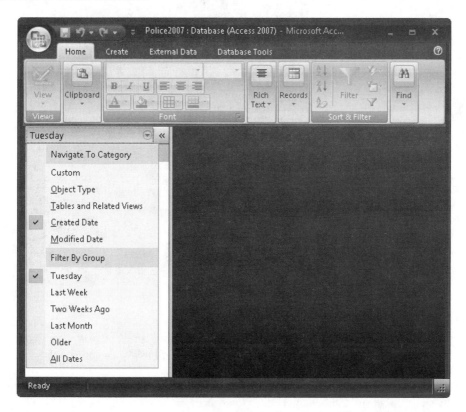

The objects are listed by type: tables first, then queries, forms, reports, macros, and modules, the list is then sorted by date. Again, you can tell the kind of object it is by the icon. In this list, there are six tables, three queries, two forms, two reports, and two macros.

17

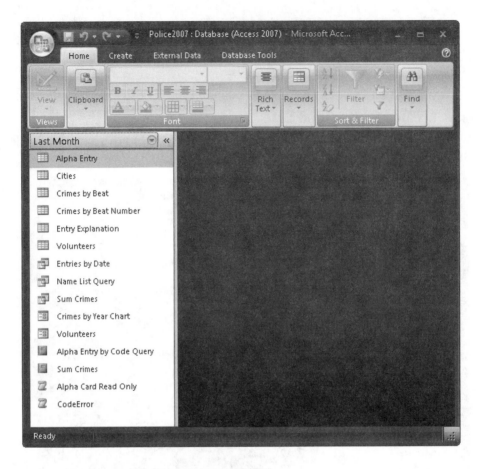

Hide/Restore Groups and Objects

You don't have to see all the groups and objects in the Navigation Pane. You may want to hide some for security reasons or just because there are some you don't use often and you would like to make the list shorter.

You can make the group or object invisible or simply displayed as dimmed in the Navigation Pane list by setting or clearing the Show Hidden Objects in the Navigation Options dialog box.

Hide/Restore a Group

To hide a group from the Navigation Pane, right-click the group name and choose Hide in the shortcut menu. The complete group is removed from the pane, including the group title bar.

To restore the hidden Queries group, for example, do the following:

1. Right-click the Navigation Pane title bar and then choose Navigation Options in the shortcut menu.

2. In the Categories list in the left pane, select Object Type as the category that contains the Queries group. In the Groups for "Object Type" pane, check the box for Queries.

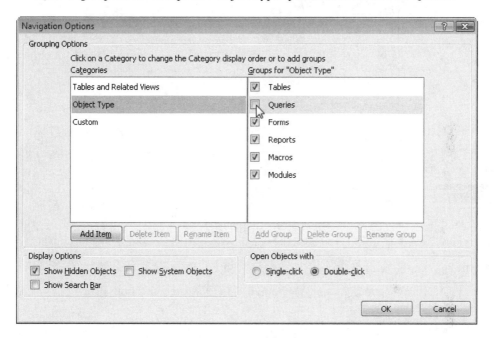

3. Click OK.

Hide/Restore an Object

You have a choice of hiding the object only from its parent group or from all the groups it may appear in. To hide the object from its parent group, right-click it in the Navigation Pane and choose Hide in this Group in the shortcut menu.

If you want an object, such as the Lookup DR form, hidden from all categories and groups, do the following:

1. Right-click the Lookup DR form in the Navigation Pane and then click Object Properties in the shortcut menu.

2. In the Properties dialog box, check the Hidden check box.

3. Click OK.

FIGURE 17-4 The Lookup DR form Properties dialog box.

To restore the hidden object, you need to open the Navigation Options dialog box again.

1. Right-click the Navigation Pane title bar and choose Navigation Options.

2. In the Display Options group at the bottom of the Navigation Options dialog box, check Show Hidden Objects.

3. Click OK.

When you return to the Navigation Pane, you will see the hidden object names dimmed in the list. To complete the restoration, do one of the following:

■ If the object is hidden only from its home group and category, right-click the object and choose Unhide in this Group in the shortcut menu.

■ If the object is hidden from all groups and categories, return to the object Properties dialog box and clear the Hidden check box.

Search for an Object

If your database is quite large and complicated, it may not be so easy to find the form or report you want to work with. The Navigation Pane provides a Search Bar to help you find any database object quickly. It actually filters the objects to display only those with all or part of the text you enter in the Search Bar.

The Search Bar is a text box just beneath the Navigation Pane title bar. If you don't see it, right-click the Navigation Pane title bar and then choose Search Bar in the shortcut menu.

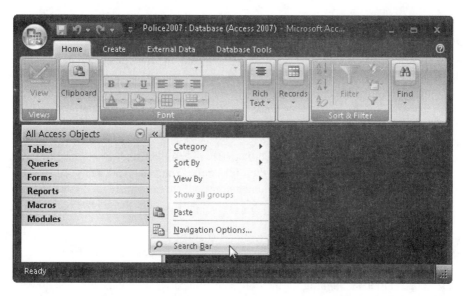

Enter part or the entire name of the object you want and press ENTER. The list of groups in the pane changes to hide all the groups except those that contain an object with the name you entered. For example, you want to find all objects relating to Volunteers in the Police database.

Clear Search String

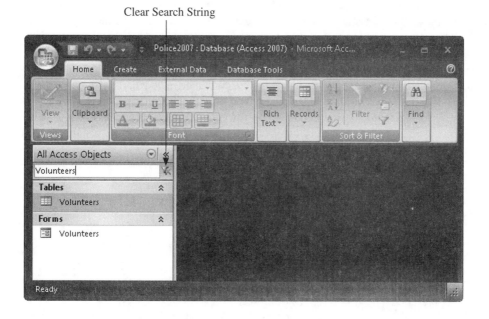

To stop the search and restore the Navigation Pane groups, delete the search text or click the Clear Search String button.

Customize the Navigation Pane

After all the forms, reports, and queries have been completed, the final piece of database development is the customized user interface. You have two ways to accomplish this: by customizing the Navigation Pane to include special categories and groups or by creating a switchboard that branches to the database activities. This section describes the process of creating a custom Navigation Pane. The next section covers using the Switchboard Manager to build the user interactive forms for your database.

If your daily staff is devoted to a few specific database activities, they don't need to scramble through all the objects in the database to get their jobs done. You can create a custom Navigation Pane with a category focusing on the department activities. Within the category, you can place custom groups relating to certain jobs. Then each group contains only the objects required for that job.

You can always revert to the generic Navigation Pane when the IT staff needs to work on the database itself. To do that, open the Navigation Options dialog box and choose one of the native categories, such as Object Type or Tables and Related Objects, and click OK.

First, let's take a look at planning for the Police custom Navigation Pane then see how to carry out the plan.

Plan the Custom Groups

To plan the arrangement of objects in the custom groups in the custom category, you need to look at what the staff does on a regular basis. For example, in the Bayview Police Department example, the staff enters incident reports and other reports of people who are involved in some way with police activities. The incidents are recorded in the Alpha Card table while the public activities are stored in the Alpha Entry table. Each of these tables has a data entry/edit form that you can place in a custom group. Other data entry forms can be included, if necessary.

On a weekly basis, they print reports for distribution of the information within the department. If mail is regularly sent to personnel, you can include the report that prints labels.

So, it makes sense to create two custom groups for these two activities. As a start, place the following in the first group, named "Data Entry":

- Alpha Card
- Alpha Entry
- Volunteers

In the second group, named "Print Reports" include the following:

- Alpha Entry by Code
- Alpha Card with Entries
- Alpha Card Report
- Alpha Entries
- Entries by Date
- Entries by Quarter
- Entries by Year
- Labels Name List

Create the Custom Category

Once the grouping strategy has been decided, modify the Navigation Pane to match. To start a new category, do the following:

1. Right-click in the Navigation Pane title bar and choose Navigation Options in the shortcut menu.

2. In the Navigation Options dialog box, under the Categories list, click Add Item.

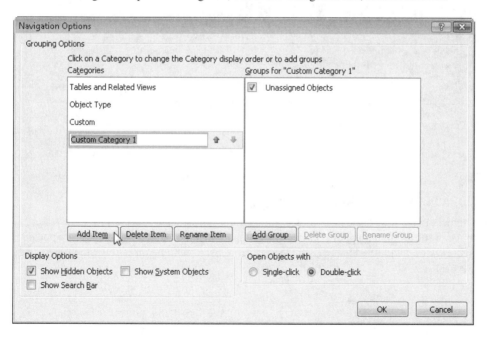

3. Enter "**PoliceDesk**" as the name for the new category and press ENTER. The Groups for pane now shows the new category name with a single item in the list of groups: Unassigned Objects.

4. Under the Groups pane, click Add Group and then enter the name of the first group (Data Entry). Next, press ENTER.

5. Click Add Group again and enter the name, Print Reports as the new group name.

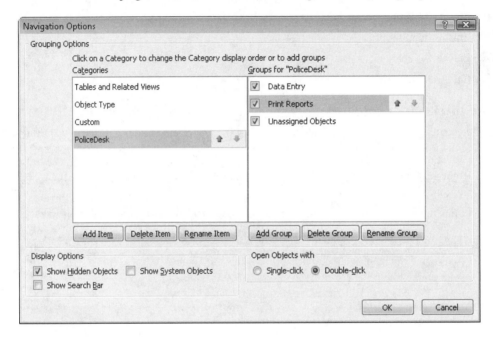

6. Press ENTER and click OK.

The next step, covered in the next section, is to open your new groups and add objects to them.

Add Objects to the Custom Groups

To add objects to the new groups, click the Navigation Pane title bar and choose the new category from the list in the upper section. The groups you added to the category now appear in the lower section with the Unassigned Objects group from which you will get the objects for each new group.

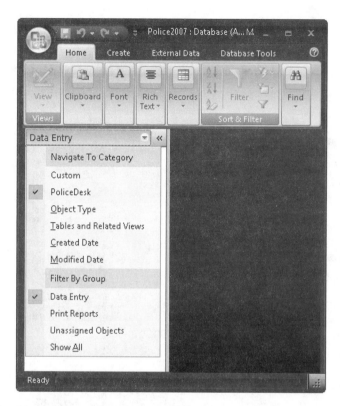

In order to be able to create shortcuts from the Unassigned Objects group to your new groups, check Show All in the lower section. Then you have three ways to move objects to the new groups:

- Drag the objects one at a time from the Unassigned Objects list to the new group.
- Select multiple items by holding down CTRL, and then drag the set to the group.
- Right-click an item and point to Add to group, then click the destination group.

To add Alpha Card, Alpha Entry, and Volunteers to the Data Entry group, do the following:

1. Scroll down the list of objects in the Unassigned Objects list and select the Alpha Card form. Next, drag it to the top of the list and drop it on the Data Entry group name.

2. Scroll down again to select the Alpha Entry form. Press CTRL and scroll down to select the Volunteers form. Drag the selections to the Data Entry group.

17

You can repeat these steps to move the eight reports from the Unassigned Objects to the Print Reports group or use the third method as follows:

1. Select all the objects you want to add to the group.

2. Right-click a selected object and point to Add to group in the shortcut menu.

3. Select Print Reports.

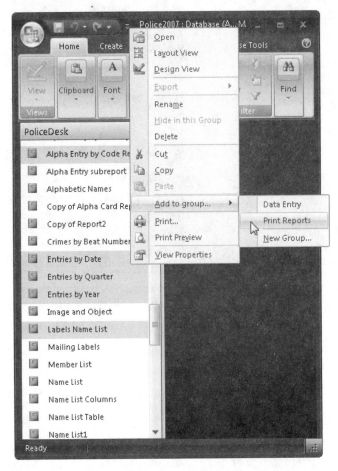

You can leave the Unassigned Objects group in the Navigation Pane if you think you may need to add more objects later or you can hide it. To hide it, do the following:

1. Go to the Navigation Options dialog box again and select the PoliceDesk custom category.

2. Clear the check box next to Unassigned Objects in the Groups for pane, leaving only the two custom groups checked.

3. Clear the Show Hidden Objects check box.

4. Click OK.

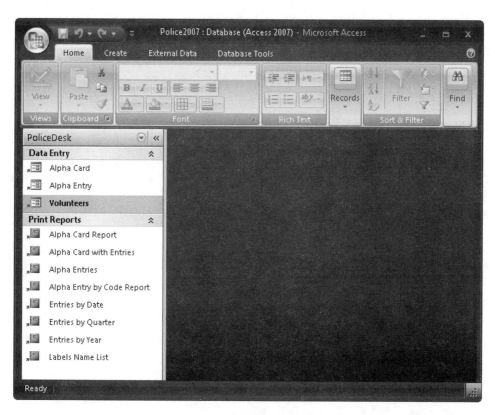

NOTE *You can tell by the icons accompanying the object names that these are shortcuts, not the objects themselves.*

Hide/Restore Custom Groups and Objects

There may be times when you don't need to see all the custom groups in a custom category. You can make them completely invisible or just have them show up in the Navigation Pane as dimmed features.

17

Hide/Restore Custom Groups

If you want to hide a custom group, right-click the group in the Navigation Pane, and then choose Hide in the shortcut menu. To restore the group, you need to use the Navigation Options dialog box as before:

1. Right-click the Navigation Pane title bar and then choose Navigation Options in the shortcut menu.

2. Choose the category that includes the group you want to restore and, in the Groups for that category pane, check the group you want to restore.

3. Click OK.

Hide/Restore Objects in Custom Groups

Even though you placed all the tables, forms, and reports in just the right custom groups when you created the database, things change and some of the groups need to be reorganized.

You can remove an object from a custom group or simply give it a different name. To remove an object from the custom group, right-click the object name in the Navigation Pane and then choose Remove in the shortcut menu. If you just want to hide it, choose Hide in this group in the shortcut menu.

Custom groups contain shortcuts to the actual objects, not the real thing. So choosing Delete removes only the shortcut, not the object itself.

If you want to give the object a new name, first right-click the object and then choose Rename Shortcut in the shortcut menu. Enter the new name in the text box and press ENTER.

To restore the hidden or removed object shortcut to the custom group, do the following:

1. If you don't see the Unassigned Objects group in the Navigation Pane, right-click the Navigation Pane title bar and choose Navigation Options.

2. In the Navigation Options dialog box, select the category and, in the Groups for that category, check Unassigned Objects. Click OK.

Then, back in the Navigation Pane, you can drag the object you want from the Unassigned Group back to your custom group.

Create Switchboards

The switchboard system for a database consists of a hierarchical arrangement of switchboard pages beginning with the main switchboard and usually branching out to two or more subordinate pages. Each page contains a set of items with commands that carry out a specified activity. Most items also include an *argument* that specifies which form to open, which report to preview, which macro or procedure to run, and so on.

When the Access 2003 Database Wizard created a new database, it always added at least one switchboard as the user interface. Figure 17-5 shows the main switchboard for the Order Entry database as created in the Access 2003.

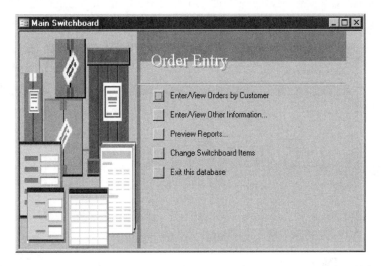

FIGURE 17-5   The Order Entry database main switchboard.

In addition to the main switchboard, two other switchboard pages were included in the user interface within the Order Entry database:

- The Forms Switchboard, reached by clicking Enter/View Other Information item.
- The Reports Switchboard, reached by clicking Preview Reports.

The ellipses (...) following each of those items tell the user that the choice opens secondary switchboard pages.

Access 2007 includes the Switchboard Manager to help create your own. Notice that one of the items on the Main Switchboard in Figure 17-5 is Change Switchboard Items, which launches the Switchboard Manager.

Use the Switchboard Manager to Create Switchboards

To start the Switchboard Manager, on the Database Tools tab in the Database Tools group, click the Switchboard Manager command. If your database already has a switchboard system, the Switchboard Manager window lists all the existing switchboard pages. If your database does not already have a valid switchboard, the Switchboard Manager displays a message asking if you want to create a new one. Click Yes.

17

The first Switchboard Manager dialog box starts with the mandatory default main switchboard page.

Add Items to the Page

If you are creating a new switchboard system, the first step is to add items to the main switchboard by selecting the page in the Switchboard Manager dialog box (if not already selected) and clicking Edit. This opens the Edit Switchboard Page dialog box, which has only one available option at this time: New. With this, you begin adding items to the switchboard.

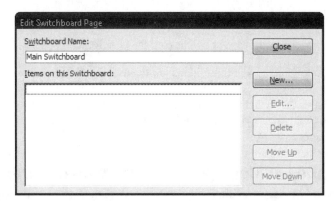

There are no items in the main switchboard for the Police database yet. Before adding them to the switchboard, enter **Bayview City Police** as the switchboard name in place of Main Switchboard. Then begin to add the list of items that you have decided should appear when the database starts up and click New to open the Edit Switchboard Item dialog box.

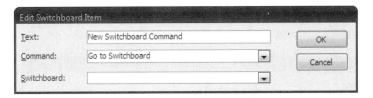

 TIP *To be able to return to the main switchboard, always add an item at the end of the list on all switchboard pages except the opening switchboard. The item moves control back up the switchboard tree to the main switchboard. The opening switchboard should have an item that closes the database.*

Three entries define a switchboard item; they are created by doing the following:

1. Enter the text you want to appear in the list of items in the Text box.

2. Choose the command you want from the drop-down list next to the Command box.

3. Depending on which command you choose, enter the command argument in the third box. The title of the box and the arguments vary with the command chosen.

To create an efficient switchboard system, place the buttons for the most commonly performed tasks on the main switchboard, then buttons for the secondary or subordinate activities on other pages. The activity most often carried out in the Police application is to look up or enter Alpha Card information in the Alpha Card form. This form also displays the Alpha Entry information in a subform. To begin the Police switchboard system, do the following:

1. Type **Enter/Edit Alpha Card Data** in the Text box in the Edit Switchboard Item dialog box.

TIP *You can use the ampersand (&) character in the item's text box to specify access keys for the items in the switchboard. For example, with Enter/Edit & Alpha Card Data, the user can either click the item or press ALT-A.*

2. Click the drop-down arrow next to Command and choose Open Form in Edit Mode from the list of eight commands.

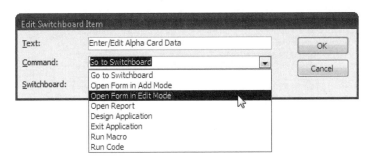

17

3. Click the drop-down arrow next to the Form (formerly Switchboard) box.

4. Choose Alpha Card from the list and click OK.

5. You return to the Edit Switchboard Page dialog box, where you now see the new item in the Items on This Switchboard list. Repeat the same steps to add the following two items to the main switchboard:

■ Enter/Edit Alpha Entry Data, which opens the Alpha Entry form in Edit mode.

■ Preview Alpha Card with Entries, which opens the Alpha Card with Entries report.

Add a New Switchboard Page

There are several more forms and reports that the Police database user might want to open but less frequently than those already added to the main switchboard. The less frequently used forms and reports can be grouped on secondary switchboard pages. To add a new page to the switchboard system:

1. Click Close to close the Edit Switchboard Page dialog box and return to the Switchboard Manager dialog box.

2. Click New. The Create New dialog box opens, in which you can start a new page.

3. Type **Enter/Edit Other Data** in the Switchboard Page Name box and click OK. Include an ampersand if you want to specify an access key for this item.

4. The new page name is added to the list in the Switchboard Manager dialog box. Select the Enter/Edit Other Data switchboard page and click Edit to open the Edit Switchboard Page dialog box as before.

5. Click New to open the Create New dialog box as before and type **Enter/Edit City Beats**. Choose Open Form in Edit Mode from the Command list and City Beats from the Form list.

6. Repeat step 5 to add the following items to the list:

    ■ Enter/Edit Name List, which opens the Name List form in Edit mode.

    ■ Enter/Edit Description, which opens the Explanation form in Edit mode.

7. Finally, add the item that returns to the main switchboard by typing **Return to Main Switchboard.** Choose Go to Switchboard from the Command list and choose Bayview City Police from the Switchboard list. Figure 17-6 shows the completed Edit/Enter Other Data page.

NOTE   *As you add pages to the switchboard tree (the logical arrangement of switchboard branches), remember to add items to the main switchboard to branch to the page and add the item to the page that moves back up the tree. Otherwise, the user has no way to move from one page to another in the switchboard.*

The items are added to the page in the order in which you define them. If you need to rearrange them, select an item in the Edit Switchboard Page dialog box and click Move Up or Move Down to change its position in the list. Each click moves the item up or down one position.

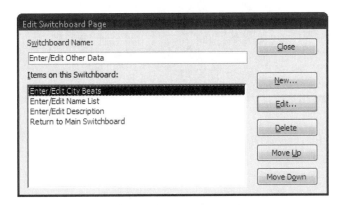

FIGURE 17-6   Items added to the Edit/Enter Other Data switchboard page.

17

To complete the Police switchboard system, create another page titled Preview Other Reports and add the items to it that will open other reports as specified in the item text:

- Alpha Entry
- Entries by Code
- Entries by Qtr
- Entries by Year
- Print Labels
- Return to Main Switchboard

When all the pages have been completed for the switchboard system, close the Switchboard Manager. The Switchboard form now appears in the Forms group in the Navigation Pane. Double-click the form name (Switchboard) to open the main switchboard form in Form view. Figure 17-7 shows the completed main switchboard for the Police database.

The Switchboard Manager has added a colored border to the switchboard template.

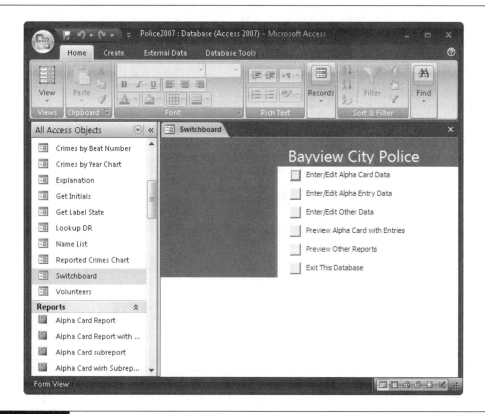

FIGURE 17-7 The new Police main switchboard.

Add a Logo

The new switchboard looks a little bare. You can add a logo to the form header and other markers to the detail section. Open the switchboard in Design view and on the Design tab in the Controls group, click the Logo command. Browse in your computer to find the logo you want and select it. Access places the image in the upper left corner of the form header section.

To add a character for each of the items in the switchboard, on the Design tab in the Controls group, click the Text command and place the new control in the Detail section opposite the switchboard item. Then type the character you want—asterisk in this case. Change the font size and color as desired.

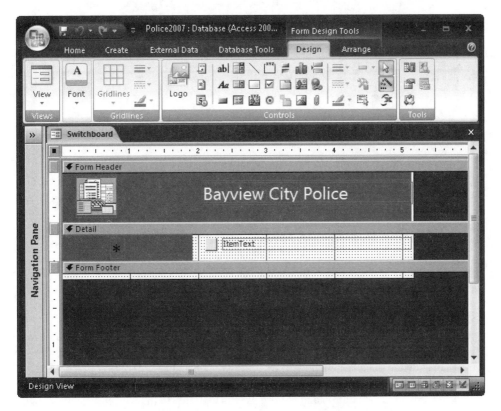

Switch to Form view to see the results of the added art (see Figure 17-8).

The picture used here is the ledger.gif file found in the Dbwiz subfolder in the Office12 Bitmaps folder.

17

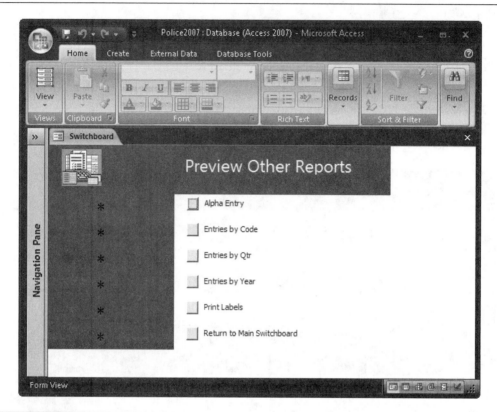

FIGURE 17-8   The completed Preview Other Reports switchboard.

Display the Switchboard at Startup

When you select a switchboard in the Switchboard Manager dialog box and click Make Default, you designate that page as the one to display when the Switchboard form opens. You still have to tell Access to display the default switchboard by setting the Display Form option in the Access Options dialog box.

Click the Microsoft Office button and choose Access Options. In the Current Database page, click the arrow next to the Display Form box, and choose Switchboard from the list and click OK. The change takes effect the next time you start the database. To bypass the switchboard display after setting it as the default startup form, hold down SHIFT while the database opens.

Modify the Switchboard

To edit any item on a switchboard page, open the Switchboard Manager as before and use the Edit buttons.

1. Choose the switchboard you want to change and click Edit.

2. To add an item, click New and enter the text, then choose a command and an argument.

3. To change an item, select it and do one of the following:

    ■ To change the displayed text, the command, or the argument, click Edit.

    ■ To delete the item, click Delete.

    ■ To move the item in the list, click Move Up or Move Down.

4. Close the Switchboard Manager.

You can also delete an entire switchboard by selecting it in the Navigation Pane and clicking Delete. You will be asked if you are sure you want to delete it. The switchboard and all the items on it are deleted.

To change the switchboard that displays when you start the database, open the Switchboard Manager and select the switchboard you want to display instead. Then click Make Default. The startup option is still set to display the Switchboard form, but the Switchboard Manager has designated a different screen as the default switchboard. This will take effect the next time you open the database.

View the Switchboard Items Table

When you use the Switchboard Manager to create a switchboard, Access creates a new table named Switchboard Items. Each record in the table represents an item in one of the switchboard pages, and each field in the record describes what the command the button that carries out and the argument it uses. Figure 17-9 shows the table created for the Police database switchboards.

Table 17-1 describes the contents of the Switchboard Items table. You can widen the columns in the table, but don't make any other changes in the table design.

Field	Contents
SwitchboardID	A sequential number assigned to the switchboard page.
ItemNumber	A sequential number assigned to each item on a page, beginning with 1. Together with the SwitchboardID, forms the primary key that uniquely identifies the item and switchboard page. Switchboards have ItemNumber 0.
ItemText	Text entered in the Text box of the Edit Switchboard Item dialog box.
Command	Number representing the command selected from the Command list in the Edit Switchboard Item dialog box. Commands are numbered sequentially in the order they appear in the drop-down list. For a switchboard page itself, the Command value is 0.
Argument	Number of the switchboard; the name of form, report, macro, or procedure to be used by the command in the Command list in the Edit Switchboard Item dialog box.

TABLE 17-1   The Fields in the Switchboard Items Table

17

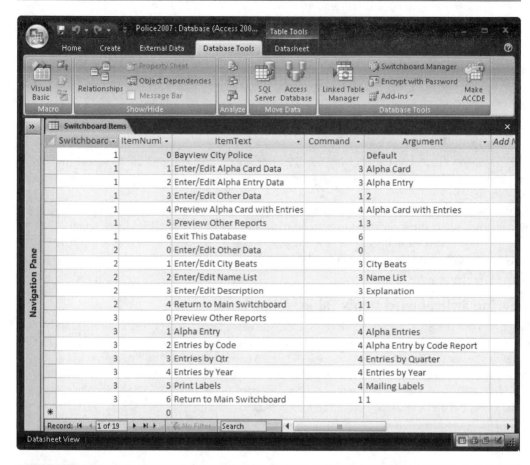

FIGURE 17-9 The Switchboard Items table.

The first row of each switchboard contains 0 in both the ItemNumber and the Command field, indicating that the ItemText is the switchboard caption and is to be displayed in the title bar. The main switchboard has a 0 only in the ItemNumber column.

The Argument field needs a little explanation. The first row contains Default in the Argument field, indicating the Bayview City Police switchboard has been specified as the default switchboard to be displayed at startup if the Display Form/Page option is set to Switchboard. A number in the Argument field represents the ID number of the switchboard as the goal of the command, Go to Switchboard. For example, the fourth row shows 2 in the Argument field, indicating that the command is to display switchboard number 2, Enter/Edit Other Data.

You Can Create a Switchboard Without the Switchboard Manager

To create a switchboard from scratch, start with a blank form not bound to an underlying table or query; then add command buttons that trigger macros or event procedures to carry out the actions you want. The properties of a switchboard form are quite different from the normal data entry form, which shows record navigation buttons, scroll bars, and other data-related features. You are not creating a "real" switchboard with a corresponding table or that you can modify with the Switchboard Manager; you are instead creating a form that works like a switchboard but one over which you have a lot more control.

Before you place command buttons on the form, change some of the form properties so it will appear more like a switchboard:

- Enter the text you want to see in the switchboard title bar in the Caption property box.
- Make sure the Default View property is Single Form.
- Leave the Allow Form View property as Yes and change the other four Allow... properties to No.
- Change Scroll Bars to Neither to remove both the horizontal and vertical scroll bars.
- Change Record Selectors to No because there will be no data on the form.
- Change Navigation Buttons to No because the user will not be moving among records.
- Change Dividing Lines to No because the form won't display records.
- Set Auto Resize to Yes so the form will always appear the same size in Form view.
- Set Auto Center to Yes to ensure the form opens in the middle of the window; and thus will be easier to view and use.

The next step is to add to the form the command buttons and labels that will carry out the desired actions:

- If the switchboard item is designed to carry out a single action, such as open a form in Form view, you can use the Command Button Wizard to add a command button.
- If the item must carry out two or more actions, you must add the button without the Command Button Wizard and create a macro or Visual Basic event procedure to attach to the button's On Click event property.

By attaching a macro or procedure to the label and the button, and including access keys in the switchboard item labels, there are four ways to trigger the action: click the button, click the label, press ALT with the access key, or press TAB to move focus to the button and press ENTER. To attach the macro to both the button and the label, select them both; then open the Event tab of the Properties sheet and select the macro from the On Click property list.

17

Part IV

Exchange Data with Others

Chapter 18

Exchange Database Objects and Text

How to...

- Copy objects from one Access database to another
- Import or link database objects and text files
- Use imported or linked tables
- Export database objects and text files

You can get your development work done faster if you don't have to create everything from scratch. Access provides a number of useful functions and tools that enable you to exchange database objects between Access databases. You can even exchange Access objects with other types of databases such as dBASE, Paradox, or SQL tables and databases that support the Open Database Connectivity (ODBC) protocol. You also can make use of text files in Access or send Access data out as text.

Copy Objects among Access Databases

It is often easier to modify an existing object than it is to develop a table, form, or report from scratch. The first step in the modification of existing Access database objects is to copy the objects you want to edit. Standard copy-and-paste operations and drag-and-drop techniques can be used to copy objects from one Access database to another.

Copy and Paste

To copy and paste an Access database object, first select the object you want to copy in the Navigation Pane. With the Office 2007 clipboard, you can copy as many as 24 objects before you need to paste them into their ultimate destination and clear space for more copied objects.

For example, to make a copy of the Alpha Card table in the Police database, do the following:

1. Select the Alpha Card table in the tables group in the Navigation Pane.

2. Use one of the following to copy the table to the clipboard:

- On the Home tab in the Clipboard group, click the Copy command.
- Right-click the table name and choose Copy from the shortcut menu.
- Press CTRL-C.

If you want to copy the table to the same database, there are three ways to paste the table:

- Click the Paste command in the Clipboard group.
- Right-click in the Navigation Pane and choose Paste from the shortcut menu.
- Press CTRL-V.

When you copy a table, the Paste Table As dialog box asks for a name for the table and presents the following options:

- Paste the structure of the table (without its data)
- Paste the structure of the table and its data
- Appending the data to an existing table

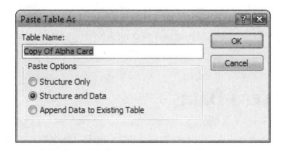

If you choose to paste the data to an existing table, you might have problems with duplicate primary key fields or unique index values. You also need to consider differing table structures. See Chapter 8 for information on solving problems with append queries.

If you want to copy an object to another Access database, instead of renaming it within the same database, do the following:

1. Start up a second instance of Access and open the destination database.
2. Resize the two Access windows to show both instances in a split screen format.
3. Copy the object in the source database.
4. Open the object group in the destination Navigation Pane and paste it into the destination database.

If you don't want to use two instances of Access, close the source database after you copy the object, then open the destination database and destination group in the Navigation Pane and click Paste.

Copying an object generates a copy of all the properties of that object. For example, when a form is copied, the format, source data, event specifications, filters, and all other properties are copied with the form.

Drag and Drop

A drag-and-drop technique can also be used to copy objects between databases. To use drag and drop, you need to have two instances of Access active at the same time.

18

Here's how to drag an object from one window to another:

1. Make sure both Navigation Panes are open to the same group, and then select the object you want to copy in the source database.
2. While holding the left mouse button down, drag the item to the destination database.
3. Release the mouse button and the table will appear in the destination Navigation Pane.
4. Enter a new name, and, if necessary, choose the desired Paste Option and click OK.

If there is an object with the same name you will be asked if you want to replace the existing one.

Import or Link Access Data

Two other important techniques for adding Access data to an Access database are *importing* and *linking*. Importing is used to actually copy Access data or other objects into an Access database from other Access databases. Linking is a way of connecting to and using data in an Access database, without actually copying the data from the other database.

You can import or link data from earlier Access .mdb or Access 2007 .accdb files to Access 2007 databases. If the source file is a locked-down .mde or .accde file, you can't import forms, reports, or modules.

If you are importing or linking a database that requires a password, you must enter the password before you can proceed.

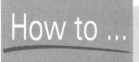 **Choose Whether to Import or Link**

You should choose to import data into an Access database if you expect to use the data only in Access and not depend on another program to maintain the data. Access is more efficient when working with its own tables and you can modify the data just the same as native-grown data.

You should link with data in another program if you rely on the source program to update the information. Linking is also useful in a multiuser environment where you split an existing database and place the data on a network server. Users can then share the database and create their own forms, reports, and other objects.

Import Objects

You can import every object in a database but let's start with the simplest case. The first case to look at is the importing of a couple of objects from one Access database to another. To import the objects, do the following:

1. On the External Data tab in the Import group, click the Access command. The Get External Data dialog box now opens (see Figure 18-1) and is the place where you can locate and select the database file that contains the objects you want to import. You can also right-click in the Navigation Pane, select Import from the shortcut menu, and then click Access Database.

2. Enter the name of the source database or click Browse to look in the File Open dialog box.

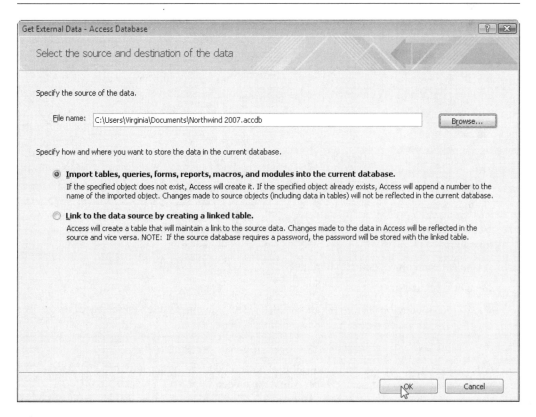

FIGURE 18-1   Choosing the source of the file.

3. After locating the database file that you want to import objects from, choose the first option to import any kind of objects and click OK. The Import Objects dialog box opens where you choose the objects to import. In this example, the Northwind database is selected from sample Access applications, and the Products and Customers tables are imported.

4. To choose which objects to import, click the desired object tab and do one of the following:

- Select each object name individually.
- Click Select All.
- To remove an object from the import list, select it again, or click Deselect All to remove all selected objects.

5. Repeat step 3 for all the desired object types.

6. After selecting all the objects you want to import, click OK to return to the Database window, where you can see the objects that have been imported. You are asked if you want to save the import procedure for later use. This is helpful if you intend to do a lot of importing. You can save export procedures, also.

Figure 18-2 shows the Police Database window with the newly imported Customers and Products tables. The imported tables are now part of the Police database and do not appear different from the native tables in the Navigation Pane.

If you import a table that includes Lookup fields, you must remember to import the tables or queries to which the fields refer and from which they get their values. If you don't want to or can't import the supporting value tables or queries, you can change the imported table design by changing the field Display Control property on the Lookup tab to Text Box for each Lookup field.

If you try to import a table that is already linked to another table, you will actually link to the source table data instead of importing it.

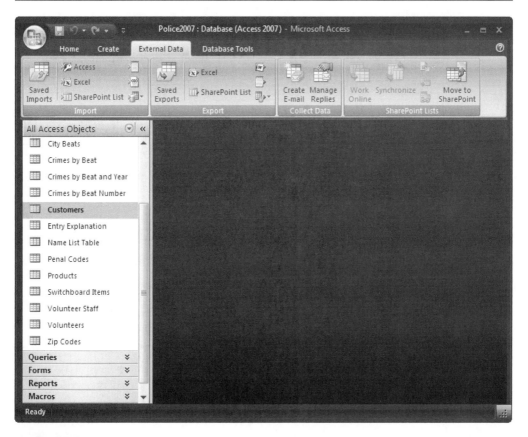

FIGURE 18-2 The Navigation Pane includes imported tables.

18

Set Import Options

There are several options you can set to customize the import process. When you click Options in the Import Objects dialog box, the box expands to show a lower pane with three sets of import options.

The first set of options presents other table features that can be imported:

- The Relationships option is selected by default and includes the relationships you have already defined for the tables and queries you import.

- The Menus and Toolbars option includes all the custom menus and toolbars in the database from which you are importing. Imported menus and toolbars are displayed on a tab named Add-Ins. Refer to Chapter 16 for information about custom menus and toolbars from earlier versions of Access.

■ The Import/Export Specs option includes all the saved import and export specifications set for the source database. See the Import and Link Text Files section for information about setting import specifications.

■ The Navigation Pane Groups option includes custom Navigation Pane groups from the source database.

The second set of options, Import Tables, determines whether to import both the table definition and the data (default) or only the definition. This is useful for creating a copy of the table structures for a new database without including any existing data.

The third set of options, Import Queries, applies to any queries you have selected to import and allows you to specify whether to import queries as queries (the default setting) or run the query and import the resulting recordset as a table.

Once opened, the Options pane remains open as you click other object tabs. Click OK when finished choosing import options and click Yes to save the details of the import operation. This saves time when you want to do it again.

When choosing which objects to import, consider the options carefully. For example, importing a form without importing its underlying tables or queries can result in problems that might be difficult to resolve. Logical, useful groupings of objects should be imported together. This means that tables should be imported to provide the field definitions and data for all the forms, queries, reports, pages, macros, and modules you choose to import.

Link Access Tables

Linking to tables in another Access database makes them available without copying them into the active database. Linking saves space and reduces the need to maintain redundant data. Linking also ensures that you always have access to current information. However, linking also means that you are dependent on an object that actually resides in another environment, where it can be renamed, moved, or deleted.

Here's how to link to a table in another Access database:

1. Open the destination database, which in this example is Police.

2. To start the linking process, on the External Data tab in the Import group, click the Access command.

3. In the Get External Data dialog box, select the database that you want to link to your active database.

4. Choose the second option, "Link to the data source by creating a linked table" and click OK. The Link Tables dialog box opens, showing only a Tables tab because tables are the only Access objects to which you can link.

5. Select one or more of the available tables and click OK.

In this example, the Suppliers table is linked to the Police database, as shown by the arrow next to the table icon.

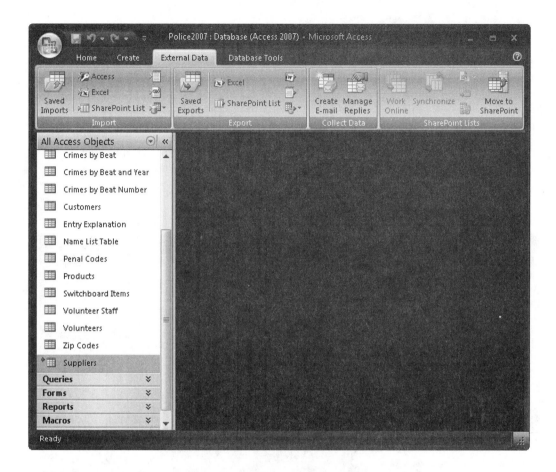

Import from or Link to Other Data Sources

Access can import data or link to existing tables in other database management systems. Access provides specific recognition of some database table formats. Acquiring data and other objects from foreign databases is not much different than importing or linking Access databases.

You can both import and link dBASE III, IV, 5, and 7 files as well as Paradox 3.x, 4.x, 5.0, and 8.0 files. For version dBASE 7 and Paradox 8.0, you'll need the updated ISAM drivers available from Microsoft Technical Support.

You can also import and link data from ODBC data sources such as the Microsoft SQL Server and Visual FoxPro. You will need a connection to the appropriate ODBC data source and the data source defined.

18

Data types are generally compatible among these database management systems, although they aren't labeled consistently. For example, dBASE Character and Paradox Alphanumeric data types both become Text fields in Access. dBASE Float and Paradox Currency types become Number fields in Access with the Field Size property set to Double. dBASE calls Yes/No fields Logical.

Use Data from dBASE or Paradox

Importing a dBASE or Paradox file into an Access database is similar to importing a table from an Access database. For example, to import a dBASE file, do the following:

1. On the External Data tab in the Import group, click the More command and then select dBASE File in the context menu.

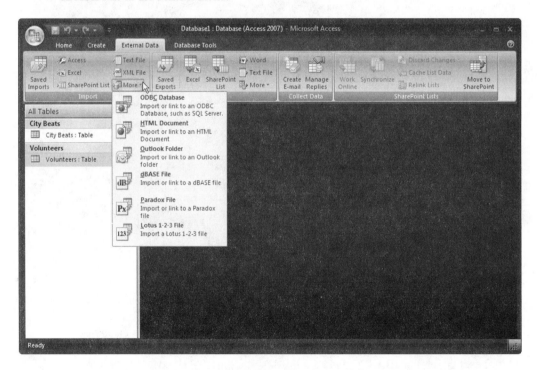

2. In the Get External Data dialog box, locate and select the file you want to import— Users.dbf in this example—and click Import.

Once the table is imported, it looks and behaves just like an Access table. You can use the same procedure to import Paradox files.

Another approach to making use of data from a dBASE or Paradox database is to use the Link Tables operation by choosing the linking option in the Get External Data dialog box. When you import a dBASE file, Access creates a table with the same name as the .dbf file and imports the data. Conversely, when you link to a dBASE file, Access also requires that the associated dBASE index files be linked. If you choose to link to a dBASE file, the Select Index Files dialog box appears, in which you can choose the indexes (.ndx and .mdx files) that are associated with the .dbf file:

- If there are none, click Cancel and proceed with the link operation.

- If you select one or more index files, the Select Unique Record Identifier dialog box prompts you to select the corresponding index field. Note that your index must have a unique value for each record, or difficulties might occur when you try to update records.

After importing or linking a dBASE file, you can set field properties for the table. If you import a file with no primary index, you can set the index in Access. When you update the file with Access, the index is also automatically updated. If you use dBASE to update the file, you must also update the corresponding index in dBASE before trying to open the file in Access.

Figure 18-3 shows a linked dBASE file in the Database window by displaying the arrow and a dBASE icon indicating that Groups is a linked dBASE file.

If you select a Paradox table to link to, you need the index (.px) file and the memo (.mb) file (if the table has any). Without these files you will not be able to open the linked table in Access. If the Paradox table does not have a primary index, you must create one in Paradox to be able to update the table in Access.

Work with Linked or Imported Tables

You can use linked or imported tables the same as any other Access table, with some precautions. Imported tables essentially have become new tables within your Access database. However, linked tables still reside within the environments in which they were created. Thus, issues such as renaming the table or changing its characteristics have implications for relating the linked table to its original source environment.

Rename a Linked Table in Access

The linked table might have a name that is not very meaningful in your Access database. You can give it a more relevant name without disturbing the link. Right-click the table in the Navigation Pane and choose Rename from the shortcut menu, then edit the old name or enter a new name.

Change Linked Table Properties

The database that owns a table usually sets the table properties of linked tables. The source database also sets the field properties and validation rules. Data entered in the table from within Access must conform to most of the properties set for the originating database fields such as default values, minimum or maximum values, field format, text options, and any other validation requirements.

Field properties that you can change in a linked table from within Access include Format, Decimal Places, Input Mask, and Caption. If you want to change other field properties in a form, set them for the controls that are bound to the fields.

18

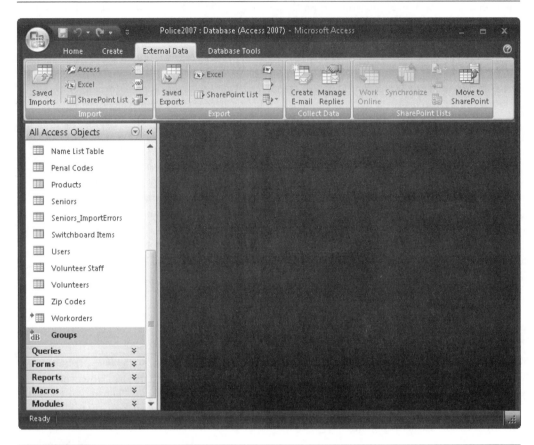

FIGURE 18-3   A linked dBASE file in the Access Navigation Pane.

Update Links with the Linked Table Manager

When the location of a linked table is changed, use the Linked Table Manager database utility to reestablish the proper path or link to the table. The Linked Table Manager does not physically move files; it only updates the path leading to the file location. There are two cases in which the Linked Table Manager might be consulted:

- To examine or refresh links
- To change the path or location of linked tables

Now I'll show you how to refresh links:

1. On the Database Tools tab in the Database Tools group, click the Linked Table Manager command. The Linked Table Manager dialog box displays a list of all tables linked to the current database with the table name and the current path.

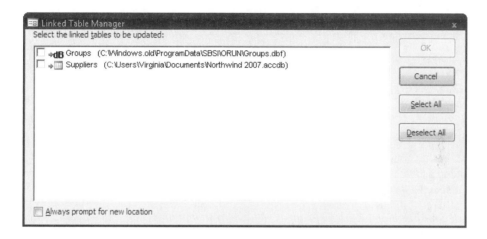

2. Click Select All or check only the table links you want to refresh, and then click OK.

3. If the Linked Table Manager is successful in locating and refreshing the file, it displays a message to that effect. If not, the manager prompts for the location of the table by displaying a Select New Location of Tablename dialog box where you can locate the file and change the path.

NOTE   *The Linked Table Manager has no way of refreshing links to tables whose names were changed in the source database after linking. Delete the current link and start over.*

To change the path to a linked table, open the Linked Table Manager as in the preceding list and do the following:

1. Select the Always Prompt for New Location option in the Linked Table Manager dialog box.

2. Check the tables whose links you want to change, and then click OK.

18

3. Designate their new location in the Select New Location of Tablename dialog box, and then click Open. The Linked Table Manager verifies that all selected tables were successfully refreshed.

4. Click OK to close the message box, and then click Close.

Unlink Tables

Unlinking a table removes the linkage only to a table in another (source) database. The procedure for unlinking a table is identical to that for deleting a table; however, the Delete function does not actually delete the linked table. It deletes only the link to the database.

If your intention is to delete a link to a table in another database and not to actually delete a complete table and its data, be sure to select a table name with the arrow indicating it is a linked table. If you inadvertently select a regular table (as opposed to a linked table) and perform a Delete, the table and its data will be lost.

Import and Link Text Files

Text files are useful when you import or link the data to Access tables. If no other common data format exists between the source of the data and Access, you can create a text file with the source program and then import that file into Access. Most relational, hierarchical, or network-oriented database management systems can generate a text version of the data using some kind of record selection function.

Text files are either *fixed-width* (files consisting of rows of data of the same length) or *delimited* text files (files containing records that use special characters to indicate the separation between data fields). Most delimited text files also use a *text qualifier*—usually double quotation marks—to delimit strings. You can use any character that does not appear in field values. After you have generated text files, you can import or link them to an Access database using the same external data importing and linking functions used for data from any source.

Use Delimited Text Files

Importing or linking a delimited text file begins with the same sequence as other importing and linking operations. However, prior to starting the importing/linking process, you must specify a table ready to receive the data—either a new table structure with the appropriate field definitions or an existing table to which this new data can be appended.

You can create a new table to receive the data from delimited text files by using basic table design techniques (see Chapter 3) or by copying the table structure from an existing table. Be careful to account for the proper number of fields, field length, and data type selection to import text data correctly.

To import a text file, do the following:

1. On the External Data tab in the Import group, click the Text File command

2. Locate and select the text file that you want to import and choose how you want to store the data, either as a new table or appended to an existing table (see Figure 18-4). Then click OK.

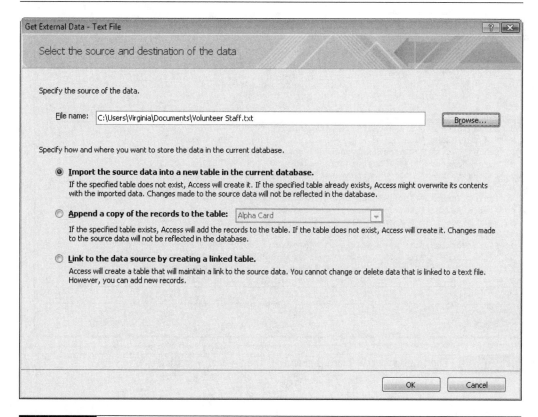

FIGURE 18-4 Choosing the text file and how to store it.

18

3. The Import Text Wizard dialog box appears displaying sample data from the selected text file. The Import Text Wizard analyzes the selected file and determines whether it is a fixed-width text file or a delimited file. Figure 18-5 shows that the text file we are importing, SENIORS.TXT, is a delimited text file.

4. Click Next to see how the file is formatted. In the case illustrated here (see Figure 18-6), the wizard has determined that the fields in this file are delimited by commas, text fields are bounded by quotation marks, and the first row does not contain field names.

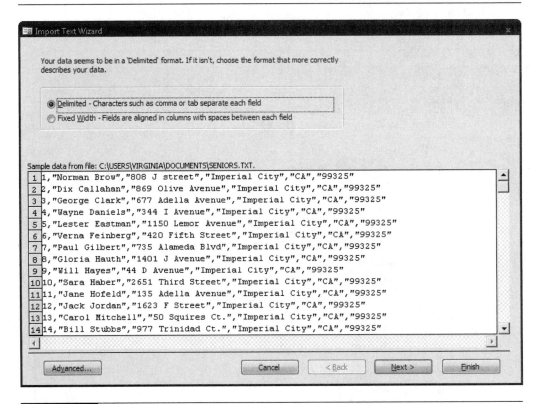

FIGURE 18-5 The Import Text Wizard determines the type of text file.

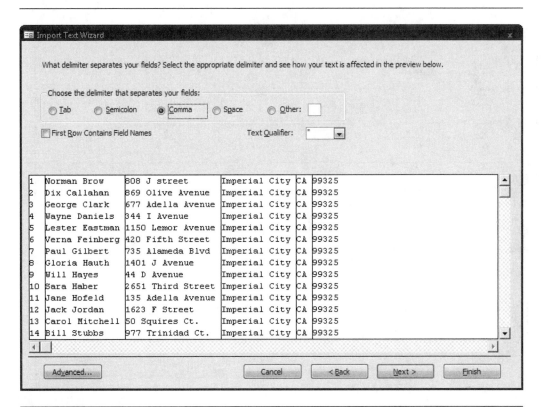

FIGURE 18-6   The Import Text Wizard determines the file's characteristics.

5. Do one of the following:

   ■ If you agree with the results of the Import Text Wizard's processing, click Next.

   ■ If you do not agree, adjust the selections (for the delimiting character, the text qualifier, and whether the first row contains field names) until you are satisfied that they are accurate, then click Next.

6. The Import Text Wizard asks you to specify information about each field in the file (see Figure 18-7).

7. Enter or verify the field name, data type, whether the field is indexed, and whether you want to import or skip that field. The wizard names the fields Field1, Field2, and so on, but you can rename them. Click in the field column to make changes.

18

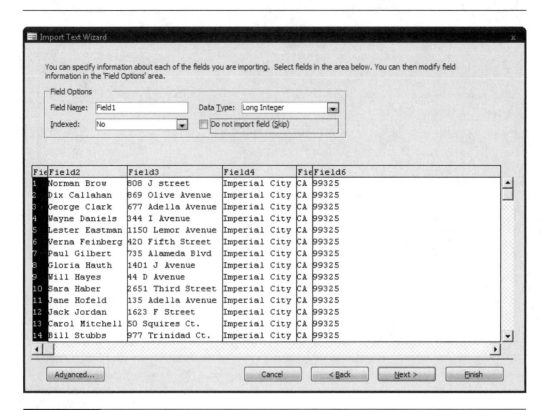

FIGURE 18-7 Setting imported field information.

After completing the field information, click Next; and the wizard will now suggest specifying a primary key field either by letting the wizard add one or by specifying an existing field. You can also choose not to have a primary key (see Figure 18-8).

8. Click Next and enter a name for the new table and then click Finish.

9. Click Yes if you want to save the import process for later use and enter a name and description for the import specifications.

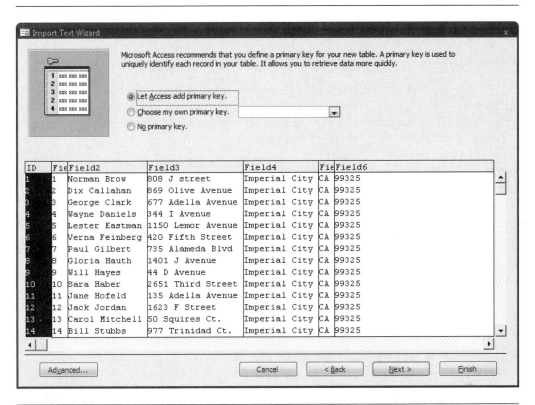

FIGURE 18-8 Adding a primary key.

TIP *If the import process seems to be taking a long time, errors could be occurring. Press CTRL-BREAK to cancel any time during the process.*

Linking delimited text files with the Link Text Wizard is the same as importing, with two exceptions: you are not asked if you want to link to an existing table or create a new one, and you are not prompted for a primary index because you are not creating a new table.

18

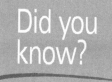

Import Errors

It is possible that improperly defined data or data of an improper length could cause errors. If this occurs, Access creates an Import Errors table containing descriptions of the errors. The table shows the field names and row numbers of the data that caused the error.

Here's a list of some of the possible import errors:

- **Field Truncation**   Occurs when the text value is longer than the Field Size property setting for the destination field.

- **Type Conversion Failure**   Occurs when a value is the wrong data type for the destination field.

- **Key Violation**   Occurs when a duplicate primary key value appears.

- **Validation Rule Failure**   Occurs when a field value breaks the rule defined in the Validation Rule property for the destination field.

- **Null in Required Field**   Occurs when the Required property of the destination field is set to Yes and a Null value occurs.

- **Null value in AutoNumber field**   Occurs when the data intended for an AutoNumber field contains a null value.

- **Unparsable Record**   Occurs when a text value contains a character specified as the text delimiter character.

If the problem is with the data, edit the file. If you're trying to append data to an existing table, you may need to change the table definition. After correcting the problems, import the file again. When a value contains the delimiter character, edit each field to repeat the character twice. When you finish, check the destination files to make sure that some of the records do not have duplicate copies.

Use Fixed-Width Text Files

The Import Text Wizard reacts a little differently once fixed-width text files are detected. The second wizard dialog box (see Figure 18-9) shows the fixed-length data with vertical lines between fields and a ruler at the top. The wizard asks you to confirm whether the lines indicate the proper separation point between fields and provides guidance for how to move or reposition the lines.

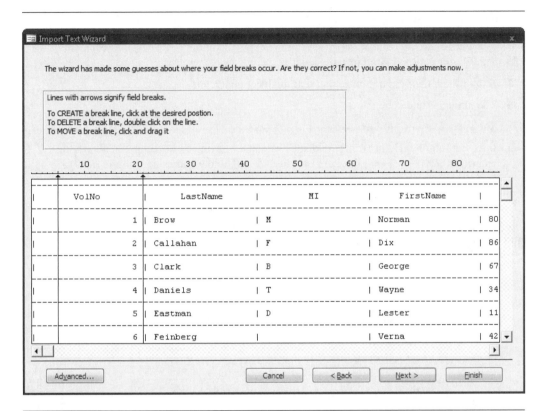

FIGURE 18-9   Importing a fixed-width text file.

- To create a line, click at the position where a field separation is desired. Two lines have been added in Figure 18-9.
- To delete a line, double-click the line to remove the field separation.
- To move a line, click and drag the line to the proper position.

Once adjustments are completed, the process of identifying the destination table and completing the import or link is the same as with delimited files.

Change Import Specifications

You can change the import specifications for a text file using the Advanced features of the Import Text Wizard. Click the Advanced button in the Import Text Wizard dialog box to display

18

the Import Specification dialog box (Figure 18-10), which enables you to specify a number of table characteristics:

- The file format (delimited or fixed-width)
- If delimited, the field delimiter and text qualifier characters
- The language and code page
- The specifications for dates, times, and numbers
- Information for each incoming field such as name, starting and ending position in the record, data type, whether the field is to be indexed, and whether to omit the field from the import

Once the text file characteristics have been satisfactorily specified, the OK button returns you to the Import Text Wizard dialog box, where clicking the Finish button will complete the text import action and place the table in your Access database.

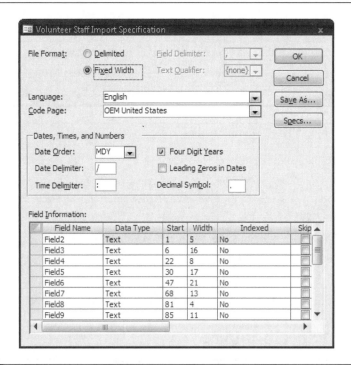

FIGURE 18-10 Setting the import specifications.

Export to an Existing Access Database

Exporting data or database objects to another Access database has the same functionality as copying and pasting. Once in their destination database, the objects look and behave like the native objects. The same data formats are supported as with importing.

To export a table:

1. On the External Data tab in the Export group, click the More command and choose Access Database in the context menu. You can also right-click the table name in the Navigation Pane, point to Export from the shortcut menu and choose Access Database in the context menu.

2. In the Export dialog box, locate and select the destination database, and then click OK (see Figure 18-11).

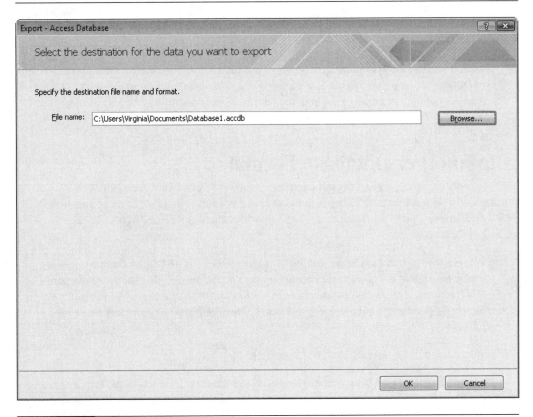

FIGURE 18-11   Choosing the destination of the table.

18

3. Accept the existing name or enter a new name for the destination table in the Export dialog box and select to export both the table definition and data or only the definition.

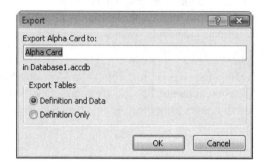

4. Click OK.

When you are exporting database objects other than tables, the basic steps are the same with the exception that the final step is not required because you are exporting only an object design without any data.

You can export only one database object at a time. If you need to export multiple objects to an Access database, it might be quicker to open the destination database and use the Import group of commands, which can be used to import multiple objects at once.

Export to Another Database Format

Access supports exporting data to the same database, and text formats are acceptable for importing and linking. Access also can export data in the proper formats for other applications such as spreadsheets (Excel and Lotus 1-2-3) and text files such as RTF and Wordfiles as discussed in the next chapter.

When you export data to older database programs such as dBASE or Paradox, both of which limit table names to eight characters (not including the file extension), the longer table names are truncated to comply with the limitation. This can result in duplicate names. To prevent this, make a copy of your table with a shorter name before exporting the copy.

To export data to these formats, do the following:

1. Select the table in your active database and on the External Data tab in the Export group, click the More command and choose from the list of files, Or, you can right-click the table name in the Navigation Pane and choose Export from the shortcut menu.

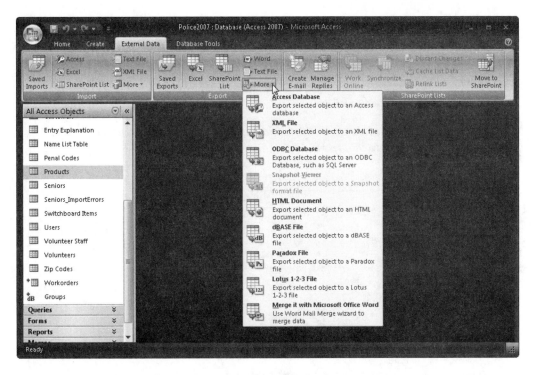

2. Choose the dBASE or Paradox file format in the Context menu.

3. In the Export dialog box, enter the destination and file format. You can choose dBASE versions III, IV, or 5. With Paradox, you have the choice of 3, 4, 5, or 7-8.

4. Enter the destination filename in the File Name box and then click OK.

Export to Text Files

When you want to export data from an Access database to a text (.txt) file, call upon the Export Text Wizard, which works much like the Import Text Wizard. The wizard helps you specify the format of the exported Access file and determine where to store the output. To export data to a text file using the Export Text Wizard, do the following:

1. In the Navigation Pane, right-click the table, query, form, or report containing the data you want to export to a text file, point to Export, and then click Text File in the context menu.

NOTE   *If the form or datasheet contains subforms or sub datasheets, only the main form or datasheet is exported. If you want the subs exported as well, you need to do them separately. Reports including subforms or subreports are all exported at once.*

18

2. In the Export—Text File dialog box, accept the default name or enter a new one. You have three export options (see Figure 18-12):

- Export data with formatting and layout

- Open the destination file when complete

- Export only selected records

If you choose to export the data with formatting and layout, you can choose the encoding : Windows (default), MS-DOS, Unicode, or Unicode (UTF-8).

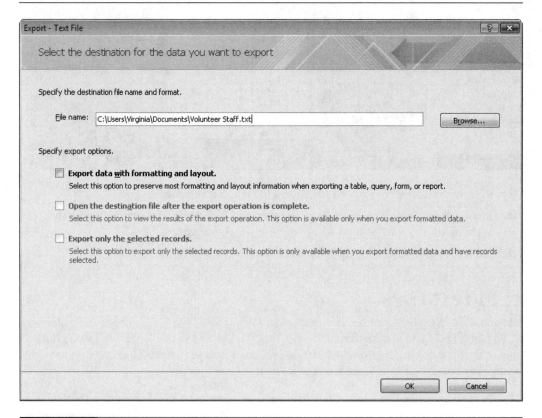

FIGURE 18-12   Choosing export options.

3. For now, choose no export options and then click OK.

4. The Export Text Wizard dialog box (see Figure 18-13) displays data from the selected table similar to the Import Wizard. You can choose between saving the data as a fixed-width or a delimited text file.

5. Click Next.

6. If you chose Delimited, the next dialog box (see Figure 18-14) contains the specifics of the delimiters, text qualifiers, and other features of each field.

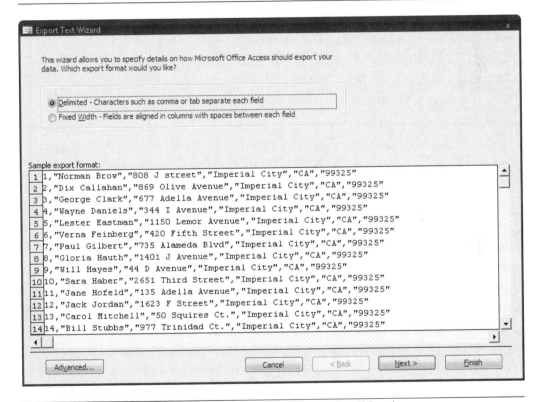

FIGURE 18-13 Selecting the text file type with the Export Text Wizard.

18

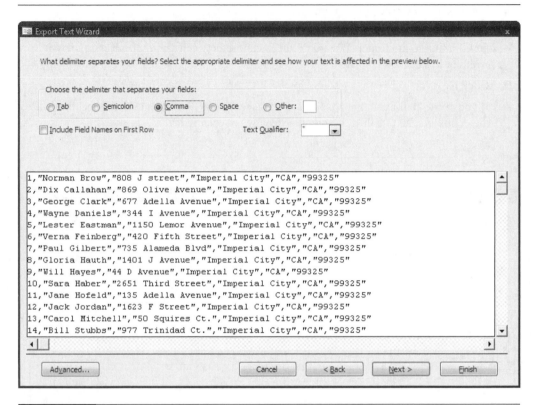

FIGURE 18-14 Setting the text file characteristics with the Export Text Wizard.

7. If you agree with the default settings, click Next.

8. If you do not agree, adjust the selections (for the delimiting character, the text indicator, and whether the first row contains field names). When finished, click Next.

9. If you chose Fixed Width, the next dialog box asks for verification of the field lengths. Figure 18-15 shows the same table being exported as fixed-width. You can drag the divider lines left or right to adjust the width of the fields.

10. Click Finish to complete the export.

You can also use the Export Text Wizard to customize the export specifications for a text file the same way you set the import specifications with the Import Text Wizard. When you click the Advanced button in the Export Text Wizard, an Export Specification dialog box appears, allowing you to specify the file format (fixed-width or delimited); the language and code page settings; the specifications for dates, times, and numbers; and field information. The options are the same as for importing.

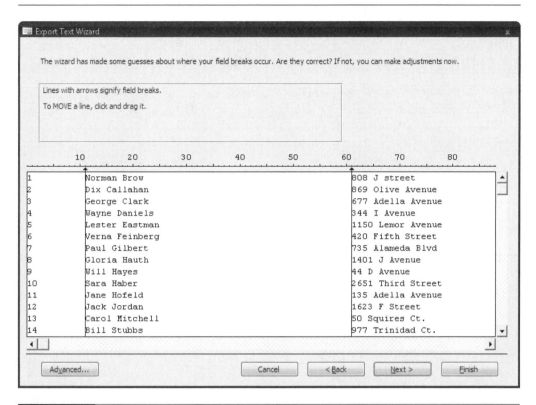

FIGURE 18-15 Exporting the text as fixed-width.

Chapter 19

Exchange Data with Outside Sources

How to...

■ Copy or move records

■ Save Access output as an external file

■ Work with Word

■ Work with Excel

■ Mail Access objects

In the last chapter I focused on exchanging data within the Access management realm, both with other database management systems, and with text files. In this chapter, you will investigate how to exchange information between an Access database and an outside source—a word processor or a spreadsheet. A successful exchange of data with these outside sources involves a sequence of steps that ensure that the end result will be useful.

Copy or Move Records

To copy or move records from other applications into Access tables, you must make sure that the data is arranged in an appropriate format and then use the selection, copy, and paste functions in Access to move the records you want. You can bring data into Access from several different word processors and spreadsheets.

Copy or Move Data from a Word Processor

There are two approaches to copying or moving records from a table created with a word processor. The first approach is to save the desired records to a text file with fixed-length or delimited records and import them into the target table as described in the previous chapter.

The second approach is to perform a copy (or cut)-and-paste operation. For this approach to work properly, you should know two major things:

■ The records in the word processing file must already be in a table or be properly separated by tab characters.

■ The columns in the word processor table must be in the same order as the fields in the Access table you are targeting.

When you copy and paste the data, you place a copy of that data in the destination file and leave the original data alone in the source file. When you cut and paste the data, you actually delete it from the source and place it in the target file. You can add new records to either a datasheet or a form.

If you are adding records to a datasheet, the columns are not required to have the same names as the fields but the data being copied or moved should be the same data type. If you are adding records to a form, the data is copied or moved to text box controls, which are bound to table fields and have the same names as those of the incoming data columns. If the column names don't match the control names or the columns have no names, the data is moved or copied to the form in the tab order.

On the receiving end, you can replace existing records or add to the records already in the datasheet or form. To replace records in a datasheet, select the same number of records to eliminate as you selected to bring in from the word processor. In a form, you can replace only the current record.

To move or copy word processing data, complete the following steps:

1. In the word processor application, select the records that you want to move or copy using the selection method provided by the application.

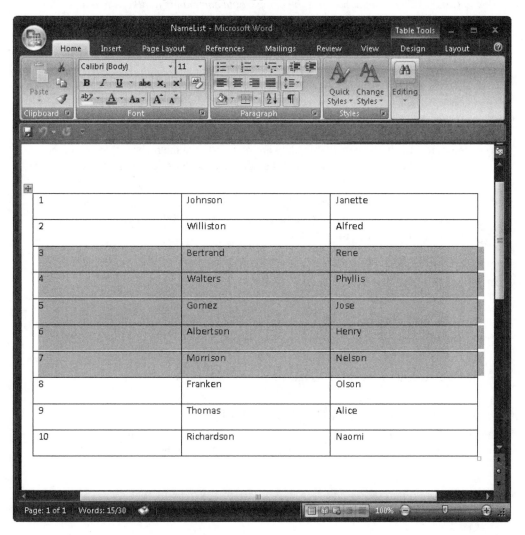

2. Do one of the following, both of which place the selected records on the clipboard:

- If you want to copy the records, on the Home tab in the Clipboard group, click the Copy command, or press CTRL-C.

- If you actually want to move the records from the word processing file to the Access database, on the Home tab in the Clipboard group, click the Cut command, or press CTRL-X.

NOTE *In Word, you can also right-click the selection and choose Cut or Copy from the shortcut menu. Other word processing programs have different methods for placing text on the clipboard. If the application from which you are getting the records does not have the Cut and Copy commands, use the comparable commands to place the data on the Windows clipboard.*

3. Open the Access datasheet or form you want to receive the records, and then do one of the following:

- To replace records in Datasheet view, select the records you want to replace and then on the Home tab in the Clipboard group, click the Paste command, or press CTRL-V. If you select fewer records in the target than in the source table, the selected records are replaced and the excess records from the source table are ignored. If you select more records in the target table, they are replaced with the records selected in the source table beginning at the top of the table; the excess selection in the target table is untouched.

- If you are replacing a record in a form, move to the record you want to replace and click the record selector, then on the Home tab in the Clipboard group, click the Paste command, or press CTRL-V.

NOTE *If you have included the column labels when you copied or moved the records to the clipboard and they don't match the field names in the form, Access asks whether you want to paste the field names in the order you defined as the Tab Order.*

- If you are adding the data to the target datasheet, select the new, blank record at the bottom of the datasheet and then on the Home tab in the Clipboard group, click the Paste command down arrow and choose Paste Append, or press CTRL-V.

4. Click Yes to confirm the paste operation.

Copy or Move Data from a Spreadsheet

Copying or moving records from a spreadsheet is similar to copying or moving records from a word processor. The advantage in the case of the spreadsheet is that the data does not have to be

 **Drag and Drop Access Objects**

You also can use the drag-and-drop method to move database objects among applications. You must have both applications running; but then you can click an Access table or query in the Navigation Pane and drag it to a Word document or Excel worksheet. Going in the other direction, you can create an Access table by dragging and dropping a range of cells from an Excel worksheet to the Table group in the Navigation Pane.

arranged in or converted to table form because it is already tabular on the spreadsheet. The same criteria apply as in the case of the word processor:

- The columns in the spreadsheet must be in the same order as the data elements in the table for the data copy/move to be useful.

- If the records are to be added to a form, the column names in the spreadsheet should be the same as the names of the corresponding text box controls on the database form.

Copy or Move Records from Access to Another Application

Copying or moving records from an Access datasheet or a form to another application is similar to bringing new records into Access from a source application. When you paste Access records to a different application, the field names appear in the first row of the table in a word processor or worksheet in a spreadsheet.

> **TIP** *If you are copying from a datasheet that has subdatasheets, only one level is copied at a time. To copy the subdatasheet, open it, then perform the same copy or move operation.*

The same four basic steps are used:

1. Select the Access data you want to copy or move and copy or cut it to the clipboard.

2. Open the other application.

3. If you are replacing existing data, select that data. If you are adding new data to existing data, place the insertion point where you want to begin pasting the new data.

4. Use the other application's command to paste or append the Access data.

19

If you are pasting Access records into a Word document, place the insertion point where you want the records to appear. The data is pasted in the document as a table. If you are copying from a form, Access includes the form and column names as well as the data.

If you are pasting to Excel, place the insertion point in the cell where you want the first column heading to be. The rest of the Access data fills out columns and rows to the right and down in the Excel worksheet.

Save Access Output as an External File

The previous chapter discusses saving Access data and objects in other database management systems or in text format. You can also export the data from Access tables, queries, forms, and reports to a number of other file formats both within and external to Microsoft Office. You can see the types of files you can export Access data to on the External Data tab in the Export group. There are commands for exporting to Excel, SharePoint List, Word, and to a text file. Click the More down arrow to see other files types to which you can export Access files.

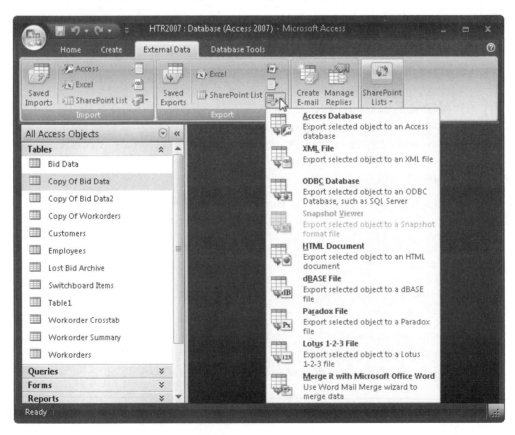

To save the data from an Access table in one of these file formats. do the following:

1. In the Navigation Pane, select the table that contains the data you want to export.

2. Click the desired file type in the Export group, which is Text in this example.

3. When the Export dialog box appears, specify the filename and folder for the destination file or click Browse to find the correct folder.

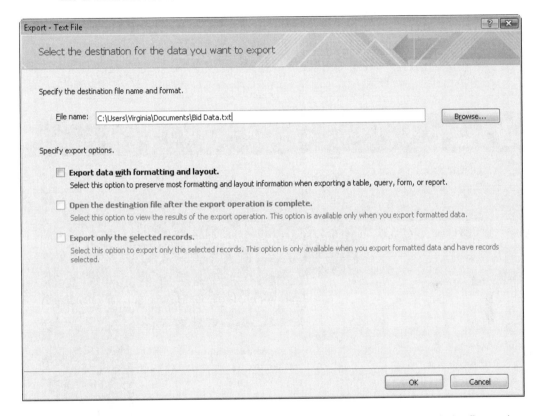

4. If you want to open the imported file when the process is complete, check the first option then the second option, and then click OK to complete the exportation.

TIP
If the file you named as the destination already exists, you are asked if you want to overwrite the file. If not, click No and rename the destination file.

If you export the Access object to Excel 5-7 or 97-2003, HTML Documents, or Text Files, you can also check three options in the Export dialog box. The first is Export data with formatting and layout, which preserves as much of the formatting as possible. The second is Open the destination file after the export operation is complete, which becomes available after you check

Save Formatted. This option launches the destination application and opens the exported file for viewing or editing when you click Export. The third option, Export only the selected records, is available if you have selected records before clicking the Export command. Checking it exports only the selected records. If you leave it unchecked, the entire file is exported.

NOTE *If you choose Rich Text Format, XML Documents, Microsoft IIS 1-2, or Active Server Pages, the Save Formatted option is checked by default. The Autostart option is available with Rich Text Format and XML Documents file type, but not with IIS or ASP.*

Many of these export formats are also available from the Navigation Pane shortcut menu. Right-click the object you want to export and choose from the shortcut menu as shown in Figure 19-1.

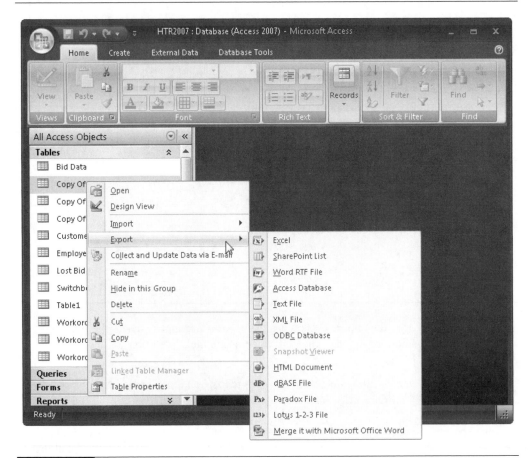

FIGURE 19-1 Choosing the destination for the exported Access data.

Work with Word

Microsoft Office has become so seamless that you almost can't tell one application from another. For example, Word works smoothly with Access to prepare form letters for an address list or helps to transmit Access data in a text format. There are a couple of ways to use Access data in Word other than the simple cut-and-paste or drag process:

- Save the Access data as Rich Text Format, then open with Word.
- Send the Access data to Word as a mail merge source file.

Save in Rich Text Format

Rich Text Format (RTF) is a standard format used by Word and other word processing and desktop publishing programs for Windows. Settings such as fonts and styles are kept intact when files are saved as RTF files.

To save the output of an Access datasheet, form, or report as an RTF file, select the object in the Navigation Pane, or open it and on the External Data tab in the Export group, click the Word command. When you choose the Rich Text Format file type, the Export data with formatted and layout options in the Export dialog box is automatically selected and cannot be cleared. The second option becomes available. If checked, this option launches Word for editing the file when you click OK to complete the process.

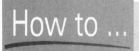 **Prepare for Mail Merge**

A query might be the ideal way to simplify Access data structures for this mail merge function. Your table for customer names and addresses might have a number of other fields, such as a telephone number or date of last order, which you don't need to pass on. You can design a query that selects only those fields relevant to addressing correspondence (Name, Title, Company, Street Address, City, State, and Zip). The Word mail merge feature also can do this after receiving the table data, but you should avoid cluttering up the exchange of data with unnecessary fields.

NOTE

You can also right-click the object in the Navigation Pane and point to Export in the shortcut menu then choose Word RTF in the context menu.

Figure 19-2 shows the Alpha Card table saved as an RTF file in the Word 2007 window.

Use Merge It with Microsoft Word

An Access database is often an ideal place to store names and addresses of customers, business associates, or friends. Once the link between Access and Word is established, you can open Word any time to print form letters, envelopes, or labels using the current data from Access.

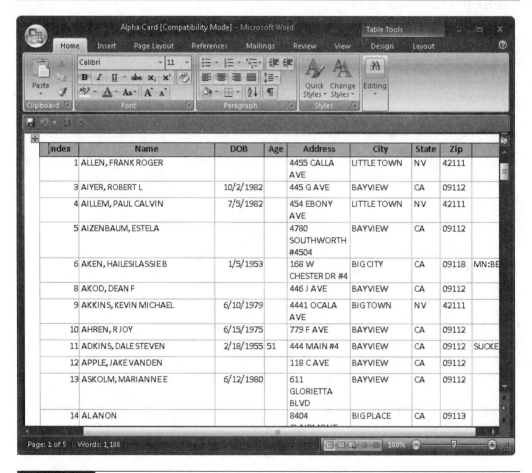

FIGURE 19-2   An Access table saved as an RTF file.

To merge data from an Access table or query using the Microsoft Word mail merge functions, do the following:

1. In the Navigation Pane, select the table or query containing the data.

2. On the External Data tab in the Export group, click the More command then select Merge It with Microsoft Office Word in the context menu.

NOTE *Once again, you can right-click the table or query in the Navigation Pane, choose Export in the shortcut menu, and then select Merge It with Microsoft Office Word in the context menu.*

3. The Microsoft Word Mail Merge Wizard dialog box appears, shown next, offering a choice of linking your data to an existing Microsoft Word document or creating a new one.

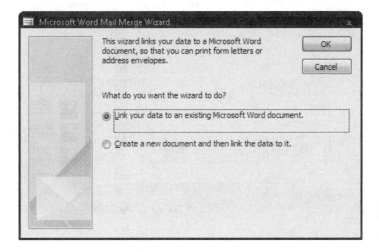

4. Select one of these options and click OK. Word starts up and opens either a new document or the specific document you have selected. Figure 19-3 shows a new Word document with the Insert Merge Field dialog box listing the fields from the Alpha Card Access table as the data source. On the Mailings tab in the Write & Insert group, click the Insert Merge Field command to display a list of available database fields.

5. Select the specific fields you want to insert in your document and place them in the document. For more information about how mail merge works, consult your Microsoft Word documentation.

19

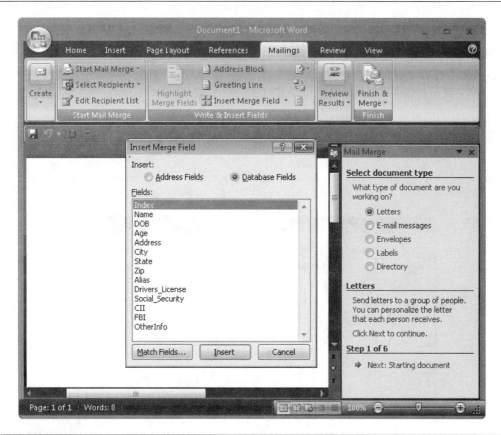

FIGURE 19-3 Using an Access table as a mail merge data source.

Work with Excel

Excel is another application of the Microsoft Office suite that can work smoothly with your data in Access. The association between Excel and Access can also be a two-way street. You can use Excel data in Access or use Access data in Excel.

You have three ways to make use of Access data in Excel or another spreadsheet program:

- Export the Access datasheet as unformatted data.
- Save the output of a datasheet, form, or report as an Excel file or worksheet.
- Load the output of a datasheet, form, or report directly into Excel.

When you use either one of the last two methods, most of the formatting is preserved. A form is saved as a table of data. If you are saving a report that includes grouped data, the group levels are saved as outline levels in Excel.

Import from and Link to Excel Spreadsheets

Before you try to import or link to data from an Excel or other spreadsheet, make sure the data is arranged in a tabular format. The spreadsheet must also have the same type of data in each column as the target Access datasheet and the rows must contain the same field in each position.

You can choose to import or link an entire spreadsheet or only the data from a named range of cells within the spreadsheet. Usually, you create a new table from the imported or linked spreadsheet data; however, you can also append the data to an existing datasheet if the spreadsheet column headings are the same as the table field names.

> TIP
>
> *Access tries to assign appropriate data types to the imported data fields, but it does not always make the correct assumption. Before you do any work on the new table, be sure the field data types are what you want. You should also check the assumed field properties and set additional properties, such as formatting, to fit the intended table use in Access. Number field formatting can differ between Excel and Access.*

If you are importing from Excel version 5.0 or later, you can select one or more of the worksheets in the workbook. You can't import multiple-spreadsheet files from Excel 4.0 or from Lotus 1-2-3. If you want one of these spreadsheets, you must open the program and save each spreadsheet as a separate file before importing.

> TIP
>
> *You can also import from other spreadsheet programs if they are capable of saving the files in Excel or Lotus 1-2-3 format.*

To import or link an Excel spreadsheet, invoke the Import Spreadsheet Wizard by doing the following:

1. On the External Data tab in the Import group, click the Excel command. You can also right-click the object in the Navigation Pane, choose Import in the shortcut menu, and then choose Excel.

2. In the File name box in the Get External Data—Excel dialog box, select the drive and folder where the spreadsheet file that you want is located. Use the Browse button, if necessary.

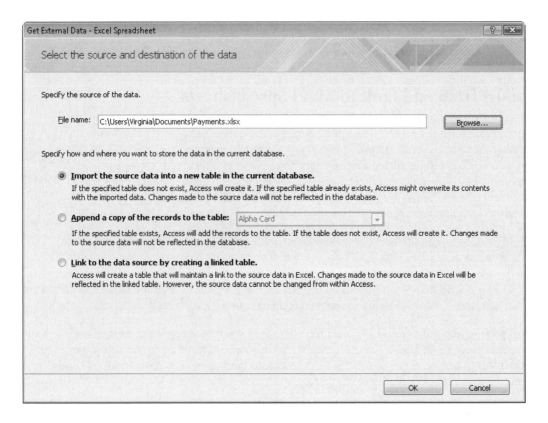

3. Choose how you want to handle the Excel data: import it to a new table, append a copy to an existing table, or link to the Excel data so that changes in the Excel file are reflected in Access. If you want to append the Excel data to an existing table, choose the table in the second option drop-down list.

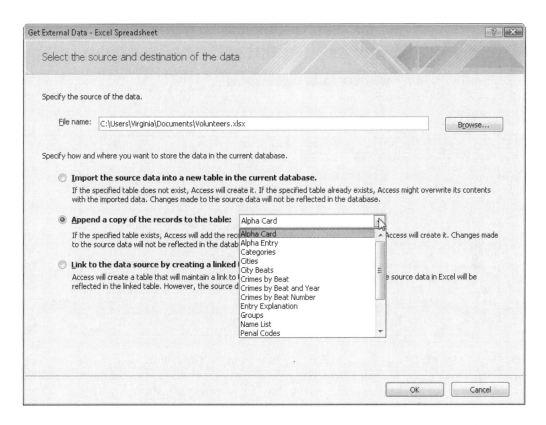

4. Click OK.

5. In the first Import Spreadsheet Wizard (or Link Spreadsheet Wizard) dialog box, you can choose to import a specific worksheet or a named range of cells, and then click Next.

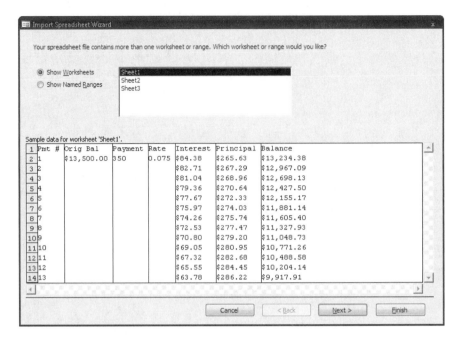

6. In the next wizard dialog box, check First Row Contains Column Headings (if this is true of your data), then click Next. Clear the check box if the first row contains field data instead of column headings. The top row moves down into the main data columns.

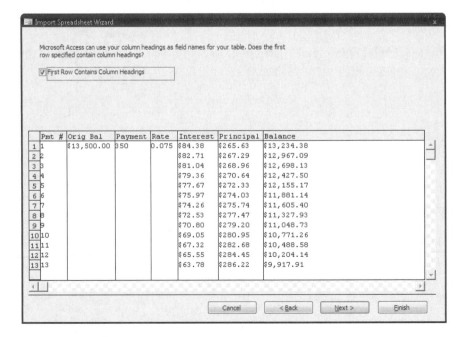

If you indicate that the first row contains the column headings and there are some headings containing data that can't be used for valid Access field names (if, for instance, the heading is blank), Access displays a message to that effect and automatically assigns valid field names.

7. In the next wizard dialog box, you can set the Field Options for each field in the worksheet:

- Click in the Field Name box and enter a new name for the field.

- Choose Yes in the Indexed box to create an index on that field.

- Change the data type, if applicable, in the Data Type box (this is not always available).

- Choose Do not import field to skip the field when importing the spreadsheet.

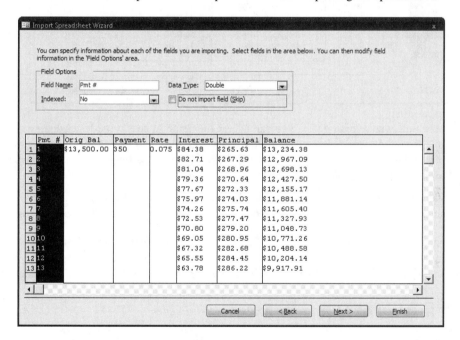

8. Click in the next field header and make other changes. After making the desired changes to each field, click Next.

9. In the next dialog box, choose one of the fields as the primary key. You can also let Access add a field as the primary key or choose not to have a primary key at all. Then click Next.

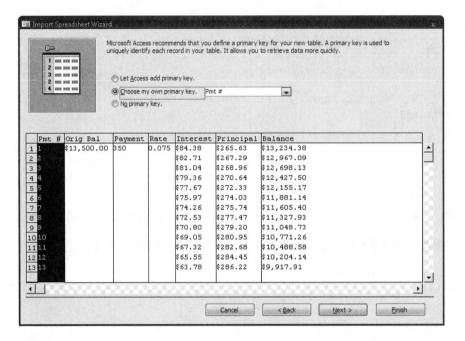

10. In the final wizard dialog box, you can accept the name Access provides or enter a new name for the Access table, and then click Finish. An option in this dialog box lets you run the Table Analyzer with the new table to see if it could be made more efficient. See Chapter 14 for information about the Table Analyzer.

11. When the import is complete, Access asks if you want to save the import steps. If you intend to use this import frequently, you can save time by saving it. Then, click Close.

The Figure 19-4 shows the new Payment Table design created by the Import Spreadsheet Wizard. Notice that the Pmt # is specified as the primary key field. Now you can change the Payment data type from Number to Currency, in order to improve the appearance of the table data.

Export a Table or Query to Excel

Exporting all or part of a datasheet to an Excel spreadsheet is similar to exporting to other file types. On the External Data tab in the Export group, click the Excel command. In the Export dialog box use the File name box to locate the folder where you want to store the exported data. Next, name the file. If you are adding the data to an existing spreadsheet, select its name; otherwise, enter a new filename in the File Name box. Then select the desired Microsoft Excel version or other spreadsheet file type from the File format list.

Check the Export data with formatting and layout option if you want to keep the same fonts and field width and preserve the data that displays in the Lookup fields. The export process takes a little longer with this option but you won't have to restore the formatting in the spreadsheet. The spreadsheet file created by Access contains the field names in the first row and data in the

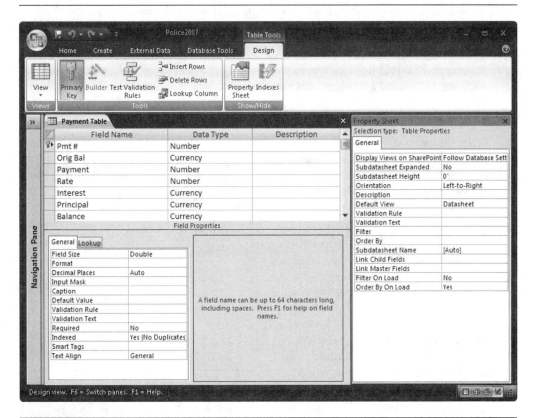

FIGURE 19-4 The new table design created by the Import Spreadsheet Wizard.

subsequent rows. If you are exporting a form, the data is saved as a table of data. If you are exporting a report that includes grouped records, the group levels are saved as outline levels in Excel.

When you choose to save the formatting and layout, the second option (Open the destination file after the export operation is complete) becomes available. This option automatically launches Excel to display the exported data on the screen when you click Export.

Mailing Access Objects

You can send Access tables, queries, forms, reports, report snapshots, and even modules attached to an e-mail message. When you attach objects or data to an e-mail message, the attachments can be converted to several versions of Excel, RTF, MS-DOS text, HTML, or report snapshot formats as part of the E-mail operation.

19

When you select an object and click the Office button and point to E-mail, you See the Send Object As dialog box, where you can choose the format you want to send.

To e-mail an Access database object, you must install an electronic mail application that supports Messaging Application Programming Interface (MAPI), such as Microsoft Outlook, Microsoft Exchange, or Eudora.

To attach an Access object to an e-mail message, do the following:

1. Select the object you want to send in the Navigation Pane. If you want to send only some of the records from a table or query, open the table or query in Datasheet view, and then select the records you want to send.

2. Click the Office button and choose E-mail from the menu. The Send Object As dialog box opens. Choose the file format you want to use for your e-mail attachment, and then click OK. If you selected only part of the datasheet in Step 1, two output formats options become available: All, which attaches the entire datasheet to the e-mail message, and Selection, which attaches only the selected data.

3. If you choose HTML, the next dialog box gives you the opportunity to attach an HTML template. Check Select a HTML Template and enter the template name or choose Browse to locate another file, and then click OK.

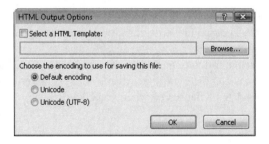

Your e-mail client program opens an e-mail message form where you can address your message, add text to the message, and send it out. The object you selected to send is automatically attached to the message.

Chapter 20

Share with Multiple Users

How to...

- ■ Share a database on a network
- ■ Manage a database in a multiple-user environment
- ■ Update and edit shared data

Creating and maintaining a database in a multiple-user environment is not a simple task. When you welcome more users to a database, you open yourself up to a whole new set of complications. Some users might not have up-to-date information; other users can try to update the same information at the same time, causing conflicts. Access includes several tools that can help ensure the integrity and security of the database and other useful features for resolving conflicts.

When many copies of the database are on different computers accessed by different users, conflicts can occur when changes are made to the same data. Access includes several tools that can help resolve the conflicts and ensure the integrity and security of the database.

Share a Database on a Network

When several users need access to the same data, there are several ways to share a single database with others. Rather than every user keeping a complete copy of the database, you can provide other means for sharing that can also improve data reliability and consistency. Some of the options for sharing an Access database are as follows:

- ■ Place the database in a central location where all users have access to all objects in it.
- ■ Split the database so that the users share only the table data.
- ■ Publish the entire database or part of the database on a SharePoint Services site.

Share an Entire Database

The easiest way to share data is to put the entire database, tables and all, on the network server or in a folder that can be shared. All users then have access to all the data and use the same database objects. If everyone uses the database for the same activities and you don't want the users to be able to customize their own objects, this is the best strategy. Figure 20-1 shows the model for sharing the entire database among multiple users. The entire database is stored on the network server, and the workstations access all the objects via the LAN.

To share an entire database on a network server, copy the database to the shared folder, then use the Advanced page of the Access Options dialog box as shown later in this chapter to set the Default Open Mode to Shared. Access must be installed on each workstation on the network to share the database.

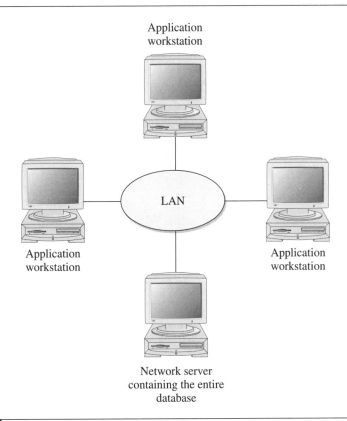

Application
workstation

Application
workstation

LAN

Application
workstation

Network server
containing the entire
database

FIGURE 20-1   Sharing a database among multiple users.

Split the Database

A faster method of sharing a database is to put all the tables on the network server and let the users keep the other objects on their own workstations. Only the data is transmitted over the network, thus reducing network traffic. This strategy is useful when the users' jobs and activities are different or the users do not all have the same versions of Access. The users maintain only those objects on their computers that directly pertain to their own activities.

The database containing the tables is called the *back-end* database; the one containing the other objects is the *front-end* database. The front-end database contains links to the tables in the back-end database. Access provides the Database Splitter Wizard to separate the tables from the rest of the database. Figure 20-2 illustrates the front-end/back-end model for sharing an Access database. All tables are stored in the back end on the network server. The workstations store all the other objects—queries, forms, reports, macros, and modules.

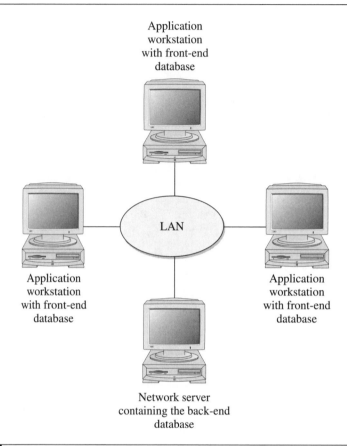

Application
workstation
with front-end
database

LAN

Application
workstation
with front-end
database

Application
workstation
with front-end
database

Network server
containing the back-end
database

FIGURE 20-2 Splitting the database into front-end and back-end.

TIP

It is not easy to undo what the Database Splitter Wizard does so be sure to make a backup copy of the database before attempting to split it.

To split a database into the front- and back-end elements:

1. Open the database and make sure no objects in the database are open, and then on the Database Tools tab in the Move Data group, click the Access Database command. The Database Splitter Wizard opens with a message describing the process (see Figure 20-3).

2. After reading the message, click Split Database. The next dialog box lets you specify where to place the back-end database.

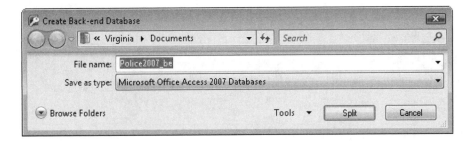

NOTE *If you are using Windows XP, this dialog box will look different but it works just the same.*

3. Click the Browse Folders down arrow to look for the network server.

4. Click the Folders down arrow and choose Network in the list (see Figure 20-4).

5. Select the network server and enter a name for the back-end database or accept the default name (the name of the current database with "_be" added).

6. Click Split. When the process is completed, a message appears announcing the successful split. Click OK to close the message box.

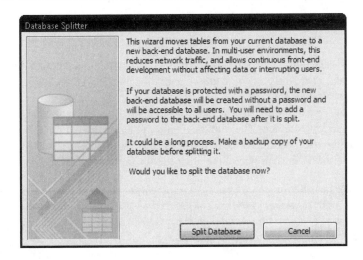

FIGURE 20-3 Starting the Database Splitter.

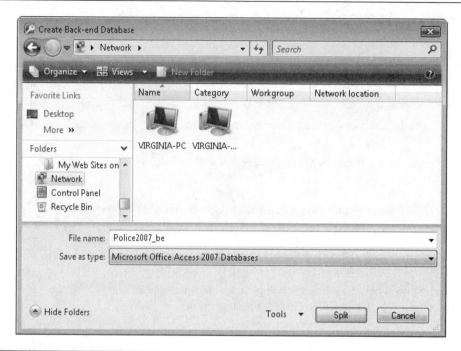

FIGURE 20-4   Choosing the network server.

It might take a while to split a large database. The wizard actually is deleting the tables from the current database, creating a new database with the tables, and then linking the current database to the new back-end tables.

When you look at the list of tables in the Navigation Pane of the current database after splitting, you can see by the link icons next to the names in the list that all the tables listed are links to another database (see Figure 20-5). If you open the new back-end database, you can see all the tables listed on the Tables tab but all the other groups in the Navigation Pane are empty.

NOTE   *To customize the distributed database environment further, you can reduce network traffic even more by moving relatively static tables—such as lookup tables containing data that doesn't change often—back to the front-end databases. If the data in the lookup table changes, you can make the changes in the back-end version and alert the users to copy the data to their own lookup tables. Temporary tables should also be stored locally to prevent conflicts and reduce network traffic.*

If you need to change the link to any of the back-end tables, on the Database Tools tab in the Database Tools group, click the Linked Table Manager command. In the Linked Table Manager dialog box, choose the affected tables and check the Always prompt for new location check box

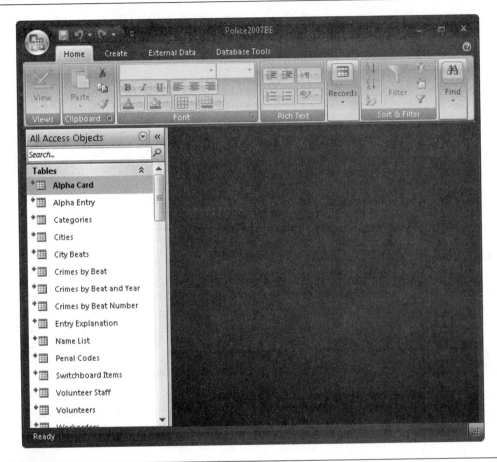

FIGURE 20-5 Tables are linked to the back-end database.

(see Figure 20-6). When you refresh the link to the table, you will have the opportunity to change the location of the linked table in the standard file location dialog box.

Prevent Exclusive Access

When multiple users are sharing a database, competition for data access can occur. If one user opens the database with exclusive access, no other user can work with it. To prevent or at least discourage this from happening, open the Access Options dialog box and on the Advanced page, set the Default Open Mode to Shared. Then instruct all the users not to open the database in an exclusive mode. See Chapter 21 for information about including security in a multiple-user environment.

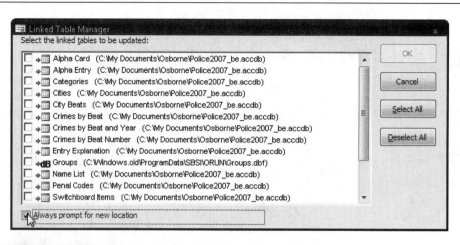

Setting to prompt for new table locations.

You can also set up a security system that prevents certain users from opening a database in exclusive mode but permits others to do so. The database administrator must be able to open the database in exclusive mode to perform duties, such as compacting and backing up the database.

You can publish your database on a SharePoint site if you have Microsoft SharePoint Services 3.0 installed and a valid path to the Document Management Server.

Access 2007 no longer supports replicating databases. If you have one that was replicated in Access 2003 or earlier, you will not be able to save it in the new ACCDB file format. You can however, continue to use it in its MDB format or recreate it in Access 2007 file format.

Manage the Database in a Multiuser Environment

As soon as more than one user can open a database, someone should be assigned as the database administrator (DBA). This person is responsible for ensuring the integrity and security of the database. The issues that the DBA needs to address include the following:

- Controlling read/write access to the data
- Setting up the user groups with the appropriate levels of access and security
- Adding new users to a group and removing users from a group
- Ensuring accurate, up-to-date record data and minimizing data-locking conflicts
- Editing database objects as necessary and ensuring that all users have current versions
- Backing up and compacting the database

Control Data Editing

If two users attempt to edit the same record at the same time, the results can be unpredictable. Some form of data locking is necessary to ensure the integrity of the database. Allowing one user temporary exclusive access to a record is called *record locking*. When a data page (a unit of data storage), recordset (table or query) object, or a database object is locked, it is read-only to all users except the one who is currently entering or editing the data in it.

Access provides three levels of record locking, ranging from no locks at all to locking all the records in the recordset. You can set the default record-locking scheme in the Advanced group of options on the Advanced page of the Access Options dialog box (see Figure 20-7).

NOTE   *To have the setting changes take effect, close and reopen the database.*

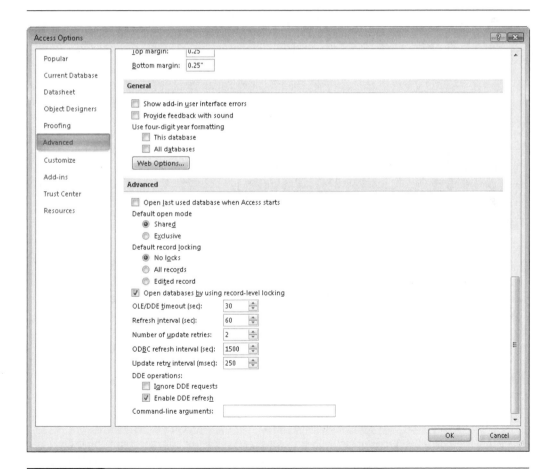

FIGURE 20-7   Setting record locking in the Advanced Access Options.

20

Set Default Record Locking

The Default Record Locking setting applies only to Datasheet views of tables and queries. If you want to set the record locking for forms or reports, set the Record Locks property on the Data tab of the object's Property Sheet. Setting record locks for a report prevents changes in records in the underlying table or query while the report is being previewed or printed. You can also set the Record Locks property for a query and override the default setting.

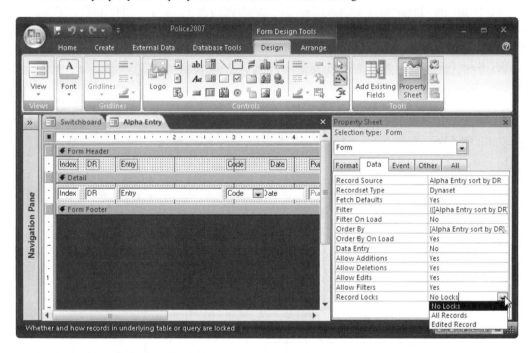

No locks is the default setting when you start a new database. It is called "optimistic record locking" because it is used where few record write conflicts are expected. Access does not lock the record during editing. The edited record is locked only at the exact moment it is being saved. It is assumed that one user most likely will have completely saved the record before another user tries to edit it. Using No Locks ensures that all records can be edited at any time but it can also cause editing conflicts among users.

The All records strategy locks all records in the form or datasheet and the underlying tables for the entire time the form or datasheet is open. No one else can edit the records. One case in which this strategy would be useful is when you are running an update query that applies to several different records and you want to make sure all the affected records are locked until the query is completed.

The Edited record record-locking strategy is called "pessimistic locking" because it is assumed that there will be much competition for access to records for editing. If it is important that all editing of a record be completed before another user has access to it, the Edited Record

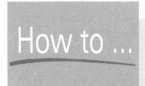

Choose a Locking Strategy

The strategy you choose depends on your data, how many users share the application, and how they use the data. For most multiuser environments, the No Locks strategy can be the most effective, even though some brief write conflict errors can occur. The overall performance of the system is more efficient than with the other record-locking strategies.

If there are more imperative reasons for locking records during editing, use one of the other locking strategies.

If the data in a form, report, or query is acquired from an Open Database Connectivity (ODBC) database, Access treats it as if the No Locks setting was selected and disregards the Record Locks property setting.

strategy is required. As soon as one user begins to edit a record, no other user can make any changes to it until the first user saves the changes. Other users can view the record, but they cannot change it.

Apply Record-Level Locking

With record-level locking in effect, Access locks only a single record in the currently open database. This applies to accessing data in datasheets and forms. If you clear this option, page-level locking becomes the default. This setting does not apply to action queries or SQL statements.

The record-level locking setting does not affect the record-locking scheme set in the Default record locking option group. The setting takes effect the next time you open the database.

NOTE *The setting does not take effect if you open the database by selecting the filename from the list of recently used files in the Microsoft Office button menu.*

Update Records with Refresh and Requery

If the data in your shared database changes frequently and it is important that the user has up-to-date data, you can use two methods to keep the data current: *refresh* and *requery*.

The refresh method updates only those records already appearing in Datasheet or Form view. When you refresh the datasheet or form, records aren't reordered or deleted; those that no longer meet the filter criteria are also not removed. To update the recordset to reflect these actions, you must requery the records.

To refresh a table, query, or form manually, open the table or query in Datasheet view or the form in Form or Layout view. Then, on the Home tab in the Records group, click the Refresh All down arrow and choose Refresh All or Refresh in the context menu. You can also press F9.

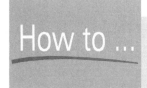

Minimize Conflicts

One way to reduce the number of locking conflicts is to arrange the workload so each user is responsible for different parts of the database. For example, one user updates records for sales in the Western states, another for the Southern area, and so on.

When two users try to update the same record and cause a conflict in the process, Access tries several times to save the record. Access first attempts to free the record from the lock before displaying the Write Conflict message. The Update Retry Interval setting specifies the period of time that elapses between tries. The Number of Update Retries setting determines how many times Access is to try to save the record before giving up. These settings are also on the Advanced page of the Access Options dialog box.

You can try different combinations of these two settings. For example, set the Number of Update Retries to 0 for Access to display the Write Conflict message at once. Set both to higher values to reduce the number of write conflicts by allowing Access to try to save the record more times with a longer interval between attempts. However, with this arrangement, users might complain that the system appears slow. Experiment with these settings to settle on the right combination for your application.

The default interval for refreshing records is 60 seconds, which might be too long in critical situations. You can reset the interval to 10 or 15 seconds. If you set it too low, Access will create a lot of network traffic.

Requerying completely rebuilds the underlying recordset. The easiest way to requery is to press SHIFT-F9.

Edit Shared Database Objects

Even if you do your best to have all of the database object designs completed before setting up the database for shared access, there are bound to be changes that must be made later. Any local objects can be modified at any time but the shared objects require special consideration.

Before you begin to make significant design changes to a shared database, be sure you open it in exclusive mode by selecting Open Exclusive from the Open button in the Open dialog box. Pick a time to do this when other users do not require access to the database, such as the middle of the night.

If the required design changes are less invasive, you can safely modify the objects while the database is open in shared mode. If the table or any query, form, or report based on the table is open, you can't change the table design. The converse is also true—if you are modifying a table design, the table and any query, form, or report that is based on it is unavailable to another user. It is a good idea to have the changes well thought-out and specific before opening the table design; then keep it open as briefly as possible.

Here are some other tips that are helpful when you need to edit shared database objects:

- When you edit a query, form, or report design that is already in use by another user, that user won't see the new version until the object is closed and reopened.

- If the objects you want to change are dependent on each other, be sure to edit them all at the same time so they will be consistent.

- Make sure no one else is using the macro you want to edit by opening the database in exclusive mode. If you change a macro that someone is using, you can cause problems.

Chapter 21

Secure a Database

How to...

- Enable/disable database contents
- Encrypt a database with a password
- Use the Trust Center
- Trust macros, add-ins, and ActiveX controls
- Secure earlier versions

The main purpose of database security is to prevent unauthorized access to the information, either for viewing or editing. Security can also prevent design modifications by unqualified individuals. Even the slightest change in a form design or a data validation rule can cause problems that can be difficult to locate and correct. Security also blocks hackers from getting into and damaging the database and spreading viruses in the system.

Access 2007 has added many new security measures that make it easier to apply security and to use a secured database.

New Security Measures

The following list covers just a few of the new security features that make it safer to manage information in a database:

- You can browse in the database without having to enable the VBA code and macros.
- You can set up a trusted location and place database files in it. Then you don't have to enable the database each time you want to use it.
- With the new Trust Center page in the Access Options dialog box, you can set and change all the security settings in one place.
- You can encrypt a database with a password to keep others from accessing the data and objects.

When you open a database that is stored in a trusted location, there is no need to choose the Trust option. If an earlier version of the database contains a valid digital signature from a trusted publisher, you can trust the contents. If you use a database from an untrusted location, it is disabled by default and you need to choose to enable it each time you open it.

A publisher is a developer who creates databases. Reputable publishers are considered to be trustworthy.

Enable/Disable Database Content

As you saw in earlier chapters, when you open a database you often see the Security Warning message bar that certain content of the database has been disabled. Then you click the Options button to see your alternatives (see Figure 21-1).

FIGURE 21-1   Security Alert warnings.

You can leave the database content (VBA macros in Figure 21-1) disabled and continue to work with the database. If you trust the source of the database, you can choose to enable all the potentially harmful contents. When you close the database, all the contents are disabled again.

You can close the Security Warning message bar without making a choice by simply clicking the Close button (X).

Encrypt the Database

The encryption security tool combines encoding the database with requiring a password to open it. Encryption actually scrambles and then compacts the database, so that it is completely unreadable by a word processor or any utility program. Encrypting a database does not restrict access to database objects but the user must enter a password to open the database. Decrypting the database reverses the process and restores its original form.

Encrypt with a Password

To encrypt the database, you must first open it in exclusive mode from the Open dialog box by doing the following:

1. Click the Microsoft Office button and click Open.

2. Locate and select the database in the Open dialog box. Then click the Open down arrow and choose Open Exclusive from the drop-down list.

3. With the database open, on the Database Tools tab, in the Database Tools group, click the Encrypt with Password command.

4. In the Set Database Password dialog box, enter the password and press TAB. Enter the password again to verify it.

5. Click OK.

To open an encrypted database, you will be required to enter the database password and click OK.

Security Problems Can Occur with Linked Tables

Security problems might occur if one of the tables in a password-protected database is linked to a second database that does not require a password. The password for the first database is stored with the linking information in the second database. Any user who can open the second database also can open the linked table in the protected database. The password also is stored in an unencrypted form in the unprotected database, making it readable to any user.

Encryption applies only to accdb database file formats. Earlier versions were encoded with a less stringent scrambling algorithm.

To remove the requirement for a password and restore the database to its original format, go to the Database Tools tab in the Database Tools group, and click the Decrypt Database command.

Use the Trust Center

The new Trust Center security system imposes strict criteria upon database components and determines whether it is safe to open the database or the database should be disabled. The Trust Center enforces the criteria on macros, add-ins, and ActiveX controls as you will see in the next sections. You use the Trust Center to set specific security options and to create or change trusted locations.

All changes in Trust Center Settings take effect after you close and restart the Access database.

Create a Trusted Environment

An Access database is made up of many components, not a single file like a Word document. The intricate relationships among the tables and other objects can create a complex security risk. One solution is to place all the database components, once they are determined to be safe, in a trusted folder. When you open a database in a trusted location, you don't have to enable its contents. Another way to eliminate the need to enable a database upon opening is to identify the developer as trusted and place the name in the Trusted Publisher list.

Build a Trusted Location

A trusted location is where you can place all the macros, VBA code, and safe expressions so that you don't have to enable them when you open the database. You use the Trust Center to create a trusted location and then to put the database itself or a copy of it in the location, as follows:

1. Click the Microsoft Office button and choose Access Options.
2. Click Trust Center, and then click Trust Center Settings.
3. Click Trusted Locations.

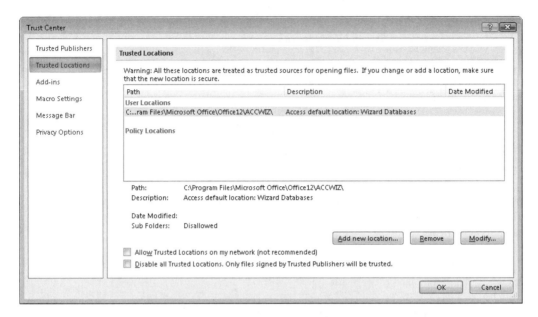

4. Click Add new location and then enter the name of the folder in the Path box or click Browse to find the folder you want.

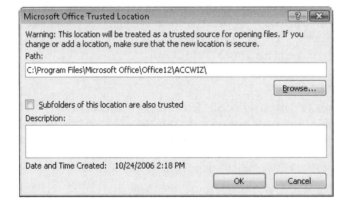

5. Check the option Subfolders of this location are also trusted if you want all subfolders also trustworthy.

6. Type a description explaining the use for the location, if desired, and click OK.

To remove the trusted location, return to the Trusted Locations dialog box, select the path and click Remove. Then click OK. You can also use the Trusted Locations dialog box to move the location to a different path by clicking Modify.

Create a Trusted Publisher List

Anyone who has created a macro, add-in, ActiveX control or some other application extension is called a "publisher." A trusted publisher is a developer who has a current and valid digital signature that is certified by a reputable certificate authority. If the developer is not involved with commercial projects, he can sign his own certificate rather that having to go through a certificate authority. (See the Create a Certificate section.)

If the publisher's signature is valid, you will see the option Trust all documents from this publisher in the Microsoft Office Security Options dialog box (see Figure 21-2). Choose that option and the publisher is added to the list.

To remove a developer from the list, return to the Trusted Publishers list, do the following:

1. Open the Trust Center.

2. Click Trust Center Settings, then click Trusted Publishers.

3. Select the name in the list and click Remove.

FIGURE 21-2   Choosing to add a publisher to the trusted list.

Trust Macros

Macros and VBA code are written by developers to carry out many types of frequently used commands. Hackers can create a macro that can invade your computer and spread a virus so it makes sense to be cautious. The Trust Center monitors for macros and checks to see if they are safe using the following criteria:

- Is the macro signed with the developer's digital signature and is the signature valid and current?
- Was the signature's certificate issued by a Certificate Authority (CA)?
- Is the developer who signed the macro trusted?

The macro is disabled if there is a problem with any of the above and the Security Warning message bar is displayed.

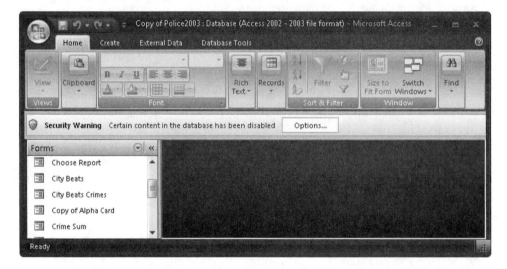

Next, go to click Options to open the Security Alert dialog box (refer to Figure 21-2). It is here that you can choose whether you want to enable the macros or not, using the following choices:

- Help protect me from unknown content (recommended)
- Enable this content
- Trust all documents from this publisher

Specific information about the disabled content is displayed in the dialog box. For example, the VBA macro under question in Figure 21-2 was signed by "heather" whose certificate was self-signed. It will not expire until January 1, 2012. You can click the Show Signature Details if you need more information.

The note in the dialog box indicates that the signature is valid but you don't have the publisher in your Trusted Publisher list yet.

21

Macro Problems

If the problem is that the macro is not signed, you should make sure that you can trust the source. You can still continue working with the database without enabling the macro.

You may get the message that the signature is not trusted if you have not added the macro source to your Trusted Publisher list. It is recommended that you do not enable any macros with invalid or expired signatures. Both of these problems can be caused by someone tampering with the macro. If the signature has expired and you have used the macro in the past, it is probably safe to enable it.

Change Macro Security Settings

To change the trust level for macros that are not considered to be in a trusted location, go to the Trust Center and click the Macro Settings button.

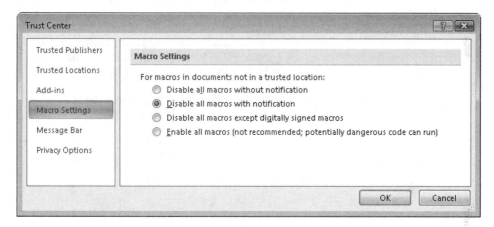

You can choose from the following four options:

- Disable all macros without notification—Blocks all macros and does not display a security warning message. However, if there are some documents you do trust even though they have unsigned macros, put those documents in a trusted location.

- Disable all macros with notification (the default)—You are notified with security alerts that some macros are unsigned. You can pick and choose which ones to trust.

- Disable all macros except digitally signed macros—Macros from trusted publishers can be run but you are alerted if you have not added the publisher to your trusted list.

- Enable all macros (not recommended; potentially dangerous code can run)—Allows all macros to run and can pose a problem with macros from hackers or other intruders.

NOTE   *A fifth option may be offered, called Trust access to VBA project object model. This option is for developers only. Developers create macros, VBA code, ActiveX controls, add-ins, and other application extensions for use by others.*

After making your choice, click OK twice to return to the database.

Trust Add-Ins

Add-ins, called "application extensions," are additional functions that add special features to the access program. For example, database templates, XML schemas, and smart tags extend the usability of Access. You can use the Trust Center to look at the add-ins that are currently installed on your computer.

Add-ins are grouped into four categories:

- Active add-ins are registered and currently running in you database.
- Inactive add-ins are in your computer, but are not currently loaded.
- Document-related add-ins are template files that are used by currently open documents.
- Disabled application add-ins were automatically shut off because of the problems they caused, such as crashing the program.

The Trust Center enforces the same criteria as for macros with respect to validity, current digital signatures, a certificate, and a trusted publisher. To change add-in security settings, open the Trust Center page, click the Trust Center Settings button, and then click Add-ins.

You have three options:

- Require Application Add-ins to be signed by Trusted Publisher—Checks the file containing the add-ins for a digital signature. If the publisher is not in the Trusted Publisher list, the add-in is not loaded and you see a message that it has been disabled.
- Disable notification of unsigned add-ins (code will remain disabled)—Available only if you have checked the first option. Then unsigned add-ins are disabled with no notification.

■ Disable all Application Add-ins (may impair functionality)—Choose this option if you don't trust any add-ins. You see no notice that they were disabled.

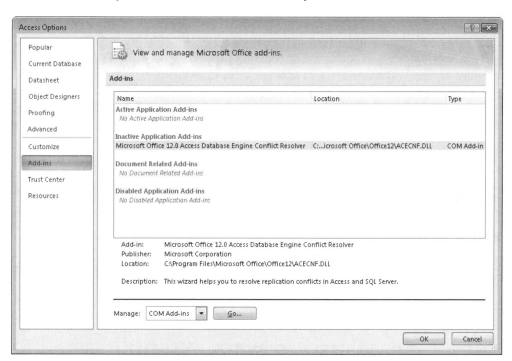

Security with Earlier Version Databases

If you applied user-level security to the database created in an earlier version of Access, it will still work when you open the database in Access 2007. If the database has no security applied, it will open in Disabled mode. In a disabled mode, many components are inaccessible:

■ VBA code and any references to code or unsafe expressions.

■ Unsafe macro actions, such as those that allow the user to modify the database or have access to outside resources.

■ Action queries that add, update, or delete data.

■ Data Definition Langauge (DDL) queries the create or alter database objects.

- SQL Pass Through queries that work with tables on the server without using the database itself.
- ActiveX controls

You can choose to enable the content each time you open the database or you can apply a digital signature. A digital signature is an encrypted electronic stamp that authenticates database components. Another option is to place the database in a trusted location.

 If you convert the database to Access 2007, all the security settings are removed and the rules for accdb and accde files apply instead.

Before you can apply your signature to the database, you need a digital certificate that authenticates the signature. If the database is only for you or your organization's use, you can use the SelfCert program to create the signature. If the database is for commercial use, you need to get the certificate from a commercial certificate authority (CA).

Create a Certificate

To create your self-signed certificate, do the following:

1. Click the Windows Start button and point to All Programs.

2. Click Microsoft Office, click Microsoft Office Tools and then click Digital Certificate for VBA Projects.

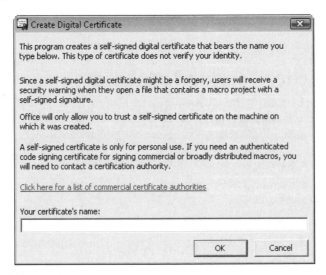

3. In the Create Digital Certificate dialog box, enter a name for the new certificate in the Your Certificate's name box.

4. Click OK twice. You will see a message that the new certificate was created.

Code-sign the Database

Applying a digital signature to a component is called, "code-signing." You can apply your signature to your database so other certified users will know it is safe to use.

Open the database you want to sign and do the following:

1. On the Database Tools tab in the Macro group, click the Visual Basic command.

2. In the Microsoft Visual Basic window, select the database and on the Tools menu, click Digital Signature.

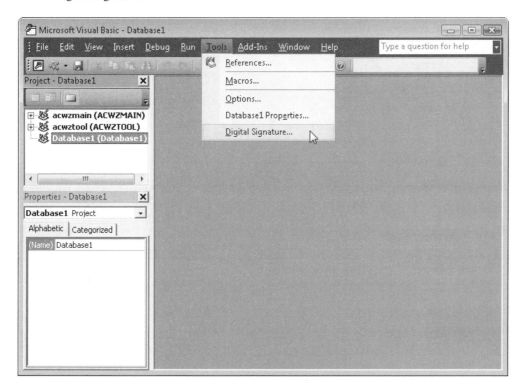

3. In the Digital Signature dialog box, click Choose.

4. In the Select Certificate dialog box, select your test certificate and click OK twice.

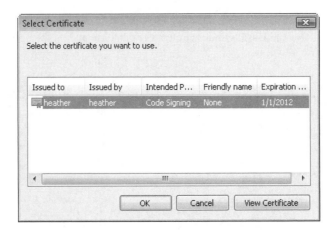

There may be reasons Access can't save your digital signature. If a problem occurs, you will see an error message with possible reasons:

- The database is under Source Code Control
- The database is opened as read-only

The database may be accdb or accde file format and you need to use the Publish method to sign it. For more information about securing databases created in earlier versions of Access, see the Help topic, "How security works with databases from earlier versions of Access opened in Office Access 2007."

Appendix

Convert to Access 2007

Y ou can convert an Access database that was created in the Access .mdb file format to the
Access 2007 .accdb format, but you might want to keep the database in the earlier version
and just run it with Access 2007 instead. This is called "enabling." This is important if your
database is used by more than one user and not all of the users have upgraded to Access 2007.
You can also convert an Access 2007 format back to an earlier file format as long as the .accdb
file does not contain any of the new features, such as multivalued Lookup fields or attachments.

Decide on a Conversion Strategy

If necessary, you can open the database and work with it in Access 2007 without conversion. If
the database is one of the later file formats (2000 or 2002-2003) you will be able to view and edit
data as well as make changes to object designs. If the database is from Access 95 or 97, you can
work with the data but you will not be able to save changes in the design of any of the objects. If
you want to modify an object, you must open the database in the original version. See the section
Open an Earlier Database for more information.

There are significant differences between the Access 2007 .accdb file format and the earlier
.mdb file format. You may want to look into the differences before converting a well-established
database to Access 2007.

For example, Access 2007 does not support replication or user-level security. If your
database relies on these, you should keep the .mdb format. If your database is shared among
several users and not all of them can convert to Access 2007 .accdb format, you can split the
database and convert part of it, while leaving other parts unchanged. This way the database can
be shared by users on different versions of Access.

Once you convert an .mdb file database to .accdb, you can't open it in the original version—
but you can convert it back. You can convert a database created in Access 2007 to Access 2000
or 2002-2003.

When the database is converted, the original database is preserved in its native file format
and a copy is created in the format you specify.

Convert a Database to Access 2007

Before you convert the database, be sure to make a backup copy. Keep this copy until you are
satisfied that the database has converted correctly and you have mastered Access 2007.

To convert the database to Access 2007 file format, do the following:

1. Click the Microsoft Office button and click Open. Browse for the file you want to
convert in the Open dialog box and then click Open. If you are operating in a multiple-
user environment, make sure all other users have closed the database.

*If the database you are opening is earlier than Access 2000, the Database Enhancement
dialog box opens asking if you want to upgrade the database. Skip to Open earlier
versions of Access files in Office Access 2007 and continue.*

A

2. With the database open, click the Microsoft Office button again and choose Convert.

3. In the Save the database in another format list, choose Access 2007 Database.

4. Then in the Save As dialog box enter a new name for the converted database and browse for a new location, if necessary. Then click Save.

NOTE   *If you are using Window XP, the Save As dialog box will look different.*

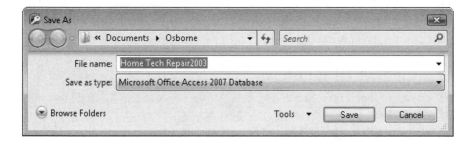

The Convert command in the Microsoft Office button list is available only if the currently open database is an earlier version.

You will see a warning message that the file has been upgraded and can no longer be shared with users of earlier versions.

You can convert the file to a different name in the same folder or use the same name in a different folder.

As the file is converted, you might see messages about compile errors during the conversion, because some of the Visual Basic commands may no longer be valid. You can correct the code after conversion.

If the database you are converting has linked tables, make sure the tables remain in the original folder so the converted database can find them. If Access can't find them, the converted database won't work properly. After you have converted the database, you can move the linked tables to another location and use the Linked Table Manager to restore the links. The linked tables are not automatically converted; you must convert them separately.

You can link a table from earlier Access versions to a later version but not the other way around. For example, you can't link an Access 2007 table to an Access 2003 database.

Convert a Workgroup Information File (MDW)

The Workgroup Information Files store permission information for secured databases. The files containing this information are .mdw files. There have been no changes made to the structure of the .mdw files in Access 2007. So when you convert to the later version, the Workgroup Manager creates .mdw files identical to those in earlier version. All such files created in Access 2000 through Access 2003 can be used in Access 2007.

Convert a Secured Database

If you applied user-level security to the database, it will still work in Access 2007.

Convert a Replicated Database

Access 2007 no longer supports replicated databases. If you have one that was replicated in Access 2003, you will not be able to save it in the new .accdb file format. You can, however, continue to use the database in Access 2007 in its .mdb file format.

A

Convert to an Earlier Version

If you want to convert the open database to a difference version, do the following:

1. Click the Microsoft Office button.

2. Point to Save As and choose from the list of formats.

Open an Earlier Database

If you are not converting the database, you can still use the database created in an earlier version with your version 2007. You can open an Access 2000 or 2002-2003 format database in Access 2007 and use it as you normally would, but keep in mind that the new features of 2007 will not be available.

If you open an Access 95 or 97 database, Access offers to upgrade it for you. If you don't upgrade, you will not be allowed to make design changes. You can view objects and change data but you cannot change any object designs. You are warned that the database is opened as Read-Only.

You must open the database using the version with which it was created if you want to modify object designs or add new objects,

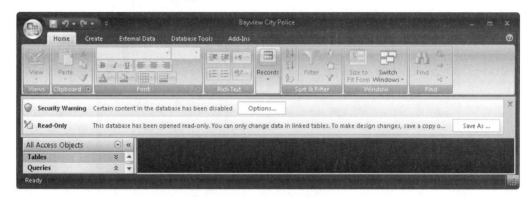

You can't link or import an Access 2007 table into an enabled database but you can go the other way and open the version 2007 database and export tables to the previous-version database. You can also cut, copy, and paste data from version 2007 tables to previous-version tables.

Share a Database Across Several Access Versions

To use a database with several versions of Access, you can create a front-end/back-end database out of it. Leave the data in the oldest version as the back end and convert the other objects to a later-version front end. To build the single-file Access database:

1. Convert the entire database to the Access 2007 file format.

2. Open the converted database and on the Database Tools tab in the Move Data group, and then click the Access Database command.

3. Split the database into a front end and back end, and then delete the back-end database created by the Database Splitter Wizard.

4. The on the Database Tools tab in the Database Tools group, click the Linked Table Manager command to link the new Access 2007 front end to the tables in the previous-version database.

NOTE   *If the database is already a front-end/back-end application, you will need to convert only the front end and leave the back end alone. Run the Linked Table Manager to link the converted front-end to the original back-end database.*

Index

Symbols & Numbers

- (hyphen) wildcard, 130
− (minus sign), 310
! (exclamation points), 130, 471
! wildcard, 130
!>L0L 0L0 input mask, 112
(pound sign), 105
symbol, input mask, 113
wildcard, 130
& (ampersand) character, 176, 186, 493
& symbol, 59, 113
(Space) formatting symbol, 59
* (asterisk), 168
* formatting symbol, 59
* wildcard, 130
… (ellipses), 18, 491
: (colon), 219
? button, 25
? wildcard, 130
@ symbol, 59
[ ] (brackets), 130, 200
[ ] wildcard, 130
+ (plus sign), 310
< (left arrow), 161
< symbol, 59, 113
<=> button, 194
<>0 validation rule, 75
<Separator> command, 453
> symbol, 59, 113
>=01/01/04 And <01/01/05> validation
  rule, 75

>> (double right arrow), 161, 261
>L<?????????? input mask, 112
>LL0000-000 input mask, 112
∞ (infinity sign), 90
; (semicolon), 215
00000-9999 input mask, 112
11-point Calibri, 122
100 Or 200 validation rule, 75

A

a symbol, 113
A symbol, 113
absolute path, 105
ACCDB file format, 420, 564, 575, 586
Access
    conversion to Access 2007, 586–590
    opening database, 7–12
    opening tables, 18–23
    overview, 3–4
    starting, 4–6
Access Database command, Database
  Tools tab, 560
access key, 18
Access language, 335
Access Options dialog box, 124, 382, 563
Access Relationships window, 33
Access Report Wizards, 302
access to shared databases, 563–564
Access window, 6–7
Action Arguments pane, 426, 429, 439
Action Failed dialog box, 430

action queries, 159, 206–215
    append query, 211–213
    delete query, 213–215
    make-table query, 210–211
    overview, 206
    update query, 206–209
actions, macro, 426–429
active add-ins, 580
Active Application Add-ins, 403
ActiveX controls, 288
Add a Group button, 323
Add Existing Fields command, 232
Add Generated Key button, 412
Add New Field, 47
Add to Quick Access Toolbar shortcut, 455
add-ins
    trust, 580–581
    viewing and managing, 402–404
Add-ins page, 403
Add-Ins tab, 460
Advanced Access options, 565
Advanced button, Import Text Wizard
   dialog box, 527
Advanced Filter Options command, 146
Advanced Filter/Sort, 137, 138, 149,
   152–153, 154
Advanced Options, 395–401
Advanced page, Access Options
   dialog box, 558
After Update property, Form and Control
   Event, 434, 438
aggregate calculations, 185
aggregate functions, summarizing
   with, 188–191
aligning controls, 245–246
alignment tools, Design window, 231–232
All Commands list, 453
All default setting, Search option drop-down
   list, 129
All Object Types tab, 413, 421
All Relationships command, Relationships
   group, 93

Allow Built-In Toolbars check box, 459
Allow Datasheet View property, Modal
   Dialog Form, 463
Allow Default Shortcut Menus setting, 387
Allow Filters property, 284
Allow Form View property, 463, 501
Allow Full Menus check box, Ribbon &
   Toolbars Options group, 460
Allow Full Menus setting, 387
Allow Layout property, 304
Allow PivotChart View property, Modal
   Dialog Form, 463
Allow PivotTable View property, Modal
   Dialog Form, 463
Allow Zero Length property, 57, 75
Alpha Entry by Code Query, 304, 314
Alpha Entry by Code Report, 307
alphabetic indexes, 332–335
Always Prompt for New Location option,
   Linked Table Manager dialog box, 519
Always use event procedures setting, 392
ampersand (&) character, 493
Analysis Notes pane, 413
analytical tools, 408
Analyze Performance command, 413
Analyze Table command, Database
   Tools tab, 409
AND operator, 75, 149–150, 177–179
Any Part of Field Match option, 129
append queries, 211–213
Applicable Filter dialog box, 155
application extensions add-ins, 580
Application Icon option, 385
Application Options, 40, 385–386
Application Title option, 385
Apply Filter command, Sort &
   Filter group, 284
Argument field, 499, 500
arguments, 424, 490
Arguments column, 425
arithmetic operators, 176
Arrange tab, 228, 245

Arrow key behavior settings, 396
arrows, on relationship line, 90
AS clauses, 363
asterisk (*), 168
attachment field, 56
Attachments dialog box, 108
Auto Center property, 463, 501
Auto Order button, 284
Auto Resize, 501
AutoCorrect options, 393–394
AutoDialer controls, 289–290
AutoExec macros, 444–445
AutoExpand property, 274, 418
AutoFormat, 257, 316
AutoIndex on Import/Create setting,
    388–389
AutoLookup queries, 200, 204–206
automatic form layouts, 263
automatic form tools, 263
automatic primary key field, 47
automation. *See* macros
AutoNumber data type, 101
AutoNumber fields, 55, 64, 83
Available Fields list, 261, 262
Axes tab, 371
Axis tab, 368

B

back ups, 206, 213, 418–419
back-end database, 559
Basic code modules, 408
Before Del Confirm event property, 442
Before Update (control) event, 299
Before Update (form) event, 299
Before Update property, 434, 436
Behavior entering field group, 396
Best Fit option, Column Width text box, 120
black-and-white bitmaps, 417
blank fields, 74–75, 131
Blank form, 226, 260, 263
Blank Report command, Create tab, 332

Border Style property, Modal Dialog
    Form, 463
bound controls, 224, 266
brackets ([ ]), 130, 200
Build button (...), 247, 255, 340, 359
Build command, Design tab, 180
Builder command, Tools group, 54, 435
built-in event properties, 278
Built-In Functions folder, 181
Button argument, MsgBox function, 441, 442
button arrangement, numeric values, 441
Byte option, Number fields, 58

C

C symbol, input mask, 113
C* Or D* validation rule, 75
C* validation rule, 75
CA (Certificate Authority), 578, 582
calculated controls, 224, 235–238, 288–289
calculated fields, 185–188, 350, 415
calculated text box control, 326
calculations, in queries, 185–193
    calculated fields, 185–188
    overview, 185
    summarizing in Datasheet
        view, 192–193
    summarizing with aggregate
        functions, 188–191
    summarizing with Wizard, 188
Can Grow property, 265, 340
Can Shrink property, 265, 332, 340
Cancel command button, 466
Cancel control property, 468
Caption property
    General tab, 184
    Modal Dialog Form, 463
    Text Field, 57
Caption property box, 183, 501
Caption property, Design View, 63
Cascade Delete Related Records option,
    87–88, 214

Cascade Update Related Fields
option, 87–88
Cascade Update Related Records
option, 209
categorizing data, 350
categorizing database objects, 474–479
cells, 123
Certificate Authority (CA), 578, 582
certificates, database security, 582–583
Chart Options dialog box, 370
Chart Type dialog box, 370
Chart Type toolbar button, 369
Chart Wizard, 352–354, 364
charts, 347–372
 See also Microsoft Graph
 adding to forms or reports, 356–358
 choosing type, 348
 creating, 348–356
  link to record data, 355–356
  Microsoft Chart Wizard, 352–354
  saving, 354–355
  selecting data, 348–351
 modifying, 358–372
 overview, 347–348
 saving disk space, 358
Check for truncated number fields
setting, 386
child tables, 35
Choose Builder dialog box, 392, 424, 436
Choose commands from: drop-down
list, 453
Choose Report dialog box, 446, 461–462
Choose Report form, 464
Clear All Sorts command, 137
Clear Search String button, 484
Clipboard commands, 99
Clipboard Task Pane launcher, 99
CloseForm macro, 470
Code value, 438
code-signed databases, 583–584
code-signing, 583
Collapse All option, Navigation Pane, 380

Collapse Group option, Navigation Pane,
379–380
colon (:), 219
color commands, 251
color palettes, 251
Color Scheme setting, 383
[color] formatting symbol, 59
Column Layout option group, Columns
dialog box, 342
Column tab options, 313
Column Width dialog box, 120
columnar form, 355
columnar reports, 341
columns
 freezing, 121
 freezing and hiding, 121–122
 hiding, 120, 121
 inserting and deleting, 125–126
 lookup, 115–118
 moving and resizing, 119–121
Columns command, Page Layout, 312
Columns dialog box, 342
Combo Box, Display Control property, 62
combo box list, 270
Combo Box Wizard, 271
combo boxes, 224
 creating, 269–273
 setting properties of, 274–275
 unbound, 273–274
Command Button Wizard, 278, 289,
417, 462, 501
command buttons, 278, 468
Command field, Switchboard Items Table, 499
commands, Quick Access toolbar, 452–457
Commands Not in the Ribbon list, 453
Comment column, 425
common report errors, 392
Compact and Repair Database utility, 420
Compact on Close option, 421
compacting database, 420–422
comparison operators, 176
compile errors, 588

complete values, filtering by, 139–141
Completion Date field, 140
concatenation operator (&), 176, 186
Conditional Formatting command, 251
Conditional Formatting dialog box, 252
conditional formatting, of controls, 251–253
conditions, 434–437
Conditions command, 435
Confirm group, 396
Contains option, 139
context filters, 137–138
context menus, 17
Continue option, Macro Single Step
    dialog box, 431
Continuous Forms, 285
Control Alignment commands, Arrange
    tab, 463
Control Box property, Modal Dialog
    Form, 463
control event, 299
Control Layout group, Arrange tab,
    232, 243, 283
Control Margins option, Control Layout
    group, 246
Control Padding option, Control Layout
    group, 246
Control Source property, 289, 326, 334
Control Wizards command, 229, 293
controls
    See also data-related controls
    adding in Design view, 232–238
        calculated controls, 235–238
        from field list, 232–233
        overview, 232
        from Tools group, 233–235
    AutoDialer, 289–290
    calculated, 288–289
    Date/Time, 316–317
    modifying, 238–254
        aligning and spacing, 245–246
        changing control type, 253–254
        deleting controls, 254

formatting conditionally, 251–253
moving and resizing, 243–244
overview, 238
selecting controls and other
    objects, 239–242
using Font group, 250–251
using property sheets, 246–250
    optimization of, 418
    overview, 224–225
    subreport, 336–338, 340
    tab, 288
    user-interactive, 278–282
    values in properties in macros, 438–441
    Yes/No, 275–278
Controls group, 229, 238
ControlTip Text property, 297, 298, 468
conversion to Access 2007, 586–590
Convert button, Microsoft Office, 587, 588
Copy command, Clipboard group, 540
copy-and-paste operations, 506, 538
copying
    data, 98–103
    database objects, 506–508
    existing table structures, 77
Create a Hierarchical Form section, 261
Create Digital Certificate dialog box, 582
Create New dialog box, 494, 495
Create tab, 424
Created Date category, 13, 474
criteria, subquery, 217–218
Criteria cell, 176, 200, 204, 217
Critical Message icon, 441
crosstab queries, 160, 195–198, 348, 360
Crosstab Query Wizard, 195
C??t validation rule, 75
CTRL-BREAK button, 525
Currency fields, 60, 69
Currency setting, 60
Currency type, 55
Current Database group, Access
    Options, 445
Current Database option, 457, 460

Current Database tab, 413
Custom category, 474
custom formatting symbols, 58–59
Custom Groups, Navigate to Category, 13
Custom Types tab, 370
Customer ID value, 205
Customize page, Access Options
    dialog box, 453
Customize Quick Access Toolbar button,
    Quick Access toolbar, 451, 452, 453, 457
customized Access workplaces, 375–406
    See also Navigation Pane; user interface
    customizing status bar, 406
    overview, 375–376
    personalizing workplace, 376–381
        creating shortcuts, 380–381
        Navigation Pane, 376–380
        overview, 376
        using ribbon, 380
    setting Access options, 381–405
        Advanced Options, 395–401
        choosing trust center options,
            404–405
        for current database, 384–388
        customizing toolbar, 401–402
        Datasheet options, 388
        Object Designers options, 388–393
        overview, 381–382
        popular options, 382–383
        Proofing options, 393–394
        searching additional resources, 405
        viewing and managing add-ins,
            402–404
customized data entry, 110–119
    creating lookup fields, 113–119
        overview, 113–115
        specifying lookup column,
            115–118
        specifying lookup list, 118–119
    custom input masks, 110–113
    overview, 110
customized Quick Access toolbar, 452–457
Cycle property, 285

D

data, 97–132
    See also customized data entry
    changing types and formats in
        tables, 48–49
    datasheet appearance, 119–125
        changing font, 122
        changing gridlines and cells, 123
        freezing and hiding columns,
            121–122
        moving and resizing columns and
            rows, 119–121
        setting default options, 124–125
    distribution guidelines, 30
    entering new, 98–110
        attaching files to fields, 108–110
        copying and moving, 98–103
        inserting hyperlinks, 105–108
        inserting pictures, 103–105
        overview, 97
    overview, 97
    record data, 127–132
        deleting data, 132
        finding and replacing data, 131
        locating records, 127–131
        overview, 127
    selecting for charts, 348–351
    sorting and filtering in forms, 284
    table definition, 125–127
    types, 516
    types of field, 54–56
    use of forms to enter, 282–285
Data Definition Language (DDL), 581
data editing control, 565–567
Data Entry property, 417
Data Labels tab, 368, 372
Data Table option, 372
Data Table tab, 372
Data Type box, 553
data validation, 71–76, 298–299
database administrator (DBA), 564
Database Default setting, Filter Lookup
    property, 416

Database Documenter, 95
Database Enhancement dialog box, 586
database objects, exporting, 529
Database Splitter Wizard, 559, 560
Database Tools tab, 413
databases, 407–422, 505–556
    See also optimization, database;
      security, database; shared databases;
      Trust Center
    Access options for, 383–388
    backing up and restoring, 418–419
    compacting and repairing, 420–422
    conversion to Access 2007, 586–589
    copying objects among, 506–508
    copying or moving records, 538–542
    creating, 27–44
        completing, 34–35
        defining table relationships, 33
        determining goals of, 30
        distributing data among tables, 30
        identifying data fields, 31
        overview, 27–28
        running new applications, 41
        specifying key fields, 31–33
        starting with blank database, 42
        with templates, 36
    design process, 28
    exporting
        to existing Access database,
          529–530
        to other database formats, 530–531
        to text files, 531–535
    importing and linking text files,
      520–528
        changing import specifications,
          527–528
        delimited text files, 520–526
        fixed-width text files, 526–527
        overview, 520
    importing or linking Access data,
      508–515
        importing objects, 509–511
        linking Access tables, 513–515

        overview, 508
        setting import options, 512–513
    importing or linking other data
      sources, 515–517
    mailing Access objects, 555–556
    opening, 7–12
    overview, 407–408, 505–506, 537–538
    saving Access output as external files,
      542–544
    sharing across several Access
      versions, 590
    steps to split into the front- and back-end
      elements, 560
    working with Excel, 548–555
        exporting tables or queries to,
          554–555
        importing from and linking to
          Excel spreadsheets, 549–554
        overview, 548–549
    working with linked or imported tables,
      517–520
    working with Word, 545–548
data-related controls, 266–275
    adding new text box controls, 266–269
    building control layouts, 266
    list and combo boxes
        creating, 269–273
        setting properties of, 274–275
        unbound, 273–274
    overview, 266
Datasheet contextual command tab, 17
Datasheet Formatting button, 123
datasheet properties, 119
Datasheet ribbon tab, 44
Datasheet view, 18, 58, 67, 162, 183, 567
    options, 388
    overview, 19–22
    to replace records in, 540
    summarizing in, 192–193
    table creation in, 46–52
        adding fields, 47–49
        adding fields from existing tables,
          50–51

Datasheet view, *(cont.)*
    field templates, 49–50
    overview, 46–47
    saving new tables, 51–52
  of the table data, 22
Datasheet view status bar, 22
Datasheet window, 364
Date Filters, 141
DateAdd function, 438, 439
dates, grouping by, 479–480
Date/Time controls, 316–317
Date/Time fields, 60, 69
Date/Time type, 55, 143
DBA (database administrator), 564
dBASE, 516–517
DDL (Data Definition Language), 581
debugging macros, 430–431
decimal fractions, 98
Decimal option, Number fields, 58
Decimal Places property, 63, 184
Decimal Places setting, 63
Decrypt Database command, Database
  Tools tab, 575
decrypting databases, 573
default button, 468
default cell effect option, 125
default colors option, 125
default column width option, 125
Default control property, 468
default control style, 249
default data format, 49
Default file format option, 383
Default find/replace behavior setting, 396
default font option, 125
default gridlines showing option, 125
Default open mode group, 400
default options, datasheet, 124–125
default property settings, 249–250
Default record locking option, 400, 567
default record-locking scheme, Advanced
  page, 565
default settings, 253
default text box property, 249
Default Value field property, 76

Default Value property, Text Field, 57
default values, 76, 249–250, 381
Default View property, 285, 501
Delete Conditional Format dialog box, 253
delete queries, 213–215
Delete Rows commands, 68, 432
delimited text files, 520–526
Description property, General tab, 184
Design view
  See also controls
  forms and reports in, 225–238
    alignment tools, 231–232
    Controls group, 229
    field list, 231
    Font group, 230
    Gridlines group, 230
    in Layout view, 238
    overview, 225
    Property sheets, 230–231
    starting new designs, 225–228
    Tools group, 230
  inserting or deleting subdatasheets in,
    126–127
  Query, 162–164
detail section bar, 264
Details option, Navigation Pane, 378
dialog boxes
  See also macros
  custom, 460–469
    designing form, 461–464
    overview, 460–461
  for user input, 469–471
digital signatures, 582
Disable all Application Add-ins
  option, 581
Disable all macros except digitally signed
  macros option, Macro Settings button, 579
Disable all macros with notification option,
  Macro Settings button, 579
Disable all macros without notification option,
  Macro Settings button, 579
Disable notification of unsigned add-ins
  option, 581
Disabled Application Add-ins, 403, 580

Disabled mode, 581–582

disk space, saving, 358

Display Control property, 61, 511

Display Document Tabs, 385

Display Form box, 385

Display Form option, Access Options dialog box., 498

display formats, 61

Display Form/Page option, 500

Display Navigation Pane option, 386

Display options, 397–398

Display Status Bar option, 385

displaytext, 105

Dividing Lines, 463, 501

Document Management Server, 564

Document Window Options, 385

Documenter, 421

document-related add-ins, 580

Does Not Contain option, 139

Does Not Equal Blank option, Selection command, 146

Does Not Equal option, 139

Double option, Number fields, 58

double right arrow (>>), 161, 261

Down setting, Search option drop-down list, 129

drag-and-drop techniques, 356, 506, 508, 541

duplicate queries, 160

duplicate values, index, 74

dynaset, 159

E

Edit mode, 127

Edit Relationships dialog box, 84

Edit Switchboard Item dialog box, 492, 493

Edit Switchboard Page dialog box, 492, 494, 495

editing mode, 282

Editing options, 396–397

ellipses (...), 18, 491

Email option, Microsoft Office button, 318

Enable all macros option, Macro Settings button, 579

Enable AutoJoin option, 391

Enable Layout View, 386

Enabled property, 298–299

encryption, database, 573–575

encryption security tool, 573

Enforce Referential Integrity, Edit Relationships dialog box, 85

Enter Parameter Value dialog box, 186

Enter/Edit Other Data switchboard page, 495

EntryNo control, 429

environments, trusted, 575–577

Equals Blank option, Selection command, 146

Equals option, 139

equijoin, 89

Error Checking options, Object Designers window, 392–393

error messages, 255

Euro setting, 60

event procedures, 299

event properties, 278, 432–434, 446

Event property box, 424

events

    data validation with, 299

    examples of, 277

exact record matches, 127–129

Excel, 548–555

    exporting tables or queries to, 554–555

    importing from and linking to spreadsheets, 549–554

    overview, 548–549

Excel command, External Data tab, 554

exclamation points (!), 130, 471

exclusive access to shared databases, 563–564

exclusive mode, Open dialog box, 574

Expand All option, Navigation Pane, 380

Expand Group option, Navigation Pane, 379

ExplainIt macro, 431

Explanation button, 431

Export dialog box, 529, 545

export formats, 544

Export Text Wizard, 531, 533, 534

exporting. *See* databases
Export—Text File dialog box, 532
Expression argument box, 438, 441
Expression Builder, 164, 180–182, 435
Expression Is condition, 252
expressions, 72, 149, 175, 177, 204, 251.
    See also selection criteria, query
External Data tab, 509, 542, 549
external files, Access output as, 542–544

F

Favorite Links pane, 7
Field cell, 218
field entry, 52
Field Has Focus condition, 252
field list boxes, 82
Field List command, 288
field list, Design window, 231, 232–233
Field List pane, 50, 91–92, 125, 228, 230
Field Name box, 553
field name button, 320
Field options, 553
field properties, 56, 298, 517
Field Properties pane, 52
Field Size property, Text Field, 57, 58, 63, 83
field templates, 54
Field Templates pane, 50, 125
Field Truncation import error, 526
field validation rule, 71
field validation rules, 71–73
Field Value Is condition, 252
field values, 188, 211, 320
fields
    adding or deleting, 67–68
    attaching files to, 108–110
    blank, 74–75, 131
    changing names of, 126
    changing names or types, 69
    changing order of, 68–69
    changing size, 69–70
    in Datasheet view table creation, 47–51
    Default Value property, 76

    in Design view table creation, 53–63
        field data types, 54–56
        field properties, 56–57
        field sizes, 58
        formatting field data, 58–62
        including captions, 63
        overview, 53–54
        setting number of decimal
            places, 63
    identifying in database creation, 31
    lookup fields, 113–119
        filtering by with Advanced
            Filter/Sort, 153
        overview, 113–115
        specifying lookup column,
            115–118
        specifying lookup list, 118–119
    names, misspelling of, 186
    navigating among in Datasheet
       view, 19–21
    in queries, 183–185
    Required properties, 74
    in select queries, 168–171, 172–173
    sorting records, 136–137
    specifying key, 31–33
    subquery, 218–219
file format, 564
File Open dialog box, 509
files, attaching to fields, 108–110
Filter By Form, 138, 146, 149, 150, 388, 416
Filter By Group list, 475
"Filter by manufacturer" drop-down list, 343
Filter By Selection, 138, 145–146
Filter command, Home tab, 320
Filter Lookup options, Access, 388
Filter Lookup property, 416
Filter Name argument, 428
Filter On Load property, 315, 318
Filter On property, 320
filter order, 256
filtered records, 137–155
    Advanced Filter/Sort, 152–153
    applying to forms and reports, 256

by context, 139–142
Filter By Form, 146–152
  combining filter conditions with OR, 150–152
  combining filter criteria with AND, 149–150
  entering filter criteria, 146–148
  overview, 146
  wildcards and expressions, 149
Filter By Selection, 143–146
Filter command, 142–143
in Layout view, 319–320
and macros, 443–444
overview, 137–138
previewing and printing, 155–156
versus queries, 157–158
removing and clearing filters, 155
saving filters, 153–155
filtered subsets, 21
filters, 284
Find a record on my form based on the value I selected in my combo box option, 272
Find and Replace dialog box, 131
Find dialog box, 284
Find Duplicates queries, 193–194
Find Unmatched queries, 194–195
First Row Contains Column Headings setting, 552
Fixed setting, 60
fixed-width text files, 520, 526–527
flow of operations, macro, 441–443
font, datasheet, 122
Font group, Design window, 230, 250–251
Font tab, 366
footer sections
  forms, 264–265
  reports, 314–315
Force New Page property, 265, 315
foreign keys, 33, 80, 84, 173, 415
Form command, 226
form design, 241, 261
Form Design command, 226

form design window, 225
form event, 299
Form Header/Footer, 227, 264, 265
Form Name argument, 426
Form Name box, Action Arguments pane, 427
form selector, 239
Form template, 392
form tools, 224, 260
Form View, 7, 238, 282, 285, 356, 567
Form Wizard, 260–263, 291–293, 468
Format | Conditional Formatting, 253
Format | Selected Legend, 367
Format | Selected object, 366
Format | Send To Back setting, 237
format chart elements, 367
Format Data Series dialog box, 372
Format dialog box, 366, 368, 369
Format function, 204
Format Painter command, 230, 251
Format property, 57, 58–62, 63, 110, 184, 275, 399
format text elements, 366
formatting
  chart elements, 366–369
  controls, 251–253
Formatting toolbar buttons, 238
Formatting toolbar, Microsoft Graph window, 365
forms, 221–299
  See also controls
  adding charts to, 356–358
  AutoFormat, 257
  common design elements, 224–225
  creating new designs, 260–264
  custom dialog boxes, 461–464
  custom user guidance, 297–298
  for data entry, 282–285
  data validation, 298–299
  hierarchical, 290–297
    Form Wizard, 291–293
    modifying subforms, 296–297
    overview, 290–291

forms, *(cont.)*
  Subform Wizard, 293–295
  use of, 296
modifying design, 264–282
  adding header and footer sections,
    264–265
  overview, 264
modifying properties, 254–257
multiple-page, 285–288
optimization of, 416–417
overview, 222
properties, 501
Simple Form and Simple Report tools,
    222–224
user input dialog boxes, 469–470
working in Design window, 225–238
  alignment tools, 231–232
  Controls group, 229
  field list, 231
  Font group, 230
  Gridlines group, 230
  Layout view, 238
  overview, 225
  Property sheets, 230–231
  starting new designs, 225–228
  Tools group, 230
Forms Switchboard, 491
Forms/Reports options, Object Designers
  window, 391–392
Freeze Columns, 121
FROM clause, 215, 217
front-end database, 559
Functions folder, 181

G

galleries, 17–18
gallery control type, 17
General Date setting, 62
General Number setting, 60
General options, 399
General tab, field property sheet, 184
Get External Data dialog box, 509, 514, 516

Get External Data—Excel dialog box, 549
Getting Started window, 9
  options, 5–6
  templates, 36
global data management operations, 206
global unique identifier (GUID), 58
Go To in the Find command group, 19
Go To ribbon command, 19
GoToRecord action, 430
Graph, Microsoft. *See* Microsoft Graph
grid lines, 123
gridlines, datasheet, 123
Gridlines group, Design window, 230
Gridlines tab, 372
Group & Sort command, Formatting tab,
  322, 333
Group By aggregate function, 416
Group By option, Total cell, 190
Group command, Control Layout
  group, 242
group controls, 242
Group Interval setting, 332
Group On setting, 332
grouped records, 322–328
Grouping & Sorting group, 313
Grouping command, Formatting tab, 328
grouping intervals, 324
Grouping Intervals dialog box, 305
Grouping Options, 305
groups, 225
  custom, 484–489
  Hide/Restore, 480–482
  macro, 445–447
  summarizing by, 190–191
GUID (global unique identifier), 58

H

handles, 241
Has Module property, 417
header sections
  form, 264–265
  report, 314–315

Help feature, 24
Help window, 24–26, 382
Hidden check box, Properties dialog box, 481
Hide Columns, 121–122
Hide Details command, Design tab, 328
Hide Duplicates format property, 332
Hide/Restore groups and objects, 480–482, 489–490
hierarchical forms, 290–297
    Form Wizard, 291–293
    modifying subforms, 296–297
    overview, 290–291
    Subform Wizard, 293–295
    use of, 296
hint boxes, 26
Home ribbon, 17
horizontal ruler, 231
horizontal scroll bar, Print Preview window, 309
Horizontal Spacing command, Position group, 246
host form, 355
HTML Template, 556
Hyperlink ScreenTip dialog box, 281
hyperlinks, 56, 105–108, 278–282, 417
hyphen (-) wildcard, 130
hyphens, 130

I

I want the combo (or list) box to look up the values in a table or query option, 271
I will type in the values that I want option, 271
Icon Browser, 385
Icon option, Navigation Pane, 379
identifiers, 175
If...Then...Else structure, 435
Ignore Nulls property, 65
image control, 358
IME Mode property, Text Field, 57
IME Sentence Mode property, Text Field, 57
Import Errors table, 526

Import Objects dialog box, 510
Import Queries options, 513
Import Specification dialog box, 528
Import Spreadsheet Wizard, 551, 554
Import Tables options, 513
Import Text Wizard, 522, 531, 534
Import/Export Specs option, imports, 513
importing
    delimited text files, 520–524
    objects and tables. See databases
inactive add-ins, 580
Inactive Application Add-ins, 403
index (.px) file, 517
Index Properties pane, 65
Indexed box, 553
Indexed property, 65, 71, 74
indexes, 64–66, 71, 74, 332–335, 415
Indexes dialog box, 71
inexact record matches, 129–131
infinity sign (∞), 90
inner joins, 89
input form properties, 469–470
Input Mask property, 57, 110, 112, 184
Input Mask Wizard, 110–111, 114
input masks, 98, 110–113
Insert ActiveX command, 229
Insert Chart command, Design tab, 352, 355
Insert Hyperlink dialog box, 279, 281
Insert Hyperlink tool, 105
Insert Merge Field dialog box, 547
Insert Rows commands, 67, 432
insertion point, 98
Integer option, Number fields, 58
invalid control properties error, 392
Is Not Blank option, Selection command, 146
ISAM drivers, 515
ISNULL function, 435
ItemNumber field, Switchboard Items Table, 499
Items on This Switchboard list, Edit Switchboard Page dialog box, 494
ItemText field, Switchboard Items Table, 499

J

Join Properties dialog box, 89
join types, 88–90
junction tables, 35

K

Keep Together property, 315
key combinations, 21–22, 88
Key Violation import error, 526
keyboard shortcuts, 392, 451–452
keys
      fields, specifying, 31–33
      foreign, 84
      shortcut, 21–22
keystrokes, 19
KeyTips, Create tab, 451

L

L symbol, input mask, 113
Label control, 326
Label Type option, 343
Label Wizard, 303, 342–346
Labels tool, Create tab, 343
LAN (local area network), 105
Landscape command, Page Layout, 312
Language Settings, 383
Layout dialog box, 336
Layout view, 223, 238, 303, 318–335, 567
      adding group sections, 322–326
      changing sort order, 320–322
      creating summary reports with Report
        Wizard, 328–332
      filtering records in, 319–320
      modifying and adding groups, 326–328
      overview, 318–319
      printing alphabetic indexes, 332–335
layouts, control, 266
left arrow (<), 161
left outer joins, 89
Legend tab, 372

legends, chart, 360–364
Limit To List property, 273
Line command, Controls group, 269
Line toolbox button, 238
Lines properties lists, Controls group, 269
Link Child Fields property, 127, 294, 339
Link Master Field property, 127
Link Master Fields property, 294, 339
Link Tables dialog box, 514
Link Tables operation, 516
Linked Table Manager, 518–520, 562,
    588, 590
linked tables. *See* databases
linking fields, 33, 339, 356
List Box Wizard, 271
List boxes, 266, 273
list boxes
      creating, 269–273
      setting properties of, 274–275
      unbound, 273–274
List option, Navigation Pane, 379
lists, lookup, 118–119
local area network (LAN), 105
Local indexed fields setting, 388
Local nonindexed fields setting, 388
Locked property, 298–299
Logical Cursor movement group, 398
logical operators, 176
logos, adding to switchboards, 497–498
Long Date setting, 62
Long Integer option, Number fields, 58
Long Integer property, 63
Long Time setting, 62
Lookup DR form, 469, 481
lookup fields, 113–119, 173–174, 511
      filtering by with Advanced
        Filter/Sort, 153
      overview, 113–115
      specifying lookup column, 115–118
      specifying lookup list, 118–119
lookup lists, 113

Lookup properties, 117
Lookup tab, field property sheet, 184, 185
Lookup Wizard, 50, 56, 115–116
LookUpDR macro group, 470

M

Macro Settings button options, 579
Macro Single Step dialog box, 430–431
Macro Tools ribbon, 426
macros, 423–447
    adding conditions to, 434–437
    assigning to event properties, 432–434
    commonly used, 437–445
        AutoExec macro, 444–445
        control values and properties,
           438–441
        filter records, 443–444
        flow of operations, 441–443
        overview, 437
    creating, 424–429
    creating and attaching to custom dialog
        boxes, 464–469
        creating macro group, 465–466
        to form controls, 466–469
        overview, 464–465
    macro groups, 445–447
    overview, 423–424
    testing and debugging, 429–432
    in Trust Center, 578–579
    user input dialog boxes, 470
Macros list, 453
magnification in Print Preview window,
    310–311
Mail Merge Wizard, 546–548
mailing Access objects, 555–556
mailing labels, 342–346
main reports, 335
make-table queries, 210–211, 416
Make-Table Query command, 210
many-to-many table relationships, 35
MAPI (Messaging Application Programming
    Interface), 556

Margin command, Page Layout, 312
Match Case option, Search option drop-down
    list, 129
Match options, 129
.mb (memo) file, 517
.mdb file format, 586, 588
Medium Date setting, 62
Medium Time setting, 62
memo (.mb) file, 517
Memo fields, 55, 59, 69
Memo format settings, 59
menus, custom, 458–460
Menus and Toolbars option, 512
Message Bar, 404
Messaging Application Programming
    Interface (MAPI), 556
Microsoft Access. *See* Access
Microsoft Chart Wizard, 352–354
Microsoft Graph, 364–372
    changing chart appearance, 366–372
        changing chart type, 369–370
        formatting chart elements,
           366–369
        overview, 366
        setting chart options, 370–372
    overview, 364–365
    toolbars, 365–366
Microsoft Office button, 6
Microsoft Office Language Settings 2007, 383
Microsoft Office Security Options dialog
    box, 12, 38
Microsoft SharePoint Services 3.0, 46, 564
Microsoft Word, 545–548
Microsoft Word Mail Merge Wizard dialog
    box, 547
mini toolbars, 17–18
MinMax Buttons property, Modal Dialog
    Form, 463
minus sign (–), 310
Modal Dialog Wizard, 462
Modal property, Modal Dialog Form, 463
modals, 467

Modified Date category, 474
Modified Date, Navigate to Category, 13
Month( ) function, 181
More command, External Data tab, 516
More Forms commands, 226, 260, 456
move handles, 241, 243
MsgBox function, 435, 441, 442
Multiple Items command, 226
Multiple Items form, 263
Multiple Pages command, Print Preview
    window, 309
multiple-column reports, 340–342
multiple-field indexes, 65–66
multiple-page forms, 285–288
multiple-user environments, 419, 558
My Computer shortcut, 419

N

Name AutoCorrect option, 204, 388
Name property, 340
names, field, 49
Nav Pane Groups option, imports, 513
Navigate to Category, 12
navigation, form, 282–283
navigation buttons, 296, 501
Navigation Buttons property, Modal Dialog
    Form, 463
navigation mode, 282, 296
Navigation Options, 380, 386, 485, 488, 490
Navigation Pane, 14–15, 376–380, 473–480
    See also switchboards
    customization, 484–490
        Hide/Restore custom groups and
            objects, 489–490
        overview, 484
        planning custom groups, 484–489
    list of tables, 562
    objects, 40–41
    overview, 12–16, 473–474
    viewing objects in, 474–484
        categorize by Tables and Related
            Views, 474–479

grouping by created or modified
    date, 479–480
Hide/Restore groups and objects,
    480–482
overview, 474
searching for objects, 482–484
networks, sharing databases on, 558–564
    overview, 558
    preventing exclusive access, 563–564
    sharing entire database, 558–559
    splitting database, 559–563
New database sort order setting, 383
New Form dialog box, 263
New Query dialog box, 193
New Record button, 282
No Locks setting, 566, 567
Northwind database, 9–10
Not CA validation rule, 75
NOT ISNULL function, 435
Not With Rpt Hdr/Ftr setting, 315
Null in Required Field import error, 526
Null value in AutoNumber field import
    error, 526
Number data type, 55
number field formatting, 549
Number fields, 58, 60, 69
Number of Update Retries setting, Access
    Options dialog box, 568
Number tab, 368

O

Object Designers options, Access, 388–393
Object Designers window, 391
Object Linking and Embedding (OLE) Object
    data type, 103
Object Linking, Embedding (OLE)
    Objects, 54
Object Name—Choose Report argument, 465
Object Type category, 474
Object Type, Navigate to Category, 13
Object Type—Form argument, 465
Object window, 12–16

ODBC (Open Database Connectivity), 506, 567
ODBC data sources, 515
ODBC fields setting, 388
Office, personalized, 383
Office 2007 clipboard, 99
Office Menu list, 454
OLE (Object Linking and Embedding) Object data type, 103
OLE (Object Linking, Embedding) Objects, 54
OLE Object control, 358
OLE Object type field, 55
On Click property, Form and Control Event, 433, 434
On Current property, Form and Control Event, 434
On Delete (form) event, 299
On Enter property, Form and Control Event, 434
On Exit (control) event, 299
On No Data property, 434
On Open property, 432, 434
On Page property, 434
One Page command, Preview group, 309
one-to-many relationship, 84, 415
one-to-many table relationships, 35
one-to-one relationships, 35, 88
Open Alpha Card macro, 430–431
Open button, 9
Open command button, 278
Open Database Connectivity (ODBC), 506, 567
Open Database Window, 458
Open databases by using record-level locking option, 400
Open dialog box, 7–8
Open Exclusive permission, 421
Open Exclusive setting, Open dialog box, 568
Open Form in Edit Mode, Command list, 495
Open Recent Database pane, 7

OpenForm action, 426
Open/Run permission, 421
operators, 175, 176
optimistic record locking, 566
optimization, database, 408–418
    controls, 418
    Filter By Form, 416
    forms and reports, 416–417
    overview, 408
    Performance Analyzer, 413–414
    Table Analyzer, 408–413
    tables and queries, 414–416
optimizing queries, 415
option group, 275–276
Option Group command, 276
Option Group Wizard, 464
Option Value property, 276
Options, Import Objects dialog box, 512
Options button, Clipboard Task Pane, 99
Options tab, 369
OR filter condition, 151
OR operator, 75, 150–152, 177–179
Order By On Load property, 315
Order By On property, 320, 321
Order By property, 321
Order Entry database, 491

P

Page Break command, Design tab, 317
Page Break Control tool, 285
page breaks, 285–286, 317
Page Footer section, 314
Page Header section, 314
Page Header/Footer, Show/Hide group, 227
Page Layout commands, 311–312
Page Layout group, Page Setup tab, 311
page numbers, report, 316–317
page property sheet, 288
page settings and report printing, 311–313
Page Setup dialog box, 156, 311, 312, 341

Page Setup options, 95, 344
Page tab, 313
page-level locking, 567
pages
    switchboard, 492–496
    viewing in Print Preview window,
      309–310
Paradox, 516–517
parameter queries, 160, 200–204
parent tables, 35
partial values, filtering by, 141–142
passwords
    database encryption with, 574–575
    for importing or linking databases, 508
Paste Errors table, 102
Paste Table As dialog box, 507
Patterns tab, 368
Percent format, Number field, 60
Percent setting, 60
Performance Analyzer, 408, 413–414
personalized workplaces. *See* customized
  Access workplaces
Phishing, 581
Picture Property Storage Format setting, 386
pictures, inserting, 103–105
PIVOT clause, 362
PivotChart command, 226
PivotChart form tool, 263
PivotChart view, 22
PivotTable view, 22
Placement tab, 367
plus sign (+), 310
Popular commands, 453
Popular Commands list, 453
pop-up modal form, 467
PopUp property, Modal Dialog Form, 463
Portrait command, Page Layout, 312
pound sign (#), 105
Preview button, 465
Preview Chart button, 352, 354
Preview macros, 464

PreviewReports macro, Choose Report macro
  group, 465, 467
Primary Key command, 64, 70
primary key field, 33, 415
primary keys, 63–64, 70–71, 80
Print Data Only command, Page Layout, 312
Print dialog box, 311
Print macros, 464
Print Options tab, 312
Print Preview commands, 309, 452
Print Preview tab, 156, 422
Print Preview window, 309–311, 465
Print Table Definition dialog box, 422
printing
    alphabetic indexes, 332–335
    mailing labels with Label Wizard,
      342–346
    relationships, 94–95
    reports, 311–313
Printing options, 398–399
PrintReports macro, 465
Product Number list, 343
Prompt argument, MsgBox function, 441
proofing option settings, 393
properties
    control, in macros, 439–441
    data validation with, 298–299
    field, 56–57
    form and report, 254–257
    input form, 469–470
    linked table, 517–518
    list and combo box, 274–275
    query, 182–183
    report and section, 314–315
    report sort, 321–322
property sheets, 126, 184, 230–231, 246–250,
  254, 267, 314, 358, 424
publisher lists, trusted, 577
publishers, 577
Purge field, 435–436
PurgeValid macro, 435, 436
.px (index) file, 517

Q

queries, 157–219
  action, 206–215
    append query, 211–213
    delete query, 213–215
    make-table query, 210–211
    overview, 206
    update query, 206–209
  adding selection criteria, 175–182
    Expression Builder, 180–182
    multiple criteria, 177–180
    overview, 175
    single criterion, 176–177
    wildcards and operators, 176
  calculations in, 185–193
    calculated fields, 185–188
    overview, 185
    summarizing in Datasheet view, 192–193
    summarizing with aggregate functions, 188–191
    summarizing with Wizard, 188
  creating special with Query Wizard, 193–198
  exporting to Excel, 554–555
  modifying, 183–185
  optimization of, 414–416
  overview, 157–158, 200
  performing calculations in, 185–193
    calculated fields, 185–188
    overview, 185
    summarizing in Datasheet view, 192–193
    summarizing with aggregate functions, 188–191
    summarizing with Wizard, 188
  select, 159–175
    adding and removing fields, 168–171
    hiding and showing fields, 172–173
    overview, 159–160
    Query Design Window, 162–164
    relating multiple tables, 165–167
    running and saving, 171–172
    from scratch, 164–165
    showing highest or lowest values, 174–175
    Simple Query Wizard, 160–162
    specifying record order, 173–174
  setting properties, 182–183
  special purpose, 200–206
    AutoLookup queries, 204–206
    overview, 200
    parameter queries, 200–204
  Structured Query Language, 215–217
  subqueries, 217–219
  user input dialog boxes, 470–471
Query Builder, 255, 267, 359, 360, 361, 362, 371
Query Design, 159, 163, 164, 184
Query Design options, Object Designers window, 390–391
query grid, 204
Query Parameters dialog box, 203
Query Properties dialog box, 182
query result datasheet, 205
Query Setup group, 163
Query Type group, 163
Query Wizard, 159, 160–162, 188, 193–198
Quick Access toolbar, 6, 254, 311, 318, 401, 451, 452–457
Quick Print command, 452
quotation marks, 61

R

random numbers, 64
record data, 127–132
  deleting data, 132
  finding and replacing data, 131
  locating records, 127–131
  overview, 127
record locking, 565
Record Locks property, 566, 567

record navigation bar, 283
record navigation buttons, 19
Record Selectors, 463, 501
Record Source property, 224, 254, 264,
 266, 267, 418
record validation rules, 71, 73–74
record-level locking, 567
records, 135–156
 See also filtered records
 changing source of in reports and
  forms, 254–256
 copying or moving, 538–542
 linking charts to, 355–356
 locating, 284
 locking, 565–567
 navigating among in Datasheet
  view, 19–21
 overview, 135
 previewing and printing, 155–156
 sorting, 136–137
 specifying order of in select queries,
  173–174
 summarizing, 188–189
 updating with refresh and requery,
  567–568
 viewing multiple in forms, 285
recordset, 159
rectangle boxes, 238
Rectangle toolbox button, 238
referential integrity, 84–88, 90
Refresh All down arrow, Home tab, 567
refresh method, 567–568
relationships, 79–95
 in database creation, 33
 defining, 80
 delete queries, 214–215
 Field List Pane, 91–92
 overview, 79
 printing, 94–95
 Relationships window, 80–91
  basic process, 83–84
  changing table designs from, 94

 creating one-to-one
  relationships, 88
 enforcing referential integrity,
  84–88
 overview, 80–83
 saving work from, 91
 specifying join type, 88–90
 types of, 35
 viewing and editing, 93–94
Relationships option, 512
Relationships window, 126
relative path, 105
Remember the value for later use option, 273
Remove command, Control Layout
 group, 245
Remove Filter command, Sort & Filter
 group, 284
Rename command, 49
repairing databases, 418–419
Repeat Section property, 315
replicated database conversion, 588
Replication ID numbers, 64
Replication ID option, Number fields, 58
Report command, Create tab, 223
Report Design command, 303
Report Design tab, 228
report design window, 225
Report Header/Footer, 227, 314
report selector, 316
Report template, 392
Report Tool, 303–304
Report tools, 224, 303
Report Wizard, 303, 304–308, 328–332,
 335–336
reports, 221–257, 301–345
 See also controls; Design view
 adding charts to, 356–358
 AutoFormat, 257
 common design elements, 224–225
 Layout view, 238, 318–335
  adding group sections, 322–326
  changing sort order, 320–322

creating summary reports with
    Report Wizard, 328–332
filtering records in, 319–320
modifying and adding groups,
    326–328
overview, 318–319
printing alphabetic indexes,
    332–335
modifying design, 313–317
modifying properties, 254–257
multiple-column, 340–342
optimization of, 416–417
overview, 222, 301–302
Print Preview window, 309–311
printing, 311–313
printing mailing labels with Label
    Wizard, 342–346
saving designs, 317–318
Simple Form and Simple Report tools,
    222–224
starting new, 302–308
    overview, 302–303
    Report Wizard, 304–308
    using Report Tool, 303–304
subreports, 335–340
    creating controls, 336–338
    creating with Report Wizard,
        335–336
    inserting existing subreports, 339
    linking reports and subreports,
        339–340
    modifying controls, 340
    overview, 335
Reports group, Create tab, 303
Reports Switchboard, 491
requery method, 567–568
Require Application Add-ins to be signed by
    Trusted Publisher option, 581
Required field properties, 74
Required property, 57, 75
resizing controls, 243–244

Resources page, 405
restoration, database, 418–419
restore characters, 132
Return command, Query Setup group, 174
ribbon, 16–18, 380, 450–452, 455–456
Ribbon Name setting, 387
ribbon tabs, 225
rich text format, 545–546
Rich Text Format (RTF), 544
right outer joins, 89
Roster form, 287
Row Height dialog box, 121
Row Source property, 119, 274–275, 358,
    359–360, 361, 371
rows, moving and resizing, 119–121
RTF (Rich Text Format), 544
rulers, Design window, 231–232
Run Query macro, 470
Running Sum property, 326

S

Save As dialog box, 52, 318, 336, 587
Save As option, Microsoft Office button, 318
Save Object As button, Save Database Object
    As group, 336
Save—No argument, 465
saving table designs, 66–67
Scale tab, 367, 368
Scientific setting, 60
ScreenTips, 17, 21, 105, 228, 382–383, 468
scroll bars, 270, 501
Scroll Bars property, 285, 463
scroll boxes, 19
Search Bar, Navigation Pane, 482–484
Search box, 8
Search Fields As Formatted option, 131
Search option drop-down list, 129
searching for records. *See* record data
second-level grouping, 326–328
section bar, 241
section selectors, 240, 257, 265

sections, report, 314–315
security, database, 571–584
    with earlier version databases, 581–584
    enabling and disabling content, 572–573
    encryption, 573–575
    new measures, 572
    overview, 571–572
security alerts, 581
Security Warning message, 11, 38, 573, 578
SELECT command, 215, 217, 229
Select Index Files dialog box, 517
Select New Location of Tablename dialog
    box, 519, 520
Select Objects button, 229
Select Place in Document dialog box, 280
select queries, 159–175, 200
    adding and removing fields, 168–171
    hiding and showing fields, 172–173
    overview, 159–160
    Query Design Window, 162–164
    relating multiple tables, 165–167
    running and saving, 171–172
    from scratch, 164–165
    showing highest or lowest values,
        174–175
    Simple Query Wizard, 160–162
    specifying record order, 173–174
SELECT statement, 215, 217
Select Unique Record Identifier
    dialog box, 517
Selected Fields list, 262
selection criteria, query, 175–182
    Expression Builder, 180–182
    multiple criteria, 177–180
    single criterion, 176–177
    and summarizing with aggregate
        functions, 191
    wildcards and operators, 176
SelfCert program, 582
self-signed certificate, 582
semicolon (;), 215

Send Object As dialog box, 556
Send Object To dialog box, 318
Set Control Defaults command, 250
Set Database Password dialog box, 574
Set Unique Identifier button, 412
SetValue action, 438, 439
SetValue macro action, 438
Shape tab, 369
shared database objects, 569
shared databases, 557–569
    management of, 564–569
        controlling data editing, 565–567
        editing shared database objects,
            568–569
        overview, 564
        updating records with refresh and
            requery, 567–568
    on networks, 558–564
        overview, 558
        preventing exclusive access,
            563–564
        sharing entire database, 558–559
        splitting database, 559–563
    overview, 557–558
Shared Default Open Mode setting, 558, 563
Short Date setting, 62
Short Time setting, 62
shortcut keys, 21–22
Shortcut Menu Bar down arrow, 387
shortcut menus, 18
shortcuts
    creation of, 380–381
    deleting, 380
    keyboard, 451–452
Show All Actions command, 438
Show animations option, 398
Show check box, 415
Show Grand Total Footer option, 324
Show Hidden Objects, 479, 480, 489
Show in Group Footer option, 324
Show Margins command, Page Layout, 312

Show Only option, Navigation Pane, 380
Show option group, 330
Show Property Update Options buttons, 389
Show shortcut keys, ScreenTips check box, 383
Show Signature Details setting, 578
Show Smart Tags on Datasheets setting, 398
Show Smart Tags on Forms and Reports option, 398
Show Table command, Query Setup group, 165
Show Table dialog box, 81, 164
Show the number of Recent Documents option, 397
Shutter Bar Open/Close button, 15, 474
Simple Form and Simple Report tools, 222–224
Simple form tool, 263
Simple Query Wizard, 159, 160–162
simple select queries, 160
"simple" sort, 137
Single Form, 285
Single option, Number fields, 58
Single Step command, 431
single-field indexes, 65
single-field primary keys, 64
Size command, Page Layout, 312
Size group commands, 463
Size Mode property, 288, 358
sizes, field, 58
sizing handles, 241, 244, 358, 366
skeleton database, 43
Smart Tags property, 57, 184
Snap To Grid setting, Control Layout group, 232, 243
snapshot, 159
Sort Ascending option, Navigation Pane, 376
Sort By command, Navigation Pane, 15
Sort cell list box, 173
Sort commands, 284

Sort Descending option, Navigation Pane, 376
sort objects, 376–377
Sort Options dialog box, 336
sort order, 256, 320–322
Sort Order command, Formatting tab, 326
sorted records, 136–137, 256
Sounds dialog box, 399
Source Object, 295
spacing controls, 245–246
Special Effect property, 340
special purpose queries, 200–206
    AutoLookup queries, 204–206
    overview, 200
    parameter queries, 200–204
spelling corrections, 394
Split Form command, 226
Split form tool, 263
spreadsheets. *See* Excel
SQL (Structured Query Language), 215–217
SQL Server Compatible Syntax (ANSI 92) option group, 391
SQL statement, 215, 217, 418
SQL view, 215, 217
Stacked command, Control Alignment group, 245, 246
Stacked command, Layout tab, 266
stacked layout, 232, 266
standalone macros, 426, 429, 431
Standard setting, 60
Standard toolbar, Microsoft Graph window, 365
Start of Field Match option, 129
startup switchboard, 457
State validation rule, 72
status bar, 7, 397, 406
Status Bar Text control property, 298
Step option, Macro Single Step dialog box, 431
Stop All Macros option, Macro Single Step dialog box, 430, 431

Store that value in this field option, 273
Structured Query Language (SQL), 215–217
subaddress, 105
Subdatasheet Name property, 127
subdatasheets, 22, 119, 126–127,
    137, 222, 541
Subform/ Subreport Wizard dialog box, 340
Subform Wizard, 293–295
subforms, 222, 296–297, 417, 531
Subform/Subreport tool, 293, 337
subqueries, 217–219
Subreport Field Linker dialog box, 340
Subreport Wizard, 339
subreports, 335–340, 417, 531
    creating controls, 336–338
    creating with Report Wizard, 335–336
    inserting existing subreports, 339
    linking reports and subreports,
        339–340
    modifying controls, 340
    overview, 335
Sum aggregate function, 352
Summarize dialog box, 352
Summary Options button, 305, 329
summary queries, 191
summary reports, Report Wizard, 328–332
summary values, 330
switchboard items, 493
Switchboard Manager, 474, 484
Switchboard Page Name box, 495
SwitchboardID field, Switchboard Items
    Table, 499
switchboards, 490–502
    creating with Switchboard Manager,
        491–498
        adding items to page, 492–494
        adding logos, 497–498
        adding new switchboard pages,
            494–496
        displaying switchboard at
            startup, 498
        overview, 491–492

modifying, 498–502
overview, 490–491
startup, 457

T

Tab Control command, 287
tab control property sheet, 288
tab controls, 287–288
tab index number, 283
tab order, 283–284
Tab Order command, 283
Tab Order dialog box, 284
Tabbed Documents option, 385
Table Analyzer, 408–413, 554
Table and Related Views, Navigate
    to Category, 13
Table command, 46
Table Design command, 52
Table Design options, Object Designers
    window, 388–390
table identifiers, 31
Table of Contents toolbar button, 25
table templates, 46, 49
Table Templates commands, 46, 456
Table Tools ribbon, 52
tables, 45–77
    arranging the data, 31
    changing definition of, 125–127
    changing designs from Relationships
        window, 94
    copying, 506–507
    copying and moving data, 99–103
    copying existing table structures, 77
    creating from templates, 46
    creating in Datasheet view, 46–52
        adding fields, 47–49
        adding fields from existing tables,
            50–51
        field templates, 49–50
        overview, 46–47
        saving new tables, 51–52

creation in Design view, 52–67
    choosing primary keys, 63–64
    creating other indexes, 64–66
    overview, 52–53
    saving table design, 66–67
delete queries, 213–215
distributing data among, 30
ensuring data validity, 71–76
exporting, 529, 530
exporting to Excel, 554–555
hiding or deleting, 93
linked to Access database, 517–520
linking, 513–515
modifying table design, 67–71
opening in Access, 18–23
    Datasheet view, 19–22
    overview, 18–19
    subdatasheet, 22
optimization of, 414–416
overview, 45
relating in select queries, 165–167
switchboard items, 499–502
unlinking, 520
Tables and Related Views category, 474–479
Tables/Queries box, 261
Tables/Queries drop-down list, 338
tabs, 371
Tabular command, 245, 246, 266
tabular layout, 232, 266
target tables, 210
Template Categories group, 36
template thumbnail, 36
templates, 36, 46, 49–50
Test Validation Rules command, 76
Text Align property, Text Field, 57
text box controls, 231, 241–242, 243, 266–269
Text command, Design tab, 497
Text data type, 55

text elements, formatting, 366–369
Text fields, 56, 59, 69
text files
    exporting to, 531–535
    importing and linking, 520–528
        changing import specifications, 527–528
        delimited text files, 520–526
        fixed-width text files, 526–527
        overview, 520
Text Filters, 140, 143, 319
Text Format property, General tab, 184
Text format settings, 59
text formatting options, 18
text qualifier, 520
Text To Display box, 281
text values, 235
tildes, 130
Tips button, 410
Title argument, MsgBox function, 441
title bar, 3–4
Titles tab, 371
To Fit command, 244
To Grid command, Align menu, 244, 245
Toggle Filter command, 138, 147, 153
toggle keys, 7
Toolbar Options, Access, 386–387
toolbars, 17–18, 401–402, 458–460
Tools group, Design window, 230, 233–235
Total cell, 190
Total Cost text box control, 252
Total On drop-down list, 324
Trust access to VBA project object model option, Macro Settings button, 579
Trust all documents from this publisher setting, Microsoft Office Security Options dialog box, 577
Trust Center, 572, 575–581
    add-ins, 580–581
    creating trusted environments, 575–577

Trust Center, *(cont.)*
    macros, 578–579
    options, 404–405
    overview, 575
Trusted Locations dialog box, 576
Trusted Publisher lists, 575, 577, 578–579
Two Pages command, Print Preview
    window, 309
Type Conversion Failure import error, 526

U

Unassigned Objects group, 486
unassociated labels, 392
unbound controls, 224, 358
unbound list and combo boxes, 273–274
Unbound Object Frame command, 357
unbound text box control, 289
UNC (Universal Naming Convention), 105
Undo command, Quick Access toolbar, 254
Undo drop-down list, 254
Unfreeze Columns, 121
Ungroup command, Control Layout
    group, 242
Unhide Columns, 121–122
Unicode Compression property, Text Field, 57
Uniform Resource Locator (URL), 105
Unit of Measure option, 343
Universal Naming Convention (UNC), 105
unlinking tables, 520
unmatched queries, 160
Unparsable Record import error, 526
Up setting, Search option drop-down list, 129
update queries, 206–209
Update Retry Interval setting, Access Options
    dialog box, 568
URL (Uniform Resource Locator), 105
Use Access Special Keys, 386
Use Control Wizards command, 271, 276,
    278, 462
user guidance, form, 297–298
user interface, 449–471
    See also dialog boxes

    customizing Quick Access toolbar,
      452–457
    overview, 449–450
    ribbon, 450–452
    using existing customization, 457–460
user interface language, 396
user-interactive controls, 278–282

V

Validation Rule Failure import error, 526
Validation Rule property, Text Field, 57, 72
validation rules, 298
Validation Text message, 75
Validation Text property, Text Field, 57, 71
validity, data, 71–76, 298–299
Value axis, 367
value lists, 113
values, 175
Verify Deletion macro, 442
vertical ruler, 231, 285
vertical scroll bar, 296, 309
Vertical Spacing command, Position
    group, 246
View | Toolbars menu, 366
View Workorder command button, 41
Views drop-down list, 8
Visual Basic event procedure, 501
Visual Basic window, 230
Visual Cursor movement group, 398

W

Warning Query icon, 442
warnings, macro, 435–437
Web Options button, 399
WHERE clause, 215, 217, 428
Where Condition, 428, 431, 435, 443
Whole Field Match option, 129
wildcards, 72, 130–131, 149, 176
window width, 450
wizards
    Chart, 352–354
    Form, 260–263, 291–293

Label, 342–346
Mail Merge, 546–548
Query Wizard, 160–162, 188, 193–198
Report Wizard, 304–308, 328–332, 335–336
Simple Query, 160–162
Subform, 293–295
Word, Microsoft, 545–548
Word command, External Data tab, 545
word processors, 538–540
Workgroup Information Files, 588
Workgroup Manager, 588
Write Conflict message, 568

X

XML Documents file type, 544
"xyz" formatting symbol, 59

Y

Y Error Bars tab, 368
Yes/No controls, 275–278
Yes/No fields, 55, 60–61

Z

Zoom box, 178
Zoom command, Print Preview window, 310